By Howard R. Lewis

WITH EVERY BREATH YOU TAKE

The
Medical Offenders

Howard R. and Martha E. Lewis

With a Preface by JAMES L. GODDARD, M.D.,
Former Commissioner, Food and Drug Administration

SIMON AND SCHUSTER · NEW YORK

FIRST PRINTING

SBN 671-20130-1
Library of Congress Catalog Card Number: 68-28916
Manufactured in the United States of America
by American Book-Stratford Press, Inc., New York

TO OUR SON DAVID

BUT FOR WHOM THIS BOOK WOULD HAVE BEEN DONE
SOONER BUT MUCH LESS PLEASURABLY

A NOTE FROM THE AUTHORS

THE NEXT TIME you visit a physician, the odds heavily favor that you will get good care at a fair fee. This point—that we are discussing a *minority* problem—is important to establish right off. Some recent lay books calling for reforms in medicine have tended to play on patients' fears. They thus do a disservice to the patient, to the doctor—and to responsible arguments for reform. Sensationalized exposés, long on overstatement and short of substantiation, only arouse laymen to disbelief and doctors to anger. They serve to put all calls for improvement in bad odor.

At the same time, bad conditions need to be focused on and warrant correcting in their own right. Few readers can fail to be impressed by the best of the recent books on economic and social aspects of medicine.

Heretofore, the problem of medical discipline has been largely unexplored, even though every patient is conceivably affected by the extremely weak policing of the profession, by the fact that standards of competence and honesty are only remotely enforced. This book seeks to tell you about the medical offenders—who they are, what they do—and about the laws and professional codes that protect them. A physician who read chapters in manuscript commented that this is also a book of medical sociology, for to put the offenders in perspective we many times look at the ways of the entire profession.

Throughout this book the word "discipline" is used in its most positive sense, implying a system of reasonable controls to uphold or bring about a high level of performance. Presented here are many recent case histories, most reported in journals and court records of the 1950s and 1960s. All doctors we refer to are M.D.s unless we specify otherwise. Direct quotations and exchanges of dialogue derive from the published court record. Except in a rare case, we have made it a rule to disguise the names of the principals; any similarity to an actual name is sheer coincidence. We see no need to embarrass a patient over an injury or a physician over a past error. These cases are designed not to point a finger at individuals but to illustrate the general weaknesses in medical discipline and the urgent need for reform.

Originally we planned to include in the section on felonious conduct a chapter on abortionists. But in researching the chapter we became convinced that the problem of abortion turns on what is essentially a religious question: whether you feel that a fetus is a living person and has a soul or other right to life. Since the thorough discussion that abor-

3

tion deserves is beyond the scope of this book, we have decided to defer it to a work in prospect on moral dilemmas in medicine.

We wish to thank the many physicians, lawyers, and medical journalists whose work we have drawn on. The citations in our source notes hardly do them justice. Special credit goes to everyone who contributed to the outstanding work of the American Medical Association Medical Disciplinary Committee, our most important single source. Largely because the A.M.A. has virtually ignored the committee's findings, the people engaged in this remarkable effort have never received the acclaim they deserve. From us they get three overdue but very enthusiastic cheers.

Additional appreciation is due the scores of doctors, medical disciplinary officials, and other authorities on the problem who were generous with information and help. We especially express our thanks to the physicians and attorneys who reviewed this book before publication. Their comments and suggestions have been invaluable. We of course bear full responsibility for any errors of fact and judgment that may remain.

Finally we want to say hooray to our editor, Jonathan Dolger, and our research assistants—Alan S. Ferman, Bill Perkins, and Karl Schaeffer.

New York City and   HOWARD R. AND MARTHA E. LEWIS
Woodstock, New York

Contents

7 CONTENTS

Foreword

As I READ THROUGH this book, there suddenly came to mind an incident in Atlanta, not too many years ago. An area-wide consumer education meeting was held and I was invited to be chairman of the session on consumer health. At that time it was my privilege to have been the Chief of the U.S. Public Health Service Communicable Disease Center in Georgia. The discussion, as I recall, was lively but not unusual; those of us who were health professionals were taking it all well in stride.

Then, toward the rear of the meeting room, an old gentleman arose and, in those mild Atlantan tones, asked me, "Doctor, why is it that airline pilots have to pass an examination every six months if they want to keep their license and fly, but once you get your license in medicine you're through with examinations? Aren't doctors as important as pilots?"

After a few tense seconds, I lamely replied that "you have certainly raised a most fundamental point and I only wish we had the time to explore it with you, but . . ." etc., etc. And somehow we got through and carried on. Now, several years later, that man's voice can still be heard— and his question remains unanswered. About all we can say is that physicians and the public are becoming aware of discrepancies among professions and of the need to correct them.

If we are going to make any progress at all in the housecleaning of the professions, it will be with the help of balanced, documented books such as *The Medical Offenders*. In here, the reader will come upon the data and the arguments that support development of greater responsibility and —to use a word frequently found in the text—discipline in the medical profession.

As the authors themselves point out, and the chapter notes amply illustrate, many physicians themselves are deeply concerned about offenders in their midst. The overwhelming majority of doctors—surgeons, internists, obstetricians, psychiatrists—remain true to the canons of practice. In its journals and in its meetings, at local, state, and national levels, a community of physicians has demonstrated an awareness of trouble and a willingness to do something about it. Mr. and Mrs. Lewis have drawn upon this community and we can be grateful that they explored it with such depth. Here the reader will find doctors who have stood up for progress and discipline—and find, also, the very real barriers to progress as well.

As the authors say, this book is about a minority of the medical community. But this is likely to be of small comfort to the public. Even though most doctors practice with competence and honor, the uneasy question will haunt the individual patient in the waiting room: "Is this doctor one of those charlatans on the fringe of medicine? Have I come to the right person?" For the charlatans, incompetents, thieves, cowards, and addicts encountered in this book may be in the minority in medicine—but the basic issue is that they remain in medicine at all. Now, more than ever before in history, the challenge is squarely up to us to raise and enforce the standards of conduct throughout the health professions—not just for the majority, but for all.

Our health manpower has been expanding dramatically. We can now describe 40 different occupational categories that span over 200 different careers, professional, sub-professional, and technical. While the population of the United States jumped 29 percent between 1950 and 1966, the increase in health manpower rose by 90 percent. Nurses, pharmacists, laboratory technicians, aides, dietitians . . . these and many others are counted among those who deliver health service to our society. But at the head of the list is the medical doctor, the man or woman who has gone the long years of postgraduate training and carries in his mind and in his hands the ability to preserve the gift of life. The doctor sets the tone, he sets the level of quality of work, he establishes the professional environment, he is the health team leader—whether he has sought that awesome responsibility or not. And as our nation commits more of its resources to health services, the role of the physician, as the one who marshals those resources at the patient's bedside, becomes even more important.

Hence, we need to know the state of medical ethics within the community of physicians. By bringing the facts out into the open and dealing with them objectively, fairly, and without sensationalism, we can break through those barriers to progress in medicine. The facts are in this book.

The authors have received their information from individual physicians, from hospital administrators, from the leaders in health care in virtually every state in the nation, and from the medical organizations and associations. It is impressive, the amount of information drawn from the American Medical Association itself in support of the thesis of this book: that there are offenders among us. This makes clear to me—as it should to every citizen—that the medical profession does have the information and the power to accomplish self-regulation, if it would only take that great step forward. Much has been accomplished in the past; but much is yet left on the agenda.

At the close of this book there is "A Call to Action," which deserves close and attentive reading. My colleagues in medicine will appreciate the authors' contention that "federal regulation of the private practice of medicine can be realistically considered only as a remote last resort." I recall my own position as a witness before a Senate committee presenting the same point of view: the practice of medicine cannot and must not be federally controlled. Does the public have an alternative for protection against those who engage in malpractice? The fifteen-point program at the conclusion of *The Medical Offenders* presents an alternative that is worth careful consideration. It is obvious, from the data in this book, that the A.M.A.'s own "Principles of Medical Ethics" is not enough. I am not sure that a "National Commission on Medical Discipline" (Point 15) is necessary; we have had a number of National Commissions in the health field, with mixed results. But I do feel that the concerns, the people, and the information for a proposed National Commission already exist within organized medicine. The task for us is to mobilize this great resource at this critical time.

This is the challenge of a generation. We have said, as a nation, that every man, woman, and child should have access to quality health care regardless of race, religion, economic condition, or geographic location. This nation can make such a bold commitment because it has lived a history of boldness and innovation. Medical practitioners can answer this challenge with courage and honor. All of them can. All of them must. This is the message I carry from this book. It is a necessary message for our time.

JAMES L. GODDARD, M.D.,

*Former Commissioner, Food
and Drug Administration*

INTRODUCTION:
The Medical Offenders

THREE CENTURIES before the birth of Christ, the Greek scholar-physician Hippocrates set forth the first principles of medical ethics: "A physician should be an upright man, learned in the art of healing . . . conducting himself with propriety in his profession and in all the actions of his life."

This requirement of competence and honor still stands as an essential to be met by every practitioner of medicine. Since time immemorial the lay community and the medical profession have been partners to a bargain. The lay public grants the profession an extraordinary amount of privilege and prestige. In exchange, the profession provides a high caliber of conduct and service.

It distinguishes American medicine that the vast majority of doctors as individuals live up to this bargain and are true to the ideals of their calling. Perhaps never before and nowhere else have so many physicians been characterized by so high a level of performance, and far and away most physicians merit the gratitude and respect they receive from the public.

Nonetheless, on at least one ground the typical physician can be faulted: He fails to enforce rigorously enough among his fellows the standards of conduct that he personally upholds. In medical societies and on hospital staffs, otherwise conscientious doctors too often decline to discipline offending colleagues. Mutual sympathy and fraternity feeling impose the so-called conspiracy of silence, often to the detriment of patients. The result is that self-policing within the profession has not substantially improved since the day Hippocrates observed: "There is no punishment for the malpractice of medicine."

But laxity *within* the profession is only part of the larger problem of medical discipline. Even if a repeated offender is expelled from his medical society and removed from his hospital staff, he can still legally practice medicine as long as he continues to be licensed. The chances are he *will* stay in practice, for nationwide the licensing of physicians is generally inadequate and ineffective as a disciplinary measure. State legislatures almost universally have failed to draft licensing statutes that keep the unfit from practicing. State medical licensing boards do not generally pursue their disciplinary functions.

The weakness of medical licensing comes as a surprise to most laymen (and most doctors as well—the subject is rarely discussed even in the medical press). Throughout the country a medical license is virtually a blank check. The licensee can perform any medical or surgical services he wishes, even if they are far beyond his skills.

Moreover, once a medical license is granted it is virtually permanent, subject only to the paying of a periodic fee. As a practical matter, withdrawing a physician's privilege to practice is nearly impossible for other than a felony conviction. Indeed, in many states the law makes no provision for suspending a license even when it is proved that the doctor is grossly negligent, or that he exploits his patients, or even that he is mentally incapacitated.

The lack of effective discipline in medicine has produced an anomalous fringe group: licensed M.D.s who are an embarrassment to their profession and a hazard to their patients. While they are, of course, a minority, their numbers are not inconsiderable. The most conservative estimate, from the profession's principal authorities on medical discipline, puts the minimum number of licensed M.D.s unfit to practice at some 15,000.

These offenders alone account for about 50 million patient visits a year. From this exposure alone, medicine's bad apples constitute a major public health problem, at least as grave a threat to patients' well-being as any single disease. But these numerical estimates are the most conservative. Other reliable sources in medicine estimate that the number of physicians who give unsatisfactory performance ranges as high as 1 out of 5 in private practice, or some 32,500 individuals.

The medical offenders are guilty of negligent and incompetent care, abandonment of the patient, and assault through unauthorized procedures—atypical, substandard acts that belong to a sphere below the level of ordinary practice. Here too are those physicians who seize upon medical service as a means of exploiting patients: the fee gougers who levy unconscionable charges; the overtreaters who perform unnecessary services; the fee splitters who buy and sell patients; the profiteers who own drugstores and drug companies and so have an interest in the prescriptions they write; the quacks who betray the canons of scientific medicine.

Also here are the mentally ill, including the sex offenders, and the narcotic addicts who have fallen prey to medicine's peculiar occupational disease. While mentally disabled physicians are often more to be pitied than condemned, they are unsuited for treating patients. Still others in medicine's underworld are the physicians who have committed felonies: fraud, narcotics violations, perjury.

The late Dr. Lindsay E. Beaton, a psychiatrist and a distinguished medical philosopher, once said that the title of physician "most of all . . . carries accountability, not only for the future of a great profession but for the very lives of our fellow sufferers from the human condition. . . . If we fail, we fail mankind."

It cannot be repeated often enough that most physicians demonstrate in their daily lives the skill and honor that should be enforced generally throughout the profession. Needed now is a concerted effort—by physicians and by aroused laymen—to deal with that minority of substandard doctors who disgrace the profession and pose a danger to patients.

In the absence of meaningful regulation, the typical physician conducts himself properly because of an agreement he makes with his conscience. This is the best regulation patients can now hope for. But one doctor's private scruples are not sufficient to curb another's incompetence or dishonesty. Medical discipline will succeed only when it is codified and enforced to the extent that the typical doctor already polices himself.

Right now the prospects for reforming medical discipline solely from within the profession are extremely poor, not only because of the resistance of those who would be disciplined, but also because of the laissez-faire tolerance that otherwise exemplary practitioners show toward offenders. This general unwillingness to discipline wrongdoers, this misplaced comradeship, erodes medicine's moral base.

How many more patients must be injured? How many more exploited? How many more crippled and killed? How much longer must picking a doctor be uncomfortably like a game of Russian roulette? The answer lies with the physicians and the laymen who can be mobilized to press for reform. Dr. Lindsay Beaton observed that "historically, idealism is an inseparable ingredient of medicine," that caring for the sick is an "act of love." It would be an expression of idealism and love were physicians to overcome a deep resistance to formal discipline and at last act against offenders. It is essential for public protection that lay groups push for reform.

Further at stake is the confidence that is at the heart of the physician-patient relationship. In urging his colleagues to clean house, the medicolegal authority Dr. Louis J. Regan warned, "The acts of the ignorant, the greedy, the callous few, threaten to destroy the merited esteem in which the profession as a whole is held." And when the patient must fear his doctor, both face disaster.

It is because of my deep respect and great admiration for the profession that I am so intolerant of those who would disgrace it.

—DR. PAUL R. HAWLEY, *Director,*
American College of Surgeons

In his relationship to his doctor the patient is often peculiarly vulnerable. . . . He may shop around for everything else he buys, from cars to cornflakes, but he takes his doctor on faith.

—Observation in *Life* Magazine

PART I

The Crisis in Medical Discipline

WHILE THE GREAT majority of physicians perform with competence and honor, thousands are guilty of substandard practices. The laws governing medicine are extremely weak, and state licensing boards generally fail to police the profession. Because of fragmentation and inertia within the medical community, medicine's much-vaunted system of self-discipline is largely a myth.

1
A Crisis for Patients

IF YOU ARE like most laymen you take comfort in the belief that doctors of medicine are kept in careful rein by stringent laws, rigorous government agencies, and exacting professional groups. Unfortunately, if you think this you are mistaken.

Actually, the privately practicing physician is largely a free agent, scarcely subject to regulation. Once he secures a license he has virtually a lifetime franchise to practice at his own discretion. There are few statutory standards he must meet, for the laws are generally silent as to what constitutes acceptable performance by physicians. Even where restrictions are clear, enforcement is spotty; the state boards charged with overseeing the profession are seldom active on matters of discipline.

Within the profession itself the disciplining of colleagues has little support; physicians do not like to police their fellows, and this reluctance is reflected at every level of organized medicine. At that, the strongest penalty a medical society or hospital staff can levy is expulsion. But removal from a society or hospital has no bearing on the doctor's license; though unacceptable to his peers, the offender retains his legal privilege to treat patients. Moreover, just as the profession is slow to prosecute violators within its ranks, so also is it loath to pursue the cause of more effective laws. As a result, the inadequate statutes currently on the books are likely to remain unamended for the foreseeable future.

The Medical Disciplinary Committee, a blue-ribbon panel commissioned by the American Medical Association, has conducted the most comprehensive investigation of the medical offenders. In essence the Committee found that (a) medicine's proclaimed system of self-discipline is more illusory than real, and (b) there are no adequate laws to fill the gap. Here verbatim, as summarized by a cooperating group, are the Committee's principal conclusions:

• Discipline in the medical profession is a vague and undefined aim at both the legislative and professional levels.
• The state medical societies are generally powerless, except to expel a member from the society in cases involving serious crimes or unprofessional conduct.

21

• State licensing boards too frequently do not have the machinery for instituting and conducting hearings on disciplinary matters.

• There is little apparent concern over such matters as narcotics addiction or fraud and deceit in practice.

• Too often a "guilty" physician is [merely] encouraged to go to another state.

• There is failure on the part of individual physicians to recognize their responsibility in reporting ethical and professional violations.

• The philosophy of present administrators of discipline . . . is very conservative and reluctant.

It merits pointing out that medicine's disciplinary vacuum creates no problem in regard to the performance of the great majority of M.D.s. The typical physician's own conscience inspires him to practice with competence and honor. Stronger regulations would probably not affect such physicians, who already represent the best that disciplinary reforms could hope to achieve.

But reform is nonetheless needed because of a minority of physicians. This fringe group benefits from the fact that few legal or professional restraints exist to curb substandard performance.

Item: A seventy-seven-year-old physician is home after being institutionalized for senile psychosis, an irreversible mental deterioration of the aged. He is incapable of maintaining a rational train of thought, much less a competent medical practice.

His memory fails him. His mind wanders. He dozes off in midsentence. He hears voices. He panics over imaginary threats. He explodes into incoherent rages.

Yet under the law of his state he can continue treating patients. The medical licensing statute contains no provision for suspending a physician's license on the ground that he is mentally incapacitated.

Item: A hospital has charged a doctor with twenty-five counts of unprofessional conduct. These incidents cost the lives of six patients.

In one operation he unnecessarily removed both adrenal glands from a woman, causing her death. After opening up another patient for cancer, he found none. Without the patient's permission he proceeded to remove a kidney, so negligently as to cause gangrene and kill her. During a tumor operation he ignored warnings that a sponge was missing. The patient later died of an internal abscess resulting from the sponge.

The doctor's hospital colleagues have documented his unfitness to practice and suspended him from the staff. But even with this documentation, the state medical licensing law permits him to stay in practice. Under the statute, substandard performance is not ground for discipline.

Item: This physician works without supervision in a hospital he owns.

He is notorious for performing unnecessary surgery, often ineptly. He also overprescribes barbiturates and neglects to administer needed therapy.

One patient came to him complaining of fatigue. Without examining him, the doctor prescribed vitamin shots three times a week. The patient actually had a rapidly worsening case of tuberculosis. Its neglect, prolonged while the doctor gave useless injections, exposed five small grandchildren to mortal danger.

This error, on top of previous ones, prompted the county medical society to expel the doctor. Although his colleagues have denounced him as a "menace to the public and the profession," he will probably remain in practice indefinitely. State law would permit the suspension of his license, but the medical licensing board, which is responsible for enforcing the law, is not vigorous in its disciplinary function. Except where doctors have been found guilty of felonies, it takes no action.

THE OFFENSES

What offenses characterize the medical offenders? In its report the A.M.A. Medical Disciplinary Committee has sketched some types of problem doctors: "There are the . . . the narcotics addicts, the mentally incompetent, and the professionally incompetent. There are those who overcharge; there are those who charge one fee when the patient has no insurance and a much higher fee if the patient is insured. There are those who perform unnecessary surgery. There are those who consort with quacks and faddists. . . . There are the fee-splitters and the rebaters."

Some less obvious offenders fall into a gray area. While a physician may not have violated a specific provision of the law or the Principles of Medical Ethics, he may nevertheless have committed an act contrary to medicine's high ideals. "These borderline cases represent the most perplexing and disturbing problem of medical discipline," the Medical Disciplinary Committee has said.

In this limbo the Committee found the doctor "who prescribes sedatives or stimulants promiscuously to all who wish to purchase them but disguises his records so that it appears that a bona fide physician-patient relationship exists between him and his customers." Also in this gray area is the ladies' man and the heavy social drinker. "Although he seems to be professionally competent," observes the Committee, "he is not a credit to the profession."

Offenses vary in intensity from region to region. To determine the major disciplinary problems in each state, the Medical Disciplinary Committee sent questionnaires to local medical societies. The commonest complaints reported to the Committee include "unjustifiably holding oneself out as being competent; deviation from the spirit of the Hippocratic Oath; . . . substandard care."

Connecticut replied that its worst problems are with physicians who overcharge and demonstrate "lack of interest or consideration for patients." Among California's problem doctors are those who are "quacks or mentally unbalanced." Iowa cites as its chief problems drug addicts and physicians suffering from mental and nervous disorders. Georgia mentions doctors who perform unnecessary surgery. Needlessly prolonging treatment is reported a big problem in West Virginia. In Maine: cheating health insurance plans. In Massachusetts: fee splitting. In Minnesota: incompetent surgery and the excessive ordering of laboratory tests by physicians who own their own labs. In Pennsylvania: improper attention to emergency calls. In Tennessee: incompetence.

Incompetence and negligence stand out as failings reported nationwide. By studying the grounds for professional liability claims, the A.M.A. Law Department has found what this wrongdoing may entail. Poor surgical results, poor medical results, and errors in diagnosis account for about half of all malpractice actions. Foreign bodies left in surgical patients constitute the next largest malpractice allegation, closely followed by burns resulting from the application of heat, chemicals, and x-rays.

Other common grounds for malpractice claims include assault (performing a procedure without proper consent), abandonment (failing to complete a medical obligation), and faulty prescribing. Poor results in neuropsychiatric treatment and improper commitment of patients are occasional causes of malpractice actions. Somewhat less frequent are cases involving malfunctioning equipment and blood transfusion accidents.

Malpractice cases often reach the courts, and the physician is held financially responsible for negligence. The most severe cases of medical misconduct may also be heard by state medical licensing boards, which are empowered to revoke and suspend licenses to practice. A summary of board actions is the closest document medicine has to a police blotter. In a typical year scores of doctors have their medical licenses revoked or suspended or are put on probation. The principal offenses include narcotics addiction, illicit prescribing or sale of narcotics, alcoholism, income tax evasion and fraud. A survey of one year's revocations shows that licenses were also lost for bribery of a public official, assault and battery, and manslaughter.

The anatomy of licensing board disciplinary proceedings is suggested by Dr. Leo T. Heywood in a study of complaints to the Nebraska Bureau of Examining Boards. Incidents of abandonment prompt a large number of complaints from patients. These cases are generally brought to the board's attention after a doctor has absented himself without notifying his patients or has refused to come to a patient's aid. Overcharging similarly spurs many protests from patients. Patients also often complain of doctors being untruthful about their qualifications to give specialized treatment.

Criminal fraud is another concern of medical licensing boards. Every board is alert to the possibility that an unqualified person may fraudulently attempt to get a license to practice medicine. Most boards have encountered a deceitful applicant who uses a real physician's name rather than his own. Or he may present a fake degree or transcript in his own name. Or he may show a concocted license, especially one from a foreign country that will be hard to check.

Dr. Heywood finds that fraud charges are registered chiefly by attorneys and by officials in insurance and government. Frauds so reported frequently involve exploitation of insurance companies, welfare agencies, and Workmen's Compensation. In recent years a number of physicians have been disciplined for entering into conspiracies with dishonest lawyers to boost personal-injury settlements. These doctors reported accident injuries that never occurred, often submitting large bills and giving false testimony as well.

In extreme cases medical societies may initiate delicensure proceedings. The grievance committee of a county medical society has referred to Dr. Heywood's board the case of a rapist who performed "immoral acts" after giving female patients "unacceptable therapeutic advice . . . concerning frustrated marital relationships." Another problem doctor was brought before the board by his medical society for mistreating psychiatric cases. He committed patients unnecessarily, then abandoned them.

DIMENSIONS OF THE PROBLEM

How large a problem is posed by the practitioners on medicine's fringe? The best-accepted estimate has been reported by Dr. Harold E. Jervey, Jr. Dr. Jervey is a past president of the Federation of State Medical Boards, the principal association of medical licensing officials. He served as a consultant to the A.M.A. Medical Disciplinary Committee.

Dr. Jervey and others with long experience in this field estimate that at least 1 physician in 20 is a severe disciplinary problem, that between 15,000 and 20,000 private practitioners (as many as 1 in 9) are repeatedly guilty of practices unworthy of the profession. Most of these physicians commit offenses that are unethical rather than prosecutable: substandard care, abandonment, overcharging, and the like. But, Dr. Jervey concludes, between 2,500 and 7,500 are actually breaking the law through narcotics violations, frauds, and other felonies.

"These figures I do not believe to be exaggerated," he adds. "If anything, they are too conservative."

In the purely clinical realm of diagnosis and therapy, an index of the amount of unsatisfactory service is suggested by the volume of medical malpractice claims filed in courts or with insurance companies. At least 2,000 professional-liability claims are brought against physicians each year, and the number may be as high as 5,000. The A.M.A. Law Department has found from surveys of the profession that at least one malpractice claim has been filed against 18.6 percent of all doctors in private practice, some 32,500 practitioners.

No less than 35 percent of these charges are valid, to judge by the number of cases resulting in an award to the plaintiff. (The percentage is the same whether the case is tried in court or settled by the insurance company.) In the courts such verdicts are decided by nonphysician judges and juries, and presumably may be swayed by sympathy for the patient and other considerations aside from the medical facts. Thus are these verdicts fair? Generally, yes, says William F. Martin, legal counsel of the Medical Society of the State of New York: "Unjust recoveries in malpractice suits are remarkably rare. The laws as laid down by most of the appellate courts in this country are, on the whole, eminently fair to both the patient and the doctor."

In the observation of some doctors these malpractice figures err on the side of meagerness. While on the staff of New York's Bellevue Hospital, Dr. Vincent J. Fisher evaluated the prehospital care given by patients' private physicians. He reports that he found "poor and even harmful care" in one case out of ten. A surgeon writing under the name of Michael V. Corio has this to say: "If patients brought malpractice suits against *all* guilty doctors—and against guilty doctors only—the courts would probably be flooded with three times the number of such suits now in litigation."

Studies by health insurance plans bear out that in some quarters of medicine substandard care is commoner than generally believed. As a means of evaluating the services performed by participating physicians, health insurers often rely on "medical audits." These are detailed reviews of cases by independent specialists, who then pass judgment on the quality of diagnosis and treatment.

In New York City, 1 out of 16 residents is covered by a health and welfare plan negotiated by the Teamsters Union. In the course of operations, the administrators of the program asked Dr. Ray E. Trussell, director of the Columbia University School of Public Health and Administrative Medicine, to conduct a medical audit. For 18 months, 35 faculty members and a panel of 7 additional physicians probed their way through a sampling of services performed by participating doctors.

From a study of 406 cases in which the patient was hospitalized, the auditors concluded that no fewer than 1 out of 5 received "poor" care. Another one fifth received only "fair" care. In surgical cases the quality of surgery in 20 percent of the cases was found "poor," in 26 percent merely "fair."

The auditors also found evidence of considerable milking of the program through unnecessary services. Twenty percent of the hospital admissions were found to have been needless. Of 60 hysterectomies, 20 were unnecessary and 10 were of doubtful need. Of 13 cesarean sections, 7 were without justification.

APPEALS FOR REFORM

"The profession of medicine is plagued . . . by a small percentage of members who fail to recognize or refuse to abide by accepted standards of conduct," wrote Dr. J. P. Medelman, president of the Minnesota State Medical Association. Dr. Medelman's remarks appeared in an editorial in *Minnesota Medicine,* his society's journal, and they constituted the journal's first comment about medicine's disciplinary problem in at least five years.

Since the profession is generally reluctant to air its dirty linen, and since discipline is not a matter of prime interest to most practitioners, comment on the subject is infrequent. When an occasional medical leader does speak out, his words are lost in the absence of a systematic campaign of information and improvement. It is a rare physician and a rarer layman who knows how bleak a picture has been painted by knowledgeable medical leaders and how little is being done about it.

Even warnings from the profession's highest echelon have resulted in few corrective measures. In his capacity as secretary and general manager of the A.M.A., Dr. George F. Lull called for a prompt cleanup. "It cannot be denied that the reputation of the medical profession is being damaged seriously by the . . . malpractitioners within its ranks," he declared. "The situation must be corrected." This was in 1953.

Nor has the problem gone unnoticed by A.M.A. presidents, and their calls for reform have similarly met with little success. When Dr. Louis Bauer was in office he sought to "drive out of the profession" all doctors guilty of unethical practices. The campaign he attempted to launch lacked general support. It lasted only as long as he held office, and so when Dr. Edward J. McCormick took up the post he started his own program to get medicine to clean house. "We cannot," he said, "protect or condone the . . . greedy and godless physicians who flagrantly violate the noble traditions of the medical profession." But Dr. McCormick's call too went unheeded.

Then, after an interval of little discussion or action, Dr. Leonard W. Larson was elected A.M.A. president. Like Drs. Bauer and McCormick, Dr. Larson recognized that reforms were now needed, first of all in the profession's attitude toward discipline. "That small fraction of undisciplined practitioners must not be allowed to remain in the body of medicine, lest it corrupt and enervate the entire profession," he warned. "We must take a vigorous position on self-discipline, for to ignore the problem would bring on ultimate catastrophe."

But, once again, zeal for reform sparked only isolated physicians and ended in next to no improvement. As a result, the malpracticing periphery of the profession remains a major hazard. And late in this decade Dr. James Z. Appel has made yet another stab at establishing a meaningful reform program. "The emphasis must now be in the field of discipline," he declared in a statement of priorities he wished to pursue as A.M.A. president. Once and for all, he urged his colleagues, let us police ourselves.

What is the effect of this lack of policing? The A.M.A. Medical Disciplinary Committee found that the situation is deteriorating. In Connecticut, Delaware, Ohio, and Utah, medical societies report that the profession's discipline problem is outpacing all efforts to correct it. In Hawaii, the problem is worse than it was ten years ago.

2
Legacy of Loopholes

ON THE COMPLAINTS of a number of patients, an M.D. was brought before a state medical examining board on charges of improper conduct. The members of the board, themselves physicians, found the doctor guilty on all counts.

In a denunciation rare for the profession, they declared him a "disgrace to the profession" who treated patients in a "cruel" manner, rendered "careless and improper" treatment, and was "ruthlessly and wantonly negligent." So unfit was he to practice medicine that the board exacted its most severe penalty: It revoked his license.

The doctor went to court to appeal the revocation. "The charges against me are not in violation of the law governing the conduct of physicians," he argued.

After studying the state's medical practice act, the judges agreed. As the law is written, wanton negligence is not grounds for disciplinary action. Because of this loophole, the doctor got his license back. And with the sanction of the law, he continued treating patients.

This Connecticut case is hardly isolated. In virtually every state, the medical practice act is shot through with loopholes, so that statutes that are supposed to regulate physicians in fact uphold the malpractitioner and victimize the patient.

"Discipline has little legal status at present," the *Bulletin* of the Federation of State Medical Boards has observed. A licensing board's authority extends only to violations specified in the law. But the typical medical practice act fails to prohibit many types of misconduct that should disqualify a wrongdoer from practicing, or at least make him subject to probation. By thus tying the hands of licensing boards, inadequate laws serve to perpetuate in practice the unskillful and untrustworthy.

The effect of this statutory weakness has been expressed by an official of the Kansas medical licensing board: "We think we do only a mediocre job in discipline." Physicians who would like to do a better job read the current medical practice acts and come away discouraged. They recognize that no great improvement can be made without substantially stronger laws and boards. A member of the New York State board has said. "Discipline . . . necessitates . . . legal authority to use punishment and revoke or suspend licenses. . . . The great weakness in many states today is that they do not have the machinery and right of discipline."

This weakness plagues even the states with the best medical disciplinary programs. California's medical practice act and licensing board are among the most powerful in the country. But Howard Hassard, executive secretary and legal counsel of the California Medical Association, must speak helplessly of a physician who is unworthy of his privilege to practice.

This doctor is called incorrigible about subjecting patients to unnecessary services and charging them excessive fees. Moreover, the quality of his services is condemned as extremely low. The California Medical Association has gone before the state licensing board to get his license withdrawn. Physician after physician testified that he is unfit to be in medicine. But under the California medical licensing law, which is strong by comparison with most other states', the offender technically violated no statute compelling disciplinary action.

WRITTEN TO BE WEAK

Medical knowledge is a public resource of the first rank, and the medical profession a public utility of prime importance. Yet the legal ties that bind medicine to the public interest are largely feeble, misdirected, and out of date.

Indeed, many state laws governing medicine were written to be weak. Today's medical practice act is generally from an age when scientific medicine was not established and substandard practice reigned supreme. Many medical licensing statutes were originally drafted with an eye to the interests of then-prevalent quacks and charlatans—and have not been significantly amended since early in this century.

The weakness in licensing regulations reflects our forefathers' paucity of medical knowledge. In early America so little had been discovered about sickness and healing that no formal education was needed to legally practice medicine. An aspiring physician might simply hang up a shingle. If not enough patients came, he would try another trade. The first surgeons combined their careers with barbering. It was usual for a doctor to make his living treating both animals and people.

If an aspirant to medicine sought training, he could apprentice himself to a senior man. Dr. Benjamin Rush, a signer of the Declaration of Independence, used to give his students a variety of suggestions, not all of them related to diagnosis and therapy. "Don't let your shoes make offensive noises when you enter a sickroom," he would advise, and "Don't make light of a disease in front of patients."

Actually, such sympathy and consideration were pretty much the best that could be offered patients by physicians. While the art of medicine was well advanced, medical science was generally undeveloped and ineffective. Thus, the first licensing codes regarded the fairness of the doctor's treatment as being more important than his training. In 1636 Virginia passed this continent's first medical-licensing act. Its chief purpose was to keep doctors from charging unreasonable fees. In 1665 the Duke of York published statutes governing territory that included New York and New Jersey. Their principal restriction on physicians was that before exerting any "force, violence or cruelty" they get the patient's consent.

Although other schools and colleges were established in the colonies, medical schools were not. Formal medical education could be gained only in Europe, a possibility for merely an isolated few. Even by the modest standards of the period, there developed a superabundance of incompetence. A scandal swelled, followed by demands for regulation. In 1772, New Jersey passed the nation's first comprehensive medical practice act. By 1800, licensing acts were passed by thirteen of the sixteen states.

But, twenty years later, a countertrend emerged. The nation, rapidly expanding westward, sorely needed doctors. A spirit of laissez-faire imbued Americans, and licensure seemed an unnecessary restriction, especially since, in the experience of many patients, licensed physicians were no more effective than unlicensed ones. State after state repealed its licensing laws. New states did not enact any. By 1850, there were virtually no regulations governing the practice of medicine in any of the states. For the most part, all that was required was a medical diploma. Even one purchased by mail from a diploma mill would do.

Now prevailed the Golden Age of Quackery. More than half the practitioners treating the public lacked the training to apply the considerable advances being made in medical science. Many of these so-called healers were virtually illiterate and mere peddlers of narcotic cure-alls. Their nostrums masked symptoms—indeed, often caused the user to float into addiction—but left the original condition untreated.

A large number of doctors were well intentioned but clung to medical theories long since outdated. One discredited school of medical practice postulated that all fevers were a consequence of inflammation of the intestinal canal. Since these doctors believed the intestines threw poisons into the blood, they drained their patients' veins. One physician used over 100,000 leeches a year in his practice.

Other doctors who were behind the times still relied on laxative "specifics." These purgatives would supposedly force the body to excrete the morbid products that were presumed to be causing the disease. Severe diarrhea was thus commonly induced, thereby further weakening and dehydrating an already ill patient.

Yet another group of physicians believed in the use of "homeopathic" drugs. In theory minute doses of these medications would displace a disease by producing identical symptoms to compete with it. The principal effect, if any, on the patient was to intensify his symptoms and so make him feel worse.

A relatively small number of enlightened doctors rose above such cultism. They pragmatically studied a disease unbound by preconceived notions. Instead of trying to fit all man's ills into a single overall theory, they experimented and observed. Case by case, these rational empiricists derived practical understanding of causes and cures. All the while, they applied to medicine the increasing body of knowledge being gained in chemistry, biology, and physics. It is from this group of nineteenth-century medical scientists that the profession of today springs.

Despite the period's great achievements in medical science, Americans continued to be subjected to much bad medicine. In 1890 the United States had more practitioners in proportion to the population than any other country in the world. More than 120 colleges were turning out doctors. But except for a handful of first-rate institutions in a few big cities, these schools were educationally submarginal, many having been established purely as financial ventures.

Most medical schools offered a meager program, totaling a mere forty weeks of part-time instruction lasting but two years. Few schools had access to large hospitals and so provided no adequate clinical instruction. Many schools blatantly wooed students by advertising low prices and easy examinations.

It was bad enough that these mills spewed forth diplomas. Worse yet, they imposed competition that deterred other institutions from giving better training. To attract students, virtually all schools of the day made courses less thorough and exams less exacting. Even potentially first-rate institutions, threatened by competition, persisted in pouring out second- and third-rate doctors. Throughout this era, a diploma from a medical college carried with it little evidence of education or ability.

Fortunately, in the twentieth century medical education has undergone radical reform. This rebirth of the profession is largely the result of an investigative report published in 1910 by Abraham Flexner, an educator and staff member of the Carnegie Foundation for the Advancement of Teaching. Flexner proposed to follow the pattern of the Johns Hopkins University Medical School, placing medical education within universities and concentrating on the quality of students and curriculum. Under the impact of the Flexner report, half the medical schools were shaken out of existence. Today M.D. degrees are given by less than a hundred schools, including recently founded institutions. In a far cry from pre-Flexner days, each school offers a program of such high quality that throughout the world an American medical degree is regarded as a certificate of excellence in training.

By contrast, a medical *license* is no such assurance of quality of performance. A Flexner-type movement has yet to upgrade the standards of medical licensure. Yet licensing has even more immediate effect than medical education on the kind of care the public receives.

THE FIGHT AGAINST LICENSING

A principal reason why state medical practice acts are weak lies in the political opposition surrounding their framing.

Throughout the last century, responsible voices in medicine called for an adequate system of medical licensing—to match the advances in medical knowledge. Sought were rigorous licensing examinations and continuous enforcement of high practice standards. One goal of the formation of the American Medical Association in 1847 was the securing of laws that would permit only qualified physicians to practice. This was in keeping with the A.M.A.'s statement of purpose: "to promote the art and science of medicine and the betterment of public health."

Licensing, however, presented a threat to most physicians of the day. Alarmed, they organized a counterattack that proved politically potent. Most quacks were in medicine because it was lucrative. To beat back restrictive legislation, opponents of licensing reform used in state houses every bit of influence they could muster, ranging from friendly visits to outright graft.

In addition to bidding heavily for legislator's favors, many doctors of questionable merit were able to exercise considerable political muscle. The A.M.A. was not the only organization around which practitioners could cluster. Homeopaths, for example, had working for them an association at least as fervent as the A.M.A. Furthermore, homeopaths could count on the students and resources of no fewer than thirteen colleges of homeopathy. With ten colleges of their own, practitioners of "eclectic" medicine—another fringe field—jumped into the foray.

Advocates of licensing reform thus met with frustration. If a state legislator was not bought or frightened, he was likely to be unsophisticated enough in science to remain unconvinced of the need for adequate licensing laws. Only persistence by responsible physicians produced any results at all. Progress through the state houses was slow. "The floors of a general assembly proved to be an ineffective place for the elevation and protection of high standards of medical care," Dr. Nathan A. Womack, of the University of North Carolina School of Medicine, has reflected in a review of the history of medical licensing.

As late as 1901, the *Journal of the American Medical Association* (*J.A.M.A.*) carried this query to the editor: "Please let me know where a graduate in medicine could practice without passing the State Board examination." In reply, the editor was able to cite as many as ten states that permitted virtually anyone who could tack up a shingle to enter the practice of medicine.

Where the state legislatures enacted licensing laws, they generally did so halfheartedly. In response to pressure from opponents, state licensing boards were virtually foredoomed to ineffectiveness. Licensure in some states was dissipated among several boards, with no unifying standards for qualification of applicants. To add to the chaos, boards were forever at the mercy of the currents in the state legislatures: now being granted powers, now seeing them taken away. Statutes were equally ill-defined regulating how and under what circumstances a malpracticing physician could be declared unfit to practice and be relieved of his license.

It was not surprising, therefore, that an editorial appeared in the *J.A.M.A.* in 1902 calling attention to the need "for overcoming present anomalous conditions regarding the regulation of the practice of medicine in the various states." True, medical licensure has been improved since then, particularly in respect to licensing examinations, and the improvement in medical schools has introduced a generally high level of medical practice.

But for the most part, especially regarding the weeding out of the unfit, that editorial could be written today.

3

License to Do Wrong

"THE LAW IS MEAGER," laments the executive secretary of one medical licensing board. Although he knows of repeated misconduct by a number of physicians in his state, his board can do little. Under medical licensing statutes it lacks proper disciplinary authority. In this his board is not unusual. Indeed, some medical practice acts could hardly be more toothless.*

For example, persons unfamiliar with the problem take for granted that at least when a medical license was issued the recipient met the licensing standards, that if the license was obtained fraudulently it can be revoked. But in no fewer than five states a medical license is no assurance that the licensee was *ever* qualified to practice.

In these states, fraud in obtaining a medical license is not grounds for revocation. An applicant may misrepresent himself or falsify his licensing examination. Once he has been granted the license it is difficult if not impossible under the law to take it back.

In taking the Oath of Hippocrates, doctors promise: "With purity and holiness will I watch closely my life and art." As a judicial matter, the U.S. Supreme Court has taken much the same position in requiring good character of physicians. The court reviewed the case of a doctor whose license was revoked after he was convicted of a felony. Upholding the revocation, the court ruled: "It is fitting that the physician should possess a knowledge of diseases and their remedies, but also that he should be one who may be safely entrusted to apply those remedies. Character is as important a qualification as knowledge."

But a medical license is not necessarily assurance that the licensee has not been convicted of a serious crime. In fifteen states the medical practice act does not consider conviction of a felony involving moral turpitude to be grounds for disciplinary action. In twelve states conviction of other types of felonies is similarly disregarded. This produces the kind of anomaly reported by one state board official: A convicted felon is in jail yet is licensed to practice medicine.

* For the findings of a survey of state medical licensing laws, see Appendix A, "Major Offenses Subject to Disciplinary Action." In this discussion, the District of Columbia, which has its own licensing statutes as well as a large number of physicians, is treated as a state.

Medical practice acts fail to deal with criminal conduct in other ways as well. In some states, the board can suspend a license only if the offender actually goes to prison. If a lenient judge gives him a suspended sentence, the board can make no evaluation of its own. By implication the law sets a rather minimal qualification for the character of physicians: All they need do is stay out of jail.

In some states disciplinary action applies only to licensees convicted of a felony. (For reports on felonious misconduct, see Chapters 10–12.) An offender guilty of a mere misdemeanor can retain his license. To cut down court work, judges and prosecutors often let defendants plead guilty to the lesser offense. Thereby the courts inadvertently help offenders slip through a loophole in medical licensing laws.

IGNORING INCOMPETENCE

Narcotic addiction presents a special problem in medicine. (See Chapter 19, "The Narcotic Addicts: Doctors' Disease.") The profession has ready access to drugs. Physicians tend to fall into addiction far more frequently than the population at large. And the use of narcotics impairs the physician-addict's judgment and dexterity.

Nonetheless, in at least three states drug addiction is not an offense under the medical practice act. Within a strict interpretation of the law, an addict can legally continue to practice.

Alcoholism is a more common and no less disabling kind of addiction. But medical licensing laws treat it even more haphazardly. Seven states make no provision for suspending the licenses of alcoholics whose habitual intoxication makes them unreliable physicians.

The members of one medical licensing board regard alcoholism as their gravest disciplinary problem. Owing to a weak medical practice act, an alcoholic's condition is not grounds for board action. The state's motor vehicle act is firmer and will suspend a driver's license on the grounds of repeated drunkenness. Ironically, then, alcoholics who are considered too unsafe to operate vehicles are left undisturbed if they operate on patients.

Not only addiction but mental illness in general plagues the profession. (See Chapter 18, "The Mentally Ill: 'Our Biggest Problem.'") The A.M.A. Medical Disciplinary Committee asked state medical associations their major disciplinary problem. Mental illness was cited from Maine ("physicians who are psychiatric problems") to California ("physicians who appear mentally unbalanced").

California has strong statutes for keeping mentally ill doctors from practicing. But elsewhere medical practice acts respond to the menace of mental illness largely by ignoring it. At least sixteen states fail to regard mental illness as grounds for suspending a license. The remaining states generally provide for suspension of a license only if there has actually been a commitment to a mental hospital.

Even then, many states fail to guard against premature or temporary release. In a study of mental illness statutes in medical practice acts, Dr. R. C. Derbyshire, of the Federation of State Medical Boards, has found that a mental patient may be legally entitled to resume practice—even though he is home merely for a visit.

Only a few medical licensing laws provide for *non*hospitalized mental disability. Thus excluded from the licensing board's disciplinary authority are all the mentally ill who have stayed out of an institution. Among these, reports Dr. Derbyshire, are the borderline schizophrenic who is enough in touch with the world to be deceptive; the manic-depressive whose peaks of elation and chasms of despair are potentially perilous to patients; the chronic alcoholic on the verge of deteriorating to total dilapidation.

"All too often this type drifts from bad to worse until he has committed a crime . . . or has done great damage to his patients," Dr. Derbyshire has said.

Some state laws are so rigid that they restrain the licensing board from even investigating cases of mental incompetence. Dr. Frederick T. Merchant, a member of the Ohio board, formerly complained that his board could not act officially even in known cases of insanity until court action was completed or the licensee voluntarily entered an institution. These procedures can take years, especially if commitment is being fought.

Professional incompetence can result from causes other than mental illness. At the first National Congress on Medical Ethics, A.M.A. president Dr. James Z. Appel cited "failure to keep up professionally" as a principal reason for substandard practices. He added: "The problem of the incompetent physician is a real one—and it must be met."

Yet, despite the rapid changes in medical science, not a single state law requires that a licensee update his knowledge or methods. Nowhere is there provision for reexamination or recertification, or any other attempt to review competence to practice. Though a medical Rip Van Winkle may grow ever more rusty and may practice a brand of medicine ever more obsolete, he need only pay his yearly licensing fee. His privilege to practice will be automatically renewed. (Incompetence and negligence are discussed in Chapters 15–17.)

Most medical practice acts also lack any means of heading off licensees made physically incapacitated by advanced age. The ravage of years is a worsening problem in medicine, for along with the rest of the population physicians are living longer. But at an age well after most laymen have retired, some physicians are still in practice attempting procedures now beyond their capabilities. And though an elderly surgeon can barely hold his scalpel, in thirty-three states there is no way the medical licensing board can remove it from his trembling hand.

A study by Dr. Derbyshire reveals that a mere eighteen states empower licensing boards to take action because of physical or professional incompetence. In the remaining states, the only hope of keeping an incompetent practitioner in check lies with his hospital or medical society. Since hospitals and medical societies have no legal authority over his privilege to practice, as a restraint this is more a prayer than a hope. What's more, many submarginal practitioners are members of neither a hospital staff nor a medical society. "These are the most dangerous kind," says Dr. James Appel, "and they can be controlled only by the state boards."

Beyond the power of virtually every state board is the offender who does not fall into any of the aforementioned categories but who nonetheless demonstrates dangerous antisocial behavior. A doctor may assault the patient (see Chapter 13, "The Assaulters: Trespassing on the Patient"). Or he may abandon him (Chapter 14, "The Abandoners: Bad Samaritans"). But technically the offender has committed no violation of the medical practice act.

Similarly untouched by medical practice acts is exploitation of the patient. It is no ground for discipline to charge an unconscionable fee (Chapter 5, "The Fee Gougers: 'Vultures in Medicine'") or subject a patient to unnecessary services (Chapter 6, "The Overtreaters: Pouring It On"). Hardly a state prohibits physicians from profiteering on patients' drug or eyeglass prescriptions (Chapter 8, "The Profiteers: Captive Prescriptions").

Dr. Derbyshire has said: "The most difficult situation is presented by the disreputable physician, not a member of a medical society or of a hospital staff, defiant of all the rules of good medical practice, who perpetrates his crimes upon an unsuspecting public in the sanctuary of his office. I know of no law which will permit systematic inspection of his office or methods. The board of medical examiners may be convinced that this physician is a menace to society but substantial evidence is difficult to obtain from either his patients or fellow physicians. The only weapon against such a person is infinite patience on the part of the board of medical examiners in investigating every complaint in the hope that eventually solid evidence can be obtained to end his nefarious practices.

"Unfortunately nothing short of a disaster will usually bring him to light."

LOOSE CONSTRUCTION

Medical practice acts are further weakened by the looseness with which they are drawn. Many laws are so vaguely worded that they give the licensing board no real authority over discipline.

For example, most medical licensing laws provide that "unprofessional conduct" is an offense subject to disciplinary action. (Five states lack even this fundamental safeguard.) But in itself this is not enough. A license to practice medicine is a "property right" and is constitutionally guaranteed due process of law. Thus the term "unprofessional conduct" must be carefully defined in a medical practice act, or a suspension or revocation may not stand up in court.

After reviewing state medical practice acts, Dr. Carl E. Anderson, of the California Medical Association, has concluded that in the laws of no fewer than twelve states the section proscribing unprofessional conduct may not be worth the space it takes up. These statutes fail to tell what unprofessional conduct is intended to mean, making it the kind of loosely worded catch-all that courts hesitate to enforce.

Already one court has warned that medical practice acts need tightening up. A District of Columbia practitioner was brought before the medical licensing board accused of committing a criminal abortion. Since abortion is not an offense in the District's medical practice act (or, for that matter, in ten other medical practice acts), the charge was "misconduct," the closest the law could come. After a lengthy hearing, the board found the doctor guilty and moved to revoke his license.

The defendant appealed, claiming that misconduct is too vague an offense to satisfy due process of law. In effect he challenged: "How could I be expected to know that abortion is grounds for discipline if the law doesn't so specify?"

The U.S. Court of Appeals upheld the revocation. But it did so mainly because "every medical practitioner knows fully that the performance of a criminal abortion is misconduct." In future, courts may not give such an interpretation to an offense that is less universally condemned. One of the Court of Appeals judges raised the question of whether the courts can "uphold and enforce" a medical practice act fogged by "broad and indefinite language."

Some medical practice acts commit the reverse error. They seek to define unprofessional conduct too narrowly and precisely—and sometimes wind up tangled in inconsistencies. Dr. Carl Anderson notes that in one state it is unprofessional conduct to advertise to treat or cure a disease that is "manifestly incurable." By implication, observes Dr. Anderson, it is permissible to advertise to treat a disease that is curable. Another state declares it unprofessional conduct to be guilty of "malpractice which results in death." If the patient is lucky enough to live, the malpractitioner is presumably safe from action.

The obstacles to professional discipline that a weakly constructed law can present are shown by a Texas case in which half a dozen women patients alleged sexual misconduct. Doing the best it could with the statutes at hand, the prosecution charged the defendant with "grossly unprofessional and dishonorable conduct of a character likely to deceive or defraud the public." In extensive proceedings, the medical licensing board heard testimony from the patients and the accused doctor. Satisfied that he was guilty, the board revoked his license.

In his appeal to the courts, the defendant denied improper conduct toward these women—and added that anyway as the law was written this was no grounds for professional discipline. The court reviewed the statute and agreed that it did not apply to his offense. It reversed the board and ordered his license restored.

Aroused that he could be let loose among patients, the board appealed the reversal. But the State Court of Appeals upheld the lower court. Explaining its interpretation of the medical practice act, the Appeals Court reasoned that the fraud and deception prohibited by the law were intended to refer only to charlatans who hold out false cures. "We think it clear this section was not meant to cover immoral conduct," the court said.

Now the board took the case to a still higher court. At last, in the State Supreme Court, the board was upheld in its interpretation of the statute. In reaching its decision, the court relied on the dictionary to determine the meaning of "deceive." The dictionary definition includes "to impose upon, to deal treacherously with." Concluded the court: If the physician was guilty of improper sexual conduct toward his patients, "They were deceived."

If this law had been well drafted, the first court might have upheld the board. As it was, the Supreme Court remanded the case for a trial on its merits, expressly stating that it was not holding the doctor guilty of anything. In some states the medical practice act is even more poorly drawn, and the licensing board has not the resolve or the funds to pursue an appeal.

Indeed, in another Texas case, the board of medical examiners canceled the license of a doctor who was a narcotics user. The physician appealed, and a jury found that—as the board charged—he prescribed drugs using patients' names and then administered them to himself. Nonetheless, the jurors restored the doctor's license. Bound by the limitations of the "deceive or defraud" statute, they could only find that he had not violated any law. Although he was a user of Demerol, the jurors decided he was not addicted nor grossly unprofessional.

INACTIVITY ON THE BOARDS

At a Medical Disciplinary Committee hearing in Atlanta, a disciplinary official of a southern state commented: "Why ask the legislatures for more law when we don't use what we've got."

Despite the undiminished need for greater enforcement of medical discipline, state medical licensing boards are actually becoming less active. In one year, licensing boards took disciplinary action in a total of 604 cases, about 12 per state. This is little enough, since included are such minor actions as reprimands. Yet even from this minimal activity the boards have slowed down: to a total of three years later of 401 cases, or only 8 per state.

In a typical year, the boards revoke a mere 75 licenses, less than 2 per state. (Recall that as many as 20,000 licensees are thought to be severe disciplinary problems.) About a third of all disciplinary actions are concentrated in just two states, California and New York. Eleven states take no actions at all.

Besides being handicapped by weak licensing laws, boards also suffer from anemic budgets, denying them essential funds and staff. The Texas board estimates that merely one hearing on the average costs $2,400. Yet some boards have budgets of merely $5,000 to $10,000 a year, barely enough to pay for office help.

The result is a flimsy effort. Without funds for investigative and legal expenses, a board will tend to act only on the most cut-and-dried offenses. Noncriminal and borderline cases are seldom touched. Explains one board member: "We can't get money from the state treasury. Since we have no money, we are afraid to tackle a difficult case." In response to an A.M.A. query, the secretary of a state board says he feels his board could do a much better job "if it had additional funds to investigate numerous borderline cases." Echoes another board: "The board could do a lot better job if there were adequate funds for investigation."

The budget squeeze also shows up in board members' compensation. Typically board members receive no payment or only a nominal sum. But most members of licensing boards are private practitioners, burdened with an overhead and already too busy. Without adequate compensation, a member often cannot afford the time for the meetings and hearing that disciplinary procedure entails; the result is that these do not take place, and offenders go unpoliced.

State governments may further shortchange medical discipline by not playing fair with funds supposedly earmarked for licensing boards. In Illinois, enforcement of the medical practice act was so ineffectual that the state medical society protested. Since the board was grossly underbudgeted, the society endorsed an increase in licensing fees, with the understanding that the increment would be used to improve the board's disciplinary activities. But the state has diverted this additional money to other purposes. The board is still underfinanced and underactive.

Other state agencies may paralyze the medical licensing board by declining to cooperate. Some boards experience difficulty in getting the attorney general's office to prosecute criminal violators.

In one western community there is an M.D. licensed to practice only in an Eastern state, who is practicing illegally without the required local license. He has a large practice, and does a thriving business dispensing a worthless preparation from the chamiso plant. Though this shrub's only value is esthetic (it has pretty white flowers), the doctor claims that his drug will cure diabetes, ulcers, and a host of other ailments.

Repeatedly the state medical board has reported him to the attorney general, seeking prosecution on charges including fraud and practicing without a license. The attorney general, however, prefers to allocate his staff and funds elsewhere—and has declined to act in this case.

Or, to save the prosecution work on a case, the offender may be allowed to plead guilty to an insignificant charge. A child with an ear infection was taken by his mother to a "nose and throat specialist." The doctor aroused her suspicions by adding sales tax to his fee. She reported him to the local medical society, which investigated and had him charged with practicing medicine without a license—a felony. The district attorney permitted him to plead guilty to a misdemeanor—engaging in the healing arts without a basic science certificate—and he got away with a small fine.

Some law enforcement agencies consider it a waste of time to go after such offenders. Even if they are arrested and successfully prosecuted, the statutes contain no real deterrents to repeating the violation. In most states, practicing medicine without a license is a misdemeanor carrying a low fine or a maximum of six months in jail. "Few states have severe enough punishments to be meaningful," says Dr. Harold E. Jervey, Jr., of the Federation of State Medical Boards. "It is ironical and incomprehensible that in a society where billions are spent to maintain health, and the death sentence is inflicted for murder, that a 'quack' can undermine health and possibly cause many deaths with no greater penalty than the payment of fifty dollars."

One impostor, whose only medical experience was as a laboratory technician, posed as a physician and found employment at a hospital. He claimed he had been an instructor of hematology and general medicine at a West Coast medical school, and in private practice before that. His mishandling of cases prompted the superintendent of the hospital to begin checking up on him. Getting wind of the investigation, the impostor fled. He took a position in another hospital's emergency room and, when apprehended, was about to substitute for a doctor going on vacation. Although he risked many patients' lives, his total penalty was a 90-day sentence, suspended on condition that he undergo psychiatric treatment.

Moreover, the example set by some boards does not inspire vigor on the part of other agencies. Even where statutory authority exists and the state provides a reasonable budget, boards often do little to discipline offenders. Board members seldom meet. When they do, they rarely pursue their disciplinary function. Instead, they concentrate on their other main function, administering licensing examinations. Generally they enforce the medical practice act only for extreme violations, sometimes only if the offender has already been convicted in the criminal courts.

"The attitude of too many [board members] leaves much to be desired," says Dr. Harold Jervey. "On more than one occasion I have heard board members state that just as long as a delinquent physician has left his state, he didn't care whether any action was taken or not. It was no longer his responsibility.

"Also, I have heard many state with pride that his board had not suspended or revoked a license in . . . years—this in heavily populated sections in the country. It must be assumed that, for whatever reason, they are just not fulfilling their responsibilities."

Much of the boards' laxity stems from the practice of appointing to the boards members who have no more taste for discipline than do doctors at large. In most states, board members are named either directly by the state medical society or by the governor on the recommendation of the state society. A board appointment is widely regarded as a form of recognition a society can give a deserving member, with only secondary importance being given to naming a physician who can do the best job.

The Medical Disciplinary Committee has reported its feeling that in general the boards have members of "high caliber." "However," the Committee goes on, "the medical profession should recognize that traits other than just being a respectable practitioner and a good fellow are required. Board work requires a flair for the judicial, for forceful, fair-minded and courageous individuals. Too often selections are made on the basis of teaching or scientific accomplishments—or as an honor to a respected practitioner. Unless an individual is interested in this field, is willing to work at mastering its complexities, and has the intestinal fortitude to withstand the many complaints and criticisms to which he will be subjected, his ability to serve is limited."

Often board members are sluggish on discipline because they are reluctant to withdraw a colleague's license to practice. "Of course the board is supposed to protect the public and not the livelihood of practitioners," one doctor has said. "But no one enjoys depriving a fellow physician of his means of making a living."

Actually, no deprivation need result from withdrawal of a license. Treating patients is only one of many well-rewarded uses medical knowledge can be put to, as substantiated by the fact that fully two out of five M.D.s are in employment other than private practice.

Medically trained personnel are in such short supply that even the physician whose license has been withdrawn can readily find administrative or scientific work. One doctor, whose license has been revoked for narcotic violations, is a narcotic addict and an alcoholic and is awaiting trial on a felony charge. Moreover, he is a poor employment risk, having run through jobs with a medical publisher, an advertising agency, and a pharmaceutical company. Despite this spotty record, he can turn down job offers. Employers feel they can still put his knowledge of medicine to profitable use.

Some licensing boards dissipate their resources by over-reacting to dubious offenses. These misguided efforts drain limited time and scarce money while more important problems are neglected.

One such ripple occurred in Nevada after a doctor new to a town offended three established practitioners. In conversations with colleagues, he purportedly described one of the physicians as "the city drunk." Another, a woman M.D., he called, supposedly, "nothing but a lousy old midwife." After being associated with the third for a while, he severed the relationship, presumably saying his standards were too high for the other man.

The board, after hearing accounts of these conversations, revoked the doctor's license. The charge it found him guilty of was "conduct unbecoming a person licensed to practice medicine or detrimental to the best interests of the public."

On appeal the State Supreme Court ordered the board to reinstate the doctor's license. Ruled the court: "It has never been held that public health . . . requires protection through the suppression of criticism."

LESS THAN THE SUM OF ITS PARTS

In this mobile nation of freely crossable boundaries, there is no effective system of keeping tabs on medical offenders. It is relatively simple for a credit bureau to discover that a housewife left a bill unpaid in an opposite corner of the country. By contrast, a medical licensing board may need to labor long and hard to discover that an applicant was removed from practice in the next state.

Across the country, medical disciplinary bodies are characterized by fragmentation and disorganization. Medical societies and state licensing boards fail to exchange information. In all of medicine there is no central clearinghouse where doctors disciplined in one locale can be learned about elsewhere.

Although the Federation of State Medical Boards is the central organization of licensing bodies, not all boards keep in touch with it. The *Federation Bulletin* publishes a news section called "State Board Actions." This is the natural medium through which boards can inform one another of revocations, suspensions, court actions, and the like. But only a few states avail themselves of it, and the Federation remains unapprised of many actions.

There is not even adequate communication between state boards that have endorsement agreements. Under such arrangements, a licensee of one state is automatically entitled to a license from another. But the lack of liaison between boards that endorse one another's licenses allows a situation like the following to develop:

A practitioner got a license from one state board by presenting false credentials. With this license, he secured another from an endorsing state. The original board found him out and revoked his license. The doctor moved his office to the second state and, using the license he got by endorsement, set up practice there.

It was only long afterward, and by chance, that the second board learned of the original fraud and withdrew the license it had granted. In some cases, a doctor who is unfit to practice has a record that is technically spotless. Board members who are fearful of libel suits may be unwilling to tell in response to an inquiry all that they know about him. Thus the board may report nothing more than the literal truth: that it has "no derogatory information" on file.

One physician illustrates the kind who can slip through on this technicality. The doctor has been arrested for drunken driving and for carrying a concealed weapon. He has been arrested and tried for complicity in an armed robbery. He is a close associate of members of the underworld. He is an alcoholic, and for three years was in a mental hospital. But officially his record is clear.

On his arrests, either charges were dropped or he was acquitted. His sole blemish is the commitment to a mental institution. However, the hospital has cleared his record by issuing glowing reports of his rehabilitation.

Not keeping in touch with law enforcement agencies is another reason boards fail to learn of doctors with criminal records. Often the board learns of a doctor's conviction only from the newspapers, and many times not at all. Dr. George H. Lage, in his presidential address before the Federation of State Medical Boards, admonished board members for being loath to make inquiries of law enforcement agencies. "Is this problem caused by an erroneous idea that a doctor is not subject to the laws of the state or fear of the board becoming involved with the law enforcement agencies?" Dr. Lage challenged, "Or, is it a reluctance on the part of the boards to direct inquiries to law enforcement agencies because they haven't learned to communicate with them?"

An equally weak line connects licensing boards and medical societies, even within the same state. One board official has said: "Medical societies don't tell us much about their discipline of members. There is no chain of communication between the board and local medical societies." Another board member reports: "The state association is extremely reluctant to sign a complaint in a disciplinary proceeding before the board."

In consequence, this has happened: A medical society expelled a member for an offense that should also have led to the suspension of his license. But the society does not let the board know of disciplinary actions it takes. The offender has thus retained his license and, even without his society membership, continues a large practice.

Communication is often blocked at the board's end as well. One board operates in secrecy, not informing the county or state medical society of its action against a member. After finding one doctor guilty of a serious violation of the medical practice act, the board censured him and placed him on probation. Shortly afterward, the unknowing members of his medical society elected him to a position of trust and honor.

In sum, then, state medical licensing laws are far too weak. State governments often do not support medical discipline. State boards in large part do not do an adequate job.

"How serious is the matter?" the *Federation Bulletin* has asked rhetorically. Its reply: "If a state cannot, or does not, for just cause revoke a license or discipline a physician, it should take a critical look at its obligation. . . . A license to practice also becomes a license to abuse."

4
Disorganized Medicine

Dr. Emil Warren (we'll call him) was one of medicine's shadow people. Over the years he drifted from one community to another. Sometimes he took a job in a hospital or in a plant infirmary. Other times he tried general practice.

Dr. Warren set up an office in a suburb. Soon the local doctors became aware of his mistakes. They rebroke bones that had been set incorrectly, attended emergencies he could have averted with good medical management, and repaired injuries he had left while attempting surgery in his office.

Warren's colleagues were embarrassed by him. "He's an obscenity on the face of medicine," declared a hospital chief of staff, and none who knew Warren's work disagreed. Yet not one of the physicians in the community seriously considered initiating action against him. And so he continued practicing undisturbed.

One day a pediatrician was brought a four-year-old girl whom Dr. Warren had been seeing for nearly two years. The girl's mouth and tongue were inflamed. Her buttocks and groin were wasted. She was so emaciated and dehydrated that her weight was less than half the norm for her age.

Warren had not recognized this as celiac disease, a reasonably common intestinal disorder of young children. Nor had he thought to seek a consultation when the girl failed to respond to his treatment.

"We've got to get rid of this guy," the pediatrician told his colleagues at the next meeting of their county medical society. After a long discussion they agreed to inform Warren that he "could not count on the support of the local medical community." A delegation was sent to Warren with this message. Shortly thereafter he closed his office and left the area.

This pleased the local doctors. Except the pediatrician. "Occasionally," he says, "I wonder where he's practicing now."

FRATERNITY FEELING

In many communities a wrongdoer can move away with the tacit understanding that his record will stay clean if only he will go. Dr. Rhett McMahon of the Federation of State Medical Boards has reported: "Frequently his transgressions are known only to his local colleagues, who sigh with relief to be rid of their 'problem' without the distasteful matter of formal complaints and actions." When the doctor applies for a license or society membership elsewhere, his former colleagues are reluctant to speak against him, especially if his offenses have never gone on record.

"Medical societies think that their job is done when a totally incompetent physician is allowed to resign from their society or moves to another community," a health insurance executive observed in his statement to the A.M.A. Medical Disciplinary Committee. "Medicine is too lenient," a medical society official told the Committee. In its report, the Committee concluded: "Organized medicine has the personnel, funds, and channels of communication to alert, inform, and stress the course of action necessary. The medical press contains too few articles in this field. There is too little factual material being promulgated to the profession and the public.

"Due to this lack of forceful leadership, the average physician and constituent and component medical society, or specialty group, have only enough courage and sense of responsibility to discipline the worst and most consistent offenders."

The law grants medical societies considerable latitude in dealing with unethical or unprofessional conduct. Court decisions have established that medical societies have the right to make their own rules on the admission and exclusion of members. Medical societies may also adopt and enforce requirements that have a reasonable connection with improving and maintaining professional standards.

Medical society disciplinary activity is limited in that only members are affected. In many communities, the worst offenders have resigned or been expelled from the local society or have not joined it. They thus practice outside the society's jurisdiction. Patients, moreover, generally attach little importance to whether or not a physician is a member of his local society. "To them we're all doctors," a member of the Medical Disciplinary Committee has remarked. "I have never yet had a patient ask me if I was a member of my county society."

A further limitation is that expulsion from membership is the severest penalty a society can impose. Unless the state licensing board also acts, the violator remains legally privileged to practice. The executive director of one state medical association recalls: "We have expelled doctors from our county and state medical societies only to find that, unless their licenses are revoked, these actions do not have much effect."

This has been demonstrated in one county where an ear, nose and throat specialist was using a discredited form of nasal surgery. To cure polyps and other nasal conditions, he stripped away the mucous membrane lining the nose. This produces atrophic rhinitis, a painful and generally avoidable wasting away of nasal tissue and mucous glands.

After many patient's noses had thus been ruined, the surgeon's specialty association asked him to improve his methods. When he refused, the association expelled him. The county medical society found him guilty of gross mistreatment of patients and withdrew his membership. He sued the society for reinstatement. To fight the suit, society members paid special assessments for legal costs. In court, with supporting testimony from the specialty association, the county society proved its charges and made the expulsion stick.

But because the doctor's license has not been revoked, he is still in practice. He continues to perform questionable surgery in a hospital he owns. From time to time the county medical society receives a letter of complaint from a patient he has injured. The society replies that the doctor is no longer a member and there is nothing it can do.

Such cases argue for stronger measures by licensing boards. But even without licensure powers, medical societies can nonetheless exert much control over members' behavior. For one thing, a society can isolate an offender from the professional and social circle he has grown to depend on. The individual doctor even more than most humans needs the cooperation and approval of his colleagues, for whom he feels a kinship to the exclusion of laymen. In *The Political Life of the American Medical Association,* Oliver Garceau discusses the rigorous disciplinary sanctions available to medical societies: "The social life of the county society is important. . . . Ostracism becomes a terrible weapon."

In studying why this is so, sociologists have found that medical school is to most physicians much as Parris Island is to most United States Marines: an ordeal so profound that it remakes everyone who goes through it. With physicians the basic training is intellectual and lasts years instead of months. But, like the leatherneck, the doctor feels a man apart, at one only with others who share his special knowledge and experience.

Medical school reorganizes the student's way of thinking from that of a layman to that of a doctor. The student becomes a trustee of medical science and its clinical applications. In his freshman year alone—after being exposed typically to anatomy, biochemistry, embryology, genetics, neurology, psychiatry, physiology and statistics—his vocabulary is increased by more than 13,000 scientific terms. During his training he becomes familiar with the signs and symptoms of many diseases. He learns how to take a medical history and how to perform a physical examination. He acquires the skill of arriving at a diagnosis by deductive reasoning—"medical logic," many physicians call it. He learns the various methods of treatment he can use for the conditions he diagnoses.

All this is accompanied by a phenomenon akin to culture shock. The medical student must adjust to a seventy- or eighty-hour study week, with the realization that despite his labors he is faced with far more information than it will ever be possible for him to learn. As part of his adjustment, he develops a tolerance for uncertainty. This is a characteristic point of view the practicing physician must have if he is to perform successfully. But it is one that flies in the face of most laymen, who need to *know* before they can proceed comfortably.

Medical students further learn to value "medical responsibility." This is the authority and accountability that a doctor has in respect to the welfare of his patient. It implies conscientiousness and the physician's recognition of the damage he can do if he performs badly. One mark of a maturing physician is that he becomes increasingly self-confident. He seeks more and more responsibility, ever more willing to answer for how he performs when acting according to his own judgment. This readiness to assume responsibility for another person's well-being is yet another point of separation between the doctor and the layman, for few laymen would willingly undertake such a burden.

Medical training also moves a student further and further from lay notions about life, death, and suffering. A study at the University of Kansas Medical School shows that freshmen start out as laymen desiring to "help" people but with no technical understanding of how to do it. As they go through school they discover specific things that need to be done. "Preserving life" is translated into individual medical procedures, each with a particular purpose. "Suffering" divides into signs and symptoms that characterize the patient's condition. By dint of his training—and his continued exposure to illness and pain—the student develops toward patients an impersonality that further differentiates him from laymen.

"Another effect of medical education is a growing tendency of the student as he moves through school to develop a professional self-image—to take on the identity of a doctor," sociologist Howard S. Becker, of Stanford University, has observed. From interviews with medical students, Constance A. Nathanson, of the University of Chicago, has seen this physician identity develop over the four-year medical curriculum. Freshmen, she found, are oriented to the interests of the patient and think close relationships with colleagues are potentially subversive to patient welfare. By contrast, seniors stress the need for preserving solidarity with fellow physicians and for protecting the interests of the professional group.

A person thus molded into a doctor often comes to rely on his colleagues for social as well as professional contacts. His private and professional lives are so intertwined that he frequently cannot see himself functioning outside the medical community. The threat of medical society censure, suspension, or expulsion may therefore be as effective a deterrent as the possible loss of his license.

An offender who is removed from a medical society loses the many positive benefits and economic advantages that accrue to members in good standing. Membership in a society has been adopted by some outside groups as a criterion of professional competence. During World War II, for example, an application to serve as a medical officer in the U.S. Navy was not considered unless accompanied by a letter certifying that the psysician was a member in good standing in a medical society. Many agencies —many hospitals, in particular—still retain this requirement. In many communities, hospital privileges are granted only if a doctor is a member of the local medical society.

A physician who loses his membership is further denied association with men in his science, and so misses out on opportunities for exchange of knowledge and for acquisition of professional status. He is not welcome at society meetings. He cannot take part in society scientific programs. He cannot be active on society committees.

Many medical societies negotiate malpractice insurance plans for their members. A nonmember almost certainly will find it difficult to get coverage on terms comparable to those enjoyed by members. He may have to pay twice as much for the same policy. Some malpractice insurers refuse to write any policies at all for nonmembers.

Expulsion so carries the stigma of unethical practice that members who have professional relations with expelled or suspended physicians may themselves be considered unethical. A doctor who has been disciplined is likely to no longer get referrals, and this loss of patients may severely hurt his practice. If he refers a patient to a society member, he may not get the patient back. A letter to the society charging patient-stealing may well go unacknowledged, for the expelled physician is very much an outcast.

This also extends into personal relations. Associating with a pariah may be regarded as so dangerous that friends may shun him. This is not only a characteristic of small, tightly knit medical communities. In Manhattan a physician was expelled from the New York County Medical Society on charges of illegal abortion. He visited a friend of long standing. "Get out of my office," he was told. "Don't visit me or call me. I don't want to see you. I don't want to hear from you. Just go."

Because the medical society can hold such sway over its members, it stands with the state licensing board as an instrument for medical discipline. Medicine's leaders often express an obligation to society at large to enforce proper conduct by physicians. "The medical profession should safeguard the public and itself against physicians deficient in moral character or professional competence," says Section 4 of the Principles of Medical Ethics. "Policing ourselves is the price we must pay for a system that allows us the free practice of medicine," adds Dr. Henry A. Davidson, editor of the *Journal of the Medical Society of New Jersey*.

When the A.M.A. Medical Disciplinary Committee asked state society officials, "What is the medical society's obligation in the matter of medical discipline?" they replied: "To protect the public's health; . . . to curtail the activities of physicians who show themselves to be a menace to the public; . . . to discipline its own members." The Committee itself concluded: "Physicians have been permitted by society to maintain discipline within the profession. This privilege places upon medicine the obligation to establish and support workable disciplinary mechanisms."

So much, then, for the great disciplinary power that medical societies have. And so much for expressions of an obligation to use it. How do the societies actually respond to the need for medical discipline?

INSIDE THE A.M.A.

At 535 North Dearborn Street, on the fringe of Chicago's commercial center, stands a plain blockish office building. This is the national headquarters of the American Medical Association.

More than 210,000—over 2 out of 3—American M.D.s belong to the A.M.A. The principal exceptions are salaried physicians. They often find professional contacts and advancement without belonging to a medical society. Other nonmembers include retired physicians who let their membership lapse after leaving practice. Some new physicians do not yet have local society membership, a prerequisite for belonging to the A.M.A. In some sections of the South, Negro physicians are discouraged or prohibited from joining the local society, and by extension are kept out of the A.M.A. And where a local society does not require A.M.A. membership, some physicians do not care to pay the additional dues or dislike the organization and prefer not to belong to it. Despite these exceptions, the A.M.A. is without parallel *the* organization of the medical profession. In all probability it lives up to its claim of being "the largest, most influential, and most active medical association in the world."

Nearly 1,000 staff employees work at A.M.A. headquarters. A visitor—noting the predominance of female clerical workers, the ubiquitous clacking of typewriters, the spare functional furnishings, the neutral-toned linoleum floors, the featureless partitions—may be reminded of the office of a government agency. The similarity is more than coincidental, for the medical profession resembles a nation within the nation, and the A.M.A. performs many quasi-governmental functions.

Laymen often associate the A.M.A. with its legislative activities and political conservatism. People who do not like the organization are fond of recalling that in addition to Medicare the A.M.A. has fought many other "tentacles of socialized medicine," a familiar phrase around A.M.A. headquarters. These tentacles have included voluntary health insurance, Social Security benefits for the totally disabled, federal-state infant and maternal health programs, federal financing of community mental health centers, federal aid to medical education, and federal assistance to states for medical examination of schoolchildren.

This, however, takes a narrow view of the A.M.A., if only because its legislative record also includes a number of progressive stands. The association has supported food and drug legislation stronger than that which

Congress passed, the establishment of a national Department of Health with Cabinet status, the setting up of the National Institutes of Health research centers, the extension of medical benefits to welfare recipients. Most bills that are proposed are not so much black and white as they are subject to revision, and the A.M.A. has engendered much respect on Capitol Hill for its suggestions on ways to improve health legislation.

Moreover, although the A.M.A. may originally oppose a measure, if it becomes law the organized profession generally takes a constructive role in its implementation. Medical advisory committees are nearly universal in government health programs. After Medicare was enacted, its first Health Insurance Benefits Advisory Council included Dr. Samuel Sherman of San Francisco, chairman of the A.M.A.'s Council on Legislative Activities. The A.M.A. similarly maintains liaison with other programs in the Social Security Administration and in the Social and Rehabilitation Service, the Defense Department, the Veterans Administration, the Public Health Service.

While the A.M.A.'s dealings with government loom large in their effect on the public, they are only a part of the association's total activity. The headquarters staff helps coordinate the entire profession, and there is virtually no area in health and medicine that is not administratively represented to some degree in the organization.

A.M.A. operations thus are extremely complex and varied. At a policy level are some 800 member physicians on about 100 committees and subcommittees. To illustrate their diversity, some deal with training (the Committee on Continuing Medical Education, the Internship Review Committee); some with specialized interests (the Committee on Aerospace Medicine, the Committee on Occupational Toxicology); some with medicosocial problems (the Committee on Alcohol and Addiction, the Committee on Medical Aspects of Automotive Safety).

To support A.M.A. operations, the headquarters staff is organized into a number of divisions that serve separate corners of the world of medicine. Names and functions change, but as of this writing: a Scientific Activities Division is responsible for technical programs relating to the various specialties and for environmental health (encompassing such matters as air pollution, water supply, radiological health). A Division of Medical Education deals with medical training and with allied health professions. A Division of Health Service handles governmental programs (federal medical services, welfare plans, disaster medical care); the distribution of medical services (insurance, manpower, forms of medical practice); medical care facilities (hospitals, clinics, nursing homes).

The A.M.A. is also a major publishing enterprise. The income it receives from advertising is by far its largest source of revenue. A Scientific Publications Division puts out the weekly *Journal* and ten monthly specialty journals. A Communications Division, besides generating reams of public relations material, publishes the *A.M.A. News*—a weekly business and political tabloid sent to all doctors—and *Today's Health*, a monthly family magazine on medical topics. Other departments of the association publish thirteen miscellaneous periodicals plus scores of pamphlets and other informational items.

Elsewhere among A.M.A. activities, a Public Affairs Division contains the A.M.A.'s "roving ambassadors." Some doctors call them "traveling salesmen." They are lobbyists and also the field representatives who promote A.M.A. programs among state and county societies. The association also keeps in touch with community organizations ranging alphabetically from Altrusa International (16,500 members) to Zonta International (18,-000). The Management Services Division—a secretariat with responsibility for funds, personnel, and facilities—maintains a data-processing center whose banks of computers and file cabinets keep tabs on every medical man in the country from the time he enters medical school until he dies. Its archive-library is believed to contain the world's largest collection on the sociology and economics of medicine. Here, too, are managed the A.M.A. conventions: the huge annual meeting, which draws about 35,000 physicians and visitors; a midyear meeting, which attracts nearly 10,000. In addition, the A.M.A. sponsors a multitude of specialized meetings. A single year's list includes a National Symposium on Venereal Disease Control, a Western Hemisphere Nutrition Conference, a Conference of State Mental Health Representatives, an Air Pollution Medical Research Conference, a Legal Conference for Medical Society Representatives, a Congress on Occupational Health.

Now: Where amid all this activity is medical discipline? Where are charges brought against offenders? Where are the investigators of doctors believed untrustworthy and incompetent? In the Law Division, which is largely concerned with corporation law and malpractice suits, is the Department of Investigation. It serves as a clearinghouse for information on nostrums and other aspects of pseudomedicine. While it combats quackery and checks the records of physicians on request from other agencies, the bulk of its work is directed against non-M.D. charlatans rather than offending M.D.s. Similarly, a Department of Medical Ethics, consisting of two professionals and their secretaries, furnishes staff support for the Judicial Council of the House of Delegates. The Department assists state and local societies on matters relating to ethics and discipline. A principal recent activity has been the organizing of the National Congress on Medical Ethics.

These activities aside, except under extremely unusual circumstances *the A.M.A. has no disciplinary authority over an offending physician.* At an A.M.A. convention that considered this lack of authority, a member of the House of Delegates protested: "This is a preposterous situation. The A.M.A. can assume unyielding positions before Congress. The A.M.A. can commit the entire medical profession to wide-ranging courses of action. Yet the A.M.A. can't proceed against some deadbeat in Podunk who's a disgrace to every doctor."

The reason for this is that the A.M.A. is set up as a loose federation of 54 independent associations comprising 1,936 county medical societies. A.M.A. leaders and the headquarters staff can and do exercise a great deal of leadership, but mostly on national matters. The constituent societies tend to regard discipline as a local matter, and for the most part grant the national association no real disciplinary power. "First and foremost," Dr. Raymond M. McKeown, chairman of the Medical Disciplinary Committee, has reported, "it is evident that in the matter of medical discipline the principle of state's rights is paramount. Each state . . . seems firmly convinced that discipline is the prerogative of the medical profession within their respective states."

The Judicial Council, the A.M.A.'s committee on ethics, is thus hampered in its disciplinary function. Reserved to it are only isolated powers. To see how special a situation must be before the Judicial Council can take action on its own authority, consider the case of Dr. Charles E. Smith.

Dr. Smith was the chief psychiatrist and medical director of the Federal Bureau of Prisons in late September 1962, when riots were taking place at the University of Mississippi over James Meredith's efforts to desegregate the school. On hand with those rioting against a Negro's admission to Ole Miss was former Major General Edwin A. Walker. General Walker had left the Army during a furor over his right-wing activities, which included his seeking to indoctrinate Army troops in Germany with material prepared by the John Birch Society. Now, because of his alleged activities during the Mississippi riots, General Walker was arrested on federal charges of incitement to insurrection.

On October 1, an attorney in the U.S. Department of Justice asked Dr. Smith to examine a file about General Walker. It contained the General's Army medical records. Also in the file were a transcript of testimony he gave before a Senate armed services subcommittee and a number of news articles quoting him and describing his behavior. According to his affidavit, Dr. Smith, after a six-hour study of the material, concluded:

"Some of his reported behavior reflects sensitivity and essentially unpredictable and seemingly bizarre outbursts of the type often observed in individuals suffering with paranoid mental disorder. There are also indications in his medical history of functional and psychosomatic disorders which could be precursors of the more serious disorder which his present behavior suggests. . . . I believe his recent behavior has been out of keeping with that of a person of his station, background, and training, and that as such it may be indicative of an underlying mental disturbance."

Largely on the basis of Dr. Smith's opinion, a U.S. District Court decided that there was a reasonable question whether General Walker was mentally competent to understand the proceedings against him and aid in his own defense. Therefore, ruled the district judge, a psychiatric examination of the General would be proper.

An examining psychiatrist subsequently submitted a report. The court found that "no opinion is expressed therein that General Walker is presently insane or presently incompetent" as defined by the law. It was therefore ruled that the General was mentally able to stand trial. The charges against him were ultimately dismissed.

Meanwhile, some doctors were reacting sharply to Dr. Smith's part in the case. Letters to the A.M.A. accused him of Communist sympathies and leftist chicanery. Two county medical societies formally alleged unethical conduct. It was charged that Dr. Smith had "made a medical diagnosis of General Walker without a personal examination, contrary to good medical practice, and that he violated the physician-patient relationship by making public statements concerning General Walker's health."

Strong sentiment on the Walker case was expressed by the American Academy of General Practice at its annual meeting. The policy-making Congress of Delegates resolved that "a protest in the strongest of terms be made condemning the actions taken by the government to accomplish mischief by designing men and to bring injustice and great personal damage to one citizen of the U.S.A., namely former Major General Edwin A. Walker."

Dr. Smith was a "service member" of the A.M.A. This is a category of membership reserved for physicians in the armed forces and in federal agencies. They belong to no local medical society but to the A.M.A. directly, and their discipline comes under the jurisdiction of the Judicial Council.

In the case of Dr. Smith, the Council consulted three psychiatrists and also the A.M.A.'s Council on Mental Health and the American Psychiatric Association. It was their unanimous opinion that Dr. Smith had merely rendered a professional opinion as physicians often do to help a court decide a technical point: whether or not Walker should be examined by a psychiatrist. The Council absolved Dr. Smith of any wrongdoing. It ruled that he "did not violate the Principles of Medical Ethics, did not violate the professional confidence, and did not make a diagnosis."

In all, the A.M.A. has fewer than 20,000 service members. Since physicians in the military and in federal employment are among the most closely supervised in the country, they raise few disciplinary problems. Even an investigation, such as in the case of Dr. Smith, is almost unprecedented. "If it weren't for the political overtones of the case, we probably wouldn't have heard of Dr. Smith at all," a member of the Judicial Council has said.

Thus, in respect to disciplining service members, the Judicial Council has extremely little to do. Proceedings against all other types of members must first go through the local societies. In June 1961 the Medical Disciplinary Committee recommended that A.M.A. bylaws be changed to permit the national organization to suspend or revoke membership of a violator regardless of whether action has been taken against him at local level. The purpose of granting the A.M.A. original jurisdiction was to provide for disciplinary action where a local society was failing to act against the offender.

The House of Delegates later passed the greatly weakened amendment that is now in effect. It empowers the Judicial Council to take action with respect only to the physician's *A.M.A.* membership, leaving his local society membership unaffected. Moreover, the Council can proceed only (1) when the state medical association requests such action, or (2) when at the A.M.A.'s request, the state association consents to it.

These provisions have not altered the highly local nature of medical discipline, and their effect has been minimal. Three years after the amendment took effect, the Council had heard but one case. It concerned international plagiarism, not one of medicine's most pressing disciplinary problems. A New Jersey physician had gone to a medical conference in Europe and there delivered a paper on electromyography, the recording of the electric potentials developed in muscle. The paper, much of it word for word, had been taken from an article published by another doctor. The fact that the member had been sponsored by an A.M.A. specialty body prompted the Medical Society of New Jersey to grant jurisdiction to the Judicial Council. It was an open-and-shut case. The Council reprimanded the doctor and had his membership suspended. A few months later he was reinstated.

AT THE STATE LEVEL

"Organized medicine, hell!" the executive secretary of a state medical association has said. "In discipline, we ought to be called disorganized medicine."

To begin with, the societies of the fifty states and four state-equivalent areas (the District of Columbia, Puerto Rico, the Virgin Islands, and the Canal Zone) each follow their own rules and inclinations on discipline. Little effort is made to coordinate their activities. State societies rarely consult one another. Although the A.M.A.'s Department of Investigation serves in part as a central repository of disciplinary information, not all states report to it or consult it. "With just the least bit of help and cooperation among the states there could be a valuable interchange of information," Dr. Raymond McKeown has observed. "There cannot be and there will not be progress or development . . . if A.M.A. is not prepared to act as a clearinghouse."

Furthermore, state society constitutions and bylaws are weak in their disciplinary provisions. No state society requires members to keep abreast of medical progress. In a survey conducted by Dr. R. C. Derbyshire of the Federation of State Medical Boards, only eight state societies report they can take action against a member for incompetence. This includes mental as well as professional incompetence. During the five years preceding Dr. Derbyshire's study, charges of incompetence were brought in a mere seven cases.

"Every state medical society suffers from timidity in matters of discipline. We've got to get more hard-boiled." Such was a comment of an official of a southern state society during a Medical Disciplinary Committee meeting in Atlanta. His observation is borne out by the sparseness of state society disciplinary activity. Over a period of five years, state societies reported an average of 126 disciplinary procedures per year, or an average of less than three per state. In the average year, these procedures resulted in a total of only 6 expulsions and 11 suspensions. In one year the actual total was merely 82 disciplinary procedures for all the states. In the final year of this period, there were 118 procedures—but 81 of these were in just two states (Massachusetts and Nebraska). In 33 states, there were no procedures at all.

One reason for this inactivity is that many state societies are slow to recognize the existence of a disciplinary problem. Dr. Raymond McKeown tells of receiving a "not atypical" letter from a state society saying, "We have no particular disciplinary problem with our members." The Medical Disciplinary Committee was "disturbed" over this letter, recalls Dr. Mc-Keown, for it also had in its files a report of a current grand jury investigation in the same state. The grand jury said that it had detected in more than one case "apathy and reluctance on the part of the medical profession to purge its own members even when a member of the profession is clearly incompetent."

Possibly the commonest cause for inaction is the state association's belief that discipline is a local matter, to be handled by the county societies. A state typically conducts disciplinary proceedings only after the case has first gone through the county society, entering a case only if it is appealed from the county level. Very rarely, the county society feels it cannot handle a complaint. More than half a county society's members were named in one allegation of improper commitment to a psychiatric institution. A state committee mediated the grievance. Similarly, a state society committee heard a complaint of overcharging that had been raised against a medical group whose members dominated the county society.

Seldom do state societies initiate proceedings. The Medical Disciplinary Committee draws this conclusion: "State medical associations have not been as effective as they could be in the area of medical discipline because of the practice of limiting their concern to matters that are appealed to them from the [county] level. . . . Considerable apathy at the county and state level in taking action against offenders [has also] contributed to the situation."

Moreover, the Committee found that despite the state societies' emphasis on local responsibility, most have "no method of encouraging county societies to be more active and no means of advising county societies of problems or procedures." Conversely, few counties report disciplinary proceedings to the state. "The states have little or no knowledge of what is being done," the Medical Disciplinary Committee has commented. As a result, an offender disciplined in one county can move to another in the same state or to one outside the state. In response to an inquiry, the state society will unknowingly give him a clean bill of health.

Even if the county society is asked directly, it may be unwilling to provide information about a violator. "It is apparent that 'trials' are kept in the family." Dr. H. Thomas McGuire, a member of the Medical Disciplinary Committee, has observed. One official, whose medical society checks applicants thoroughly before granting membership, reports being obstructed on this account. The A.M.A. is cooperative in promptly supplying what information it has. State societies usually tell what they know. But he has found: "Local societies just do not cooperate. They are reluctant to supply derogatory information about a physician. . . . The people who can give you information are either afraid to do so or don't care once a problem doctor moves out of their area. As long as he is no longer their problem, they don't care."

IN THE COUNTIES

"The present dilemma over discipline comes largely from weakness at the County Society level." Thus the *Federation Bulletin* has summed up why organized medicine is generally failing to police itself: Effective disciplinary powers are concentrated in the county societies. But local societies as a rule are lax in discipline.

The basic unit of county society discipline is the "grievance committee." In counties where a grievance committee is functioning, a typical case is likely to follow this course: A patient, usually a woman, first phones the society office to register a complaint. "Have you talked the problem over with the doctor?" she is asked. If she hasn't, she is requested to do so.

This direct contact resolves about half the complaints. Remaining complaints need to be submitted in writing, and the doctor is asked to submit his side of the story. If there is a conflict as to the facts in the case, the committee will probably ask the contenders to come in for a hearing. Otherwise, to save time, cases are settled from the written evidence, with possible supplementation by telephone.

The typical case concerns the doctor's fee. Often the committee finds that the fee was fair but the doctor neglected to explain that it included an injection or laboratory work, or was for a more extensive service than the patient understood. The committee will explain this to the patient. If the fee was actually above the going rate, the committee will generally advise the doctor to make an adjustment.

Allegations of rudeness are another large area of patient complaints. In Ohio, a woman at her husband's bedside was angered when the doctor told her, "Move it away, honey." In Pennsylvania, a woman describing her symptoms was asked, "What medical school did you say you went to?" Some patients are oversensitive. A Chicago woman complained her doctor was "arrogant." She had offered him a cigarette. Absent-mindedly he pocketed the whole pack. Grievance committees generally are adept at soothing patients' feelings, sometimes with a noncommittal apology like, "We are sorry you were offended."

Ideally, grievance committees provide satisfaction for aggrieved patients and a means of disciplining offending colleagues. For these reasons, the A.M.A. has long encouraged local societies to implement grievance committee procedures. In December 1949, an A.M.A. convention adopted a resolution commending associations that had grievance committees and urging all others to adopt comparable programs. An A.M.A. president, Dr. David B. Allman, said, "If we individual physicians do not keep medicine's house in order, outside organizations—like . . . government—will do it for us. That is why medical grievance committees are protecting the honest and capable physicians as much as they are the patient." The A.M.A. *Public Relations Manual* calls grievance committees "the solution" to most physician-patient disagreements. "In addition," the *Manual* goes on, "they provide one kind of machinery by which the profession can police its own ranks, to eliminate professional incompetence and economic abuses."

Yet county societies are not generally using grievance committees as effective disciplinary mechanisms. Some 40 percent of county societies replying to an A.M.A. survey lack such committees. Even among the large county societies, with 500 to 1,500 members, there are two that have yet to establish a grievance committee.

Societies that have grievance committees often render them ineffective. Some societies relegate a miscellany of functions to the committee, impeding its disciplinary activity. Societies also minimize the grievance functions of the committee by calling it the Welfare Committee, the Public Liaison Committee, the Committee on Professional Relations. The A.M.A.'s *Guides for Medical Society Grievance Committees* holds that misleading titles and extraneous duties divert a committee from its real job: " 'Grievance committee' is unquestionably the most realistic title and the one best understood by the profession and the public. Any unfortunate disguising of a grievance committee's true purpose, by the use of inappropriate titles or by ascribing to it a multiplicity of functions, negates realization of valuable benefits to the profession and the public alike."

Many societies further obscure the committee by failing to let the public know about it. An A.M.A. study of county society activities shows that only about one in five societies publicize their grievance programs. The *A.M.A. Public Relations Manual* notes: "It is highly inconsistent for a medical society to set up a . . . committee and then keep it a secret from the public. . . . Some physicians fear that a grievance committee will evoke complaints from a great number of cranks and psychopaths. This has not proved to be the case in areas where . . . committees function and are well publicized."

At the opposite extreme, some societies, mindful of the publicity value of the committees, tend to give them more play than they are worth. One Medical Disciplinary Committee member has observed: "Many grievance committees are valuable for public relations but are not doing the job that needs to be done. Some are toothless watchdogs that bark but don't bite."

Many grievance committees are further handicapped by cumbersome procedures and negligible authority. Often the grievance committee is nothing more than an informal advisory body. It lacks power to discipline the membership. It receives some complaints but not others. It cannot initiate investigations. It cannot compel a member to respond to a charge. Because such procedural weaknesses are widespread, the Medical Disciplinary Committee has heard from far-flung county societies remarkably similar calls for better methods. For example, from the Omaha-Douglas County Medical Society in Nebraska: "There is a need for more effective procedures of professional discipline." From Dade County (Miami), Florida: "There is undoubtedly need for more effective procedure for professional discipline in this area." From Hartford County, Connecticut: "Inasmuch as professional discipline is a most difficult thing at best, we certainly would like to have more effective methods of carrying out this type of control."

Under most societies' bylaws, the most a grievance committee can do is advise an offending physician to follow its recommendations. Only a rare committee is empowered to take direct action: to censure, suspend, or expel the offender if he fails to accept its findings. Far more typically, if a violator ignores the committee, bylaws make it necessary to refer him to the society's ethics committee or governing board for a hearing and possibly to the total membership for final action.

Few grievance committees care to do this, preferring to feel they have already succeeded in bringing "moral weight" against the colleague. Thus the matter ends. One society secretary told the Medical Disciplinary Committee: "Members of the grievance committee do not have sufficient respect for their position or their responsibilities." An official of an Ohio county society has said that disciplinary procedures in his area sometimes fail to achieve their intended purpose because of a "natural reluctance on the part of the committee to take immediate and strong action."

Rare too is the ethics committee, governing board or membership at large that will act vigorously against an offender. This hesitancy discourages grievance committees from referring cases or attempting effective action. "All too often, violations go unpunished . . . because a board or committee judging an alleged violator is timid," said Dr. Franklin J. Evans, president of the Florida Academy of General Practice. Extreme leniency characterizes county society disciplinary actions—"a tendency to whitewash," a Maine society officer calls it.

One society official has reported how a county disciplinary committee dealt with an alcoholic physician. Patients had objected to the doctor's poor technique and had complained that he often had the odor of alcohol on his breath. The society attempted to resolve the problem by recommending that the doctor "seek a cure for alcoholism." In another case, a doctor was found guilty of selling narcotics to high school students. The committee voted that he be expelled—and then suspended the sentence.

Elsewhere, a committee brought about an adjustment, but covered up for the offending colleague. A woman complained that the $750 charged her by a doctor was too high. The committee agreed that the fee was excessive.

"We think $400 is adequate," the chairman told the doctor. "Will you make a reduction if she calls you?" He said he would. However, the chairman wrote the woman: "You have been charged a reasonable fee. But in view of your financial condition it is suggested that you contact your doctor for the purpose of arriving at a mutually satisfactory charge."

Yet another instance of disciplinary timidity resulted in a good deal of buck-passing. After charges were filed against a physician, his county society's ethics committee declined to take action because of the "prominence of the accused in the society and in the community." The committee asked the society as a whole to consider the charges. The society membership voted to refer the case to the councilor for their district in the state society. The district official sent it on to the president of the state society. He in turn asked the A.M.A. Judicial Council to decide the matter. The Judicial Council sent it back with the message: "If local societies fail to curtail unethical practices, ethics lose their effectiveness."

Fear of litigation inhibits much medical society disciplinary activity. Society officials, worried that a disciplined doctor will file a libel or antitrust suit, hold back on taking actions they feel are justified. Such fears of suit are generally groundless, however. While C. Joseph Stetler was general counsel of the A.M.A. he advised disciplinary officials not to be "too impressed" by threats of suits. "The possibility of legal repercussion has been greatly overplayed," Stetler said. "If the cause for disciplinary procedure is valid, this is the easiest kind of case to defend." California has one of the most active disciplinary programs in the country. But even there only four doctors have fought their disciplinary committees through the appellate courts during the past twenty years. Each case was won by the society.

Nonetheless, the Medical Disciplinary Committee found of societies that the "mere fear of litigation seemingly deters them from acting in a number of cases." In upstate New York, a county medical society official has said that fear of legal action against the society or committee members has resulted in "a tendency to slight or overlook some problems." A Massachusetts Medical Society official has noted "deterioration" in professional discipline in the state because doctors, "partly as a result of legal advice, are less willing to publicly criticize or punish members."

Officials of local societies sometimes have other practical reasons for not wishing to discipline colleagues. Dr. Orlen J. Johnson, while president of the Michigan State Medical Society, told of one prominent physician who refused to have any part of ethics enforcement. He feared that doctors he might help discipline would stop sending him referrals.

COLLEAGUES AND HOSPITALS

Dr. James H. Berge, chairman of the A.M.A. Judicial Council, was once asked how his colleagues reacted to his activities in medical discipline. "With relief that they don't have to do it," Dr. Berge replied. "Most of them tell me, 'I wouldn't take your job for a million dollars.'"

Such reluctance on the part of individual physicians is a major obstacle to medical discipline. The membership's support is needed—to set up disciplinary committees, to man them effectively, to prosecute offenses. But disciplining colleagues is something the typical physician does not care to do. Under any circumstances he does not like being a judge, prosecutor, or witness. He has toward fellow physicians a natural sympathy that further makes a punitive role repellent to him. Moreover, he already feels too busy merely conducting his practice, keeping up with his field, attending to his private life. Since disciplinary activity offers him nothing economically, clinically, or personally, he is likely to be uninterested even in the subject.

In listing disciplinary deficiencies within organized medicine, the Medical Disciplinary Committee reported as its most important finding: "apathy, substantial ignorance, and a lack of a sense of individual responsibility by physicians as a whole." This disciplinary blind spot is most pronounced in small communities where all the doctors know each other. The smaller the society, the less likely it is to have disciplinary machinery. Of societies with 15 members or less, only 28 percent have grievance committees. Nearly 70 percent lack any organized program for handling complaints from the public. Dr. Wallace S. Brooke, president of the Utah State Medical Association, told his society that it is "unworkable" to require doctors in a small community to discipline their colleagues. In large areas of the country, this bodes ill for the success of disciplinary efforts, for most county societies are small: An estimated three quarters of all county medical societies have under 50 members. Nearly half have 15 members or less.

Even in larger societies, doctors are loath to take action against a colleague. At the National Congress on Medical Ethics, Dr. John H. Burkhardt of Knoxville, Tennessee, explained why: "Personalities enter in, friendships bias, previous favors modify, intimate contacts persuade, and an unwillingness to cast the first stone asserts a strong effect. Thus it is that although members of a local society are usually the first to be aware of a fellow member's dishonesty and unfairness they are often the least likely to accuse or to indict."

Physicians who are reluctant to act against a colleague are inconsistent in their thinking. Almost every physician knows doctors whom he thinks so little of as practitioners that he would never send them a patient. He may even discourage patients from seeing these men, often in the positive manner of strongly recommending other doctors in the same field. On the other hand, the same physician will rarely take steps to discipline doctors he deems substandard. Nor does he extrapolate from his own experience with substandard physicians, and so does not recognize the scope of medicine's disciplinary problem.

The Medical Disciplinary Committee has protested the "hear no evil, see no evil" attitude of many doctors. Disciplinary officials complain that doctors do not report violations or cooperate in investigations of offenders. "Unless a colleague flagrantly violates the rules, doctors tend to protect him," says Dr. Leo T. Heywood of the Nebraska Bureau of Examining Boards. Dr. Heywood feels that complaints initiated by physicians tend to be "incomplete and petty." And if the complaining physician takes the witness stand, adds Dr. Heywood, the "presentation is timid . . . [and] little more than a warning can be given to the offender."

Often the physician, after reporting an offender, refuses to testify or give a deposition. This absence of usable evidence can kill the disciplinary body's case. Much of the time physicians will in effect suppress a case. A surgeon who was president of his local society charged a patient of limited means $5,000 for a gallbladder operation. The local doctors were aghast. Yet, an A.M.A. official recalls, none of them was willing to bring a formal charge against the surgeon.

Reluctance to act against colleagues impedes discipline in yet another medical setting: the hospital, which even more directly than the medical society influences the kind of care patients receive. The relationship between a private practitioner and his hospital bears clarifying. The hospital is the physician's workshop, an institution whose facilities he can draw on for himself and his patients. Administratively, however, the private practitioner is not an employee of the hospital, rather, he is an "attending" physician, in the sense that he is visiting in a professional capacity. In most hospitals, attending physicians are organized into the "medical staff," a largely self-governing association. Among the staff's responsibilities is the disciplining of its members.

In a hospital a physician's work can readily be reviewed and supervised by colleagues. Thus the hospital is widely considered the most logical place to apprehend the substandard performer. Often evidence of incompetence can be detected early and corrected by a simple admonition. If circumstances justify it, the physician's privileges can be curtailed; for example, he may be limited to only specific types of surgery or restricted to handling only certain kinds of medical cases. Or he may be required to work under supervision. It can be made incumbent on him to consult with a specialist or operate only when a senior surgeon is present.

These are the mildest forms of hospital discipline. They do not interfere with the doctor's means of livelihood, and both the patient and the physician benefit. Dr. R. C. Derbyshire, of the Federation of State Medical Boards, tells of one inadequately trained surgeon who was constantly expanding the number and scope of his operations with "disastrous results." When he was called to account, some members of the medical staff wanted to expel him immediately. But one staff member argued: "If we kick him out, who's going to keep an eye on him? He'll go somewhere else where he won't be controlled." The staff voted to sharply curtail his privileges and require supervision. "Consequently," reports Dr. Derbyshire, "for the past ten years he has been a useful and respectable member of his profession."

The Joint Commission on Accreditation of Hospitals, the principal body enforcing standards in hospital care and administration, recommends that hospital privileges be granted for only a year at a time. Before a physician is reappointed, advises the Commission, his performance should be reviewed in case supervision should be required or privileges should be reduced or withdrawn. Also, the Commission recommends, medical staff committees should regularly review the competence of staff members, with the intention of instituting disciplinary action when necessary.

The General Principles of Medical Staff Organization, adopted by the A.M.A. House of Delegates in December 1964, similarly states that the medical staff has the duty to see that proper standards of medical care are maintained. Toward this end, the A.M.A. resolved, the staff's elected officers should enforce an ongoing program of discipline.

Despite such urgings, hospital medical staffs are generally much like medical societies in being hesitant to use disciplinary powers. In many small communities, the reason for this similarity is obvious: The hospital staff and the local society have substantially the same members, to the point that society and staff meetings are combined into one joint session. In some areas the medical society has taken the lead in trying to reform hospital discipline. The New York County Medical Society has urged medical staffs to establish watchdog programs to reduce inadequate performance by physicians. "There are more than enough faults by all concerned to provide an ample inventory of errors of omission and commission," the New York Society's report says. But, characteristic of the state of medical discipline, the society has no power to force medical staffs to make the improvements. Dr. John Cotton, president of the society, said: "We cannot put teeth into these suggestions because we're toothless. We cannot punish a doctor or a hospital who doesn't comply."

In most accredited hospitals, a physician's qualifications are systematically reviewed only when he applies for privileges. Thereafter his performance may be reviewed while he is still new to the staff. Checking on applicants is a function of the credentials committee, which is often the only active disciplinary committee in the hospital. Its activity reflects a prevailing willingness in medicine to be strict toward the newcomer, and progressively more lenient as he builds up seniority. "With respect to the older, well-established member of the staff, not much attention is given . . . until some tragedy occurs," observes Dr. James F. Regan of California, an authority on medical discipline.

Nonaccredited hospitals often are undiscriminating even as to a doctor's initial qualifications. In many cases seen by Dr. Regan, a physician of questionable competence quits a hospital rather than submit to a reduction of privileges. He goes to a smaller, nonaccredited institution where his privileges are unrestricted. Injuries and deaths often result.

Dotting the country are hospitals that provide an ironic contrast between a structure and its contents. Often tax-supported, the institution makes available first-rate facilities for doctors. But for all its gleaming facade and up-to-date equipment, the building is a hollow shell professionally. Nowhere within is medical discipline enforced. In a confidential communication, a surgeon who went from a medical school faculty to a South Dakota city of 5,000 has written: "I am appalled at what goes on in small hospitals where only one or two doctors work behind closed doors. No one in these small communities has any way to judge what kind of medicine is being practiced, and there are no policing methods such as are available in large hospitals."

But even in larger hospitals, the available methods often are unused because of staff reluctance to discipline a colleague. Dr. Robin C. Buerki, executive director of Henry Ford Hospital in Detroit, declared the lack of self-discipline among medical staffs to be one of the big problems facing the modern hospital. The staff in effect abdicates its responsibility to enforce quality standards, Dr. Buerki asserts. Staff chairmen are "elected not to enforce rules and regulations . . . but rather to wink an eye at them so that the doctors in the hospital can practice medicine as they see fit." The typical staff "resents pressures that force it . . . to say that Dr. Smith is qualified to do work in a given field and that Dr. Jones is not."

Unwillingness to discipline colleagues can paralyze important watchdog committees. For example, a tissue committee reviews the pathologists' analysis of tissue removed in surgery. The committee's purpose is to detect misdiagnoses and unnecessary operations. If it notes a pattern of offenses, it is expected to start a disciplinary proceeding against the surgeon.

But in some hospitals the tissue committee exists only on paper. Election to it is regarded as a formality, for it never meets and it performs no reviews. Even if it does meet, its reviews may remain a formality: The members decline to make disciplinary recommendations. In a study of one hospital, all the tissue committee members agreed that "nothing has ever been done even if continuing poor standards of practice or recurrent surgical errors were observed." One reason this hospital was studied was that its medical staff had an extremely high rate of malpractice suits.

Tissue committee activity may be thwarted by the pathologist's reluctance to cast a shadow on a colleague. The pathologist has been called the keeper of the surgeon's conscience. Pathology, the scientific study of the alterations produced by disease, is one of the relatively exact branches of medical practice. Diagnostically, the pathologist is expected to call a spade a spade. This does not always happen. Instead, the pathologist may conceal his finding with a euphemism. Dr. Robert S. Myers, of the American College of Surgeons, has said: "Euphemisms, which are a denial of the basic integrity of the pathologist, have become accepted and not uncommon methods of tissue diagnosis."

These euphemisms are often used by the pathologist when he finds that the operation probably should not have taken place because the tissue was essentially normal. The camouflage is usually applied to parts of the body that lend themselves readily to surgery and thus are frequently removed: the appendix, uterus, fallopian tubes, and ovaries. Thus, reports Dr. Myers, to conceal the fact that an appendix was normal, a pathologist may use such disguises as acute appendicitis, acute ulcerative appendicitis, acute suppurative appendicitis, acute catarrhal appendicitis, acute peri-appendicitis, acute-chronic appendicitis, chronic ulcerative appendicitis, fibrosing appendicitis, and appendicitis Type X.

Similar concealment in pathologists' reports was uncovered during an American College of Surgeons audit of a hospital with an extremely high rate of unnecessary surgery. The A.C.S. investigator found that virtually every uterus was "fibrotic," every fallopian tube showed "chronic salpingitis," every ovary was "cystic"—all terms that are regarded as too general to mean much medically. In one case the pathologist returned a tissue diagnosis of "acute or chronic ulcerative appendicitis." He was being unnecessarily obliging. At the time of the operation, the surgeon had reported the appendix was normal; removing it was a standard step incidental to other abdominal surgery. Another surgeon told the A.C.S. auditor that, in the course of an operation, he had to remove some normal stomach tissue. Routinely this was sent to the pathologist. Two days later the pathologist called him and asked: "What diagnosis do you want returned on this stomach?"

Other hospital committees instrumental to discipline often are similarly impeded. The committee may not meet. If it meets, it may not act. If it is prepared to act, it may not get the help it needs from sources of information within the hospital. Thus, in many hospitals, discipline is anarchic at the committee level.

But even if the committee is conscientious and exacting, even if it recommends disciplinary action whenever it seems needed—even then, the medical staff itself may be obstructive. A common complaint of diligent hospital committees is: "The medical staff won't back us up."

Dr. Richard H. Blum, a psychologist, was commissioned by the California Medical Association to study eight hospitals in depth. Dr. Blum interviewed scores of staff members at these institutions, and his sampling gives much insight into staff attitudes toward discipline. One of the best hospitals Blum studied is a highly respected institution whose attending physicians have a very low rate of malpractice suits. Another of the hospitals in the Blum study offers low-quality care and has a medical staff whose members are frequently sued for malpractice.

Despite the considerable difference in the caliber of each hospital's staff, Blum reports, most doctors on both staffs said that "they would feel uncomfortable if they, personally, had to take an open stand in their own staff which would call for restriction of privileges to a colleague. Most said it was important to them that they avoid open and individual conflict with their colleagues—either in calling for censure or in censuring. They said further that it was so important to achieve harmony, i.e., avoid dispute or individual stands, that they would favor compromise or even the avoidance of issues as preferable to disputation. Indeed, in both hospitals the staff agreed that they felt so bad—as individuals—about restricting privileges that they did not often—or ever—do it. And as one said, 'I hope I never do.'"

An exceptional case of personal reluctance to discipline a colleague has been reported by a physician in Alabama. An aged surgeon was making mistake after mistake. He could not hear; his vision was poor; sometimes he could not even find his car in the hospital parking lot. At a hospital staff meeting, the doctor who tells the story moved that this surgeon's privileges be withdrawn. A vote was called. The elderly man's mind was so clouded that he raised his hand to vote for his own retirement. His vote was the only other one for the motion. The rest of the staff elected to keep his privileges unrestricted.

Other pressures on a staff militate against effective discipline. A major conclusion of the Blum study is that good hospitals are largely the result of good administration. Some hospitals are so badly administered that staff discipline suffers along with many other functions of the institution. Discipline is one of the first considerations to fall by the wayside when a hospital is marked by poor leadership or by conflicts between physicians.

Where there are strong personality clashes on the medical staff, cliques tend to form that destroy disciplinary enforcement. At such hospitals, doctors often fear reprisals if they report unfavorably on another's work.

Discipline may also be obstructed by the board of trustees, which governs the corporation controlling the hospital, and by the administrator —the hospital's chief executive, usually a layman, who reports to the board. If the trustees and the administrator are overconcerned with finances, they may reject the medical staff's disciplinary recommendation against a doctor who brings a large number of patients into the institution. If they are too mindful of politics, they may not care to offend a physician who is influential in the community.

Hospitals sometimes squelch physicians who criticize staff performance. This was the charge a thoracic surgeon made against a proprietary hospital. According to the court, evidence showed that he warned the physician-owners of the hospital that a nurse-anesthetist was incompetent. Two days later a baby died during surgery as a result of an anesthetic given by the nurse. After reviewing the record, the thoracic surgeon declared that "on its face" it showed malpractice. He added to the owners: "You're also responsible because you were informed that the nurse was incompetent."

The surgeon's relationship with the owners was not improved by a later occurrence. A patient bleeding badly from a gunshot wound was brought into the emergency ward. "It's too late to save him," one of the proprietors said. But the surgeon insisted that they take the patient into the operating room. The patient's life was saved. Shortly after, one of the owners told the surgeon that he would be "blocked" in all hospitals in the community.

When the surgeon applied for privileges at the town's general hospital, he was rejected on the ground that he was "not temperamentally suitable for hospital staff practice." A principal reason was that he "could not get along with" the owners of the proprietary hospital. The surgeon took his case to court. In ordering the town hospital, a public institution, to grant him privileges, the court noted: "The goal of providing high standards of medical care requires that physicians be permitted to assert their views when they feel that treatment of patients is improper or that negligent hospital practices are being followed."

Residents and interns, as trainees in a hospital, work closely with attending physicians. Often these "house staff" members are in a position to point out errors in judgment. But house staff discipline dictates that the attending physician is in charge of the patient, that the house physician (resident or intern) should merely follow instructions even though he may actually be more experienced in a problem than the private practitioner. In one such case, the patient was bleeding profusely from a peptic ulcer. As the sixth bottle of blood was being run in, the resident asked the attending physician if a surgeon should not be consulted.

"No," said the physician. "The patient's in good shape. We can get the bleeding under control."

Although the resident felt otherwise, the attending physician was in command. On the twelfth bottle of blood, the patient went into shock. The attending physician finally called in a surgeon, but it was too late to save the patient.

Inevitably, weakness in discipline produces poor patient care. Most major malpractice claims originate out of medical services rendered by physicians in hospitals. By the time a medical staff cancels or limits an offender's privileges, a great deal of damage has generally been done. One malpractice insurer has observed that a "significant number of malpractice cases would never have occurred if diligence had been exercised in limiting the privileges of physicians who had demonstrated carelessness or incompetence."

The Blum study of hospitals in California has shown how an institution can deteriorate in the absence of effective discipline. At one of the most poorly run of the hospitals, a Blum researcher was stationed in the operating-room area to observe a full day's operations. "Although these observations might normally be expected to provide a dull day's work," the researcher later reported, "the standards of medicine at [this hospital] are always of a type to keep one's mind alert—if not on edge."

Immediately after the first operation of the day, an operating-room nurse found a broken surgical tool. The head surgical nurse called the doctor from the dressing room with urgency. She showed him the broken piece and suggested that an x-ray be made to determine if there was any matter left in the patient. The doctor refused, largely because he felt the patient would not be able to pay for it.

Out of eight operations observed at this hospital, six were marked by evidence of laxness or misconduct. Two patients had to wait on the operating table more than half an hour before the surgeon showed up. There was an error in reading an order written by one doctor; his 150 cc. looked like 100 cc. and was so administered. In another incident, the surgeon violated basic rules of keeping operating rooms sterile. After the operation, he dressed in street clothes and left the ward. He returned and—without scrubbing, dressing in a robe, or putting on a mask—he entered the operating room.

At another hospital Dr. Blum found a near-total breakdown of staff discipline. One surgeon had removed fifty normal appendixes. He was disciplined only after the administrator, in desperation over the institution's plummeting standards, asked that the hospital's accreditation be withdrawn. Another doctor admitted that when he was president of the medical staff he knew of several cases of normal uteri being removed, but he kept it secret. Now he is on the hospital's tissue committee.

Once a pair of physicians got into a fight during surgery. One reached across the patient, grabbed the other, and knocked him out. Two doctors on the staff were so in fear of a third one that they carried guns. A narcotic addict applied for privileges at the hospital. Despite knowledge of his condition, the credentials committee gave their approval.

At the same hospital, the medical records committee attempts to do its job but is blocked by the medical staff as a whole. One doctor simply refused to maintain records, which are essential to the continuity of patient care. He was usually 100 cases behind in his record-keeping but just laughed at the records committee. A member of the records committee tried to initiate action against physicians responsible for three cases of negligence, two of which resulted in death. He was attacked for "picking on" the offenders.

Two doctors on the staff were in partnership. One of the partners was to do a tonsillectomy on a child. To get the anesthesiology fee for himself and his partner, he wanted his partner to administer the anesthesia. The hospital administrator refused permission on the grounds that the partner was not qualified. The partners now went over the administrator's head, to the chief of surgery. He gave his permission—and reprimanded the administrator for interfering. The child died during surgery in cardiac arrest, heart stoppage which is a frequent result of improperly administered anesthesia.

A badly burned patient was rushed to this hospital. He had lost all the skin from the top half of his body and was screaming in agony. When the doctor learned that the patient was a member of the Kaiser medical plan, a health care arrangement opposed by many private practitioners, he ordered that the patient be put back into the ambulance for the long trip to the Kaiser plan hospital. He refused even to give a drug to relieve the patient's pain.

Some days later the hospital's board of trustees met to consider suspending this doctor. The trustees were met by protests from the medical staff, who opposed this disciplinary action.

PART II

Exploiting the Patient

MANY OFFENSES are financial in origin. Most common is the charging of excessive fees, but other forms of exploitation compromise the patient's care as well as his pocketbook. Some exploitative physicians subject patients to unnecessary services, including surgery. Fee splitters are likely to refer patients to substandard practitioners, chosen mainly because they will pay a kickback. Physicians who own drugstores and drug companies are tempted to profiteer from their prescriptions. Quacks, motivated by the dollar, betray the principles of scientific medicine and dispense worthless treatments.

5

THE FEE GOUGERS:
"Vultures in Medicine"

IN CALIFORNIA there is a doctor who keeps a cash register near the front door of his office. If you don't pay in advance toward your visit, you don't get in.

Medical societies frown on the use of cash registers by physicians, feeling that a machine that clangs No SALE does not honor the profession. The biggest problem, however, is not with the doctor who has a cash register openly in his office—but one secretly in his heart.

The Massachusetts Physician calls fee gougers "medical vultures" whom the profession should "call to task." Medical society presidents have made special efforts to discipline this fringe group. As president of the Colorado Medical Society, Dr. Gatewood C. Milligan tried to stem the "uncontrolled inflation" he was seeing in bills his own patients received from gougers. "I get the very disquieting feeling that dollar amounts have no meaning at all," he said. "The unreal, nightmarish feeling that [accompanies a fee of] $50 for a fifteen . . . minute consultation." After Dr. Donald M. Dowell was elected president of the Missouri State Medical Association, he attacked the crippling fees charged by gougers. He warned that fee gougers are "driving us right into socialized medicine." While president-elect of the Medical Society of the State of New York, Dr. George A. Burgin reported on medicine's "bad citizens." Through extreme overcharges, he noted, fee gougers threaten the survival of some private health insurance programs.

Concern over fee gouging has been expressed by yet another president, Lyndon B. Johnson. Under the Medicare program for financing care for the elderly, physicians can collect fees directly from the government. "Responsible medical society and professional leaders must take the lead to prevent unreasonable costs for health services," President Johnson said. "And the best prevention is intelligent self-restraint by doctors."

DOCTORS AND DOLLARS

Some three thousand years ago the Greeks of Thessaly recounted the legend of Aesculapius, son of Apollo and the nymph Coronis. The centaur Chiron taught young Aesculapius the art of healing. Finally Zeus, fearful that Aesculapius would make all men immortal, slew him with a thunderbolt.

The Greeks honored Aesculapius as the god of medicine. Temples erected to him in many parts of Greece were visited by the sick. Those who came would present offerings.

And so, from the beginning, medicine was linked with payment. Fees are still an extremely sensitive area of physician-patient relations. Worry over the cost of an illness can cause as much anguish as the sickness itself, and anxiety over looming expenses can impede a patient's recovery.

The Principles of Medical Ethics give the doctor great leeway in how he handles the business side of his practice. About setting charges, Section 7 of the Principles says only: "His fee should be commensurate with the services rendered and the patient's ability to pay." The great majority of physicians are mindful of the special obligations their skills impose on them. As a result, the profession has evolved a guideline as to how much doctors can in good conscience charge.

Physicians increasingly feel that the only fair fee for a given service is the "going rate." This is the approximate fee charged within a community by most doctors of comparable training. The A.M.A. Judicial Council sanctions the going rate, ruling that "although . . . some services . . . are invaluable, nonetheless, their practical value lies within a range . . . above . . . which a fee is unconscionable." If a physician charges considerably more than the going rate, he may be called to account by his medical society's grievance committee. Health insurance plans use the going rate as their guide to reasonable charges. Courts seek testimony as to the going rate in deciding complaints of overcharging.

In time of inflation, local doctors in the same field are likely to raise their fees by about the same amount within a short period. This results not from a conspiracy; rather, each man keeps one eye on rising costs ("NOTICE OF RENT INCREASE") and the other on the competition ("Charlie, what do you ask for an office visit these days?").

Medical fees have actually lagged behind inflation. Sometimes appearances are to the contrary, since fee increases tend to come in spurts that attract attention. Also, laymen often fail to distinguish between the amount actually received by the doctor and such other health costs as hospital, laboratory, and pharmaceutical expenses.

Thus since 1940 the general cost of living has outstripped doctors' fees by about 11 percentage points, making physicians' services relatively less expensive than before World War II. In sharp contrast, hospital charges have risen about five times faster than the cost of living and are the largest health expense.

UNWHOLESOME SHADOWS

"The fee situation is becoming so bad that patients fear to go to some physicians . . . because of their reputation as fee gougers," *The Massachusetts Physician* has said. "It is very unfortunate that the few who do not follow the traditional concepts of the true physician cast an unwholesome shadow on the whole medical profession." Some shadows:

• An internist billed a patient $5,000 for care of a heart condition. For the same treatment, most cardiologists would charge no more than $400.

• A surgeon charged $2,000 for working on a woman's bunions, calluses, and toes. At most, comparable work should cost $200.

• A gynecologist's fee for a routine dilation and curettage was $1,200. Few specialists in the field would ask even $150.

At the First National Congress on Medical Ethics, participants generally agreed that excessive charges are the leading cause of patient complaints to medical society grievance committees. A substantial number of these complaints are found justified. Grievance committee officials in Illinois and Pennsylvania estimate that no fewer than one out of every three doctors named in fee complaints do in fact overcharge and must be advised to reduce their fees.

One such case involved a gouger in Ohio who invented a $25 "admission fee," a totally nonstandard charge, to pay for his phone call for having patients admitted to the hospital. Another was an obstetrics case in which a Kentucky doctor did not see the patient for a single prenatal visit. Moreover, he was absent when she delivered. Yet he pressed the patient for his full fee of $150.

Some types of medical service are especially subject to fee abuses. One problem area is emergency care. Medical disciplinary officials would like to curb a group they call "hotel doctors," practitioners who exploit tourists. Not uncommon are charges double and triple the going rate.

Other kinds of transients were overcharged by an orthopedist on the West Coast. He treated the cuts and bruises of a college football team that was training in his town. All told, he saw nine players in two catchall visits. He charged $25 for each patient, even when the sole condition was the minor rash that athletes are prone to. For a total of two hours of office work, he billed the team $265. "Your fees are hurting us all!" the college's regular doctor protested to him.

Especially exploitative are charges for emergency care made by a doctor who is not even present. A father took his fifteen-month-old daughter to a Portland, Oregon, hospital emergency room to have a cut in her eyebrow treated. A resident physician phoned their family doctor. "Go ahead without me," the doctor said.

But besides the bill from the emergency room, the father received one from the family doctor for $17.50, for "supervising and directing" the treatment.

Robert H. Elsner of the Multnomah County Medical Society in Portland helped prompt the society to rule that a member cannot bill emergency room patients unless he is actually present at the time of treatment. Many local societies, however, remain permissive about charging for treatment in absentia, although the A.M.A. Judicial Council has ruled that a doctor may ethically bill the patient only for services rendered under his "personal observation, direction, and supervision."

The hospital is often a setting for exploitation by fee gougers. In many locales, shortage of specialists forces hospitals to make costly arrangements with pathologists to oversee laboratory services and with radiologists to supervise x-raying and radiotherapy. In turn, the inflated charges for these services are passed on to the patient.

Conditions in at least one city came to light when Charles G. Brooks of the *Washington Star* did an exposé of the "highly peculiar—and very expensive" arrangements in District of Columbia area hospitals. The highest paid doctors in the area, the *Star* found, were usually anesthesiologists, pathologists, and radiologists—specialists without whom few hospitals can function.

Since physicians in these specialties are scarce, some choose to contract only with hospitals that will provide them with equipment, office assistance, and a virtual monopoly. Under such contracts, the specialist often gets a share of every dollar hospital patients spend for services in his field. Pathologists, for example, keep as much as 40 percent of the profits of a hospital laboratory although they make no investment. Widespread abuse by pathologists has spurred the Justice Department to file an antitrust conspiracy action charging the College of American Pathologists with illegally monopolizing and restraining the medical laboratory trade.

A small group of radiologists was found to be keeping a stranglehold on Washington hospitals, investing virtually nothing in facilities but drawing as much as $80,000 a year. At least one radiologist earned over $200,000 a year, more than six times the net earnings of the typical radiologist in private practice.

Sometimes an arrangement proposed by a hospital specialist is so excessive that his specialty society trims it down. The American College of Radiology was asked by one of its members to help him in his negotiations for furnishing services to a hospital. The College does this routinely, but it drew back when it learned the terms the member was proposing.

He would work at the hospital two days a week. He would use the hospital's equipment, supplies, personnel. In exchange, he was asking to be paid half the x-ray department's gross income. This would have netted him over $60,000 a year, no less than $575 a day.

The College officials assigned to help him reported that they "disagreed with the radiologist's valuation of his services." The counselors felt that the volume of work at the hospital not only was too great for one part-timer but would require the services of at least two full-time radiologists, whose salaries could be met from the ample percentage the doctor was proposing. College officials strongly recommended that he associate himself with two such colleagues to provide optimum x-ray services to the community.

The radiologist rejected this recommendation. Instead, he offered to retain a part-time associate who would assist him in this hospital—and also other hospitals he was serving.

The College responded they could not be a part of this. "It represents exploitation of patients in the community," the counselors said.

The radiologist then broke off his discussion with them. "Don't help me anymore," he told them.

Later, the College was pleased to learn that the hospital refused to consider the radiologist's proposal.

ROBIN HOOD RIDES AGAIN

The increasing standardizing of doctors' fees at the going rate has largely made medical Robin Hoods disappear into Sherwood Forest. As recently as the 1950s, some 60 percent of private practitioners varied their fees according to what the traffic would bear: charging the poor less, the rich more. Now an estimated 90 percent routinely stick to the going rate, reducing fees if a patient cannot pay, but raising them rarely or never.

In Louisiana, a medical Robin Hood was called to a hospital after a corporation executive suffered a heart attack. The doctor remained with him for less than three hours. His fee for this visit: $225.

For eight days the doctor visited the patient daily. But for each visit, instead of asking his usual $8, he billed his patient $25. After the patient left the hospital, the doctor made house calls. His fee was usually $10. He now charged $25. For glucose and terramycin, costing about $4, he charged $25. For a dosage of gamma globulin, ordinarily $15, he charged $75. In all, the doctor billed the patient for $1,939.

The bill landed in court. There the doctor testified that his bill was based on four factors: his special skill, the twelve miles between his and the patient's home, the "demanding attitude" of the patient, and the patient's "great wealth."

On the testimony of other doctors, the judge ruled that the first three reasons were untrue or did not apply. As for the patient's financial condition, his wealth consisted of a salary of $25,000 a year. This, ruled the judge, did not justify excessive charges. The doctor's bill was reduced by two thirds, to $650. At that, local physicians had testified that even less would have been fair.

Yet another gouger is a big-city specialist whose home is in a suburb. He cooperated in a magazine's exploration of his case on the condition that identifying details be disguised. Assume he is a forty-year-old gynecologist and that one Saturday he was called from his home to aid a neighbor, a well-to-do middle-aged woman whom he found in shock from a uterine hemorrhage.

The doctor ordered an ambulance, then rode with the woman to the medical center where he had privileges. He stayed with her several hours, seeing that she was admitted to the intensive-care section and started on measures that would control the bleeding and bring her out of shock. A few days later he performed a hysterectomy on her, thus removing the fibroid tumors that had caused the trouble.

The woman left the hospital after thirteen days. During her stay, the doctor had visited her twice a day. She had nothing but praise for him—until she received his bill. His fee was $5,500.

The woman consulted other doctors she knew, and they agreed: The bill was much too high; a charge of $800 to $1,000 would be reasonable. Following their advice, the woman sent the doctor a check for $950 with a note suggesting this was fair payment.

By then, the story of the $5,500 fee had spread throughout the community. Local colleagues of the doctor voiced strong criticism of him—for, they said, his excessive fee had made the community wary of all physicians. "Every doctor in town is taking a beating for a guy who doesn't even practice here!" was how one internist summed up their feelings.

As a result of such reactions, the doctor returned the woman's check and canceled the bill. Why was the charge so high in the first place? Someone put the question to him. "It's really quite simple," he explained. "After all, I'm not a rural G.P. I'm a specialist—an excellent one—and I command high fees."

Valid reasoning? Not according to most physicians who took part in a subsequent discussion of this incident. One doctor expressed the majority view when he said: "I can't remember seeing a case in which a $5,500 fee was justified, no matter how skilled the doctor may have been."

Often the more astronomic the fee, the greater the overcharger's comeuppance. In Hollywood's heyday, the late W. C. Fields was one of the country's most sought-after stars. At the age of fifty-six and at the pinnacle of his career, he was under contract for three different movies for $100,000 each, and he had another $700,000 in the bank.

But momentarily his career was in jeopardy. From overconsumption of alcohol, he had polyneuritis and liver disease, and his continued heavy drinking was causing even more damage. Finally he contracted bronchopneumonia. His physician, a G.P., demanded that he be hospitalized.

At Fields' insistence, the doctor accompanied him to the hospital and for twenty-three days and nights lived in an adjoining hospital room. After Fields recovered, he received a bill that nearly made him ill again. The physician was asking $12,000.

Fields refused to pay, claiming that the fee had been set with one eye on his bankbook. The doctor sued to collect—and won. Fields appealed, and the higher court reversed the decision. In setting forth the reasons for the reversal, the court emphasized the doctor's failure to state his income for recent years and his customary charges. These were factors to aid in ascertaining his professional standing and the reasonable value of his services.

PAYMENT ON DEATH

Perhaps the most questionable financial interest a physician can have is an opportunity to profit from a patient's death. Counting on a piece of the patient's estate is always a tricky business, as a doctor in Michigan learned. He claimed he treated an elderly woman free for the last months of her life on her promise that she would leave him all her possessions when she died. When she did die, no will was found. Her $16,000 estate passed to relatives.

The doctor sued for the entire estate. The courts found against him, largely because there was no written record of the alleged promise. Moreover, the court said that even if the patient had made such a promise, the doctor would have to show it was fair and that he exercised no undue influence. Evidence submitted by the doctor revealed that in suing for the whole estate he was seeking compensation amounting to at least eight times what he would normally charge.

Strong doubts are bound to be raised when a physician has the patient's finances sewn up and has only to wait for the patient's death to collect. According to evidence presented by a state licensing board: Dr. Herman Daines (names in this account are disguised) had practiced in a Connecticut city for some seventeen years before he and his wife separated. He moved into a boardinghouse owned by Dora Herlie, a seventy-year-old spinster. Before long, she was treating him like a son. She let him know that she planned to leave him her considerable estate.

Over the next four years, Miss Herlie's health suffered the usual ups and downs. Then she developed severe diarrhea, persistent vomiting, and a rapidly worsening mouth infection. Daines examined her, applied routine medication, and called Dr. Carl Parsons, a local colleague. Dr. Parsons found her heart weak and a hard mass in her abdomen, "suggestive of cancer" he said.

As Miss Herlie's condition grew worse, Parsons tried to have her sent to a hospital for diagnosis and treatment. "At least, get nurses for her," he told Daines. But the heir-apparent kept her at home. The only nursing care he provided was from his mother—an unskilled woman in her seventies—and from his brother-in-law, a clerk.

For more than two months, Miss Herlie grew weaker. Finally, Daines expected her to not last the day. From another physician he secured a partially filled-in death certificate, highly irregular when the patient is still alive.

That afternoon Miss Herlie died, and Daines inherited over $70,000. Ignoring her expressed wish to be buried, he shipped her body to a medical school for use as a cadaver.

Helped by evidence brought forward by Dr. Parsons, the Connecticut Medical Examining Board brought about the revocation of Daines's license. The board explained that his behavior had been "unprofessional."

6

THE OVERTREATERS:
Pouring It On

IN GIVING TREATMENT the doctor of course calls the shots. An exploiter, however, may call too many. Illustrative is the overtreater who gave a woman useless injections once a week for five years. The woman chanced to develop serum hepatitis, a severe liver disease during which needless medication can be especially dangerous. Even then, he continued the injections.

Overtreating, the deliberate performing of unnecessary services to justify a higher bill, is harder to prove than fee gouging. Fees can reasonably fall only within a fairly narow range. But in matters of medical judgment, doctors enjoy extremely wide latitude.

Thus it is relatively easy to show that a fee gouger charged about twice the going rate for an injection. It is far tougher to prove that an overtreater has given twice the number of injections actually called for. Indeed, the overtreater may defend his poured-on services as being "good medicine" or "conservative care." That is how some overtreaters seek to justify needless diagnostic studies.

Patients are rarely in a position to judge if laboratory work or x-rays are needed, especially since painstaking physicians often order many studies to pin down a diagnosis. But completeness of diagnosis is hardly what motivates overtreaters like the one to whom a little Washington State girl was referred. She was sent to him for only a cystoscopy, a visual examination of the bladder. The girl's doctor had already made several studies—x-rays, a bladder-measurement test, and the like—and sent along with her all the pertinent reports. Even though the evidence was complete and current, the overtreater pushed the family into the considerable expense of repeating all the tests.

Even if diagnostic tests are negative, an overtreater may submit the patient to extensive treatment for a disease he does not have. For example, according to the findings of a court, this case of a man who was troubled by spots on his scalp and face: "Such spots are caused by syphilis," the doctor said. He took a blood specimen for a Wassermann test.

A few days later he received from the laboratory a negative report. He got in touch with the patient.

"The test shows positive. Come down as soon as possible to get started on treatment."

When the patient showed up, he was informed that the cost of the treatment would be $150, itself a gross overcharge.

"Can I see the report?" the patient asked.

"The lab doesn't keep a record of its reports," the doctor lied.

When the patient came for his next appointment, he again asked to see the report.

"Okay," the doctor said at last. "I'll get a copy for you."

That week he paid a visit to the lab, ostensibly to see the manager. While on the premises, he took a blank report form. On it he composed a report showing the test positive and handed this to the patient as justification for the treatment. He was found out because the patient, still suspicious, consulted another doctor.

Given a genuine condition—perhaps a simple injury—an overtreater may really make a frontal assault on the patient's pocketbook. A medical society grievance committee forced a refund in this case: A cabdriver was in an accident, but his injuries were minor and needed little treatment. Even so, an exploitative doctor made daily house calls for several weeks.

Then for several months the overtreater had the patient come daily to his office. For a year after that he gave the patient physiotherapy as often as five times a week. The fee charged for each of these services individually was within acceptable limits, except that the service itself was unnecessary. For the unneeded treatment, the cabdriver paid over $700.

UNNECESSARY SURGERY

The hospital had a particularly high rate of emergency surgery. Was much of it unnecessary? Were many patients being rushed into the hazards of major surgery needlessly? Was money, not medical necessity, prompting some surgeons to operate?

Other doctors at the hospital suspected as much. To find out for sure, they formed a committee to analyze the tissues removed during operations. The findings: Fully one out of every three operations performed at the hospital was unnecessary—the organs taken out were normal.

The committee warned the most flagrant offenders. Before long, needless operations dropped to about one in ten, a rate close to irreducible, given the limitations of diagnostic accuracy.

This episode in a Passaic, New Jersey, hospital has gone down in medical annals to illustrate the value of active tissue committees. Usually an audit of a hospital with from ten to fifty doctors on its staff shows that two or three are doing a great deal of inexcusable surgery. The Joint Commission on Hospital Accreditation and the American College of Surgeons consider unjustified surgery a far more serious problem than fee gouging. "Because," says one investigator, "the patient's body is at stake."

The overtreater who does unnecessary surgery is usually a good salesman, persuading patients of something they "ought to have out." Often he becomes the biggest operator in town. At most, conservative surgeons do 300 to 500 major operations a year. But performers of unneeded surgery may do 1,200 to 1,500, even 1,800 a year, often spreading them over several hospitals.

The work of so busy a surgeon can hardly help but be spotty: He hasn't the time to give adequate attention to the patient before or after the operation. His performance in the operating room tends to be hurried. He is often unavailable when postoperative emergencies arise.

The patients whom overtreaters sell most successfully are neurotic women. A gynecologist new to this country observed: "In Europe it is all the doctor can do to persuade a woman to have a needed operation. In America it is difficult to dissuade her from having an unnecessary one."

Some women have had six, nine, or sixteen major operations in search of relief from their anxiety, malaise, and all-around misery of emotional immaturity. Dr. Walter Alvarez of the Mayo Clinic wrote of a "frail, constitutionally inadequate girl" who had four exploratory operations of the abdomen before she was out of her teens. Her appendix went in the first of these operations. Adhesions (stuck-together tissues) from the first operation were broken up in the second. She gave up her ovaries and fallopian tubes in the third. In the fourth, nothing was removed. Despite the lack of indications for surgery, an overtreater was willing to cut her open anyway.

CHRONIC REMUNERATIVE APPENDICITIS

The most commonly performed unnecessary operation is the appendectomy. Overtreaters welcome the chance to remove the appendix, since this wormlike extension of the intestine serves no purpose in the body.

"You'd better have it out now before it gets infected," the overtreater is likely to say. By contrast, medical authorities feel that a healthy appendix is less of a threat than the surgery for taking it out. The frequency with which healthy appendixes are removed has led to the coining of a term, "chronic remunerative appendicitis," to describe the normal appendix that is removed merely to enrich the surgeon.

True, it can be virtually impossible to distinguish acute appendicitis from other conditions that cause pain in the lower right abdomen: a ruptured ovary, a glandular inflammation, an intestinal infection. Many surgeons have an erroneous diagnostic rate of not more than 6 percent. The American College of Surgeons allows a margin of error of 12 percent before it levels a charge of unnecessary surgery.

Yet among some surgeons one pathologist finds that as many as 25 percent of the appendixes removed show no traces of inflammation or obstruction. A study of one surgeon's work shows that no less than five out of six appendixes he takes out are normal or show only minimal signs of pathology.

Although very young children rarely suffer from acute appendicitis, some overtreaters make a practice of removing any child's appendix, needlessly bringing on a frightening experience and days of pain. One overtreater preyed on the anxieties of parents to get consent to perform "prophylactic" appendectomies on at least eighteen children under four years of age. Seven of the children were under two. One was a baby of ten months. Another overtreater set about removing the healthy appendix of a two-year-old child. The youngster was suffering from pneumonia, which the surgeon had overlooked. For the appendectomy the child was given a lung anesthetic, and from this he died.

THE RAPE OF THE PELVIS

A twenty-three-year-old woman complained of pain in her lower abdomen. The doctor diagnosed the condition as a pregnancy occurring in the fallopian tube. Standard procedure for such cases is merely surgical removal of the fetus. But this overtreater removed both ovaries, both fallopian tubes, and the uterus as well. This left the young woman sterile. "The rationale [for this operation] is perplexing . . . since the . . . pelvic organs were otherwise normal," remarked Dr. James C. Doyle, a professor of gynecology who reviewed the case.

Such wholesale removal of a woman's reproductive organs has been called "the rape of the pelvis." After the appendix, the organs most frequently removed without medical cause are the uterus, the ovaries, and the fallopian tubes.

A study of 246 hysterectomies at 10 hospitals reveals that fully 31 percent of the uteri removed were normal. In more than 9 percent of the cases, the uterus was removed for such nonspecific complaints as fatigue, irritability, nervousness, and headache. Women operated on for these reasons could not be helped by a hysterectomy any more than by a manicure. An additional 17 percent of the patients had no complaints at all. Dr. Norman F. Miller, of the University of Michigan School of Medicine, has called such operations "hip-pocket hysterectomies," beneficial only where the overtreater keeps his money.

Some women who are rushed into sterilizing operations come with complaints entirely unrelated to gynecology. A surgeon removed both ovaries, both fallopian tubes, and the uterus of one twenty-five-year-old woman when she was, in fact, suffering from eye trouble.

Some overtreaters use the threat of cancer to justify a hysterectomy, particularly where there is a fibroid tumor in the uterus. But gynecologists point out that more than half of all women past child-bearing age develop such nonmalignant growths. Indeed, studies show that women with fibroids are actually *less* likely to develop uterine cancer than women without.

Even when ostensibly performed to ward off a malignancy, many hysterectomies do not truly eliminate the threat of uterine cancer. In about two out of three cases, the overtreater does only a partial hysterectomy, removing the uterus but not its cervix (or neck). This leaves the patients as likely to get cervical cancer as before.

The operation for so-called fallen womb is also rarely justifiable. This major surgery is done by overtreaters purportedly to relieve backache and fatigue. After making an abdominal incision the surgeon pulls up the uterus by tucking in the supporting ligaments—in effect, a suspension of the organ—but relief, if any, is only temporary. The ligaments are elastic and eventually stretch again. The overtreater may then perform a hysterectomy, obliterating the first operation.

The actions of one group of overtreaters show the extent to which the fee is the prime motivator of uterine suspensions. In a private hospital these doctors were doing several uterine suspensions a week. They also did work in a nearby hospital where all the patients were on charity. There they did not find it necessary to do even one uterine suspension.

Hasty and unconfirmed diagnoses account for much unneeded surgery. In 112 cases studied by one investigator, doctors preoperatively diagnosed ovarian cyst, then removed the ovaries. But in no less than 90 of the operations, pathologists found there were no ovarian cysts and the patient had needlessly lost her reproductive capacity.

Physicians at one small hospital were concerned about the apparently unnecessary surgery being performed by two surgeons. The staff set up a tissue committee, but the two surgeons refused to recognize its decisions. So the trustees asked the American College of Surgeons to audit the surgery done at the hospital.

For five days the College investigators did an on-the-spot study of the 879 surgical operations performed during the preceding 14 months. The investigators found that the two surgeons in question churned out more than half the surgery done at the hospital. No less than 24 percent of their surgery was unnecessary, constituting about one operation of every eight performed at the hospital.

Particularly striking was their needless removal of reproductive organs. Fully 80 percent of surgeon A's sterilizations had no diagnostic justification; and surgeon B was not to be outdone: Of his sterilization operations, a solid 100 percent were unnecessary.

7

THE FEE SPLITTERS:
Patients for Sale

ONE BITTERLY COLD January afternoon, a physician from an out-lying Iowa town came to the office of Dr. Evarts A. Graham, a surgeon.

"I have a young woman with acute appendicitis that I'd like operated upon," the visitor said.

"Where is she?" asked Dr. Graham.

"Oh, I left her at the station."

Dr. Graham was shocked. "Do you mean you'd leave a girl on that exposed platform in this zero weather while you came here to talk to me?"

"Well," explained the other doctor, "I didn't want to bring her here until I knew what kind of deal you'd make. I usually receive 50 percent of the surgical fee."

Dr. Graham recalled that episode while chairman of the Board of Regents of the American College of Surgeons and a leader of the College's crusade against fee splitting. In this underhanded practice, a physician pays for a referral by slipping to the referring doctor a portion of the fee he gets from the patient. The payment is a "split," "rebate," "kickback," "commission," or (most genteelly) "referral fee." By whatever name, the patient is sold to the highest bidder. In the bargaining, little regard is given to the competence of the receiving physician—or, indeed, to whether the service is needed in the first place.

"Fee splitting is a little like fornication," says Mac F. Cahal, executive director of the American Academy of General Practice. "Everybody knows it's going on, but nobody knows exactly how much." The A.M.A. Medical Disciplinary Committee got one indication of how much when it analyzed questionnaire responses from the medical societies of thirty-eight states and twenty-two large counties. Fee splitting turned up among the six major infractions committed by local offenders.

According to Regents of the College of Surgeons, fee splitting is especially bad in New York City and in Pennsylvania and New Jersey. In New York, a state investigating commission has reported: "Kickbacks ranging from 15 to 50 percent were paid to more than 3,000 physicians in New York, Queens, and Bronx Counties alone." While the South Atlantic States are fairly clean, several hotbeds of fee splitting are known. Worst of all are certain cities on the West Coast and in much of the Middle West.

While in many places fee splitting is limited to only a few conspirators, in some areas the practice is rampant. The journal *Medical Economics* has been able to document an article titled "The Whole Town's Splitting Fees!"—which exposed how virtually all the G.P.s and general surgeons of a sizable eastern city split fees as routinely as they sent out monthly bills.

CORRUPT DOCTORS, DEBASED SERVICE

A referral fee for passing along business may be thoroughly acceptable in the world of commerce, for there the guiding motive is the sheer making of money. But in medical practice the doctor is expected to refer in accordance with the patient's best interests, uninfluenced by a desire for a piece of the action. "The venality of fee splitting is all the worse because most people trust doctors," Dr. Ralph Johnson commented as president of the Wayne County (Detroit) Medical Society. "If the doctor says you must have your gallbladder taken out, you do. You can't have financial chicanery in back of such a relationship."

Fee splitting always threatens to corrupt the doctor and debase his service to the patient. For one thing, kickbacks encourage the fee splitter to refer patients for unneeded treatment. Dr. Dean A. Clark declared before a meeting of the American Public Health Association: "The result of hidden fee splitting, naturally, is that the physician may be tempted to refer patients more frequently than is medically necessary if a sizable split is in the offing."

On the receiving end, the surgeon (or other specialist) getting the patient compromises medicine for money. The ethical surgeon believes his job is as much to prevent surgery as to perform it. Like the good lawyer who tries to keep his client out of court, the proper surgeon takes his patient into the operating room only after more conservative therapy fails. By contrast, fee-splitting surgeons as a matter of routine cut into the patient without trying other measures first. Even if tempted to let a patient off without surgery, the fee-splitting surgeon must contend with the referring physician, called a "feeder," who is out for a cut of the surgical fee. If the surgeon does not operate, the feeder may not send him any more business.

A typical case of feeder-surgeon exploitation of the patient has been described by Dr. James B. Blodgett of the Detroit Surgical Society. A general practitioner examines Mrs. Smith and finds a lump in her uterus. He sends her to a surgeon with whom he has a kickback arrangement.

When the surgeon examines Mrs. Smith, he thinks, "That's a harmless fibroid. Ordinarily I wouldn't recommend surgery here at all." But what he tells the patient is: "We'll operate as soon as possible."

He removes the fibroid unnecessarily and sends Mrs. Smith a bill for $300. The feeder then gets $150 of the payment.

The practice of fee splitting is generally accompanied by the practice of low-caliber medicine. "Where fees are split, the patient is routed not to the best medical care, but to the most satisfactory financial arrangement for the referring doctor," observed Dr. William Bromme, council chairman of the Michigan State Medical Society. Since submarginal practitioners tend to offer the highest kickbacks, split-fee cases largely go to doctors who have the least ability. The feeder is often no great shakes as a physician either—which leaves the patient between a referring Scylla and a receiving Charybdis.

In split-fee surgery, shoddy care often begins before the patient enters the operating room. Ethical surgeons insist upon a preoperative examination as a necessary procedure. As well as being skillful with a scalpel, the surgeon should be a consultant who, because of his training and experience, can give an objective and independent opinion. Except in an emergency, the conscientious surgeon would no more operate without having seen the patient than without having washed his hands, for without an examination the surgeon cannot confirm, disprove, or refine the referring doctor's diagnosis. Fee-splitting surgeons, however, may abdicate this essential of their calling.

Indeed, the split-fee surgeon may not know what his patient looks like before he starts cutting. Dr. Eugene Hoffman, former head of the fee committee of the Los Angeles County Medical Association, tells of a case in which the surgeon got a call from the feeder about a patient with appendicitis. The feeder told him, "I'm bringing the man in at eight A.M."

When the surgeon arrived, the patient was already prepared and taking anesthesia. Far from having examined the patient thoroughly, the surgeon never even saw the face of the person he was operating on.

When a fee-splitting surgeon fails to perform a preoperative exam, after he has opened the patient up he may well find that the operation was unnecessary, that he now will remove an organ that need not have come out. One type of corrupt physician who frequently cuts out healthy tissue is the "ghost surgeon."

Like the ghost writer who does the work while the by-liner gets the credit, this phantom of the operating room is hired by other doctors to perform surgery in their name. This allows the original physician to collect the fee rather than refer the patient to an outside surgeon. Trouble is, the surgeon who would consent to be a ghost is generally not as competent as the outside man would be. Moreover, the ghost surgeon slips up on preoperative procedure by virtually never seeing a patient. Often he appears in the operating room after the patient is anesthetized, then disappears without the patient's ever learning that he was there, much less who he was.

The mother superior of one hospital stopped in a room to chat with a woman recovering from surgery. The patient mentioned a general practitioner who she thought had operated on her.

"He didn't operate on you," the mother superior said, recalling the operating room record. "Dr. Brown did."

The patient was shocked. "Who is Dr. Brown?" she asked. "I've never even heard of him."

The mother superior called for Dr. Brown and asked him about the case. He admitted working regularly as a "ghost" for two general practitioners in the hospital. He was fired from the hospital and eventually expelled from the American College of Surgeons.

In another variety of ghost surgery, the ghost may be visible in the operating room—but introduced to the patient as merely the doctor's assistant. One woman was told by her physician that part of her stomach needed to be removed. Before the operation, the doctor introduced the woman to another doctor who, he said, would "assist" him with the operation. Afterward she found that the so-called assistant had actually performed the operation, though he had never examined her.

Splitting the cash fee is not the only method of payment in feeder-surgeon conspiracies. In one way of paying for referrals, the fee-splitting surgeon calls the feeder a "surgical assistant" and has him stand around the operating room or hold an instrument.

Thus the feeder is entitled to bill the patient for an assistant's fee. This stratagem is widely preferred by fee splitters. No money changes hands between doctors—and, despite strong suspicions, proving that the assistantship was a payoff is nearly impossible. Equally appealing to the fee splitter is the fact that in this arrangement the *patient* pays the kickback, in the form of an additional charge for the assistant's services.

Having the feeder as the surgical assistant can be disastrous for the patient's health as well as harmful to his finances. A main purpose of engaging an assistant is to have present a second man competent to continue the operation if the surgeon in charge is suddenly incapacitated. Comments Dr. Paul R. Hawley: "I rather shudder for the patient when the surgeon suffers a coronary or a cerebral hemorrhage with a bowel anastomosis [link-up of two severed ends of the intestine] just started, or a lobectomy [removal of a lung] half completed, with only a G.P. with him."

Because the feeder lacks surgical skill, he often merely adds to the operating time and increases the likelihood of complications. Furthermore, engaging the feeder keeps the fee-splitting surgeon from using a regular assistant, since any capable second man would suspect why this incompetent is "assisting." Fee splitting therefore stands in the way of a goal of good surgeons: the development of a smooth surgical team made efficient by constant working together. Even if the feeder were competent, his off-and-on-presence would snarl the continuous practice a team needs to best serve patients.

Another kickback arrangement can similarly injure the patient. Ordinarily the surgeon is responsible for the patient's care following the operation. Unless notice is given to the contrary, the surgeon's fee should cover all postoperative services. To pay for a referral, the fee-splitting surgeon may have the feeder needlessly supplement the aftercare and bill the patient accordingly. Dr. Robert S. Myers of the American College of Surgeons has an apt name for this method of greasing the feeder's palm. He calls it "featherbedding."

Or the feeder may take over the aftercare entirely. This practice can be dangerous to the patient. Even among physicians who wouldn't dream of splitting a fee, the referring doctor is often no more competent to handle postoperative care than he is to perform the operation. For just this reason, Dr. Leland S. McKittrick, a clinical professor of surgery at Harvard Medical School, has stopped doing any surgery for which he cannot personally handle the aftercare. He has found that referring doctors miss complications—an intestinal obstruction, for example, or problems relating to fluids—that a well-trained surgeon would catch.

In one case that Dr. McKittrick recalls, the surgeon handed over the postoperative care of a young man who had had an uncomplicated appendectomy. The convalescence should have been uncomplicated. But it was not—and the referring doctor could not handle the problem. Because the doctor failed to spot a warning sign involving fluids, the patient died.

In communities where fee splitting is widespread, the practice tends to depress the quality of care for *all* patients. Superior and ethical surgeons tend to avoid such places. Conversely, the inferior and the unscrupulous are likely to be drawn where they can flourish.

A general tawdriness prevails in medical circles where doctors are corrupt. In one city, both hospitals were hotbeds of fee splitting. An American College of Surgeons inspection found that each institution failed to meet even minimal standards of medical acceptability.

Not only were kickbacks rife. Cases in the hospitals were inadequately reviewed. Records were left incompleted. Unjustified surgery was common. Moreover, neither hospital imposed any system of qualifying, supervising, or reviewing the performance of doctors who chose to do major surgery. Literally any physician on the staff who could hold a scalpel could perform any operation he wished. In regard to the competence and conscience of some members of the staff, the College of Surgeons inspector found evidence of "shocking inadequacies."

NONSURGICAL SPLITS

Surgery is not the only field in which fee splitting flourishes. Corrupt doctors are on the take in a host of services. Some offenders, for example, demand kickbacks of up to 50 percent from oxygen-supply companies.

Radiologists live almost wholly on referrals from other physicians. Investigations reveal that in communities where competition between x-ray specialists is stiff, some men will usually be willing to split fees with feeders who exploit the situation. Referring physicians told one New York radiologist that they could not afford to send him their patients if there was no money for them. Consequently he wound up kicking back 50 percent of his fees to more than 200 doctors.

Many companies supplying trusses, braces, and other appliances admit handing over to referring doctors one third of the price they charged the patient. Laboratories are also expected to cut some doctors in—for example, 30 percent for urinalyses.

The eyeglass industry in particular is vulnerable to graft. Eye doctors —medically trained ophthalmologists as well as non-M.D. optometrists— have among their number a minority notorious for demanding kickbacks from the dispensing opticians. One tax case shows how much a part of ophthalmology fee splitting has been. Judging purely the tax angle, the U.S. Supreme Court ruled that an optician could deduct his kickbacks to ophthalmologists because kickbacks were a business expense that was "ordinary and necessary." The court found that the optician was forced to give local ophthalmologists fully one third the amount received from patients. Otherwise, concluded the court, the doctors would send the patients to opticians who would fork over.

Robert J. Bauer, head of the Better Business Bureau of Los Angeles, put a stop to the eyeglass racket there. He found that kickbacks to ophthalmologists were forcing patients to pay 25 to 50 percent more since opticians inevitably tacked the cost onto the price of the glasses. Bauer sent the Los Angeles County Medical Association an open letter that charged:

"Literally hundreds of your members are receiving secret . . . rebates. . . . The doctors . . . , in the interest of personal gain to themselves, channel their patients' prescription business to certain firms which reward the doctors for doing so. . . . The practice of such firms is to charge the patient about double the amount the firm wishes to retain and remit the overcharge to the doctor."

Bauer also plastered Los Angeles with posters that showed an eye doctor reaching for a stack of kickback money. The poster said: "DOES YOUR OCULIST GET A KICKBACK? Ask Him! . . . Some dispensing opticians kick back 40 percent or more of your payment for eyeglasses!"

The effect of Bauer's campaign was felt across the country. The Houston, Texas, Better Business Bureau began its own campaign. "The evidence is hard to get," it reported, "but we have found that rebates to eye doctors by opticians furnishing glasses to patients amounts to as much as 25 percent of the retail price." One Houston optician admitted that he had been kicking back $18,000 a year to doctors.

The U.S. Department of Justice took its cue from Bauer and began investigating kickbacks from opticians. It found a doctor in Minneapolis who had collected $15,000 in rebates, one in El Paso who had collected $20,000, and four in Fort Dodge, Iowa, who had raked off $40,000.

These investigations have ended the kickbacks in many areas and lowered eyeglass prices to their proper amount. In Los Angeles, for example, prescription prices dropped from $25 to $16, no less than 36 percent.

LIFE IN THE JUNGLE

Fee splitting pollutes a sanctuary that should be safe from commercial exploitation. While under the doctor's care, a sick person wishes to be removed from the marketplace. But fee splitting turns the patient into a piece of merchandise and the fee splitter into a hustler. One family doctor, referring a patient for surgery, waved aside any offer of payment. "I've known you for twenty years," he said. "I wouldn't take anything for this." But he was willing to take half the surgeon's fee under the table.

A physician may meet up with the murky world of fee splitting practically the moment he hangs out his shingle. While head of surgery at the Chicago Medical School and Mount Sinai Hospital, Dr. Richard A. DeWall grew increasingly concerned over the "unfortunate quiet" relating to ethical abuses in surgical practice. He was especially troubled since, as an educator, he felt responsible for the trainee who was unprepared for life in the jungle.

Accordingly—"because someone has to light the fire"—Dr. DeWall wrote in the prestigious journal *Surgery, Gynecology and Obstetrics* a much-discussed editorial attacking this situation: In some parts of the country the young surgeon starting practice will be approached by a doctor and asked to see a patient in surgical consultation. The subject of "arrangements" is soon brought up. At first the young surgeon may not be clear as to what is meant. But he will soon find out that it amounts to an invitation to split fees.

When a new doctor comes to town, the first question fee-splitting old-timers may ask is, "Do you or don't you?" One young surgeon in New Jersey barely opened his office door when—along with sellers of drugs, equipment, and supplies—hordes of would-be feeders began descending on him. He kept careful count. Before he gave his last refusal, he had been propositioned by no fewer than thirty-three G.P.s.

The enticements put forth by fee splitters are often tempting. A new surgeon was invited to the home of a suburban G.P. "I'd like you to look over my books," the host said suddenly. "I want to prove to you that you can make $10,000 in six months by handling all my surgery. All you need do is split the fees fifty-fifty."

"No thanks," the surgeon replied.

Later he calculated that building his practice was taking about ten times longer than if he had elected to split fees.

"As far as I could determine the American College of Surgeons hasn't made a dent in fee splitting," a young surgeon has written in a letter to his former teacher. The young man had toured the South and Southwest hoping to find a good location. Unexpectedly, his trip gave him a panoramic view of shady practices in surgery.

"I visited my friends in Kansas, Oklahoma, Texas and Arkansas . . . to find out the possibility of doing their surgery if I started up in their town," the young man's letter continues. "All said sure—for 50 percent of the fee. That was the standard."

The young man proceeded through Texas, where he met a group of doctors on the hunt for a ghost surgeon. "I had a wonderful offer, as far as money goes. . . . The head doctor wined and dined my wife and me . . . before he finally told us the setup. What it amounted to was that each of the doctors scheduled their own surgery and told the patient they would do the case; then I would do the surgery."

On a fifty-fifty split, the young man was told that he would earn about $40,000 a year. He would replace their current ghost, a member of the faculty of a nearby school. Concludes the young man: "Probably more . . . ghost surgery goes on than we know about."

It is not only the feeder who seeks out the surgeon. Conversely, fee-splitting surgeons hunt for new sources of referrals. To seduce newcomers into feeding him patients, one fee-splitting surgeon has offered kickbacks actually higher than the fees he received. Generally he would pay 110 percent commission until the young man got established, then would gradually level off to a fifty-fifty split. In the parlance of merchandising this surgeon offered feeders a loss leader.

Some fee splitters go even further in using techniques of high-pressure salesmanship. They engage in fee-splitting price wars. One general practitioner moved to a midwestern town and began a surgical practice, although he had had little training in it. He found that he was competing with another G.P. who also was practicing surgery. The two doctors began running their practices with discount-house competitiveness.

One began offering the town's physicians a 20 percent kickback for referrals. The other raised to 30 percent. The first doctor countered with 40 percent. The two surgeons finally reached a truce, offering all doctors 50 percent of the surgical fee.

Sometimes, without bothering with preliminaries, jaundiced fee splitters simply assume that a new man is a member of the club. Dr. Edwin M. Limbert was fresh out of specialty training when he took over a deceased surgeon's practice. His predecessor's nurse began introducing him to the doctors who had been sources of referrals. As is customary in getting established, Dr. Limbert told them that he would like to see their patients, that he would not charge for consultation, and that the patients would be returned to their family doctors after surgery.

"Money was not mentioned," Dr. Limbert recalls, "and I was innocent enough to think that such a program would appeal to all of them."

Before long he got patients from the doctors he spoke to. Nothing unusual occurred for a while. Then, after one operation, the referring physician followed Dr. Limbert and asked to see him in private.

Alone, the physician came right to the point: "I've been getting my 35 percent, and I want it now."

Thereafter, reflects Dr. Limbert, "I got disillusioned, and fast."

Another source of referrals complained to him: "I'm used to my 50 percent and I ain't been gettin' it."

Yet another demanded: "Did so-and-so pay you? How much of that is for me?"

And still another fee splitter threatened the young surgeon: "Goddamn you, you'll starve. You'll never get another patient from my part of the country. There isn't a doctor in the state who doesn't get his cut. You'll come begging for patients."

Such ruthlessness is not uncommon in the fee splitters' dealings with ethical doctors. The nonsplitter may be exploited no less than the patient.

A general practitioner referred a patient to a surgeon who was not a fee splitter. After the operation the G.P. told the surgeon that he would collect the $300 surgery fee from the patient "as a favor, because I know these people."

When the surgeon received the $300, he routinely mailed a receipt to the patient. Soon he received an irate phone call. "What do you mean by sending me a receipt for only $300," the patient demanded. "Dr. M. told me your fee was $1,000 and that's what I gave him."

The fee splitters' most unscrupulous acts are often reserved for the colleague who won't play ball. A new surgeon in a hospital may find his work maligned and himself frozen out of practice if he turns down feeders' proposals. "The young surgeon will never see another patient from the referring physician and likely may have to give up practice at that particular hospital as no patients will be referred to him," Dr. Richard DeWall reported. "To stay in his community at his chosen hospital, the young surgeon must either conform or not practice the profession for which he has spent many years in preparation."

Where fee splitting is entrenched, it can take on the dimensions of a conspiracy. One unusually courageous doctor went to a meeting of the

American College of Surgeons and tried to expose the fee splitting engaged in by virtually every surgeon and G.P. in his city. Soon afterward, he had to go elsewhere to remain in practice. One of the fee splitters who helped force him out explained blithely: "He didn't fit in, so he moved away."

The acceptance of corruption that accompanies widespread fee splitting may take hold of even the laymen on hospital boards of directors, who normally are expected to operate their institution in the public interest. After becoming chief of surgery of a hospital, one conscientious physician found himself in a dispute with a surgeon who insisted on continuing to split fees.

At length the fee splitter took his large surgical practice to another institution. This left his old hospital with empty beds and a consequent deficit.

The hospital board of directors called the chief of surgery on the carpet. "If you'd played ball this would not have happened," they admonished him.

Part of the chief of surgery's job is to initiate appointments to the surgical staff. He appointed two orthopedic surgeons who would not split fees. The board, however, was not convinced that their patients would take up enough empty beds. Over the chief's protests, the board brought in a surgeon known as a fee splitter on the theory that his kickbacks would generate more patients.

"In other words," observed the beaten chief, "they didn't give a damn about the morals of the situation."

GLOOMY PROGNOSIS

"We are fighting very hard," Dr. Preston Wade, a current board chairman of the American College of Surgeons, said of the College's efforts to wipe out fee splitting. But the College is almost certainly fighting a losing battle. The prospect is that fee splitting will become increasingly widespread. More and more referring doctors will demand kickbacks. Ever more surgeons will be willing to pay for patients.

That gloomy prognosis is based on a projection of current trends. The economic conditions that lead doctors to split fees are intensifying. No easing off is in prospect. Nor are adequate controls in sight.

Like a weed, fee splitting flourishes despite being nearly universally condemned. "The secret division of a fee between two physicians . . . is dishonest, against the public interest and has long been considered unethical by responsible doctors of medicine"—such is how the American College of Surgeons sums up the feeling predominant in the profession. Most other specialty groups forbid the practice; the American Academy of General Practice calls it "morally reprehensible." Some organizations, like the College of Surgeons, have more or less ongoing campaigns to root out violators. For the guidance of all members of the profession, the Principles of Medical Ethics specifically prohibit the practice, and the A.M.A. Judicial Council has painstakingly elaborated on the many types of fee splitting, every one of which is forbidden.

In addition, at least twenty-three states regard the practice as illegal and subject to criminal penalties. While there is no conviction on record, the statutes at least make it clear to the fee splitter that he is not comporting himself within the law. The Internal Revenue Service too has declared against fee splitting. It has ruled that the doctor who gives a kickback must pay income tax on the full fee he receives, not merely on the portion he retains. This makes kickbacks a nondeductible expense, putting them in the same category as bribes.

One surgeon who fell afoul of the tax rules was one of the last fee splitters in his city, following a decision by other surgeons to stop the practice. He was deluged with referrals from feeders—sometimes doing twelve or more operations a day. One day an Internal Revenue agent appeared. The tax audit showed that he had been concealing large amounts of cash, which he used to pay off referring doctors. He was assessed over $100,000.

This surgeon, who had already suffered two heart attacks, felt he could earn what he owed by operating on more patients. But he could not increase his volume without splitting fees, and if he split he could not file an honest tax return. Furthermore, the more he worked, the higher would be his income tax bracket. A College of Surgeons official who tells this story concludes: "Doctor X found an alternative solution, by paying his debt to nature. He died of coronary thrombosis."

In the face of such opprobrium, fee splitters show a remarkable ability to rationalize their behavior. "Almost *no* doctor [engaged in fee splitting] failed to mention some kind of justification for the fee splitter," a report on the practice has noted.

Many fee splitters further advocate that fee splitting be "legalized." Most physicians feel that the splitter, who obviously has a scalpel to grind, presents a weak case for sanctioning the practice. Dr. Paul R. Hawley, for example, snorted over any such proposal. Quoting from *Measure for Measure*, he called any attempt to legalize fee splitting an effort to "condemn the fault, and not the actor"—and added: "It is to be hoped that this is not a measure of the profession's willingness to compromise with evil solely for the purpose of filling the wallets of doctors."

So much for the cloud the medical kickback is under. Why, then, do fee splitters risk the scorn of colleagues and punishment by the law? What promotes this underhanded practice so at odds with medical ideals? How prevalent will this brand of corruption be in the near future?

Some answers to these questions can be found in a comprehensive study which the American Medical Association came close to keeping from the public. The study began as a response to public outcries against medical kickbacks. To investigate the problem, the A.M.A. convened a Special Committee on Medical Practices. Many observers would not have been terribly astonished if the committee report came out heavily coated with whitewash. But the panel—called the Truman Committee after its chairman, Dr. Stanley S. Truman of California—did a thorough and objective job.

Committee members and representatives interviewed scores of doctors across the country. An interviewer would frequently spend hours probing a physician's experiences and opinions, and these interviews would be recorded and transcribed. The committee report drawn from this evidence runs to well over 15,000 words. Dr. Dwight H. Murray, chairman of the A.M.A. Board of Trustees, called the findings "the most constructive and exhaustive relating to the problem of fee splitting ever written."

Then, despite the acknowledged importance of the study, the A.M.A. suppressed it. Instead of carrying even a respectable fraction of the report, the A.M.A.'s *Journal* published a résumé of exactly one page.

Several doctors who had copies of the report took issue with the A.M.A. leadership. They felt that the profession as a whole, which spent some $15,000 for the study, was entitled to see what it had paid for. These dissenters therefore made an unabridged version of the report available to the independently published *Medical Economics,* which printed it in detail. Were it not for these free spirits within medicine, the Truman Committee report might never have come to light.

Among the committee's conclusions was an implied accusation that medical leaders were not doing their job, specifically that "the present supervision of organized medicine over the ethical standards of doctors is not adequate to protect the public or the good name of the profession." The committee added that it wished to "call this forcefully to the attention of the Board of Trustees." Six years later, in a broader study, the A.M.A. Medical Disciplinary Committee found little improvement in medical discipline and detected essentially the same weaknesses.

The Truman Committee has provided an authoritative report as to why doctors split fees. Combined with other data, the report helps show why the practice is almost certain to become more widespread. The reasons have to do with worsening financial problems faced by G.P.s and surgeons. To wit:

General practitioners more and more are becoming medicine's second-class citizens. Laymen tend to attach considerable glamour to surgical therapy. Witness, for example, one story in the *Time* magazine medicine section. The article was replete with compelling color photographs of surgery in progress. Proclaimed the legend across the cover of the issue:

"IF THEY CAN OPERATE, YOU'RE LUCKY." By contrast, diagnosis and medical therapy seem to many misguided patients like mere pill-pushing: lack-luster, routine, even an easy out for the unskilled M.D.

No medical man—be he internist, pediatrician, or G.P.—likes playing second fiddle to the surgeon. Moreover, the public matches its esteem for surgery with a willingness to pay highly for it. The differential between surgical and medical fees especially galls the medical practitioner.

"Take a child with an [inflamed] appendix," a G.P. told the Truman Committee. "You make the diagnosis, call the hospital, arrange for the admission, maybe for an ambulance, and you get $5. You refer the case to a surgeon who takes the appendix out in fifteen or twenty minutes, sees the child four or five times afterwards, and gets $150. I think the differential is too great."

Similarly, an internist expresses his doubts that the surgeon's services are really worth his fees. "I think it would be much easier," he said, "to do four tonsillectomies and make $400 instead of doing one difficult diagnostic workup for $25."

The medical man's urge, then, is sometimes to reduce through fee splitting the differential he resents. This may be all the excuse he needs to hold out for a kickback. Or, to quote Dr. Paul Hawley: "A certain portion of G.P.s . . . want a slice of what they consider the surgeon's gravy."

Furthermore, hospitals are increasingly requiring that physicians have specialty training before they can use hospital facilities. G.P.s particularly are being banned from the operating room.

G.P.s resent diminishment of their hospital privileges. Besides being a slap in the face, it cuts them off from the larger services that pay better and are professionally more satisfying. The money lost from being shut out of an operating room can have special meaning if the G.P. practices in a pocket of poverty or in an area overpopulated with medical practitioners. Often local G.P.s tell themselves they would starve if they depended solely on their income from house calls and office visits. Ergo, to protect their standard of living, they may make it the practice in the community to demand part of the surgeon's fee.

The Truman Committee has thus found that the squeeze on the G.P. is threefold: having to do with prestige, fees, and privileges. In combination, these encourage the G.P. to seek a split fee.

All indications now are that the squeeze will get worse. Though non-surgical therapy increasingly works wonders, the public is unlikely to lose its fascination with surgery. And as long as a scalpel remains more photogenic than a pill, the press is bound to play up the surgeon as the folk hero of medicine.

Consistent with the aura surrounding the surgeon, surgical fees most likely will stay comparatively high. To a great extent surgeons' fees are buttressed by health insurance plans, which have always been more liberal in payments for surgery than for medical services. In all probability this will continue. Surgeons also find it easier than medical practitioners to raise their fees. A patient is not likely to quibble over whether the removal of a breast should cost $300, $350, or $400—but may protest if a formerly $8 house call now costs $10. Thus the fee differential that irks medical men is almost certain to persist.

So too is the withdrawal of G.P. privileges at many hospitals. Indeed, the G.P.'s decline seems as inexorable as the advance of specialism. Already his hospital privileges have so shrunk that G.P.s—who not long ago did nearly all surgery—now do little more than an estimated third. There is strong evidence that they should not be doing even this much. The progress of good surgery dictates that restrictions on G.P.s intensify.

In sum, the G.P. who finds the operating room door locked to him must face the problem of how to live on smaller fees from assorted lesser services. Many G.P.s are likely to decide to make their referrals pay through fee splitting. Will their solicitations for kickbacks be welcomed by surgeons?

Possibly, for *surgeons face ever stiffening competition for patients.* In 1930 there were no more than 4,500 general surgeons. Now there are at least 26,000, plus about 8,000 others who claim surgery as a part-time specialty. This burgeoning has created an anomaly: at a time when the nation suffers from an overall dearth of physicians, there is a plethora of general surgeons.

Surgeons themselves feel their specialty is too full. The American College of Surgeons has asked its members for opinion on the supply of manpower in the major specialties. Some 13,000 surgeons responded. The field they most often singled out as overcrowded: general surgery.

Right now there are over 5,500 resident physicians training to be surgeons. In cycles of roughly three years, these young surgeons pour out of their training institutions into an already jampacked field.

Nor is there any sign of a letup in the production of general surgeons. It is probable that every surgical trainee will be succeeded by another, who in turn will enter practice and the scramble for patients. What's more, the number of surgeons entering the field may even increase. Over 7,000 surgical residencies are now approved—and the triennial output of surgeons may well rise to that number.

The competition for patients would be severe enough even if the number of ailments requiring surgery remained static. But because of advancements in nonsurgical therapy and improvements in surgical methods, these more and more surgeons are having less and less to do.

Surgeons used to joke that they could live off the complications of appendicitis, what with a patient requiring ten weeks in the hospital for an abscess and then a second hospitalization for an appendectomy. Now it is a rare appendicitis that requires more than ten days in the hospital—and operations done in two or three stages are generally a thing of the past.

Mastoiditis shows how drugs can wipe out the need for scalpels. This inflammation of a bone behind the ear used to be cured principally by surgery. Now the operation is very rare because antibiotics make it unnecessary.

As drug and x-ray methods improve, much the same is likely to happen for many types of cancer. The cancer operation, another staple of the surgeon's practice, will then become a less usual occurrence. The competition among surgeons for remaining services will become correspondingly more fierce.

The loser in the rat race is often the young man attempting to establish a surgical practice. Since the newcomer simply adds to the glut, he is unlikely to find local practitioners welcoming him with open arms. "General surgeons are pretty easy to come by in a community of this sort," one doctor told the Truman Committee. "And for anybody to come in and say 'Stop sending your surgical referrals to the other surgeons with whom you are working and send them to me,' would be presumptuous."

Before he can earn a living, the young surgeon must gain a hospital staff appointment. But in communities oversupplied with surgeons, hospital privileges may be hard to come by. "I've been having trouble getting on the staffs of the hospitals," one new surgeon has written a colleague. "The applications are being held up in a committee by one person who just doesn't want new surgeons. . . . [Because I have no hospital in which to operate] I've already lost two gallbladders, two hernias and one appendectomy. I have not made even one cent since being here."

One survey, conducted by a surgeon who uses the pseudonym Dr. J. Ray Thomas, has sought to measure the extent of the difficulty surgeons have in getting started. "Most young surgeons are well capable of and would like to do at least 250–300 major surgeries annually," Dr. Thomas has said. "This amount of surgery would justify the limiting of their practice, their long years of training and would help to perfect their surgical judgment and technique."

But the Thomas survey shows that even surgeons who are no longer newcomers—having been in practice three to five years—are almost universally doing less than 250 major operations a year. Fully 80 percent do less than 200. Indeed, at least 36 percent are so limited in opportunities that in a full year they do less than 100.

Thus, for increasing numbers of hard-pressed surgeons, what is likely to be the solution to their financial dilemma? The Truman Committee states its conclusions using doctors' own words, and so shall we.

Says a G.P.: "The young surgeon who tries to set himself up in an area very soon finds himself without a referral reservoir unless he is willing to split the fees with the referring practitioner."

Another G.P.: "The ideals get a bit tarnished or rubbed off when the economics of making a living for a wife and family hit you."

And a surgeon: "It is simply a question that when a practice is so widespread, as it is at the present time, and there are so many surgeons who have a tough time getting surgical cases, the economic factor overcomes ethical factors."

8

THE PROFITEERS:
Captive Prescriptions

SENATOR PHILIP A. HART of Michigan glanced around the hearing room of the Senate Subcommittee on Antitrust and Monopoly. He was bringing an end to six days of testimony on physician ownership of pharmacies and drug companies. The Senator was troubled by the effects of doctors profiting from their prescriptions.

"Frankly," he said, "if I could stop the practices I have heard described during these hearings as of this moment, I would do so."

He went on: "What amazes me is that a great and noble calling such as medicine has members who are apparently willing to besmirch the public image of the greater majority of dedicated doctors for the possible extra financial rewards involved.

"What further amazes me is that this same overwhelming majority of dedicated physicians let their colleagues get away with it."

Thus Senator Hart summed up the feeling of many who have explored this corner of medicine's underworld. In a typical case, a woman goes to her doctor for a stomach ailment. The doctor examines her, then gives her a prescription for medication.

To the patient, the prescription is a paper bearing meaningless marks. She assumes she is getting the proper medication in the right amount.

Perhaps the doctor mentions: "This can be filled at the drugstore down the street." It seems a thoughtful suggestion. The woman leaves the doctor's office satisfied. She stops at that drugstore to get her medicine.

In this case, what she does not know is that the doctor owns the pharmacy he recommended. Or he may have an interest in the company that packaged the drug he prescribed. He would thus profit from the prescription. And he is therefore tempted to write prescriptions that are not in his patients' interests but his own.

HOW YOU PAY

Owning a drugstore can be extremely lucrative for physicians. Most independently owned pharmacies net a profit of no more than 5 percent. By contrast, a pharmacy owned by a group of 21 doctors is netting 23 percent. One California doctor nets $50,000 a year from his pharmacy alone, about twice as much as the typical private practitioner nets from his total practice.

In physician-owned pharmacies, much of the substantial profit may come from a captive market: the owner's own patients. James Robert Nielson, general counsel of the California Pharmaceutical Association, asks: "Is there any other business where the owner of a store can direct the customer as to what he must buy, how much he must buy, and how much he must pay for it at the expense of the customer's health?"

If a physician steers you to a pharmacy he owns you may be hurt in at least three ways:

1. *You are likely to pay higher prices.* A spot check in a midwestern state shows that doctor-owned pharmacies charge as much as two dollars more than independents to fill the same prescriptions.

The reason for the higher price is twofold: A patient directed to a pharmacy by his doctor seldom checks the prices at other drugstores. The profiteer thus need not charge competitively. Too, many thoughtful doctors make a point of prescribing the brand that will cost the patient least. But with their own profit at stake, pharmacy owners generally feel little incentive to save the patient money. Profiteers tend to prescribe a higher-priced drug even when one less expensive would do.

2. *You may buy drugs you don't need.* Studies show that doctors start writing more prescriptions almost as soon as they acquire a pharmacy. One such doctor was uncovered by the Hart Committee. Since he began operating a pharmacy, the volume of his prescriptions has jumped by 500 percent.

A related finding shows that doctor-owners generally prescribe smaller quantities if the patient insists on taking his "Rx" to an independent store. One West Coast medical group owns an adjacent pharmacy. A woman undergoing treatment was given nine prescriptions and told that she should have them filled at the group's pharmacy. When she informed the physician that she was employed at a local pharmacy and preferred to have her prescriptions filled there, she was told to have only three of the prescriptions filled—that she didn't need the other six prescriptions.

As a taxpayer, you may get stung still further. Tax-supported health-care programs seldom challenge a doctor's prescriptions. Thus government programs fall easy prey to profiteering pharmacy owners. In one Kansas county, 94 percent of all welfare prescription claims are submitted by a single doctor-owned pharmacy. A California welfare agency has been studying claims submitted by a physician who recently opened a drugstore next to his office. Since entering the pharmacy business, his prescriptions for the same welfare patients have risen from $10,000 a year to $50,000.

3. *Competition may be killed off.* Since profiteers can funnel prescrip-

tions to their own drugstores, independent pharmacists often are unable to compete. In one Kansas town the wife of a doctor runs a drugstore. In fifteen years the town's other pharmacist, an independent, has filled only two prescriptions that the doctor has written.

In a North Dakota community two thriving drugstores employed five pharmacists. Then a three-doctor group opened its own pharmacy, rewriting all old prescriptions and refusing to authorize refills at any outside pharmacy. The number of prescriptions filled at the independent drugstores dropped from seventy daily to a mere ten. Within nine months two of the pharmacists were laid off.

In yet another town, two independent drugstores have suffered a 70 percent drop in prescriptions despite an increase in population. The main reason: Local physicians now have their own pharmacy. Still elsewhere, in Wisconsin, eight physician-owned pharmacies fill the same number of prescriptions as the combined total of twenty-eight independents.

Besides cornering patients' drug purchases, profiteers can compete unfairly by stocking a smaller inventory. While the independent pharmacist must stand the expense of a wide selection of drugs to meet prescription demands, a doctor need carry only one line—and prescribe only what he carries. One physician-owned pharmacy in California thus makes a profit of $90,000 a year on an inventory of less than $10,000. A deliberately restricted inventory is also unfair to the patient, since he may wind up not with the drug he needs, but with the one the prescriber has on hand.

Furthermore, while independent pharmacists must buy all their stock, physicians get many free samples from pharmaceutical houses. Some profiteers sell the samples at regular prices. One patient who had a prescription filled at a physician-owned drugstore found marked on three fourths of her pills the words "COMPLIMENTARY" and "NOT FOR SALE."

When independents are forced out of business through unfair competition, patients are left with less choice than ever. A small town in a large midwestern state once boasted three well-stocked pharmacies. Within three years, the independents have been replaced by one medical-group pharmacy with a limited stock of drugs. The nearest independent drugstore is twenty miles away.

UNDERCOVER TIE-INS

Physician ownership of pharmacies is on the rise. In Wisconsin in a mere five years the number of doctor-owned pharmacies has doubled. In California in only fifteen years the number of known physician-owned drug stores has jumped from 39 to 252. Already in Hawaii physicians or physician-owned pharmacies dispense between 60 and 70 percent of all medicine.

Monopolies and near-monopolies have taken hold in many communities. Of the twelve doctors in one New Mexico community, eleven have gathered together as partners in one of two drugstores there. In a South Dakota city, eighteen of twenty-one physicians own pharmacies and routinely direct patients to them. In some cities, especially in the West and Midwest, *every* physician is associated with a pharmacy. Increasingly, groups of physicians are establishing their own clinics, an integral part of which is their own drugstore.

Nationwide, the number of known physician-owned drugstores has grown from 1,200 in 1960 to more than 2,200 now. But profiteers often use ruses to conceal their tie-in with pharmacies. Not unusual is the pharmacist who is registered as the owner, while in reality a physician holds the title and gets the profits. Also common is the pharmacy that is registered in the name of the doctor's wife or another family member. The state of Washington has learned of at least fifty pharmacies controlled by physicians under dummy corporations.

Exploitative physicians need not necessarily own a pharmacy to share in its profits. Rather, they can be landlords who receive as rent a percentage of pharmacy receipts. Often doctors in partnership, calling themselves "medical associates" or a "clinic" or "group," have space in their office building for a pharmacy. If the pharmacy pays a fixed monthly rent and is run by an independent pharmacist, it can serve as a fairly operated convenience to the patient. But often the partnership rents out the pharmacy in return for a percentage of the gross income. A seven-doctor group in Colorado, for example, solicited bids from prospective tenants. Over and above a $400 monthly rental, the pharmacist who would pay the highest percentage of gross receipts would get the lease.

Such arrangements, of course, mean that the more the pharmacy takes in, the more the partners make. One independent pharmacist told the Hart Committee of a clinic of seven doctors in South Dakota who get "a large percentage of the gross profits or in other words a kickback. The more prescriptions they write, the more the kickback. We now have five drugstores in town, and I am sure we don't fill as many all together as one clinic."

In one case described before the committee, a California medical group thought the kickback insufficient. In the partners' original arrangement with a pharmacist, they got 6 percent of the gross. Then the partners doubled the rent, to receive 12 percent. Shortly thereafter, they put pressure on the pharmacist to sell. The pharmacist refused. One of the partners warned him: "Well, you're going to sell, or else."

"Or else what?"

"Well, we could put another pharmacy in this building somewhere. If you don't sell to us, we will open a pharmacy on the second floor, or in the parking lot, and send everyone there."

Ultimately the doctors forced the pharmacist out. They approached another pharmacist and asked him to run the store for them.

"Why don't you sell or rent it?" he asked.

"That isn't our point," a senior partner replied. "We want the money. In simple language, what we want you to do is hang your license on the wall. But we will take care of all the financial interest, and we'll pay you a salary."

As incentive to front for the doctors, he was offered $15,000 a year plus a percentage of the gross. Moreover, he was assured the gross would rise. One of the partners told him: "You know, I have never been too interested in the pharmacy before, but I will, since we are going to have a percentage. You know, I can write two prescriptions instead of one for these people. I can write them bigger. I can see all my patients get down there."

SUBTLE AS A SLEDGEHAMMER

To make sure that their patients "get down there," profiteers may employ subtle and not so subtle manipulation. "Smith's Pharmacy will give you a good break on this," a doctor backing Smith's may say. Or, "Smith's knows how I like my prescriptions filled." Or, "I find Smith's more reliable than Jones'."

About as subtle as a sledgehammer is the physician-owner who promotes his pharmacy right on his prescription blank, printing such directions as "Take this to Advance Drugstore" or "Have this filled at City Drugstore." Similarly unsubtle are profiteers who do away with the written prescription altogether. Many such physicians, especially those in groups, have direct phone connections with their drugstores. The doctor calls his pharmacy and places the order while the patient is in the office. A witness told the Hart Committee of one doctor who takes patients by the arm and steers them into the pharmacy adjoining his office. There he verbally gives the prescription to his pharmacist-employee. Observed the committee: "It is the rare patient who, when informed of where he can pick up his prescription, can summon the will to ask the busy physician to write out the prescription because he wishes to make his purchase elsewhere."

In such cases, if a strong-minded patient decides to go to an independent pharmacy, he may find himself out of luck. Prescriptions written by some doctors are in a code that is understood only at the doctor's pharmacy.

Indeed, the medicine prescribed may simply not be available at any pharmacy except the doctor's own. A profiteer may prescribe obscure brands available only on his own shelves. To fill the prescription, other local pharmacies need to purchase the product from him.

The profiteer himself may concoct the product. One physician, for example, prescribes a drug of his own devising for expectant mothers. If a patient brings the prescription to her own druggist, he has to buy the medication from the doctor's pharmacy.

Some medical groups allow patients to fill prescriptions *only* in the group's own pharmacy. Often doctors in the group refuse to see patients who have their prescriptions filled elsewhere. Since doctors in a Colorado town established a pharmacy, they have systematically tried to run all their prescriptions through their own store. They denigrate the local independent pharmacies, order prescriptions for patients over direct lines to their own pharmacy, and chide objecting patients for "not being cooperative." Patients have brought petitions to the state legislature protesting the coercion.

In one southern Illinois town, a bitter controversy has arisen over the prescribing methods of doctors in a local group. The nineteen partners share the profits of a pharmacy which is located behind the counter just inside the front door of their clinic. In the latest year for which figures are available, the pharmacy had gross sales of $333,208 and yielded a profit of $110,000.

The town's independent druggists protest that the partners use intimidation to insure that prescriptions they write are filled in the captive pharmacy. In a typical instance, the prescription for one patient called for Neo-Synephrine, a common nose drop that can as easily be purchased over the counter—that is, prepackaged without a prescription. The group doctor's prescription specified a limited supply and also directed "No Refills." If the patient wanted more of the medication, she would have to ask the doctor for another prescription, entailing another office visit and fee. Moreover, by being dispensed as a prescription, this over-the-counter item cost $1.50 to $2.00 extra, the usual professional surcharge.

This medical group has been widely accused of refusing to allow patients to take prescriptions elsewhere. One woman recalls asking a nurse for her prescription. "No," she quotes the nurse as saying, "we'll just send it around to the pharmacy desk."

Another woman instructed her daughter to ask for her prescription. "But the nurse told her she would have to have it filled at the clinic pharmacy—she couldn't take it with her. It turned out to be only for vitamins."

Some exploiters dispense drugs directly as part of an office visit. Two physician-partners have been treating young acne sufferers with an antibiotic called tetracycline. They sell the drug to patients themselves. There is nothing wrong per se with physicians dispensing drugs; doctors often act as their own pharmacists in areas where drug service is inadequate. But these partners are in a large city with satisfactory pharmacies. In addition, they have been charging as much as thirty-two dollars a hundred for the pills—more than six times what independent pharmacists charge, more than twelve times what the pills cost wholesale.

Profiteering is also found among ophthalmologists who sell as well as prescribe eyeglasses. According to a survey of the American Association of Ophthalmology, more than 40 percent of the country's 7,500 M.D. eye specialists (who are also called oculists) sell the glasses they prescribe. The Guild for Prescription Opticians of America has found only two states, Alaska and North Dakota, where ophthalmologists do not sell glasses.

The practice is contagious. In Tucson, Arizona, only two doctors sold glasses before 1959. A more recent count shows seventeen out of nineteen ophthalmologists in the business. In some cities, ophthalmologists own the optical stores.

After performing an eye examination, the ophthalmologist has the patient select his frames and tells him to come back in a week or so to pick up his glasses. The prescription is then sent to a wholesale house to be filled. Like physicians who own drugstores, the dispensing ophthalmologist can easily exploit patients by writing unnecessary prescriptions. If a patient already wears glasses, the doctor is often tempted to make minor changes in the prescription so that a new pair is required.

Since dispensing ophthalmologists enjoy a monopoly position in the patient's eyeglass purchase, they are under little pressure to charge competitive prices. A study in Los Angeles shows that ophthalmologists who sell glasses charge about nine dollars per pair more than opticians, who do not prescribe and so are in no special position to exploit the patient.

"Many times we see patients who definitely do not need glasses," says Dr. John William Dickerson, an ophthalmologist in Norfolk, Virginia. "How can one clearly decide whether a patient does not or does need glasses when one can make money by giving him glasses? It muddies the waters. It makes the profit motive an important part of the medical decision. It is wrong."

EXPLOITATION, INC.

All the abuses of the doctor-owned pharmacies are committed on a larger scale by physician-owned drug companies. These "repackaging" companies buy established drugs in bulk and market them under their own brand names. Many do not even repackage. The company gets the drugs already packed and labeled and merely distributes them to pharmacies.

Since druggists must follow a prescription to the letter, at the stroke of a prescriber's pen the pharmacist can be forced to buy drugs of a specified brand—either that or lose the prescription, for the law does not allow the pharmacist to substitute even an exact equivalent without the doctor's permission. A pharmacy, of course, represents a much larger purchaser of drugs than an individual patient. And many exploitative physicians put the squeeze on pharmacies, a squeeze that is felt by patients in the form of higher prices and inferior drugs.

The president of a Salt Lake City drug repackaging company testified before the Senate Subcommittee on Antitrust and Monopoly. Senator Hart asked him: "In the first two years of your activity about how many stockholders did you have?"

WITNESS: "Over 450."

SENATOR HART: "And of those, how many were physicians?"

WITNESS: "244."

Or more than half. This company is by no means unique. Doctor-owned or -controlled drug companies operate in at least 30 states. One Texas company is owned exclusively by physicians. A South Carolina company has 365 stockholders, 198 of whom are doctors or members of doctors' families.

Thus far, no fewer than 140 drug companies have been identified as wholly or largely doctor-owned. The actual number of companies controlled by physicians is thought to be around 300. Ownership by physicians is often difficult to ascertain because many doctors own stock in the name of a wife, child, or other relative. Or a doctor stockholder may list his name but not his M.D., obscuring the fact that he is a physician. "Indeed," the Hart Committee reports, "where there is a desire to conceal ownership, the number of subterfuges available is endless."

Counting only doctors whose stockholding is known for certain, the committee has determined that more than 5,000 physicians have interests in drug companies. These do not include large pharmaceutical houses such as Pfizer, Lilly, and Squibb, where stock owned by doctors is a negligible fraction of the whole. Rather, these are small, regional repackaging companies in which stockholders profit directly from prescription sales.

Many drug repackaging companies embark on campaigns to sell stock to doctors. The expectation is that the physician-stockholder will then prescribe the company's products. The Hart Committee subpoenaed the stenographic proceedings of one repackaging company's board of directors. In one transcript, the directors were discussing getting their salesmen to sell more stock.

"I've been pushing these fellows to put as much as possible in the hands of physicians," said the company president, himself a private practitioner. "Then . . . [I'd] write a personal letter once a month: sold so many drugs, made so much profit."

"I want some publicity," interjected one of the directors, a salesman. He went on to outline an idea of his: giving stock to medical students, perhaps as a prize to the top student in each graduating class.

The physician-president of the company was elated. "That's a brand new idea," he exclaimed. "When did you dream it up? The first thing that occurred to me is that if we are going to do something like this it might be wise to spread it around a little more—three or four fellows instead of one, and that will give us that many more prescribers."

Later one member of the board estimated the value of selling stock to physicians in terms of what their prescriptions were worth. "If twenty or thirty of them bought shares," he observed, "they represent a minimum of $100,000 worth of business."

This company has especially tried to sell stock to doctors at prison camps. A physician on the board explained that the prison doctor is desirable because he has a literally captive market and "is free to write for any amount of drugs needed to look after the prisoners in his care. . . . I really think this could be a bonanza strike." On behalf of the company, this doctor arranged telephone calls to eighty-two purchasing authorities for prison camps.

The telephone campaign was extended to purchasing agents of other institutions. A hospital business manager has recounted his experience with the calls. "The suggestion . . . was made again and again that the medical staff be advised to purchase substantial quantities of the common stock . . . and that the hospital then switch its entire drug business to [the company]. We were 'guaranteed' that the stock would triple and quadruple if we took such action because [the company] had already made similar arrangements in other states and they implied that they were on the road to achieving such an arrangement with the North Carolina Prison Division.

"The conference lasted more than thirty minutes and was the baldest proposition I have heard in seventeen years of bulk purchasing."

"PUSH OUR PRODUCTS"

At the Hart Committee hearings, one of the investigators suggested to the president of a drug company: "If you have doctor-stockholders . . . they might on occasion prescribe some of your drugs or at least be more favorable to your products."

The president's reply: "I would hope they would be more favorable."

"Hope" is an understatement. Management typically exhorts the doctor-stockholder to prescribe more of the company's products. Medilite Laboratories (a pseudonym like all company names in this account) included this appeal in its report to stockholding physicians:

> Sales generated per Doctor Stockholder were only $1.03 per day . . . This represents approximately 1 Medilite "script" per day. . . . Many doctors see 40 to 50 patients a day.

> IF—Each Doctor Stockholder would have written a scant 2 "scripts" per day—sales would have been $118,000—with estimated profits of between $35,000 and $40,000!!

> JUST IMAGINE IF—Each Doctor Stockholder would have written 3 "scripts" each day—sales would have been a walloping $168,000—profits for November over $65,000.

Therewith Medilite launched a "three in one" campaign—calling upon doctor-stockholders to write at least three Medilite prescriptions in one day, with the intent of tripling the company's profits.

In the same spirit, a doctor who held stock in Medilite has written his colleagues: The company is "America's budding opportunity stockwise" and "a rosebud about to bloom, stockwise." He elaborated: "I take this opportunity . . . to urge that we actively protect and promote our stock interest by way of actively 'penpushing' Medilite products. . . . I hope I can persuade you to help in the promotion of the company. . . . You have great influence upon several colleagues and you could interest them both in the stock and in the use of the products. . . . Let's push the pen for Medilite together and make it grow."

Surginate, Inc., entertains stockholding physicians twice a year. A member of the board has reasoned: "If we feed them a dinner, pay 7 cents per mile here from home and back, and even give them $10 to make them feel paid for their time, [they'll] make the prescription end of it more than pay off." The president of this company, a physician, ended one such invitation to doctor-stockholders with "If you can't come—write (prescriptions, that is)."

So, then, many drug companies calculatingly sell stock to physicians. Does the scheme work? Do stockholding doctors actually prescribe their company's products?

Evidently they do. "Not to be overlooked," reported the Hart Committee, "is the testimony in the record that not only were doctors encouraged to prescribe on their own companies for financial gain, but the doctors often did just that." The files of doctor-owned companies bulge with letters from physicians who wish to show that they are doing their part to make their company grow. A Louisiana doctor has written Medilite's president: "I want to assure all of you that I will continue to help in the only way that I have been able to . . . i.e., by continuing to prescribe as many Medilite products as I possibly can for the benefit of my patients."

Another letter, from a doctor now in Oklahoma, says: "When I was practicing back in Arkansas, I wrote all Medilite prescriptions. If we have more physicians with stock in Medilite who will write prescriptions for the company it will immediately go in the black. The only solution is to have a great number of physicians who own stock in the company to write for their own company."

Still another doctor-stockholder writes: "I do agree to prescribe and to encourage my associates to use our products." And from Tennessee: "I believe a check of my previous orders . . . both direct and from Nashville wholesale companies will verify my previous help to the company."

Many doctors abruptly start prescribing their own brand as soon as they buy stock. Just a few weeks after a drug company moved into an area in the West and sold stock to several hundred doctors, druggists began to notice a marked change in the doctors' prescribing habits. A survey of pharmacies has turned up instance after instance in which stock-holding physicians suddenly changed to their own company's products. Some doctors are writing as many as twenty prescriptions a day for their own brand.

The willingness of physician-stockholders to boost their companies has proved highly profitable. In a mere eight years, the stock of one doctor-owned company has skyrocketed from $1 a share to $22. Stock was sold in blocks of 500. So a doctor who invested $500 now has stock worth $11,000. An impressive return on a relatively small initial investment. And an inducement to keep right on turning out those prescriptions.

OF EXPENSE AND INSECTS

A number of physicians told the Hart Committee that they own their own drug companies only to guarantee patients high-quality drugs at lower prices. But, the committee reports, "the hearing record refutes the doctors' own rationalizations. . . . What has been shown is that the drugs are often of questionable quality and prices are generally high."

Indeed, if a doctor-stockholder prescribes his own company's products, his patients can expect to pay more than if the drug were bought from competitors. The main reason for this is that the doctor's brand specification is inviolate; if he designates Chemipen, say, instead of Darcil, Pax-ipen, Syncillin, or Ro-Cilin, the pharmacist may not fill the prescription with a different brand even though each is merely another company's name for the identical synthetic penicillin. With a stockholder-written prescription so protected, doctor-owned companies need not fear losing the sale. Thus they tend to ignore competition in setting their prices.

"Doctor-owned companies, selling in the captive market created by their own prescriptions, sell at higher prices and retain the entire spread," the Hart Committee has declared. Typical is the doctor-owned company that charges, item for item, some 20 percent more than its closest competitors.

One doctor-owned company, the Mirinol Pharmaceutical Company, buys one thousand tablets of dextro-amphetamine sulfate (an appetite depressant) for 85 cents. Mirinol sells them under the brand name Miri-nex for $11.30—an astronomic markup of 1,230 percent.

Another doctor-owned company sells the sedative butabarbital sodium for $1.80 a hundred; a wholesale house sells the same tablets for $1.40 a *thousand*. For reserpine, a tranquilizer, Medilite charges $30 a thousand tablets; the identical pills are widely sold by wholesalers for 65 cents a thousand—some 4,500 percent less.

Moreover, stockholders may prescribe company items that can be bought less expensively over the counter. Surginate bought about fifty gallons of sodium salicylate, a common over-the-counter product akin to aspirin. At its board of directors meeting, a doctor-stockholder was asked: "Charlie, how often do you write prescriptions for salicylates?"

Charlie's reply: "Hardly ever, but I can start."

For the next year and a half, he and other doctor-stockholders wrote prescriptions for salicylates, always specifying the Surginate brand. At last the Food and Drug Administration forced a halt, charging that "an article of this composition is not entitled to be restricted to prescription dispensing." In the meantime, untold numbers of patients were put to the expense of unnecessary prescriptions, all so Surginate could get rid of an overstock.

The patient may further suffer if the stockholding physician prescribes his own product instead of a more suitable drug of another company. This is a major hazard, since half of all prescriptions are for the patented drugs of the major pharmaceutical houses. These drugs are not normally available to repackaging companies. The drugs include most of the wide-range antibiotics, the newest steroids, the potent tranquilizers, the newer sulfa drugs, and most antidiabetes drugs. A patient denied these drugs by a doctor-stockholder is in effect being kept years behind modern advances in pharmacology.

Patients also may wind up with drugs that are inferior and dangerous. The Food and Drug Administration has found that doctor-owned drug companies tend to be small, inadequately administered enterprises that fall short on essentials of safety. A frequent failing is the improper labeling of drugs.

Without information about when and, at least as important, when *not* to use the drug, doctors may unwittingly prescribe the patient into serious complications. For mineral-oil laxatives, the F.D.A. requires that labels warn: "Do not administer to infants or young children." By contrast, one doctor-owned company distributes mineral oil with a label that *recommends* its use for babies and young children.

Similarly, labels give incorrect statements of contents and recommended dosage. They also omit standard cautionary notes. Vitamin B_{12} is normally given to pernicious anemia patients by injection. One doctor-owned company promotes a vitamin B_{12} capsule for the treatment of pernicious anemia. Left out is the F.D.A.-required warning that for pernicious anemia such capsules are not reliable substitutes for injections and that periodic examinations and laboratory studies of pernicious anemia patients are essential.

The F.D.A. has similarly found doctor-owned drug companies that stint on quality controls. Rare is the small repackager that examines incoming materials or tests finished products.

At one doctor-owned company—the Solar Pharmaceutical Company—the F.D.A. has found that the week's chemicals are mixed by a chemist working part-time on his day off. No one helps him, supervises him, or goes over his work. When he is through the batches are poured into bottles and, without being checked, are shipped to drugstores. In a full year, the company recorded sales of $235,381 and spent a meager $237.50 for what it described as quality tests.

Contaminated products thus slip through. F.D.A. inspectors have found evidence of the actual yield of a batch being greater than the amount that could result from the mixing of components. This is a sure sign that foreign matter has entered the process. In one case, nose drops were mixed, packed, and sold, and only afterward was it learned that they had been contaminated by oil.

Another doctor-owned company has a long history of violations of F.D.A. sanitation and quality-control regulations. One F.D.A. inspector has characterized the company as showing "complete disregard for the requirements of the law." Investigators have found continued misbranding of products, so that labels described different contents than were actually in the drug.

Raw materials were contaminated. Wood shavings were found in one drum; wrappings from an employee's lunch in another; a paper cup was fished out of a third. Pharmaceuticals were dusty, discolored, and moldy; one carton contained a green encrusted spoon. Cans had rusted, and the rust had mixed in with materials waiting to be used.

Other chemicals were contaminated by insects. Dead insects and insect holes were found in several containers. There were also insect webs and discarded skins, remnants of insects that had made nests in the pharmaceuticals. When the F.D.A. inspector lifted the top of a can of liver extract, he found a live insect larva crawling across the surface.

9
THE QUACKS:
Practitioners of Witchcraft

THE GLORY OF modern medicine springs from its application of science to healing. Medicine's union with biology, chemistry, and physics distinguishes it from chiropractic and naturopathy. Only in medicine does the scientist's cold eye search out the truths of nature for use in promoting human health.

"A physician should practice a method of healing founded on a scientific basis," states the Principles of Medical Ethics. No physician would doubt that this axiom is the sine qua non of his services to patients. And no activity more honors the organized profession than its unrelenting war on quacks.

Yet there are M.D.s who are so professionally bankrupt that they betray their patients and their calling by engaging in quackery. They are to be condemned even more than the laymen who take up quackery after hustling low-grade insurance, trashy securities, shoddy stormwindows. The medical graduate has superior training and has pledged to use it. He knows the perils his charlatanism can impose on patients.

If the M.D. quack is licensed to practice medicine, he enjoys all the protections and privileges society accords holders of medical degrees. The law's inability to curb charlatans in the profession points up sharply the weakness of medical licensing statutes. After completing one of the most comprehensive studies of quack M.D.s, the California Senate Interim Committee on Public Health reported: "There is no doubt that quackery exists among licensed practitioners. . . . Here the quack is apt to be the most dangerous, yet it is here that . . . laws are least effective because they do not adequately define the scope of permissible conduct under the professional licenses, nor do they provide effective means of revoking licenses."

"TAKE THIS INSTEAD OF INSULIN"

The chief lure of quackery is the riches it promises. Limited only by his imagination, the quack may well pull in a gullible public. But in the course of practicing pseudomedicine, quacks may not only bilk patients with fraudulent treatments. Often they also direct the patient away from the medical therapy he may need to stay alive.

Thus, according to a court's finding of facts, in Chicago Dr. Roger F. Wagmann (a pseudonym) listed himself in the classified telephone directory not only as an M.D. but also as a chiropractor and naturopath. He had an arrangement with a shop selling trusses for the relief of ruptures. Customers entering the shop were steered to his office for examinations and fittings. In a further effort to attract business, Dr. Wagmann, though trained only as a general practitioner, held himself out as a specialist in the treatment of diabetes.

On one office visit, a woman came to Dr. Wagmann and told him she was a diabetic. As quacks often do, he went through the routines a patient would expect of an ethical practitioner. According to her testimony, he gave her a physical examination. Then he took her blood pressure, analyzed a urine specimen, and proceeded to inquire as to her history and habits.

"What about candy?" he asked her. "Do you eat much?"

"Oh no," she said. "When I want something sweet, I just eat dates."

'You can use honey, too," he advised.

Then she told him the purpose of her visit. "I'm tired of taking insulin shots," she said. "I've heard I can get medicine from you that I can take by mouth."

The doctor seemed to hesitate. "I don't know," he said. "I don't normally give that medicine to anyone who hasn't taken it before. But," he resolved, "if you want to try it, I guess there's no reason why you shouldn't. This is new stuff—and the people who make insulin are fighting it because they have a good thing in insulin."

He began telling her the advantages that the new medicine had over insulin. "Insulin just controls diabetes. It doesn't cure it. You have to keep taking it. Why, the discovery of insulin probably set back research for a diabetes cure for a hundred years.

"But this new medicine reactivates the glands," he went on. "So cut down on insulin gradually, probably at the rate of five units a month. If you're taking twenty-five units a day now, you can take twenty next month, and in five months you won't have to take any. I first learned about this wonderful new medicine from a patient of mine named Mrs. Blatt, and through her I've been able to make the medicine available to other diabetics. Now I'm organizing a research institute to find a cure for diabetes. At the institute we're working on this new medicine."

The woman was handed a gallon jug of fluid. "Take three tablespoons a day," Wagmann told her. "Figure on coming back for a refill in about three months. That will be thirty dollars."

Later it developed that the doctor was cracking a private joke when he said a patient named Blatt had introduced him to the medicine. Arthur

Blatt and George Blatt had run a phony diabetes clinic in Indiana. They were now in a federal prison, having been convicted of shipping fraudulent diabetes cures across state lines.

Chemical analysis revealed that the medicine Wagmann purveyed was nothing more than saltpeter, vinegar, and a malt product similar to beer. In court a physician specializing in the treatment of diabetes testified that the medicine could not possibly have any therapeutic value. If it were substituted for insulin, the diabetic could undergo the grave effects of too much sugar in the blood—developing gangrene, entering shock, even dying. These complications could be intensified if the patient ate honey, which can impose an excessive burden of sugar on a diabetic's blood.

THE DOCTOR IS A LAYMAN

Some quack M.D.s put the diagnosis and treatment of patients into the hands of unskilled laymen. In the City of Brotherly Love, according to a Pennsylvania court's statement of facts, an M.D. named Maxwell Tiberius Putty (a pseudonym) published the *Philadelphia Trolley, Motor Bus, Street and Health Guide*, featuring extensive advertisements of his abilities. The booklet illustrates why advertising is prohibited among physicians.

"Consult a good physician today," advises one advertisement. It goes on to suggest you call Dr. M. T. Putty.

Under the heading "NERVOUS DISEASES" appears a self-test that would draw at least one yes from any living person:

ASK YOURSELF:

Do you get dizzy?
Are you easily dazed?
Are you easily excited?
Do your hands tremble?
Does your heart flutter?
Are you easily irritated?
Are you easily frightened?
Is your temper irritable?
Is your sleep unrefreshing?
Do you suffer from neuralgia?
Is there a twitching of the muscles?
Do you forget what you read? . . .

If so, urges the message at the bottom, visit Dr. M. T. Putty.

"Lose no time in consulting Dr. Putty," proclaims another page, "if you have belching of gas, discomfort or pain . . . nausea . . . dizziness, headaches, poor appetite . . . bitter taste in the mouth."

"DON'T GROW OLD TOO SOON," cries a column heading. "By having your disease treated, you will retard old age and make life worth living." The treatments of Dr. M. T. Putty are then recommended: "Sick people consult me . . . Don't delay, call today . . . This means you."

Dr. Putty's booklet was not his only means of attracting patients. In newspapers he inserted this advertisement:

PILES

HEMORRHOIDS

TREATED

No Cutting or Burning
There is no loss of time from work or
home. Careful rectal examination, $1.

And this:

Varicose veins, varicose ulcers treated
painlessly without loss of time.

And this as well:

Piles get well our safe way without operation including bleeding, itching, external and internal piles. No cutting, no burning, no pain. Relief of symptoms in 3 to 6 days in majority of cases. Cost of treatment within the reach of working people.

If a patient visited Putty's office, he generally was treated not by Putty but by Lincoln Mead (a pseudonym), a $75-a-week lay employee. As many as 70 patients a day came to see Putty. Mead would treat most of them. He had access to the drug room and, without supervision, dispensed medicine he decided the patient needed.

One of the patients treated by the Putty-Mead team visited the office because of stomach pains. He was examined by Mead, whom he believed to be a physician. Mead took the patient's blood pressure and x-rayed his stomach, then said: "I'll treat you for $150. You'll have to pay $50 as a down payment."

Paying in advance of treatment is hardly standard practice. But gullible patients are often desperate for a promise of help. This patient agreed, although Mead made no statement to him regarding the nature of the ailment or what was needed by way of therapy. Thereafter he visited Mead twice weekly and got an injection and a supply of medicine.

At the end of the sixteenth visit, Mead told him: "I'm not satisfied with the results. You'll need more treatments. This will cost another $150."

The patient continued seeing him for another two months. By then he was suffering difficulty in urinating. He lost confidence in Mead and Putty and quit. During all this time his condition was never diagnosed. He had been examined by Putty only once.

Quacks often string a patient along, counting on the self-limiting nature of most diseases to produce the "cure." If an ailment takes a turn for the worse, the quack is likely to unload the patient as fast as possible. Another of Putty's victims was a deaf mute who visited the office complaining of pains in his stomach. He was greeted by Mead, who took his blood pressure. Throughout his collaboration with Putty, Mead ran grave risks in his promiscuous use of radiological devices. In the hands of an untrained operator, these can be deadly to the patient. Now Mead x-rayed and fluoroscoped the deaf mute's stomach and chest. After the examination, he announced: "You've got gallbladder trouble."

The patient began visiting Mead twice a week. On each visit, Mead gave him a bottle of medicine, a box of laxative pills, and ointment for rectal massage. For these worthless products, the patient paid five dollars.

One year and about a thousand dollars later, the patient's condition was getting worse. He staggered in for one visit, and for the first time Putty saw him. Without needing to perform an examination, Putty said: "Get into a taxicab and go to a hospital." There the patient finally underwent the abdominal surgery he had long needed.

SCENES FROM FLASH GORDON

Modern medicine has acquired an armamentarium of mysterious machines, magical drugs, and wondrous procedures. These therapies from Tomorrowland tickle the lay imagination, so much so that slightly hoked-up remedies sometimes work better than the simpler, more straightforward ones that orthodox doctors prefer. Many patients respond more favorably to an injection than to a pill, which may be equivalent in dosage but not in drama. Similarly, a machine that is obviously complicated is likely to engender the patient's confidence, whereas a trimmer model performing an identical function may leave him cold.

Dr. Paul Williamson, a prominent Texas physician and cracker-barrel philosopher, is forever amused at how often the mortar of medical science crumbles until it is strengthened by the sand of human imagination. In a field in which a red pill can succeed where the same pill in blue fails, observes Dr. Williamson, every doctor must expect to act a bit like a magician.

Quacks, however, take advantage of the soft spot some patients have for medical hocus-pocus and use it as a substitute rather than a supplement. To lead patients on, the quack may concoct flashy paraphernalia suggestive of science.

In California, the courts have found, an M.D. named Sheldon R. Mondell (a pseudonym) dazzled patients with an electric "diagnostic machine," a metal box about two feet long and a foot square. The front looked like the instrument panel of an airliner: two gauges, ten small dials and four larger dials, three on-off switches, a removable fuse, several sockets and jacks, any number of lights.

Dr. Mondell used this machine on nearly every patient. One woman came to him complaining of a pain in her chest. He seated her next to the machine and told her to hold a small metal plate that was connected to the machine by wire.

"This receives invisible signals like a radio or television," he said. "It's electronic, not electric, so you probably won't get any sensation from it."

If the patient did feel anything, it would have been the doctor who got the shock. Inside the box, the wires were hooked up to empty air. Electricity entering the machine did little more than light the bulbs, making this device essentially a highly embroidered lamp.

Now the doctor turned his attention to the dials. In the best Man of Science fashion, he adjusted one dial and studied the gauges. Then, ever so precisely, he adjusted another dial. At last he told the woman: "You have staphylococcal and streptococcal infections. What you need is an hour of my electronic treatment five days a week. That will cost you only thirteen dollars a week. And don't you worry: I'll keep checking you with the diagnostic machine to see if you're getting the right treatment."

Dr. Mondell also injected patients with a so-called drug he labeled "Glyoxylide, 12X." The liquid was distilled water. Mondell termed his injections "Koch shots" and claimed they would cure cancer, arthritis, and a host of other ailments.

Mondell often administered his Koch shots in series of six. For each shot, he charged $100. If a patient balked at the price, Mondell would assure him that other doctors charged $800 a shot, adding: "I can give a better price because I get the material in quantity."

At least as big an asset as Glyoxylide, 12X, was Hedwig Hellerman (a pseudonym) who worked as a nurse and receptionist. One of her duties was to tell patients her "true story."

She had cancer several years earlier, she would say, and went to a hospital in Georgia. Not responding to treatment there, she came to California, expecting to die. "I was so sick that I couldn't even be operated on," she would say. But then her family took her to see Dr. Mondell. "And after six Koch shots, I was cured!"

If the patient resisted treatment, Nurse Hellerman would shift from her testimonial to threats of a ghastly fate. She would warn of submicroscopic creatures eating away at the patient's insides. One patient, who had been prescribed extensive therapy despite perfect health, suggested: "Perhaps I needn't come back quite so soon."

"What?" roared Hellerman. "Don't you realize that the virus Doctor found can multiply fifteen times every five minutes? I don't believe you realize how serious your condition is. You should start your new treatment at once."

A woman passer-by, evidently noting Mondell's M.D. shingle, dropped in because of a sore leg and hip. To her surprise, she was taken into an examining room and was given the full treatment with the diagnostic machine. As she later described it, the scene was out of Flash Gordon. Nurse Hellerman methodically read off a list of the organs of the body. In response, Mondell adjusted dials on the machine and called out gauge readings, which Hellerman recorded.

After each reading, Mondell shook his head and said, "That's terrible. That's too bad." With the examination over, he told the patient: "The machine shows you are full of malignant virus from your head to your toes. It isn't cancer yet, but it is the beginning of cancer. In a short time the virus will spread, and then there will be no hope for you. You're going to have to have a Koch shot."

The patient was handed a diet book and some tablets.

"But," she told them, "I don't know if I can get $100 for the shot."

Hellerman grabbed back the tablets and diet book. "You won't need these right away," she said. "But you will need that shot; otherwise there will be no help at all for you. Don't you know that between 6,000 and 7,000 people die of this virus every month? Without the shot, radium and surgery won't be able to help you. Even God won't be able to help you. You'll die a horrible death."

Mondell could ordinarily rely on the patient's not having cancer. Like many quacks who exploit the cancer fears of healthy people, he figured he couldn't lose. If the fraud were uncovered by a responsible physician, the patient would normally believe that Mondell's finding was an honest error. At any rate, the patient would usually be so relieved not to have cancer that he would be unlikely to make trouble. Conversely, if the patient stayed on in ignorance, Mondell could effect a cure at will. At the first hint of restlessness, he could examine the patient, announce, "You're now well," and get the credit for miraculous treatments. Mondell's luck held until one day a patient came to him who really did have cancer.

George Hawkins (a pseudonym) sought help for back and hip pains. For an hour Mondell and Hellerman went through one of their routines. She called out numbers from a book, as if reading a formula. He repeated each number and twirled dials on the diagnostic machine.

After an hour, Mondell looked very grave. Hawkins, he announced, had twenty-three different ailments. These included problems with his heart, spleen, liver, and colon, and such diseases as arthritis, neuritis, staphylococcal infection, and cancer.

"In view of the seriousness of your condition," Mondell went on, "a Koch shot is the best treatment."

Hawkins paid the $100 and received the shot. On his second visit, his wife was diagnosed with the machine. Mondell told her she had thirteen illnesses, involving the heart, liver, and bladder. Also, she was told, she had a brain tumor. "I'd recommend you receive the same treatment as your husband," Mondell said.

Thereafter, with his wife undergoing the same procedures at the same rates, Hawkins visited Mondell's office for hour-long treatments. He was placed in a room with a dial-encrusted box that was a smaller version of the diagnostic machine. At the instruction of Mondell or Hellerman he would hold a lead plate over one of his supposedly affected organs. After his spleen got a fifteen-minute dose, Hellerman would poke her head into the room and say, "Okay. Now do your liver."

Hawkins' cancer in the meantime was spreading throughout his body. Even after he became so weak that he could no longer get out of bed, Mondell did not call in a physician who might help. Instead, Mondell rented Hawkins one of his smaller machines to use at home for a dollar a day. He discouraged the couple from seeking competent help, telling them the Koch shot had done for them all they could expect from medical science.

Day after day, Hawkins wasted away. Mondell continued Hawkins on treatments with the machine. As Hawkins grew still weaker, Mondell prescribed aspirin as well. With a moribund state approaching, Mondell took a leaf from chiropractic. This physician, with the grandeur of medical knowledge at his disposal, attempted to save his patient with spinal manipulation.

Inevitably George Hawkins died. Small good it does him, but Mondell and Hellerman were convicted of the fraudulent conspiracy that ended in his death.

PART III

Felonious Conduct

THE FOREGOING OFFENSES—overcharging and overtreating, fee splitting, profiteering, quackery—are ways of exploiting individual patients. While all such occurrences are violations of the public trust, most fall within the law as the statutes now stand. There are types of medical misconduct that are clearly illegal. Swindling health-insurance carriers is one such offense; another white-collar crime, evading income taxes, also occurs with disproportionate frequency in the profession. Doctors alone can be expert medical witnesses in court, and some commit perjury. A few medical offenders traffic in drugs, catering to addicts by abusing the physician's legal authority to prescribe narcotics.

10

THE SWINDLERS:
Blank Form, Blank Check

To THE PATIENT it's a piece of paper that the doctor fills out so he will be paid by health insurance. To the insurance carrier it's a means of learning what services the doctor has performed. To some doctors it's temptation.

A physician's conscience is his chief restraint as he completes a health insurance form. Within limits, almost any carrier will pay the doctor for the services he sets down. To this extent, insurance carriers are open to exploitation, and a small minority of doctors treat an insurance form like a blank check. The amount they swindle and the costs of policing them lead to higher premiums for policyholders. Among insurance swindlers turned up recently are:

- A doctor who billed Blue Shield for removing his daughter's appendix —twice.
- A physician who used an ordinary styptic pencil to stop minor bleeding—but charged an insurance company for cauterizing a major wound.
- An M.D. who billed an insurance plan for doing a certain procedure 29 times at $400 apiece—whereas all the other physicians in the program performed a total of one.

All of which explains why personnel who review health insurance claims may cast a cold eye not only at the fee the doctor charges but also at the services he lists. Overtreating is a favorite way for insurance swindlers to milk a program.

One doctor billed the Veterans Administration for weekly injections he was giving a former serviceman who suffered from flat feet. When the V.A. questioned the validity of such treatments, the doctor said that the shots contained "vitamins to tone up the muscles of his feet."

"Poppycock!" replied the V.A.'s chief medical officer. "There is no justification in all of medicine for such 'therapy.'"

"Look here," responded the doctor. "You bureaucrats don't treat patients. So don't tell *me* how to treat them!"

Another doctor snowballed the costs of treating an insured case after a policyholder wanted a small wart removed from the back of his hand. The doctor arranged to have the procedure done in a hospital, thereby raising the insurance payment to him from $15 to $37.50.

This simple operation required only Novocain, which the doctor himself administered by injection. But the hospital's anesthetist billed the insurance company for $25, and the hospital charged for a day's room and board even though the patient was never in a hospital bed. The bills for removal of a wart measuring less than a quarter of an inch totaled about $200, all so the doctor could collect the higher insurance payment.

Some doctors bilk insurance plans by giving unnecessary diagnostic tests. One doctor was doubling his income from the routine office visits of Blue Shield subscribers by performing extra "diagnostic" procedures—an examination of the rectum and bowel, for example, even if the patient had a sore throat.

IN NEVER-NEVER LAND

While those tests were unnecessary, they were at least performed as reported. Some insurance cheats, however, perform merely token services, then report major procedures for payment. In this medical never-never land, sprains become fractures, bumps emerge as concussions, scratches deepen into cuts.

One New York dermatologist put in a claim for removing a breast tumor. When Blue Shield investigated, it found that he had actually treated a benign skin condition. In another pseudosurgery, a G.P. submitted 157 claims for the incision and draining of carbuncles (severe infections that burrow beneath connective tissue). On investigation, Blue Shield found he had treated not a single carbuncle. Rather, he had cared for skin pustules of the minor sort common in acne.

Insurance carriers have special problems with physicians who own their own hospitals, reports A. B. Halverson of the Occidental Life Insurance Company of California. Proprietors of these institutions stand to benefit if procedures are blown up to require lengthy hospital stays. It is a rare appendectomy that requires even ten days' hospitalization. But at one Southern California hospital, Occidental found that the physician-owner took out a normal appendix and kept the insured patient hospitalized for twenty-four days.

At the same hospital, investigators found, a supposed "seven-inch wound requiring hospitalization" was really a minor cut less than an inch long. As a result of Occidental's detective work, this hospital withdrew claims totaling more than $3,000.

More obvious to claims reviewers is the physician who reports performing complicated surgery in his office. To get the substantial insurance payment for surgery, exploitative doctors have claimed they surgically removed internal hemorrhoids, excised pilonidal cysts, even took out organs. If true, the lack of hospital facilities and staff would have constituted a grave threat to the patient's life. In most cases, Dr. Arthur A. Fischl of Group Health Insurance has found, the office "surgery" is a minor procedure inflated in the insurance report by a physician who lacks hospital privileges.

In a six-month period, one general practitioner submitted eight claims for repairing dislocations of major joints. Blue Shield became suspicious when it learned the doctor had accomplished the treatments in his office, without the aid of x-rays. In each claim, the "dislocation" proved to be a strained ligament.

As a matter of routine, many insurance plans inform the patient of the payment that has been made to the doctor. Sometimes the patient recognizes that the doctor has exaggerated his service. In Arkansas, a policyholder learned that his doctor had been paid $150 "for performing an appendectomy." The patient replied:

"I'm glad you paid my doctor $150 but he didn't take out my appendix. He removed a wart from my neck."

In policing claims, insurance carriers rely on such reactions from patients. Laymen, who generally expect high standards of behavior from doctors, are often quick to blow the whistle on a suspected swindler. One otolaryngologist billed an insurance plan for extensive nasal surgery and bone removal. He got the usual fee of $350. Routinely the insurance carrier sent the patient notification of the payment. Almost at once, the patient wrote to complain.

"How come so much money?" he protested. "The doctor did nothing but pack my nostrils."

INFLATED FEES

After Dr. Morton E. Berk, of Honolulu, finished three years of service on his medical society's health insurance committee, he was asked the worst problem he encountered. His reply:

"Abusers of health plans. Until . . . they are castigated by their colleagues and treated like the thieves they really are . . . abuse will undoubtedly continue."

Insurance carriers estimate that between 1 and 5 percent of all claims submitted suggest abuse. A principal type of tampering entails charging a higher fee than normal because an insurance plan and not the patient will pay. An Occidental Life Insurance study of 6,000 claims has shown that, comparing patients with equal incomes, physicians charge an average of as much as 20 percent more when the coverage permits them to set their own fee for a service. This is in contrast with what they would charge if the coverage incorporated a fee schedule, generally based on prevailing rates.

As a result of such findings, the Health Insurance Council, an industry group, has made this observation:

"Some physicians apparently feel that a patient with insurance protection . . . has moved beyond the financial bracket which normally would be determined by his annual income. On that basis and following the pattern of charging according to the ability to pay, the fees charged sometimes appear to be higher than might be expected in the absence of insurance."

An example of such fee raising in action has been reported by Joseph M. Adelizzi, managing director of the Empire State Highway Transportation Association, whose members provide health insurance coverage for employees. Originally a surgeon set $75 as his fee for a service for a patient connected with the association.

"Good," the patient said. "I have health insurance that will pay up to $75."

"In that case," the surgeon told him, "my fee is $125 and you'll have to pay only $50."

The Santa Monica, California, local of the International Association of Machinists provides a health insurance plan for members. A physician treated one machinist with 28 days of house calls. The bill he submitted was for $1,625, or some $60 per visit. The union refused to pay, so the doctor reduced his bill by $1,000, to $625. This netted him over $20 per house call—and other local physicians declared that he was still getting away with robbery.

In another California case, a surgeon operated on an eleven-year-old boy for a hernia and undescended testicle. Believing the family carried insurance, he submitted a bill for $3,500. Although the policy had not yet gone into effect, the insurance company protested in behalf of the boy's parents. Ultimately they got a revised billing of $500.

According to insurance company evidence presented in court, fee disputes surrounded a New Orleans surgeon who submitted a bill for an elbow operation on a patient insured by the Hartford Accident and Indemnity Company. The company protested that the $4,550 fee was excessive. The surgeon agreed to reduce it to $3,000, and the company sent him a check for that amount.

But, in a bookkeeping error, the company failed to record that the sum had been paid. Thus the company later sent the doctor another check for the same amount.

Meanwhile, the same patient required another operation. Instead of submitting a bill for the additional surgery, the surgeon credited the mis-sent check toward his fee. The insurance company now went to court to get back the duplicated payment.

"Not only should I not give the $3,000 back," the doctor said. "I demand an additional $900 because the second operation was worth $3,900."

The court, however, disagreed. It instructed the doctor to return $1,500, leaving him $1,500 for the second operation. Even that, said the Court of Appeal, "is more than ample for the services rendered."

Five months later, the doctor was back in the Court of Appeal. This time he was suing the Travelers Insurance Company for $4,325 for operating on the arm of a man injured in a motorboat accident. The fee was "unreasonable and excessive," said the company. During the trial of the case, two surgeons took the witness stand.

"What would be a reasonable charge for the services this surgeon rendered?" each was asked.

"A thousand dollars," answered one.

"Six hundred dollars," said the other.

Striking its own, more liberal compromise, the court ruled that the fair fee would be $1,275, less than a third of what he had asked.

SOMETHING FOR NOTHING

Claims reviewers occasionally spot insurance frauds who perform no service at all for the fees they seek to collect.

In Louisiana, a physician treated many patients who were employees of the same company and thus were covered by the same insurance carrier. The doctor became suspect after he filed so many false claims in their names that the carrier had to raise the premium it was charging the employer. The evidence gathered against the doctor was transmitted to federal authorities, who successfully prosecuted him for mail fraud.

Similarly, a New York ophthalmologist submitted 170 claims in a single year for removal of foreign bodies from the cornea, the transparent coating of the eyeball. Blue Shield investigators found that in none of the claims were foreign bodies removed or even present.

Nor is the presumed patient necessarily present. Federal officials charged that a private practitioner in Dallas got $6,654 from the Veterans Administration for allegedly treating patients. At least $258 had been claimed for treatment while the veterans were actually being cared for in government hospitals. One of the supposed patients had died before the dates on which the doctor reported seeing him.

In exchange for the privilege of using a hospital's facilities, attending physicians customarily perform chores for the institution. Some of these duties can be onerous, such as serving in clinics or on burdensome committees. By contrast, one of the most nominal of assignments is general stand-by service. In effect this merely requires the doctor to be reachable by phone in case the regular staff needs help.

Although the stand-by physician's connection with the hospital is generally just that uninvolving, some doctors use stand-by as an unauthorized excuse to bill for services performed during the period by the hospital staff. Two Baltimore doctors thus collected $480 from Blue Shield for presiding at deliveries—though the doctors on stand-by were no closer to the hospital than their home phones. They were found out after a

Blue Shield subscriber complained that $80 for delivering his child had been paid to a physician who had never even seen his wife.

Claims reviewers also watch for physicians who are obligated by their hospitals not to charge for their services yet do so anyway. A Newark, New Jersey doctor was found guilty of defrauding a medical-surgical plan of over $5,500. The state successfully contended that he had collected insurance fees for surgery performed at a hospital that was supported by the county to provide exclusively free medical care.

The return from defrauding a health-care program can be greater than from robbing a bank. One Long Island doctor was indicted on 373 felony and misdemeanor counts, including 122 counts of grand larceny, for filing false claims for the treatment of Welfare Department beneficiaries..

The doctor ultimately admitted cheating the program in almost every way possible: He filed claims for patients he had not seen. He billed the county for treating whole families when he had actually seen only one member. He charged for tests he never performed and for injections he never gave. He exaggerated services beyond resemblance to what was really done. He even entered into collusion with two druggists to submit to the county fraudulent prescriptions.

In all, the doctor confessed to offenses totaling over $100,000.

THE TAX CHEATS

The health insurance form is not the only document that some dishonest physicians abuse before signing. Form 1040, the federal income tax return, also comes in for occasional swindling.

The medical profession produces a disproportionately high number of tax evaders, about four times the rate for the public at large. In a typical year, between 20 and 25 of some 1,400 persons convicted of tax violations are M.D.s. While only 1 out of every 240 taxpayers is a physician, doctors account for about 1 out of 60 taxpayers convicted of tax evasion. Almost always the doctor is a respected citizen. Charles K. Rice of the Justice Department's Tax Division has reported that tax fraud is a white-collar crime. Most convicted defendants are business and professional people who have never had previous trouble with the law.

"It may seem strange, but as a group the percentage of fraud cases arising among doctors of medicine is far out of line with other professions," commented Judge Ernest H. Van Fossan after retiring from the U.S. Tax Court. Judge Van Fossan went on to speculate: "Why this is so would be an interesting study, but possibly the table drawer into which [a physician] tosses fees which he receives in cash or the deep pocket in which he places them may be the answer."

Every year a half dozen or so physicians go to prison as a result of criminal violations of income tax laws. Deliberate concealment of income is the principal offense. After practicing abroad for a number of years, one G.P. settled in a New England city. Feeling that cash payments would be too hard for tax agents to trace, he recorded only a fraction of his cash receipts. The rest went for living expenses and acquiring new possessions.

During a routine audit, a tax agent noted that the doctor owned a large house, a flashy car, and other trappings of high living. The doctor's reported income would not allow him to consume quite so conspicuously, so the I.R.S. man investigated further. As new facts were uncovered, the doctor attempted to misdirect the investigation by continuously changing his explanation of where he got his funds.

Finally the agent reconstructed the doctor's income for the previous eight years, showing that he had failed to report an average of $13,000 a year. The doctor pleaded guilty and paid $15,000 in fines and back taxes. He also served 90 days in jail.

A tax-evading physician with other sources of income sometimes reports only his earnings from his practice and conceals the rest. A California practitioner provided special services for an insurance company and a county old-age program. He reported his income from his private patients. But—according to charges to which he pleaded nolo contendere—he converted his monthly checks from the insurance company and the county into cashier's checks. These were as good as cash (and safer), and he turned them into currency whenever he needed money.

This method enabled him to hide about two thirds of his income one year and over half his income the next. With his unreported earnings he bought jewelry, household furniture, a trip to Hawaii. Ultimately his spending called attention to him. He was required to pay back taxes and fines totaling $34,000. Moreover, his state board of medical examiners ruled that he had committed a felony involving moral turpitude, put him on probation, and suspended his license to practice for 180 days.

Anyone in business needs a bookkeeping system to keep track of who has paid how much and what is owed by whom. Tax evaders, to disguise their true income, often keep secret records. In a southern community, an internist resigned from the staff of a local hospital. Word got around that he had refused to keep medical records the way the hospital required. The story reached the ears of a Treasury agent. Suspicious, he followed up the case for two years.

The doctor had been concealing income by recording small fees for minor services while actually receiving large fees for major services. Thus a $350 hysterectomy would go down as a $75 dilation and curettage, and the $275 difference would be stashed away. This concealment was the reason the doctor could not submit to the cross-checks that the hospital demanded on its records.

A jury convicted the doctor of willfully failing to report total income of some $23,000. His penalty: payment of back taxes and fines of $17,000 and a prison sentence of five years.

Another physician who tampered with his books was a West Coast surgeon. His financial records seemed meticulous, but an I.R.S. agent was puzzled by strange symbols that kept recurring. Treasury experts deciphered the hieroglyphics as an elaborate code that denoted payments not included in the surgeon's tax reports.

The doctor also misrepresented his deductible business expenses. "What about this gift you deducted?" the agent asked.

"It was a promotional expense, for practice building," replied the doctor.

"Really?" said the agent. "Then why did you have the gift shop enclose a card saying 'Happy Mother's Day'?"

To the charges, the doctor pleaded nolo contendere. He was sentenced to pay $20,000 in fines and back taxes and received a six-month prison term.

To lift the curtain on a tax evasion, the I.R.S. may need outside help. In one case, the intervening force was death. A New York City gynecologist lived modestly with his wife in a three-room apartment on the lower East Side. He spent little of his earnings from his thriving practice. Instead, he put most of his income into thirty-seven trust accounts that he secretly maintained in as many savings banks. On his income tax returns he mentioned none of the amounts he deposited.

The accounts came to light after the doctor died. Tax agents discovered that he had been accumulating the extra money by falsifying his records. One year he listed only 200 patients on his books. Actually he had treated 600.

The Tax Court ruled that the beneficiaries of the trust accounts would need to satisfy back taxes and penalties totaling over $150,000. The office nurse, who had inherited 11 of the accounts, thus had to surrender some $50,000.

Often tax evaders are revealed by informers. Over many years of practice one doctor regularly concealed cash and juggled his books. With each $1,000 of unreported income, he bought investment bonds under fictitious names. He placed these bonds in safe-deposit boxes that he rented under assumed identities.

Meanwhile, someone who knew the doctor became more and more interested in his financial affairs. The Treasury Department will not reveal the precise identities of tax informers. It will say, however, that informers are often bookkeepers, accountants, and employees of banks and brokerage houses—persons in a position to sense that income is not being properly reported. With physicians, informers are also frequently disgruntled patients, colleagues, even wives and children.

Whoever it was in this case developed a comprehensive file on the doctor's dealings, including many of the fictitious names the doctor used and the location and amounts of many of the concealed bonds. He (or she) informed the I.R.S. The agents found the report was true and pressed charges against the doctor.

For his efforts the informer received a near-record $41,000. The doctor's back taxes, interest and penalties totaled no less than $2,400,000.

11

THE PERJURERS:
Witness for the Highest Bidder

MULTIPLE SCLEROSIS is a slow, progressive paralysis that has no known external cause. Nonetheless, a doctor testified in support of a plaintiff who contended an accident had caused him to develop multiple sclerosis.

By lying on the witness stand, such physicians subvert everyone's right to justice. Medical testimony plays an essential role in litigation; only by presenting the expert opinion of doctors can the principals in a case resolve such questions as the extent of an injury or the likelihood that it resulted as claimed. But introduce for either side a physician who is willing to perjure himself, and the case may wind up decided on false testimony rather than true merit.

While Dr. Paul R. Hawley was director of the American College of Surgeons, he commented that "vicious practices" by "ambulance-chasing" doctors had grown to huge proportions.

"More and more doctors of questionable integrity are appearing in court," Dr. Hawley observed. "We know that actual perjury is committed almost daily in medical testimony."

The harm that physician-perjurers do extends beyond the cases they personally corrupt. The adjudication of *all* personal injury claims is suffering in a kind of Gresham's law of medical testimony: Perjuring doctors are driving ethical ones off the witness stand.

The typical physician shies away from court appearances to begin with, since they disrupt his practice routine. Moreover, notes Dr. Kent L. Brown, the dislike the typical doctor has for his "prostituted colleagues" serves to strengthen his distaste for medicolegal details. Many doctors are loath to testify in court, give medical depositions, serve as an expert witness, or in any way cooperate with lawyers. Thus, notes Dr. Brown, most doctors "have defaulted to a small group of physicians, some of whom are better known for courtroom appearance than for the practice of medicine."

One surgeon cited by Dr. Paul Hawley has testified for plaintiffs in claims totaling over $6,300,000 in six years. His fee is reported to average 10 percent of the damages awarded. Dr. Hawley castigated the profession for its laxity in dealing with such physicians. "Brand them as unethical and cast them out of organized medicine," he urged—for a physician who "sells his support on the witness stand to the highest bidder" is "morally unqualified" to practice medicine.

A SHARE OF THE TAKE

Early one Sunday morning, an office worker we'll call Leonard Peters lay in bed half awake. Not long before, Peters had collected several thousand dollars in a personal injury suit. The doctor had padded his bill to increase the settlement, and his medical report had been a fabric of lies. The pieces of false evidence had been so effective that Peters felt the doctor well deserved his share of the settlement.

Now Peters' front doorbell rang. The caller was a detective. He handed Peters a document and told him: "This is a warrant to take you in for questioning."

Across Brooklyn, dozens of similar scenes were taking place. They marked the first steps in a large-scale investigation of fraudulent injury claims. Because of the lightning opening move, none of the claimants like Peters could tip off lawyers or doctors who took part in the frauds.

The investigation was to give a hint of the scope of doctor-lawyer conspiracies nationwide. Called the Arkwright Investigation—after its head, State Supreme Court Justice George A. Arkwright—the probe was carried out in great secrecy. Judge Arkwright's first report was conservative, merely stating that his commission had uncovered a great number of instances of collusion between attorneys and doctors to defraud insurance carriers through fraudulent medical reports and bills. Named in the report were but eight doctors, all from Brooklyn.

Gradually the investigation extended throughout the state. The number of implicated physicians grew: to 16, to 100, to 300. At last the New York State Medical Society announced that no fewer than 1,300 doctors would be brought up on charges of unethical and possibly criminal conduct. The frauds they were accused of perpetrating totaled an estimated $3,-000,000.

A surprising aspect of such scandals is the generally good reputation of the doctors involved. Many of the guilty physicians are men of recognized standing who have good practices and top-notch hospital connections. "The petitioner has borne a good record in the community and in the medical profession," an Appeals Court said of one of the first doctors to lose his license as a result of the Arkwright disclosures. Despite his good record, the court declined to restore him to practice. In such cases it is often implied that the confidence a doctor is held in provides all the more reason he should not allow himself to be seduced.

Seduction is often mainly a matter of money. One physician's arrangement with an attorney allegedly worked like this: Long after an accident, the lawyer would send him patients who at most had only superficial injuries. The doctor would report to the insurance companies that he had given extensive, expensive treatments with total charges generally over $100. The doctor later told authorities that in the four cases at issue he received $25 to $35 in cash from the attorney. Some doctors in collusion with attorneys do not even see the patients for whom they submit medical reports. The doctor may supply his attorney-partner with letterheads on which the lawyer himself types up a false report.

One doctor, whose medical reports the court found were ghost-written by two lawyers, signed a statement attesting to the grave condition taking hold of a woman as the result of an accident. The numerous injuries listed on the report substantiated the need for the doctor to make nine house calls and see the woman in his office on thirty-one occasions. His bill: $218. During an investigation, the woman testified that she had never seen the doctor once.

Fraudulent reports often have no relationship to the patient's condition. One physician was found by a court to have signed medical reports, which were written by a lawyer, listing eight injuries including a brain concussion. The patient actually had twisted his back and bruised one of his legs.

Fee splitting by lawyers and doctors in collusion is not uncommon. In a declaratory action the Massachusetts Board of Regents charged the following: A physician would urge injured patients to see a certain attorney to press accident claims. The lawyer would then have the doctor beef up the case with unnecessary visits and treatments. After a settlement, the two men would compute what each had received in legal or medical fees. Then the higher would pay the lower (usually the lawyer paying the doctor) to achieve a 50-50 split. Investigators found splits had occurred in at least 138 cases, for which the doctor had received kickbacks totaling over $8,000. The court held that if true, the physician was guilty of gross misconduct.

Doctors in a conspiracy to defraud occasionally get left holding the bag. That is what happened to a physician who operates his own hospital and used it to help inflate an accident claim.

One afternoon in late August a woman passenger was injured in a train derailment. After receiving treatment from the railroad, she entered the doctor's private hospital to have bruises and sore muscles cared for. At the end of two weeks, the doctor told her: "You are completely recovered and can go home today."

The woman, however, stayed at the hospital for six more months. This extended hospitalization resulted from a scheme to get a large settlement from the railroad. The plan—involving the woman, her lawyers, and the doctor—was to get $50,000, in which the doctor would share. The longer the hospitalization, the more serious the injuries could be made to appear.

When the case was settled the woman got only $3,500. She refused to split any of it with the doctor. Indeed, she would not pay for her hospital and medical care, which had been provided at the doctor's expense.

Now the doctor sued to recover over a thousand dollars merely in out-of-pocket payments. This was a mistake, for, after hearing the story, the judge declined to help him collect for any charges not medically necessary and told him at least part of his services were "tainted with fraud."

STOOPING FOR PEANUTS

The typical physician, if he pursues his practice honestly and diligently, will earn a lifetime total of about a million dollars. Since virtue is so much its own reward, it is puzzling why some doctors will stoop so low for relative peanuts.

For a gain that was unlikely to exceed a few hundred dollars apiece, four doctors were charged with conspiring to sell license applicants the questions and answers to the New York State medical licensing examination. One of the indicted doctors was the secretary of the state board of medical examiners, which had prepared the test. He allegedly passed copies through two other physicians to a fourth who acted as salesman.

The head of a large state mental hospital allegedly was caught systematically padding his expense account and resigned. This noted psychiatrist received a salary of $25,650 a year and was provided a house and generous maintenance allowance. The amount by which he was allegedly cheating the state: $20 a month.

Another physician became involved with a gang that had stolen $428,000 from an armored truck. One of the gang had been shot in the leg while fleeing and the gunmen were hiding out in a rooming house. The injured man was in bad shape, and this doctor was called in.

The physician, a court found, treated the wound. He accepted payment, and—though the law requires doctors to report gunshot wounds—he said nothing to the police. The robber died. Now the doctor agreed, for a price, to provide a death certificate and a proper burial. The plan hit a snag when he had trouble engaging an undertaker. To get rid of the body he dismembered it so it could be packed in a small trunk. Three days after the death, the gang carried the trunk away and abandoned it in an untraveled area.

Ultimately the trunk was found. Starting with this as a clue, the police followed the trail—and eventually were led to the doctor.

Occasionally a physician will be involved in the crime of mayhem, the deliberate maiming of a person. One North Carolina doctor invited criminal charges when, the court held, he went along with a patient named George who proposed a plan to defraud an insurance company.

"I'm going to cut off my fingers to get insurance money," George said. "Just give me a little something to kill the pain."

The physician gave him an injection to anesthetize his fingers. George then had his brother James cut the fingers off with an electric saw.

A few months later, George was back at the doctor's office. With him was a friend, Walter. "I didn't feel a thing," George recalled approvingly. "How about deadening Walter's fingers now?"

"No," said the doctor.

"Why not?" asked George. "You did it for me."

"You owe me $65," the doctor replied. "Besides, Walter would be foolish to cut off his fingers."

George paid the $65, plus another $29 for Walter. The doctor gave Walter an injection of procaine.

Shortly afterward, state's evidence showed, Walter noticed that the injection was wearing off. With feeling restored to his fingers he underwent a change of heart. "I don't want my fingers cut off," he announced to George and James.

"Like hell you don't," they replied. They grabbed for him. Walter ran into the house and tried to hide. The brothers gave chase. They found him cowering and crying. "Don't cut them off! I don't want them cut off." But James sawed four fingers from Walter's left hand.

Months later, Walter was the key witness at the trial of the doctor. Gazing at his mutilated hand, he recalled: "I asked James not to cut them off and I told him I didn't want my fingers cut off. He cut them off anyhow." The doctor was found guilty of being an accessory before the fact to the felonious maiming.

In another case, the maiming was done by a doctor seeking to raise an insurance settlement. It all began with an innocent mistake by another doctor, a conscientious surgeon. One of his patients had been in and out of hospitals for ten years because of a bilateral hernia. The surgeon decided that the rupture could be repaired permanently only by removing the left spermatic cord and testicle, an accepted remedy for the problem.

Routinely he drew up a consent form for the patient to sign. But on the form he absent-mindedly wrote "right" as the testicle to be removed. In the operating room he realized his slip of the pen and removed the left testicle as he had intended. He neglected, however, to draft a corrected consent form after the operation had been successfully completed and have the patient sign it.

Because the patient had been hurt on his job, his case came before an industrial accident commission. Here the lawyer representing the patient found the uncorrected consent form and saw a chance to strike it rich.

The lawyer filed a $100,000 assault suit against the surgeon, charging that the left testicle had been removed without the patient's consent. What's more, charged the lawyer, the testicle had been healthy.

The lawyer had a son-in-law who was a surgeon. This doctor was willing to testify that the original surgeon had been negligent in removing the left testicle, that it was the right one that should have been removed. But what if a doctor who did not happen to be the lawyer's son-in-law examined the patient and found the remaining testicle healthy? Before that could happen, it too had to be cut off.

On his father-in-law's advice, the surgeon sent the patient to a psychiatrist. This consultation established evidence of the mental trauma that would result from the operation. Then the surgeon castrated the patient.

With the case now almost foolproof, the lawyer raised the claim to $500,000. "The only remaining question," he told his son-in-law, "is how much we get."

The maiming, however, proved to benefit no one—least of all the patient, who had knowingly submitted to it. The day after the new claim was filed, he died of a heart attack.

A MURDER IN MISSISSIPPI

Money is not the only reason some doctors will lie in a matter before the bar. Racial sentiment also can prompt a physician to falsify important findings.

Most Americans recall the murder in Mississippi of three civil rights workers. When their bodies were recovered, a private pathologist and the University of Mississippi Pathology Department examined the three bodies and reported that all three of the young men had been shot, but that there was no other evidence of mutilation or bodily injury. Dr. David M. Spain, a New York City pathologist, was asked by the families of the deceased if he would conduct an independent autopsy. After great difficulties, Dr. Spain was able to examine one body, that of the Negro, James Chaney. Here is the incident, described in his own words:*

> One of the University pathologists stepped forward, silently, and helped me slide Chaney's corpse . . . to the stainless steel examining table in the middle of the room. He stepped backward, and lined up with his three comrades on one side of the table, facing me. The only sound in the green-tiled room was the rough noise of the zipper of the protective plastic bag as I pulled it away from Chaney's body.
>
> I was immediately struck by how slight and frail this young man was—
> . . . I looked at his wrist, the one that was reported broken in the unofficial examination, and I couldn't find the bullet hole the newspapers mentioned. The wrist was broken, all right. Bones were smashed, so badly that his wrist must have been literally flapping when he was carried.
>
> But there was no indication of any bullet hole.
>
> I looked up at the three doctors opposite me. Their faces were stone.

* Reprinted by permission of *Ramparts*.

I motioned to the wrist. I asked where the bullet hole was. One of the stone figures facing me offered a mumbled explanation, something about how Chaney's hand had been across his chest when the first examination was made and the examiner must have mistaken the bullet hole in his chest for the one in the hand.

I looked at him in amazement.

Then I noticed Chaney's jaw. It was broken—the lower jaw was completely shattered, split vertically, by some tremendous force. I moved the shattered pieces of his jaw in the vertical direction for the three doctors to see. They remained silent. I couldn't catch their eyes.

I carefully examined the body, and found that the bones in the right shoulder were crushed—again, from some strong and direct blow.

. . . One thing was certain: this frail boy had been beaten in an inhuman fashion. . . . I surmised he must have been beaten with chains, or a pipe. . . . It was impossible to say if he had died before he was shot . . .

I examined his skull and it was crushed, too.

I could barely believe the destruction to these frail young bones. In my twenty-five years as a pathologist and medical examiner, I have never seen bones so severely shattered, except in tremendously high speed accidents or airplane crashes.

It was obvious to any first-year medical student that the boy had been beaten to a pulp.

I have been conducting examinations of this type for a quarter of a century, but for the first time I found myself so emotionally charged that it was difficult to retain my professional composure.

I felt like screaming at these impassive observers still silently standing across the table.

But I knew that no rage of mine would tear their curtain of silence. I took off the green surgical smock . . . and left the room as fast as I could.

12

THE DRUG TRAFFICKERS:
"To Gratify the Appetite"

DURING THE CIVIL WAR men who had been injured in battle were given large doses of opium to ease their pain. Soldiers often left the hospital cured of their wounds but addicted to narcotics.

Their affliction acquired the name "soldier's sickness." But it was even more widespread among civilians. Apothecary shops sold habit-forming drugs with no restriction. Even women and children were swallowing massive amounts of narcotics in tonics dispensed by apothecaries and traveling medicine men.

In 1914 Congress passed the Harrison Narcotic Act, which is designed to restrict narcotics to medical uses. When the law first took effect, a number of doctors interpreted it to mean merely that they now had a corner on the market. U.S. Commissioner of Narcotics Henry L. Giordano recounts that some physicians "thought the limitation meant nothing more than restricting to practitioners the right to prescribe or dispense narcotics and that the individual practitioner could exercise this privilege at his personal discretion. There was evidence that some physicians were prescribing and dispensing morphine to so-called patients who had no need for it except to gratify their addiction."

Actually the Harrison Act authorizes physicians to prescribe drugs for no reason other than to cure disease or alleviate suffering. Narcotic prescriptions may not be written solely "to gratify the holder's appetite," a U.S. Circuit Court of Appeals has ruled. An addict can legally receive a narcotic only if he is suffering from an acute painful condition, or if he is so ill that sudden withdrawal would threaten his life, or if he is tapering off to cure his habit.

In the realm of narcotics control, an uneasy relationship has developed between physicians and enforcement officials. The Harrison Act holds the physician responsible for the supervision of any narcotics he handles. The law puts doctors on notice that anyone dealing in drugs does so "at his peril."

A private practitioner who wishes to prescribe or dispense narcotics must register each year with the federal government. The doctor is accountable for all narcotics he brings into his office. He is expected to report his purchases and uses, and any thefts or other losses.

In many states, physicians are required to report the name and address of any person who appears to be a narcotic addict. Despite possible penalties, this law is honored by doctors more in its breach than its observance. Physicians tend to regard it as oppressive and a violation of the confidentiality of the physician-patient relationship. In Nassau County, New York, police files contain the names of about 500 addicts. Perhaps 12 were reported by doctors.

Physicians furthermore must bear up under the constant scrutiny of the Federal Bureau of Narcotics. Large narcotic prescriptions or purchases are likely to launch a Bureau investigation. Most inquiries establish that the apparently excessive amounts are used by patients with incurable, painful diseases. Generally the patient is dying. Although the prescribing physician is cleared of wrongdoing, he often is left with the feeling that he is being watched by Big Brother. Commissioner Giordano has explained the Bureau's position: "Many physicians strongly protest a police officer making inquiries into professional practice. . . . But, in fulfilling our responsibilities imposed by the legislators and the courts, narcotic agents must make inspections, ask questions and seek appropriate explanations."

While no doctor doubts the need for narcotics control, enforcement agencies are widely resented for the manner in which they sometimes exercise their police powers. The Federal Narcotics Bureau or a local agency is likely to send an undercover agent to a doctor's office in an attempt to get an illegal prescription. Although this tactic can be the most practical way of securing evidence against an offender, it smacks of entrapment. It does not sit well with physicians, who fear that although they act in good faith they may be charged with a violation. Many doctors have heard of one physician who was convicted on evidence furnished by an addict. The addict had been sent to the doctor's office by enforcement officials. The doctor told the court that the addict feigned illness so cleverly that any physician would have prescribed a narcotic drug for him in good faith.

The narcotics problem is a special burden to doctors in areas with large numbers of addicts. In New York City, for example, there are roughly three addicts to every practicing physician. Many addicts specialize in "hitting" doctors' offices. Physicians are advised to keep their prescription pads out of sight. A blank pad lends itself to an addict's forging narcotics prescriptions, and stolen Rx blanks bring a good price in the addict underworld. A physician is also unwise to keep a large stock of narcotics in his bag or office, for this invites not only the first theft but many repeated ones. Some doctors, weary of having addicts break into their cars in the hope of finding drugs, have given up their

MD license plates. In New York, to discourage burglars some physicians post on their car windows signs in English and Spanish that say NO DRUGS HERE.

Addicts subject physicians to a wide variety of ruses. Dr. Edward R. Bloomquist of the A.M.A. Committee on Narcotic Addiction, has observed: "The experienced addict is in every sense of the word a clever confidence man, and the physician who prides himself that he is incapable of being tricked is due for a dent in his ego."

In a typical case described by Dr. Bloomquist, the addict ingratiates himself with the doctor, then mentions casually that he must remember to have a prescription filled for a member of his family.

"Funny," he will say feeling his pockets, "I thought I had it right here. Some stuff called ditalid or gitalid or something like that."

"You must mean Dilaudid," the doctor says. "Here." He takes out his prescription pad and does the "patient" a favor.

Addicts are often extremely skilled at manipulating others to gratify their addiction. Dr. Bloomquist believes that the physician's sympathetic instinct—ordinarily one of his assets—often puts him at a disadvantage in dealing with addicts. Compared to the addict, comments Dr. Bloomquist, the typical physician is "naïve." One addict maintained a list of eighty doctors from whom he extracted occasional prescriptions. When he built up a large enough stock of drugs, he sold his surplus to other addicts. Addicts learn to produce bloody sputum and simulate bad coughs, and can convincingly describe the symptoms of back strain, tic douloureux, migraine headache, asthma, angina pectoris, and renal colic. An unsuspicious physician is likely to treat many of these conditions with a narcotic.

Narcotics Bureau investigators frequently learn from informers when a well-intentioned doctor is getting a reputation in addict society as an easy mark. A narcotic agent is likely to visit the doctor and suggest that he be more judicious in prescribing. Of greatest concern to the Bureau, however, is the doctor who is not so much duped by the addict underworld as a willing accessory to it. These physicians abuse their privileges to prescribe and dispense narcotics. They exploit the addict's craving at great profit to themselves.

EASY MONEY

Doctors at one hospital were surprised at the lavish gifts a colleague was receiving from a wealthy patient—presents on the scale of yacht cruises and a winter cabin. Finally the doctor admitted the patient to the hospital's psychiatric service. There it was found the patient had been a narcotic addict for years—"and," recalls one staff physician, "had been getting monthly prescriptions for 'pain' from guess who?"

The temptation such physicians face springs in part from a U.S. Supreme Court decision of 1919. In one of the first cases tried under the Harrison Act, the defendant physicians claimed that it was good professional practice to prescribe narcotics for an addict, not in the course of treatment to help him cure his habit, but merely to maintain his customary use. The court replied: "To call such an order for the use of morphine a physician's prescription would be so plain a perversion of meaning that no discussion of the subject is required."

This ruling permanently shut off physicians as a legal source of supply. Subsequent proposals to legally provide addicts with free or low-cost drugs through "clinics" have met little success. Supporters of clinic programs argue that narcotic addiction is similar to alcoholism, and of itself an addict's taking drugs is no more a criminal act than is an alcoholic's consuming liquor. Purely on pragmatic grounds, it is reasoned, a clinic plan would cut crime. Many addicts now steal to support their habit. In the course of thefts, addicts commit hundreds of assaults and about a dozen homicides a year. A clinic program is in operation in Britain. While it has many shortcomings, the British generally regard it as the least objectionable alternative in a problem that defies solution.

The Bureau of Narcotics has taken the position that narcotic addiction is "unacceptable and utterly repugnant to the moral principles firmly infixed in the moral character of our people." The Bureau insists in respect to addicts that it is "medically unwise to maintain them in a constant state of disease, rather than to seek cure and rehabilitation." One difficulty is that addicts need larger and larger doses to get the same effect. Government-supported clinics would need to either provide an addict with increasing amounts—which could threaten his life—or provide doses only up to a maximum level, which would stimulate a whole new illegal traffic. Moreover, addicts tend to seduce others into the habit. In a clinic plan, the government would be maintaining the addict, whom the Narcotics Bureau calls the "primary agent of contagion."

Vehement opposition to relaxing narcotics rules has also been expressed in Congress. After holding hearings on addiction, a Senate subcommittee concluded that making free or low-cost narcotics widely available would "tend to increase the present problem." The House Subcommittee on Narcotics has called any clinic plan "doomed to failure."

For a narcotic-dispensing program to stand half a chance of being passed, it would at least need strong support in medical and scientific circles. But a White House Conference on Narcotic and Drug Abuse called clinic plans "unpromising and dangerous." The American Medical Association and the National Research Council, in a joint committee report, have opposed the furnishing of drugs to addicts as being "generally inadequate and medically unsound." Further, the joint committee is not optimistic about large-scale ambulatory treatment plans, in which addicts would presumably withdraw from drugs while receiving care on an outpatient basis. These plans too are "unsound," for addicts generally require being institutionalized in a drug-free environment before they can kick the habit.

The Narcotics Bureau, the A.M.A., and local enforcement agencies warn doctors in private practice not to try to cure an addict through outpatient methods unless the physician has special experience. Even then, the doctor should dispense only a day's supply at a time, and only enough to reduce withdrawal distress to a mild level. An effect of all these strictures is that the rare doctor who is willing to cater to addicts will soon find them beating a path to his door. One Bronx, New York, physician issued over 1,000 narcotic prescriptions to addicts and drug pushers. Max Schaffer, an investigator for the Narcotics Control Bureau, said this doctor "attracted them like magnets." Bureau agents, posing as addicts, went to the doctor's office and requested drugs. Asking no questions, the doctor whipped out his pad and issued a prescription.

The humorist Alexander King went through a long period of morphine addiction in which doctors supplied him with prescriptions. "One of these crocodiles," King recalls, practiced in Staten Island, and getting to him and back by ferry took several hours of travel. (King once flew to Chicago to cash a prescription a visiting Chicago doctor had written for him.) One week King made the trek to Staten Island and was told that the doctor had just died. King wept so hard that others present consoled him tenderly and sat him with the principal mourners.

A doctor who sells narcotics or narcotic prescriptions often charges what the traffic will bear. Fifteen dollars a week merely for a filled-out prescription slip is not uncommon. Narcotics sold through legitimate channels are seldom expensive. A quarter-grain morphine sulfate tablet costs under a dime. But a physician's prices to addicts can be exorbitant. One doctor charged a state narcotics officer $125 for 40 morphine tablets, a profit of at least 3,000 percent. Another doctor, indicted on some 88 counts of narcotic violation, is alleged to have made between $10,000 and $20,000 in three years from his sales.

Like other pushers, doctors who traffic in narcotics can be unscrupulous about raising prices. Exploitation of addiction sometimes occurs despite a physician's good background and reputation. One internist with a large practice was married and the father of two children. He had an excellent war record and was respected by his colleagues as a conscientious physician who spent a great deal of time doing charity work in hospitals and clinics. According to testimony, the following occurred:

One day, a couple came to his office and got on the subject of narcotics. The woman hinted that she was addicted to morphine and asked: "Is there anything you can do to help us?"

"I haven't any now," the doctor replied. "You know I can't write prescriptions for you people." He turned to the man. "Do you use it, too?" The man replied that he did. "Well," the doctor said. "Call me in the next couple of days and I'll let you know."

A week later the couple returned. This time, the doctor gave them three tablets of morphine in a tissue, and charged twenty dollars for a few minutes' visit. He had yet to examine either of them, or take a medical history, or ask about previous medication.

The following week the man came again. The doctor gave him three tablets and said: "It's fifty dollars now."

The man handed him a fifty-dollar bill.

"In small bills," the doctor told him. He added: "Make sure these bills aren't marked. And don't carry my name and address on you."

For weeks thereafter, the doctor charged the man fifty dollars for tablets costing under fifty cents. The man did not pretend to be other than a criminal type. On one occasion, he mentioned he made his living "hustling a girl."

A jury acquitted the doctor of criminal charges—but, in a separate proceeding, his license was revoked. On appeal, the court upheld the revocation, saying that although the doctor was a respected citizen, he had violated the law and his duty as a physician "for the sole motive as shown by the evidence—money."

AN ELEPHANT UNDER WRAPS

To avoid suspicion, drug-selling doctors often falsify records and write prescriptions for concocted diagnoses. A doctor thought to be selling narcotics was visited by an agent of the Federal Bureau of Narcotics posing as an addict. His testimony according to the court: The doctor asked, "What is the matter with you?"

"Nothing," the agent replied. "I am addicted."

"I will have to treat you for something," the doctor said. "I'll put down kidney colic."

"There is nothing wrong," repeated the agent. "I am addicted."

The doctor explained: "If the federal men come around they will pick me up and I can show I treated you for something." The doctor wrote a prescription for sixty quarter-grains of morphine. On the Rx he noted: "Diag.: Renal Colic."

Another agent posing as an addict came to the same doctor. He, too, received a prescription for morphine. And although the doctor did not examine him either, he wrote "renal colic" on the prescription blank.

In all, the doctor wrote five morphine prescriptions for the two men. All gave renal colic as the diagnosis. At a hearing, the doctor was asked why he indicated this diagnosis. "A druggist told me a diagnosis was required on prescriptions for narcotics," he said. "Renal colic was the first thing that occurred to me."

Some doctors try to cover themselves by going through the motions of an examination. According to testimony at a trial, one physician put a stethoscope to the chest of a purported patient and said: "It appears you have a cold." He prescribed a narcotic. At a later visit, the doctor examined the patient's nostrils. "It appears you still have your sinus," he allegedly said, and then wrote a narcotic prescription.

This ruse did not help the doctor. He was convicted of unlawfully prescribing and selling narcotics. In upholding his conviction the court observed drily, "The examinations were not very thorough."

Because of the ready market found among addicts, illegal drug traffic can quickly develop into a high-volume operation. Hiding tens of thousands of illegal doses from the watchful eye of the authorities is like keeping an elephant under wraps. In attempts to cover illicit narcotics sales, some doctors enter into collusion with pharmacists. This helps obscure the large volume of drugs that might otherwise show up in the physician's own records. One physician and a druggist have been charged with selling 35,000 narcotic tablets to addicts in a nineteen-month period. The doctor would allegedly route an addict to the pharmacist, who would fill the prescription from stock.

A classic court case alleging a large-scale operation involves a doctor who maintained a sanitarium for drug addicts. Charged the prosecution: In three years he had only 38 patients in the sanitarium. But during the same period he supplied narcotics to between 1,000 and 1,500 addicts.

At his trial, the doctor admitted that in a single day as many as 80 addicts would come to him for drugs. Each would pay cash for a day's supply. In one year, records assertedly showed, the doctor dispensed 95,000 grains of heroin and 215,000 quarter-grains of morphine.

Two doctors with a similar business sense planned to open a clinic and use it as a cover for their narcotics sales. For two years, using official narcotic order forms, the doctors bought more cocaine than is required by most large hospitals. They sold doses to addicts, getting $6,900 for a quantity they had bought for $180.

The order forms alerted the Narcotics Bureau, which sent undercover agents to the doctors. After succeeding in making a purchase, the agents put the physicians under arrest. With remarkable effrontery, the doctors offered the agents a bribe. "If you let us go," one said, "we'll give you an opportunity to invest money in our clinic."

Some doctors trafficking in drugs have made a profitable business out of providing narcotics to teen-agers. A grand jury investigation in New Jersey charged that a Manhattan physician who was issuing hundreds of prescriptions for barbiturates to students, some in junior and senior high school. The teen-agers would drive to the doctor's office in groups of four or five. For about three dollars, he would sell them prescriptions for thirty tablets.

In another case, parents registered a complaint with the State Narcotics Bureau that a doctor was making opiates available to their children. Agents for the Bureau turned up evidence that the doctor had sold some seven hundred prescriptions in two years, mainly to teen-agers. The district attorney on the case commented: "At times it looked like a line-up in the doctor's office with the kids waiting to buy prescriptions."

SIDE EFFECT: ADDICTION

Not all mishandling of narcotics by doctors results from criminal intent. Much narcotic abuse is a product of errors. When administering narcotics, doctors have a responsibility to be especially careful. Most of these drugs dull a patient's perceptions and responses. A patient can be endangered if the doctor leaves him unaware of the potential effects.

In an accident on a construction job, the courts have found, a thirty-three-year-old steelworker was cut on the scalp. He went to a doctor, who sewed up the cut and gave him a prescription for the sedative Nembutal. The proper prescription for the relief of pain would not have been a sleeping pill like Nembutal but a drug pharmacologically classified as a narcotic. However, the doctor had lost his narcotics permit because of violations of narcotics laws. Now, according to testimony, this ensued:

The doctor directed the patient to take a pill "when necessary for pain," evidently not alerting him to the dangers of an overdose. Nor, apparently, was the patient made aware that Nembutal will make a person drowsy and may cause a reaction much like extreme drunkenness. After having the prescription filled, the steelworker took a pill and returned to work. On the job his injury bothered him, so he took another pill.

At 5:30 P.M. he left for home fifty miles away, driving a truck. About halfway home, he lost control of the wheel and ran the truck into a field two hundred yards off the highway. A farmer who came to his aid observed that he was not in control of his faculties, although he did not smell of alcohol.

A nearby garage pulled the truck in for minor repairs. When it was ready, the patient climbed in to continue his trip home. He is thought to have taken yet another pill to relieve his headache. Two miles down the road he again lost control of the wheel. The truck crashed into the guardrail of a bridge. His injuries were fatal.

In prescribing narcotics, doctors are expected to guard against a patient's falling into addiction. Standard precautions include issuing drugs in limited amounts and making prescriptions unrefillable. Some doctors, however, authorize patients to refill drug prescriptions indefinitely. In effect, these doctors contribute to the patient's addiction. A study of thousands of addicts at the Public Health Service Hospital at Lexington, Kentucky, shows that 27 percent of the addictions were iatrogenic, or originated by physicians. Often, patients become addicted after surgery, or in the course of being treated for such diseases as asthma, migraine, sciatica, arthritis, and heart disease.

Most patients who receive narcotics in treatment have little need for them afterward. But in some patients the first exposure to narcotics triggers a craving that leads to long-term addiction. After undergoing a kidney operation, a forty-year-old illustrator of children's books was given morphine injections every six hours to dull her pain. "I began to like that feeling of just floating away," the woman recalls. She looked forward to the injection and began asking for it more frequently. The nurse objected, since the surgeon had specified they were to be given every six hours.

The woman complained of increased pain, and so the surgeon complied with a more liberal drug order. By the end of six weeks, she was getting a morphine injection every two or three hours. Although the surgeon questioned her need for the drug, he failed to cut the dosage. When the woman left the hospital, she was addicted to morphine. She has resisted rehabilitation and now lives in a slum tenement, barely earning enough to support her habit.

Because the danger of addiction is inherent in the use of narcotics, good practice calls for doctors to prescribe these drugs sparingly, only when necessary to relieve pain. But some doctors use narcotics when the patient's condition does not justify it, then persist after the patient's addiction is obvious. In a successful negligence suit brought by a New England woman, the courts found the following: The woman was complaining of nausea. The doctor did not perform a physical examination but gave her an injection of morphine. Twice more that day he gave her a morphine shot.

The woman did not know what the medication was. About a year later she again suffered nausea and went to the doctor. Once more he gave her morphine. She received occasional injections for half a year, then moved up to two injections a week. She suspected that she was receiving a narcotic. But by now she had become accustomed to feeling "pretty high," and she looked forward to her shot.

Toward the end of August, she was getting morphine every day. In September the doctor gave her an injection twice a day. In October, three times a day, sometimes even more. Finally, the woman's husband ordered the doctor out of the house.

The woman, now aware that she was addicted to morphine, became jumpy. She called every doctor in town asking for an injection. Two days later, after every doctor had turned her down, she blacked out. At the hospital she was treated for her addiction, and cured. Thereafter, her gallbladder was removed. Her nausea disappeared with it.

There is a strong suggestion in many such cases that the doctor uses narcotics to mask the pain resulting from inadequate treatment. A woman gave this testimony in a negligence charge upheld by the courts: Following an operation to relieve intestinal obstruction, she continued to complain of severe pain even after she returned home. In response, her doctor prescribed morphine for self-administration. For three months, she and her husband, son, daughter, and son-in-law all administered morphine by injection to relieve her pain. The doctor saw her three times. He did not look into the cause of her suffering. When the family ran out of morphine, the doctor would order more for them by phone. He told them to judge for themselves when it was needed.

"Aren't we using too much morphine?" the doctor was asked.

"Don't worry about it," he replied. "She's improving." The woman was now taking morphine every three hours day and night.

At last, the family decided she was not recovering properly from the operation and wished to see another physician. "That's not necessary," their doctor told them. "Her recovery is satisfactory." The family insisted and made preparations for the woman to fly to a consultant. By now her addiction was so advanced that the doctor gave her thirty morphine tablets and thirty-six sleeping pills merely to tide her over.

The consultant performed surgery and found she was suffering complications from the original operation as well as intestinal obstruction that had supposedly been corrected. Under his care, she underwent a long and painful withdrawal from the drug.

A doctor is in a position to addict a patient without the patient's realizing it. Criminal records show that some doctors take advantage of this opportunity to exploit the patient, who now needs a continued supply of the drug.

One doctor, convicted of making false statements and using false names in prescriptions, claimed that morphine was necessary to relieve the urinary discomfort a woman was suffering. But, physicians testified, the amount of the drug he prescribed was three times that needed for even the most excruciating pain. To conceal these violations he prescribed for the woman using both her married and maiden names. The woman's habit increased by stages to sixty quarter-grains a day. Before the doctor was apprehended, he had kept the woman on narcotics for nine years.

Another woman went before a Senate subcommittee investigating narcotics traffic to testify how a physician had made her a narcotic addict. He then became her supplier and charged high prices for the drug. In all, she paid him over $40,000. To make this money, she testified, she became a prostitute.

PART IV

Assault and Abandonment

NONCRIMINAL OFFENSES like medical assault or abandonment are likely to affect the typical patient even more than the felonies just discussed. Assault is an error of commission, in which the doctor acts without the patient's consent. Abandonment is an act of omission. The doctor fails to fulfill his obligation to perform necessary services.

13

THE ASSAULTERS:

Trespassing on the Patient

LET'S SAY THAT while walking down the street you were physically attacked. The law affirms that your body is your most precious possession and that you should be guarded against invasions upon your person. Thus your attacker would be charged with the crime of assault.

Much the same principle applies in medical jurisprudence. Here the law recognizes that physicians are in a position to inflict on patients unneeded or unwanted services. The law therefore requires that except in emergencies doctors treat patients only with permission. If a doctor fails to get proper authorization, he is liable for civil action on grounds of assault and battery.

Justice Benjamin Cardozo has offered this classic judicial statement of the rule: "Every human being of adult years and sound mind has a right to determine what shall be done with his body, and a surgeon [or other physician] who performs an operation without his patient's consent commits an assault." The matter of the patient's consent also has important philosophical ramifications. Dr. Herbert S. Ratner of the Stritch School of Medicine of Loyola University has said: "The patient is a free agent; ultimately his consent must be obtained before anything is done to him. . . . A fundamental human right is at stake."

MISTAKEN IDENTITY

On rare occasions a physician is accused of assaulting a patient with the use of brute force. In one court case, three witnesses testified that a psychiatrist lost his temper with a schizophrenic young woman and beat her until she was bruised and bloody. More typically, medical assaults spring from carelessness. Sometimes such errors make a reality of the perennial nightmare that haunts persons awaiting surgery: that the wrong operation will be performed.

In a memorable case in Pennsylvania, two children were brought to the operating floor of a hospital at the same time. Fred was there for a tonsillectomy, Billy for a circumcision. The children got mixed up, and the wrong operations were performed.

Later one of the surgeons swore he had done everything possible to avoid such a mistake. "I went up to the boy and double-checked," he recalled. "I asked him his name. I asked, 'Are you Fred?' And he said, 'I sure am.'"

155

Investigators probed further. They went to Billy and said, "Before you went to the operating room, did the doctor ask you anything?"

"Yes, sir," replied Billy. "He asked me, 'Are you afraid?' and I told him, 'I sure am.'"

Because of such mistaken identities, in Illinois a limb was amputated from the wrong patient. In California the right patient was treated but the wrong limb was taken off. In Michigan a woman was taken to a hospital for treatment of an infected finger. She wound up in the operating room with her gallbladder removed.

Physicians contribute to such blunders by failing to respect hospital precautions against wrong-way runs. In one hospital, a nurse told an orderly: "The patient is in bed number two." The orderly started counting from the wrong end and wheeled the wrong patient into the operating room.

According to hospital rules, the surgeon is supposed to identify the patient before anesthetic is administered. Then, to verify the patient's identity, the anesthesiologist is supposed to ask: "What's your name?"

But on this day the surgeon was late and the operating-room routine began without him. Without checking the patient's name, the anesthesiologist merely said: "Just take a few breaths now and you'll soon be sound asleep." Finding the patient asleep, the surgeon started cutting without determining that this was the right patient.

The result: The patient, who was in the hospital for an injured hand, lost a healthy kidney.

A healthy organ similarly lost is the subject of a complaint filed by a Tennessee railway electrician. He was scheduled for the removal of hemorrhoids on the same day another man was to undergo surgery for correction of a hernia and removal of a diseased left testicle.

That morning each patient received preliminary anesthetic and was trundled off to the operating floor. Through an error their charts were switched, and each man went into the other's operating room.

In violation of standard surgical procedure, neither doctor checked that the draped figure on the operating table was the correct patient. Nor, once the tissue was revealed, did either doctor question why surgery seemed uncalled-for. Thus one of the men got a needless hemorrhoid operation. In the other operating room, the railway electrician's abdomen was cut into for the repair of a nonexistent hernia. And though it showed no abnormality, his left testicle was removed.

FALSE PROMISES

In law and in medical ethics it is a cardinal principle that the patient fully understand the nature and effects of the procedure that he is being advised to undergo. This requirement of *informed* consent with full knowledge of the alternatives is part of the patient's right to determine what shall be done to him. "The term 'doctor' means teacher," Dr. Herbert Ratner has said, "and one of the main functions of the physician in his relationship with the patient is to . . . educate him to a right decision."

Yet, to get consent, some doctors lead patients on by virtually guaranteeing an unrealistically good result. To sell patients on nose reshaping, surgeons have been known to exhibit photographs of movie stars—implying that a woman will resemble a screen goddess after the recommended rhinoplasty. Some cosmetic surgeons also retouch the patient's photograph to suggest what she would look like if she underwent the operation. Courts have ruled that this practice constitutes a guarantee and makes the doctor liable to a breach-of-contract claim.

Guaranteeing cosmetic surgery became an issue when a physician in New York urged a woman to undergo an operation to remove a scar on her shoulder. In a letter to the county medical society, the woman charged that he had guaranteed the scar "would disappear, except for a thin and barely visible line" and that the healing process "would take only about four months."

After the woman underwent the operation, however, the scar was more unsightly than ever. A raised, colored scar had replaced the flat, fading one, and the scar was now between a quarter and half an inch in width.

"When asked by me what he proposed doing to rectify this situation," she wrote, "he suggested another operation at additional cost."

The society's grievance committee, although the woman's complaint was expressed in a "courteous, fair and reasonable fashion," rejected it.

Instead, the physician sued her for libel in a suit that was eventually thrown out of court.

UNDISCLOSED RISKS

Informed consent implies that the patient or his family be advised of the risks inherent in a procedure. The doctor need not terrify the patient with the nth possible complication, but he is expected to discuss dangers the patient is reasonably likely to face. Yet in recommending a procedure, doctors sometimes fail to mention its hazards. The patient thus may authorize one course of action although he would prefer another if he knew the relative risks.

This is especially likely to happen if the doctor says with a certainty that the procedure is so safe as to be without danger. One District of Columbia woman recalls questioning her doctor about the shock treatments he recommended and being assured by him, "They are perfectly safe." At the beginning of her first treatment, she was struck by a convulsive seizure. This is a strong risk of electroshock therapy, and most doctors mention it for the consideration of the patient and his family. In the seizure, the woman's arm was fractured, causing permanent and painful injuries.

A patient suffering impaired hearing has claimed in a suit that he felt similarly assured that no harm could result from treatment. A physician he consulted told him that his hearing might be improved by a stapes mobilization operation, the surgical freeing of a tiny bone in the ear. "In any event," he testified the doctor told him, "the operation will not damage your hearing."

During the next seven months the patient underwent two operations on his right ear and one on his left. At the outset he was able to hear normal voices. Now, according to the suit he brought, far from improving his hearing or having no effect, the operations have left him totally deaf —unable to distinguish any sounds, even with a hearing aid.

In many cases the doctor simply neglects to mention the risks. With no hint that he should think twice, a patient submitted to having a tumor on his neck removed by fulguration, a treatment employing electrical sparks. Only after a hemorrhage occurred, with considerable scarring, did the family learn that such was a possibility. "If the doctor had advised us of the risks," they said afterward, "we would have asked about another method."

A nine-year-old boy who had hallucinations was taken to a neurologist. To determine whether the boy's trouble was emotional or organic, the doctor recommended an arteriogram, an exploratory type of surgical process that involves x-raying the arteries. Physicians ordinarily point out that an arteriogram is a dangerous procedure. A significant minority of such operations result in paralysis, other injury, or death.

The boy's parents alleged in a suit that the doctor gave them no such indications. If he had, they say, they would have first tried to get the information they needed through a less hazardous course, such as submitting the boy to psychiatric observation. With the parents presumably unaware of the dangers and alternatives, the boy underwent the arteriogram and now is partially paralyzed.

Another hazardous exploratory procedure is the cerebral angiogram, an operation for x-raying blood vessels of the brain. Allegedly as a result of an angiogram, a patient who had only an eye problem has suffered brain damage that rendered him paralyzed and unable to speak.

He has charged in a suit that the doctor neglected to tell him that cerebral angiograms involve great risks and that nonhazardous procedures might have made the angiogram unnecessary. Moreover, physicians have testified that the operation was performed in a hospital with inadequate equipment. If a cerebral angiogram were in fact called for, medical witnesses said, the patient should have been sent to a better-equipped institution.

Yet another type of hazardous procedure is cobalt irradiation. Rays emitted by radioactive cobalt can penetrate the body more deeply than x-rays and thus are useful for treating certain types of cancer. But cobalt irradiation is extremely tricky. The rays are at their strongest about a fifth of an inch beneath the skin—unlike x-rays, whose maximum strength is at the skin itself. If not precisely administered, cobalt rays can be tremendously destructive to healthy internal tissue. The problem can be even more critical if the beam is moving so as to distribute a dosage over a section of the body.

Physicians are obligated to summarize these hazards to any patient to whom they recommend cobalt radiation therapy. But one woman has made this allegation in a suit: She had a cancer remaining after the removal of her left breast. The doctor she consulted recommended cobalt radiation without mentioning the dangers or discussing alternatives. Believing that the procedure presented no special risk, she entered into treatment at a medical center.

For twenty-three days, using a rotating beam, the doctor irradiated an area extending from the patient's breastbone around to her left side. The first hint of danger came from a skin ulcer that was an aftermath of the breast surgery. At the start of her exposure to the radiation, the sore was about the size of a quarter and was draining. She understood that the cobalt radiation therapy would shrink the ulcer and help it heal. Instead, discharging pus, the sore spread across her chest.

Other symptoms soon followed. By the end of the treatment it developed that the dosage she had been receiving was too large for healthy tissue to survive. As a result of excessive radiation she was left a deformed invalid. Her entire chest—skin, cartilage, and bone—was destroyed.

PATIENTS IN THE DARK

Among colleagues, physicians spend hours conversing in terminology barely comprehensible to most laymen. Unmindful physicians also use medical terms in proposing procedures to patients. The patients thus often authorize a treatment without having actually understood what is entailed. According to the charge in one suit:

A man suffering a genital disorder was given sulfa salve for temporary relief. "I'd recommend circumcision," the doctor told him.

Some months later the patient and his wife returned. "I'd like to stop using the ointment," the man said. "As soon as possible I'd like that operation you told me about."

Shortly thereafter, his wife called to make final plans. Trying to recall the case, the doctor asked: "Does he want a circumcision or sterilization?"

"I don't understand," the wife replied. "We want what you recommended."

"The tube-tying operation?" the doctor suggested.

"I guess that's right," she said.

It was only after the patient awoke from the surgery that he and his wife discovered that the operation had been not a circumcision but a vasectomy—a tying off of the spermatic tube, rendering him sterile.

The requirement for informed consent obligates doctors to disclose the effects of the treatment being authorized. Not unusual is the woman who agrees to the removal of a fibroid tumor from her uterus without the doctor's having made the consequences clear to her. After the operation she is often shocked when she learns that she will no longer be able to bear children.

Men, too, may consent to a sterilization procedure without being made aware of its effects. One patient complained of the diminished size and force of his urinary stream and the increased frequency of urination. According to his subsequent complaint in court: The doctor asked him to undergo examination with a cystoscope, a tube for peering into the urinary tract and bladder. "I want to see if you need a prostate operation," the doctor told him.

Next day the patient was on a hospital operating table, where the cystoscopy was performed. The doctor now came to the head of the table to report the results of the examination. "In my opinion a transurethral prostatic resection should be done," he said. "Do I have your consent to proceed with that operation?"

"Yes," the patient replied, under the impression that this was a simple correction of a bladder difficulty. The doctor admitted later that he had not discussed the operation with the patient in "particular technical detail." One of the details left undiscussed was that to reduce the possibility of infection the patient's spermatic cords would be severed.

The patient sought redress, charging that he had been sterilized without his consent. Ordinarily, the courts hold in such cases that if there was no emergency the doctor should have told the patient all the facts of the procedure. He then would have been free to reject the surgery altogether. Or, electing it, he could choose to risk infection rather than undergo severing of the spermatic cords.

IGNORING THE PATIENT'S NO

Implicit in the requirement for patient's consent is the patient's right to *prohibit* a procedure. The patient's body is first and foremost his own possession, the courts have ruled; to violate his specific prohibition is to aggravate assault. Some doctors, however, have gone ahead and done precisely what the patient has forbidden. Moreover, such disregard of the patient's expressed wish has caused tragedy.

In Oklahoma a housewife was to have her appendix removed. "I don't want a spinal anesthetic," she told the surgeon.

"Very well," he replied. "I'll see that you're given a general anesthetic instead."

At the hospital he followed the proper routine for bringing this about. He noted on her chart that she did not want a spinal and was not to be given one. A chart stays with the patient and is the principal medium of communication between members of a hospital staff. Unless specifically countermanded, orders written on a chart are generally regarded as inviolable. But a suit won by the housewife against an anesthesiologist charges the following:

On the morning of the operation, she was given a shot of morphine as a preliminary anesthetic. Barely awake, she was taken to the operating room. There her chart was read by the anesthesiologist. He admitted later that no emergency precluded a general anesthetic or made a spinal anesthetic imperative.

The anesthesiologist may or may not have talked with the patient. According to his version, she said: "Don't give me a spinal."

"It's a safe anesthetic," he says he told her.

"Well," he claims she finally said, "I won't be obstinate, but I want to go to sleep." This, the anesthesiologist has maintained, gave him the permission he needed to go against the orders on the chart.

The woman recalls no such conversation. In any event, physicians have testified, she was under the influence of a   strong sedative and in her drugged state was in no condition to think through a change of mind. Whether or not the anesthesiologist spoke to her, witnesses said, her original objection to spinal anesthesia should have stood.

Despite that objection, the anesthesiologist proceeded to give a spinal. The patient was placed on her right side and pulled into a bowed position. While the nurse held her, the doctor introduced the needle into her spine and injected the anesthetic.

The woman felt a sting, then a grating sensation. Pains shot through her legs and feet. She was rolled onto her back. In her right arm she received an injection of thiopental sodium (Pentothal) to complete the anesthetization. She went to sleep immediately. She was not conscious again for three days.

There was testimony that the needle giving the spinal anesthetic punctured the spinal cord, tearing soft tissue and allowing spinal fluid to leak out. This has resulted in a chronic inflammation of the cord.

The patient is paralyzed from the waist down. Her hip joints have become grotesquely misshapen. Her legs have shrunk. When her braces are taken off her legs, her feet drop and cannot be raised or controlled. Nor can she control her bowel movements or her bladder. This necessitates her wearing protection at all times to absorb the leakage.

Her condition is permanent. At the time she received the spinal she was thirty years old.

Another woman, worried about lumps in her right breast, consulted a physician and has filed this charge in court of what ensued.

"Can you take out part of a lump to test whether or not it is cancerous?" she asked.

"Certainly," he said. "I'll call the hospital and arrange for a room."

The patient heard him talking on the phone. He ordered a tray "for the removal of a right breast."

"If that's my breast you are talking about," she said, "you are not going to remove it."

"I have no intention of removing your breast," he told her. "I wouldn't think of doing so without first making a test. It takes the same instruments to make a test as it does to remove one."

As part of the process of being admitted to the hospital, the woman signed a consent form. This blanket document authorized the doctor "to perform an operation for mastectomy . . . upon myself, and to do whatever may be deemed necessary in his judgment." The doctor had not explained the word "mastectomy" to her, she asserts, and she did not know the term.

But, her complaint goes on, she did know that she did not want her breast removed. "Are you sure you understand that you're just to make a test of the breast?" she asked the doctor that evening.

"I have no intention of doing anything different," he replied. "I'm to make a test only."

She was concerned enough to repeat this several times. "If you go ahead and remove the breast, it can't be put back on," she added. "But if we just make a test, maybe it won't have to be taken off."

The next day in the operating room the doctor did not perform a biopsy or any other test. Rather he removed the breast straight away. His reasoning, as he explained it afterward, was that he had the patient's written permission on the consent form and also that there was no point in doing a biopsy because there was no pathologist in the community to analyze the tissue sample.

Other physicians in this community took issue. They testified that it had long been the practice at the hospital to submit biopsies to a pathologist not far away, then wait for his report. This the doctor could have done since no emergency was involved to warrant rush surgery on an uninformed patient. The woman's allegation continues:

After the operation the doctor went to her room and told her: "You had cancer, but I removed it. I got it early and got every bit of it."

"Are you sure you got it all?" she asked.

"Yes. Every bit of it."

"How long would it have been before it started to spread?"

"That I can't say. Maybe two days. Maybe a week."

The patient left the hospital. She regretted losing her breast. But she was consoled by knowing that she had been rescued from cancer.

The doctor had assured her that the cancer would not spread or recur. Nonetheless, she remained worried. Some lumps developed on her ribs, and she returned to the doctor.

"The cancer is spreading, isn't it?" she said.

"It couldn't be," the doctor replied.

"How can you be so sure?"

"Because," he allegedly confessed, "you didn't have cancer in the first place."

This was confirmed by a tissue study made at the hospital. What she had had were noncancerous cysts. Even if these needed to be removed, she need not have lost her breast.

PLAYING GOD

Injuries can also be caused by procedures a doctor decides to do on his own authority, without consulting the patient or family. While performing an appendectomy on a young girl, a surgeon noticed her ovaries were swollen. Thinking they might be cancerous, he snipped them out—without first checking with her parents or submitting a sample of the suspected tissue for analysis. Had he, he would have learned that the girl was undergoing her first menstruation, which was causing the swelling. The girl, barely blossoming into womanhood, was now rendered permanently unable to bear children.

Some physicians perform a hysterectomy during any entry into a female abdomen. They justify this as "good preventive surgery," a view generally discredited among surgeons. For six years a Louisiana doctor treated a woman to help her and her husband conceive. The furthest thing from her mind, she charged in a successful suit, was to have her reproductive organs removed.

Now the doctor had her under his scalpel for an appendectomy. Her husband was in the hospital waiting while the operation was going on. But, the woman testified, without asking him or having any other permission, the doctor cut out her ovaries, uterus, and uterine tubes because it was his notion that this was "good surgical procedure." After the operation, he visited her room. She recalls sobbing at him distraughtly: "You've double-crossed me!"

Sometimes a hysterectomy is not only performed without consent but botched as well. The courts have found that a young mother, here named Alice Day, was swept into a nightmare after she consulted a physician we'll call Dr. Norton about a pain in her right side. She won a malpractice action which charged the following:

"You have a small tumor," he said. "It will have to be removed."

That afternoon he admitted Mrs. Day to the Norton Hospital, a small proprietary institution he owned. Within an hour or so, she was taken to the operating room. Contrary to standard medical procedure in non-emergencies, he made no preoperative studies to determine if his diagnosis was correct, if surgery were necessary, if the patient were physically fit for it. Nor, in contrast with the usual practice in major surgery, did he have a physician present to assist him.

He was minutes from a first-rate hospital and practiced in a California community loaded with medical talent, yet he exposed the patient to battlefield operating conditions. If bombs were bursting overhead, this doctor could not have rushed things more.

Mrs. Day had given Dr. Norton permission to remove only the suspected tumor. Now, without seeking her further consent, he cut out her appendix and uterus, both of which were healthy. It was while performing this unauthorized surgery that his scalpel slipped and he severed an artery. He neglected to tie off the blood vessel before sewing her back up.

Mrs. Day thus continued to bleed internally. During her ten days in the Norton Hospital she was overwhelmed by nausea and could eat no food. Sleep was impossible. There was a constant roar in her head and crackling in her ears. Dizziness engulfed her. A severe backache kept her in anguish. She suffered an insatiable craving for water. Her thirst was due largely to the fluid she was losing as she hemorrhaged and also to the fact that she was pouring forth sweat. The heavy perspiring made her gown wringing wet and her bed foul.

Despite her deterioration she was made to walk the day after the operation on the general theory that a patient should be up and about. The following day, over her protests, she was again taken from bed to walk. This time she fainted.

Dr. Norton had gone out of town, having supposedly arranged for two physicians to cover the hospital. One of the substitutes noticed that Mrs. Day's red blood count had dropped by about 25 percent and her hemoglobin count was also perilously low. From blood samples, he determined that she was suffering from microcytic anemia, a severe condition marked by shrunken red blood corpuscles. He recognized that she should be checked for possible hemorrhaging. But, reluctant to involve himself in her care, he made no effort to treat her. "I am here merely to observe for the benefit of the original doctor," he insisted.

The other substitute also noticed the danger signals in Mrs. Day's blood count. Moreover, he discovered that she had started bleeding from her vagina. While he realized that this demanded immediate attention, he also refused to take action. He felt that Dr. Norton should bear the full responsibility for her decline.

Dr. Norton, however, saw Mrs. Day only twice: on the day after the operation, then on the day he discharged her. He knew of her deterioration and of the warnings in her blood count. But he sent her home without even taking her blood pressure.

At home, Mrs. Day experienced gushings of blood from her vagina. Suddenly she expelled five large clots. Her husband rushed her back to Norton's hospital, where she was taken immediately to surgery. For the first time Norton had her blood typed. This safeguard is considered fundamental in surgery.

Taking one other basic precaution, Norton had a physician assist him. It was from the assistant that Mrs. Day learned what had gone wrong.

After her pelvic cavity was opened, more than two cups of blood were sponged out and a number of large clots were removed. Two weeks of steady bleeding had saturated the tissues, making them spongy and swollen. "The blood had just by pressure eroded through the entire area," the physician assisting later recalled. First one organ, then another was deemed unsalvageable and cut out.

The destruction and removal of tissue left Mrs. Day with a vaginal vault shortened to less than two inches. In the malpractice suit growing out of this episode, the judge commented at length and with great sympathy over the misfortune befalling her and her husband: "There is no amount of sentiment or of gold that . . . so [preserves] the comfort, the tranquility and the happiness of a man and woman united in wedlock for a lifetime as does their conjugal relationship."

Before this experience, Mrs. Day was a cheerful, normal woman. She had been active socially and adept at running a smooth, pleasant household. The surgery produced the symptoms of menopause. From this and other effects of the operation, Mrs. Day became more and more nervous and depressed. Her happy home underwent an upheaval. She suffered a complete breakdown and had to be confined to an institution.

Yet another suit over a physician's proceeding without permission concerns Martin Cromwell (pseudonym), whose feet occasionally hurt him. According to his testimony: During one interval of discomfort he consulted the outpatient clinic of a hospital. A doctor he saw there urged him to undergo surgery.

"I've never had an operation before," Mr. Cromwell replied. "I'll confess I'm scared stiff of the knife."

"It's a very minor operation," the doctor assured him. "It requires only a small incision in your back and the clipping of a nerve. You'll be in the operating room only forty to forty-five minutes."

Thus persuaded, Cromwell entered the hospital for a lumbar sympathectomy. This operation entails the severing of a nerve of the sympathetic nervous system, which controls the muscles contained in the walls of blood vessels. Presumably the sympathectomy would cause the muscles surrounding the blood vessels in Cromwell's legs to relax. The expanded vessels supposedly would then increase the flow of blood to his feet and end his pain. Continuing the allegation:

The physician who examined Cromwell and began the operation we'll call Dr. Harris. He was an assistant resident in training to be a surgeon. The only other physicians present in the operating room were two interns.

Dr. Harris scheduled the operation for a time when no supervisory surgeon was in the hospital in case advice or aid was needed. On the hospital staff was a foremost specialist in the surgery of the sympathetic nervous system, the developer of the most extensive operation to be performed on sympathetic nerve tissue. It would have been valuable for an inexperienced surgeon to at least have him on call. Dr. Harris, however, performed the operation when this senior specialist was not available.

Cromwell had consented to the operation with the understanding that it would be small and simple, an inch-long incision in his back. Now, in the operating room, Dr. Harris cut an opening eight inches long into Cromwell's abdomen and lifted out all the internal organs. Instead of merely clipping a nerve, Harris set about removing an entire nerve chain.

His hand was unsteady. Weakened by his scalpel, the nerve chain snapped. Part of it, a grayish knot of nerve tissue called a ganglion, disappeared into Cromwell's abdominal cavity. In searching for the broken end, Harris came across the large artery and the large vein that carry blood to and from the legs. He probed under these vessels. Suddenly a gush of blood erupted from Cromwell's abdomen. The doctor had punctured the vein. Blood was pouring into the abdominal cavity.

The artery and the vein were bound together by tissue composed of layers of fiberlike threads. This fibrous tissue was in Harris's way. So he could get at the puncture, he tried to separate the fibers from the vessels. In working at the tissue with a scalpel, he tore the vein again and again. The flood in Cromwell's abdomen became more and more profuse.

Harris now made an incision in Cromwell's left thigh near the groin. Cutting from that point, Harris traced the vein until he was close to where it was torn. There he tied it off. To his surprise, the bleeding continued uncontrolled. The other big vessel, the artery, had been perforated as well.

Because of the protracted operation and great loss of blood, Cromwell's condition became critical. He went into shock, his blood pressure and body temperature nosediving. The operation came to a standstill while Harris sent out a desperate call for help.

The chief of the hospital's surgical service responded, rushing from his home. Upon discovering Cromwell's condition the chief surgeon abandoned all efforts to repair the artery and vein. Instead, he directed all his attention toward saving Cromwell's life. To meet the emergency he tied off the torn blood vessels and clipped them. With these main vessels severed, the blood supply to the lower part of Cromwell's body was greatly reduced. That night, on awakening from the anesthetic, Martin Cromwell discovered he was paralyzed from the hips down.

With the large vein and artery clipped, the only way his lower left leg and thigh could get circulation would be through the remaining but smaller blood vessels. These could not provide sufficient blood, and gangrene developed. Cromwell's left leg needed to be amputated. To salvage the joint, the amputation was blow the knee.

This amputation was defective and Cromwell had to undergo debridement, surgery for the removal of foreign and contaminated matter from the stump. Then, in yet another operation, his leg had to be re-amputated, now above the knee.

Shortly after the re-amputation, Cromwell suffered a heart attack. This left an infarct, an area of dead tissue in his heart. A blood clot entered his right leg and obstructed circulation there. Gangrene resulted, forcing the amputation of his right leg.

In the first operation alone, Cromwell had spent seven and a half hours in the operating room and received seventeen pints of blood in transfusions. The heavy medication he received to relieve his pain caused him to become addicted to narcotics. When he entered the hospital, he weighed a robust 180 pounds. Over four months went by before he left. On the day he was released he weighed 94 pounds. He was a physical and emotional wreck with stumps for legs, a severely impaired heart and a predilection toward narcotic readdiction.

If any person were so assaulted on the street instead of in an operating room, the person who crippled him would probably be sent up for life. But there is a further irony: Martin Cromwell very likely should not have been operated on at all.

His hospital record shows that his condition had never been diagnosed. Speculation as to what troubled him ranged from hardening of the arteries to Buerger's disease, an ailment resulting from excessive smoking. If any disease were present, it was in its early stages. Except for isolated periods of discomfort, Cromwell could walk and work without distress. Nonsurgical treatment ordinarily would have been tried before surgery was even considered.

But chances are Cromwell would never have needed an operation. As his medical history shows, he suffered one particular condition that in all likelihood accounted for much of the pain in his feet. Though obvious, it was evidently overlooked. He had fallen arches.

14
THE ABANDONERS:
Bad Samaritans

A BOY we'll call Jerry Robins broke his leg playing football. He was taken to a hospital where a physician we'll name Dr. Frankel reduced the fracture and set the leg in a cast. The next day, the courts found, Jerry's father told the doctor that the boy had a throbbing sensation in his ankle, as if a tight band were around it. "Maybe the cast is too tight," Mr. Robins suggested.

Without examining the cast, the Robins' charge goes on, Frankel shook his head. "No," he said emphatically. "It's not too tight."

Shortly afterward, Frankel left on a trip. He did not tell the Robins family he would be gone. Nor did he arrange for any other physician to look in on the boy. He was away for a week.

Meanwhile, the pain in Jerry's ankle became continuous and almost unendurable. He developed a fever raging up to 103 degrees. "I can't feel my toes," he told his father.

When Frankel returned, Mr. Robins again asked him to examine the cast. "The cast is fine," Frankel insisted. He declined to see the boy and instead discharged him from the hospital. After Jerry had been home a week, Mr. Robins called Frankel and told him the boy's condition was no better. "Won't you come examine him?" Robins asked.

"There's nothing wrong with the boy's leg," Frankel repeated. He refused to come.

At last, the father called in another physician. Dr. Stillman loosened the cast and found deep layers of dead tissue. In a common reaction to fractures, the leg had swollen. As the leg expanded, the cast became tighter, exerting vise-like pressure on the nerves.

Ordinarily doctors guard against this possibility and check any feeling of tightness in the cast. If kept under surveillance, simple leg fractures in young patients generally heal in a matter of weeks. But in Jerry's case, nearly three weeks of unrelieved pressure caused severe complications. The boy was incapacitated for twenty-two months. Then, because of gangrene setting in, the leg was amputated.

Patients are sometimes victims of a physician's refusal to provide necessary medical attention. Under civil law this can amount to the offense of

168

abandonment, for patients are entitled to a doctor's diligence in staying with a case until he formally withdraws or is dismissed. In actions that the Robins family brought against Dr. Frankel and won, the Virginia Supreme Court of Appeals restated this legal principle: "After a physician has accepted employment in a case, it is his duty to continue his services as long as they are necessary. He cannot voluntarily abandon his patient."

If there is no doctor-patient relationship already established, a physician technically has no obligation to accept a patient. An extreme example is a psychiatrist in Arizona who refuses to treat certain types of people. He turns away the alcoholic and the obese. Out of a personal aversion, he will not treat promiscuous women. Nor does he care for poor people. His attitude is deplored by many other physicians who feel he "seems to treat his specialty as a hobby" and is "anti-human-being." Nevertheless, he is perfectly within his rights.

According to the letter of the law, in many states, a physician may refuse to treat a critically ill patient even if he is the only doctor available and is doing nothing else at the time. As long as the doctor is not already on the case, the Indiana Supreme Court has ruled, he can withhold his services "even without any reason whatever." On the other hand, not coming forward in emergencies is so alien to professional ideals that the Principles of Medical Ethics specifically prohibits it: "A physician may choose whom he will serve. In an emergency, however, he should render service to the best of his ability."

Thus, while morally bound, physicians are legally free. Some doctors take advantage of the loophole.

THE LEGAL SPOOK

The scene was the Caribbean paradise of St. Thomas in the Virgin Islands. Dr. Robert S. Thrope, a Massachusetts internist, was on his last day of vacation. A few hours before he was to fly home, he was called to aid a boat captain who had been electrocuted. Dr. Thrope tried to restore the captain's heartbeat with external cardiac massage. After ten minutes he opened the captain's chest and began internal massage. He continued in the ambulance and kept at it until they reached the hospital. Despite his efforts, the patient died.

Criminal charges were brought against Dr. Thrope for practicing medicine without a Virgin Islands license. When this charge was dropped, Dr. Thrope was threatened with prosecution for homicide if an autopsy revealed he had contributed to the captain's death. Dr. Thrope was ordered not to leave the islands until the autopsy was completed. But the autopsy needed to be done in Puerto Rico and would take weeks. At last the doctor was allowed to return to Massachusetts with the understanding that if indicted he would come back to St. Thomas to stand trial.

The autopsy report was completed two months later. It concluded that the exact cause of the captain's death could not be determined. Hence Dr. Thrope could not be held criminally responsible. Shortly before he was finally freed of charges, Dr. Thrope made a remark memorable as a masterpiece of understatement: "I've had a hard time keeping my mind on my work. It is very disturbing."

Besides the obvious injustice this case represents, it is notable on several counts. It has led ever more physicians to resolve not to get involved in emergency calls. It has prompted a number of states to pass "Good Samaritan" laws for the protection of doctors who respond to emergencies. And despite the reaction it has aroused, it is highly exceptional. Physicians actually need have little worry that being a Good Samaritan will lead to litigation.

"Would you stop at the scene of an accident?" is a frequent conversational topic when doctors gather. Usually at least one physician says he would offer help without hesitation. Another will say that he would stop only if he were first on the scene or only if the injured looked in bad shape. Almost certainly one or two will reply, "You're crazy if you do even that. Why invite a malpractice suit by trying to work under difficult conditions?"

The belief that emergency care is a special malpractice hazard is so prevalent in medicine that it amounts almost to a folkway. In a Boston University poll of Massachusetts physicians, about 12 percent of the surveyed doctors replied that out of fear of being sued they would refuse to answer the call, "Is there a doctor in the house?" Others said they would answer the call only after waiting a few moments for another physician to volunteer. The A.M.A. asked some 7,500 physicians if fear of a claim makes them unwilling to furnish emergency care away from their office or hospital. Fully 46 percent said they would not stop, and many of those who said they would stop expressed serious concern over the legal risk.

To resolve doctors' apprehensiveness over the risk of suit, California in 1959 passed the nation's first Good Samaritan statute. It provides that "no person . . . who in good faith renders emergency care at the scene of the emergency shall be liable for any civil damages as a result of any acts or omissions." At least thirty-three other states have since enacted similar legislation. The laws vary widely in detail. California's statute does not apply when the physician is "grossly negligent," but New Hampshire's law protects a doctor from any damages. The Massachusetts law is limited to motor vehicle accidents. Indiana's protects only doctors licensed in the state. Montana's applies to anyone who gives first aid in the state, whether doctor or layman. All the laws, whatever their precise provisions, are intended to ease doctors' minds.

These laws have been endorsed by the National Safety Council and the American College of Surgeons. Many other groups have hailed Good

Samaritan statutes as constructive, long-needed measures. But not everyone is enthusiastic about them. Eight state legislatures have voted down Good Samaritan bills, and in Illinois a Good Samaritan statute that passed the legislature was vetoed by the governor.

The major criticism of Good Samaritan laws is that they are unnecessary. Under existing law, a doctor is not expected to render the same caliber of care at the scene of an accident as he could in his office or at a hospital. The standard of care applicable in an emergency is much the same for the physician as it would be for a layman who renders first aid. In most situations this is tantamount to guaranteeing that a court would throw out any negligence suit.

Nor need a doctor fear he will be charged with abandoning an emergency patient if he does not follow up the on-the-spot care. Legal precedents hold that the mere rendering of emergency treatment does not establish a doctor-patient relationship. The physician has no continued obligation that can lead to abandonment. A spokesman for the A.M.A. Law Department has summed it all up: "In a roadside emergency or any similar case there'd be absolutely no special legal risk for the doctor."

Fear of a malpractice suit for care in emergencies thus adds up to what Professor Marcus L. Plant, of the University of Michigan Law School, calls a "legal spook." The A.M.A. Law Department, which ordinarily goes to great lengths to warn doctors of malpractice risks, regards Good Samaritan suits as a phantom threat. An A.M.A. survey of members has produced "only a few" reports of claims arising from Good Samaritan situations. No more than two are reported to have resulted in payments to the claimant. The A.M.A. Law Department considers even these few reports unverified, for after scouring legal records, the department has been unable to find any case or any judgment against physicians growing out of emergency care. Moreover, an A.M.A. inquiry to all major malpractice carriers has found no company that has ever settled a malpractice claim for Good Samaritan services. "It's pretty obvious that such claims have been so rare as to be nonexistent," an A.M.A. attorney has said.

Though the A.M.A. has not taken an official stand on Good Samaritan laws, a spokesman has said: "There's no actual evidence a doctor has ever been required to pay damages for being a Good Samaritan, so we don't really see a necessity for this type of legislation." In New York, the state medical society refused to endorse one attempt to enact a Good Samaritan law. One medical leader—Dr. James E. Donnelly, a member of the Colorado State Senate—helped kill a Good Samaritan bill in his state by declaring: "Let's knock off the malarkey. There's no need for this bill. There's never been a malpractice suit in this state against a physician as a result of his emergency services." And the reasoning given in Governor Otto Kerner's veto of the Illinois Good Samaritan legislation: "This has resulted from literature, widely circulated among doctors, recounting the dire consequences in terms of malpractice litigation that can result from a physician's humanitarian act in rendering emergency roadside care. . . . The attendant danger to the physician is largely, if not wholly, imagined. A systematic inquiry into all of the reported malpractice decisions has failed to disclose a single such 'roadside' instance."

Howard Hassard, executive director and general counsel of the California Medical Association, helped draft the first Good Samaritan law. He did this not out of legal necessity (there is a "relatively small risk of suit," he says) but so that doctors should not be "beset with fears." Hassard thinks he knows the actual case that has caused much of the current worry over litigation following emergency treatment. A surgeon happened to be in a hospital when a mother came in with a little girl who had a broken arm. The surgeon applied a temporary splint and told the mother to take the child to their family physician.

The mother did not follow instructions. The arm healed improperly and the surgeon was sued. He was so irate, recalls Hassard, that he paced up and down the corridors of the courthouse cursing out loud. He also cursed in front of the jury. The result was a $10,000 verdict against him.

"The word spread throughout the medical profession that if you're a Good Samaritan you'll get sued and have a judgment against you," Hassard says. "The fact that this physician behaved as he did never got into print. But his bad temper has probably been the hidden cause of a lot of unnecessary worry about emergency care."

Doctors commonly refuse to respond to an emergency on the grounds that the patient does not fit the doctor's specialty. The A.M.A. Law Department regards such reasoning as specious. "It is a fair assumption," the department has said, "that more knowledge of how to handle a person's emergency medical problem has brushed off on a person who has had four years of medical school plus a year or two of internship than on one who has only had some first aid courses."

Nonetheless, some specialists are unwilling to treat even an accident victim who comes to their office. A gun enthusiast who was target shooting with a rifle accidentally shot a Brooklyn postman in the hand and thigh. The postman subsequently told the following story to the county medical society: He saw a doctor's office. Bleeding from the wounds, he made his way in and told the receptionist, "I'm shot and I need help."

"One moment," the girl replied. "Doctor's with a patient." She called the doctor over the intercom. "There's a postman here who's been shot."

"Tell him I can't help," the doctor said. "I'm an internist with no surgical equipment." He gave her the name of a surgeon to send the postman to.

The postman turned around and limped out. He found a phone and called the police for help. Some weeks later the doctor was suspended for one month by his medical society for failing to treat the injured man. The doctor defended himself, saying, "He wasn't bleeding to death." The doctor, who worked by appointment only, also said it was not his policy to "treat surgical problems or anyone walking off the street."

Just as an internist can be expected to provide emergency treatment for a bullet wound, so some courts say any surgeon should be prepared to deal with cardiac arrest, a known risk of surgery. But according to the allegations in one suit: an ophthalmologist was about to begin surgery on a six-year-old boy to repair crossed eyes when the anesthesiologist called out: "His heart has stopped." The anesthesiologist massaged the boy's heart externally. There was no response. After a minute, he told the ophthalmologist: "The only thing to do is open his chest and massage the heart manually. You'll have to do it quickly." Brain cells are the first to die, and danger of permanent brain damage is increased by every second of delay beyond three minutes in restoring circulation.

The ophthalmologist hesitated. Some time earlier, the county medical society had presented lectures, movies, and demonstrations on the procedure. They were presented not only to members of the society but also to specialist groups such as ophthalmologists. Plaques with directions for handling this emergency were placed in every operating room in the county. But the ophthalmologist said: "I'm not qualified for that kind of surgery."

He rushed from the operating room and found a general surgeon, who came into the operating room and got the boy's heart beating again. The general surgeon had never done an open-chest massage before either. By this time the brain had been damaged. As a result, the boy is now blind, mute, and totally paralyzed.

EMERGENCY DISSERVICE

The police in Suffolk County, New York, tried to find a doctor for a man who had suffered a heart attack. They phoned more than twenty doctors. None were available.

Before a doctor was finally reached, the man died. A medical society officer said he thought the emergency-call system was working "very well," and the police neglected to use it. But local police said: "This sort of thing happens about once a month."

Few communities are well organized for handling emergencies. While many county medical societies have after-hours emergency services, these generally are informal arrangements. Typically, an answering service keeps a list of physicians willing to see patients who have no doctor or cannot reach their regular doctor.

In only a rare emergency-call system are doctors assigned to coverage. The system tends to fall apart on weekends and holidays, when few physicians are available, and almost none are willing to take patients other than their own. Even if a system starts out working well, it is likely to soon become overburdened. Physicians tend to slip up on arranging their own after-hours coverage with colleagues, figuring that the society's emergency service can handle any calls.

If unable to locate a doctor, patients often turn to the emergency room of a nearby hospital. But because of overcrowding and understaffing, emergency rooms often have inadequate coverage. Good practice dictates that any emergency patient be treated within fifteen minutes of his arrival at a hospital. After surveying 325 emergency rooms for the American College of Surgeons, Dr. Robert Kennedy found that even in hospitals with house staffs, emergency patients often suffer delays of thirty to sixty minutes.

Occasionally, a patient does not get treated at all. One case where this was alleged goes as follows: Around five o'clock one morning a New Yorker we'll call Mr. Grady awoke perspiring and pale, with severe pains in his chest and arms. His wife found him standing at an open window with his mouth open, trying to gulp as much air as he possibly could. She helped him dress. Slowly they made their way three blocks to the hospital. In the emergency room, Mrs. Grady told the nurse in charge: "I think my husband is having a heart attack."

Mr. Grady mentioned that he was insured with the medical-coverage program H.I.P. (Health Insurance Plan), which maintained an independent treatment center in the hospital complex.

"The hospital has no connection with H.I.P. and does not take care of H.I.P. patients," the nurse said. "But," she offered, "I'll try to get you some H.I.P. doctor."

She located one and Mr. Grady described his symptoms to him. Their conversation is in dispute. The doctor says that he offered to come to the hospital, but that Grady said he felt better and preferred to see his regular doctor. The allegation charges that the doctor replied: "Go home and come back when H.I.P. is open, at eight o'clock and you can see your regular doctor." The charge continues:

"I could be dead by eight o'clock," Mr. Grady said.

"Please," Mrs. Grady said to the nurse. "Can't a doctor examine my husband. It's an emergency."

"Come back at eight," the nurse told the couple. "A doctor will see you then."

"I could be dead by eight," Mr. Grady repeated.

Giving up on getting treatment at the hospital, Mr. and Mrs. Grady left and walked home, pausing frequently to let Mr. Grady catch his breath. At home, Mrs. Grady was helping her husband undress when he fell to the floor. Before a doctor came, he was dead. It was an hour and a half before eight.

Many emergency rooms are supervised by private practitioners on call from their homes. Such a system of emergency care often breaks down, especially when the doctor on call attempts to manage a case by phone.

Dr. Charles E. Letourneau, a hospital consultant, tells of a G.P. on call who was phoned in the middle of the night and asked how to treat a cut hand. The doctor gave unclear instructions, and the emergency room got them wrong. The hand is now paralyzed.

Sometimes a doctor on emergency call deserts a patient by sending him away without providing for his care. One California G.P. came from his home to the emergency room to treat a man who had suffered a head wound in a car accident. The doctor decided to send the patient to a neurosurgeon at another hospital for x-rays. However, he did not inform the other hospital that the patient was arriving.

Had he called, he would have learned no neurosurgeon was available. As it was, the patient was subjected to an unnecessary seventeen-mile ambulance trip and was dead on arrival. The doctor was found not negligent. But a court reviewing the case commented: "To us, as laymen, the handling of the decedent is shocking, even though it may not have caused the death in this particular case. He was shipped off, unattended by any qualified nurse or doctor, and with no instructions to the ambulance crew."

Emergency care was also withheld in a case with strong racial overtones. Testimony in a successful suit related this account: A forty-two-year-old veteran had lost his left eye and forearm in World War II. Now, in a brawl, a bullet entered the stump of his arm, tearing away an artery. He bled profusely on the street and in the ambulance. At the community hospital, ambulance attendants carried him into the emergency room. There one of the nurses merely looked at him and walked away. The veteran was a Negro, and this was Mississippi.

Blood streamed from his arm to the floor, forming a puddle over two feet in diameter. After about twenty minutes, another nurse came. She too looked at him, then walked away. Finally, the nurse in charge of the emergency room took the wounded man's blood pressure and pulse. She called a doctor from home. He arrived half an hour later. Meanwhile the nurse placed a towel on the wound to soak up the blood, but made no attempt to stop the bleeding.

The doctor looked at the wound but did not try to stop the flow of blood either. On learning the injured man was a veteran, he recommended transfer to a veterans' hospital. "I'll arrange for an ambulance," he told the nurses, and left.

Although the wonded man had not stopped bleeding, the nurses did not again check his blood pressure, nor did the doctor ask about it. Thus they were not alerted to the sharp drop in pressure that would indicate his going into shock. The man's skin became cold and clammy. He sweated heavily and pleaded for water. He asked to see his little boy.

The first medical attention he received was at the VA hospital, more than two hours after he had been brought to the community-hospital emergency room. He died soon after. An autopsy showed he had bled to death.

"ACCEPT PERSONAL RESPONSIBILITY"

The medical emergency most families are familiar with surrounds the birth of a baby. The courts view the patient's relationship with an obstetrician as ending only after the infant's arrival. If the doctor plans not to attend the delivery, he needs to give reasonable notice or provide a competent physician in his place. The patient is entitled to be properly attended and, say the courts, she must not be abandoned.

In a rural area, a woman has alleged in a suit that she was abandoned by her doctor an hour before delivery. Her complaint sets forth these details: She went into labor on June 18. Her husband got in touch with the doctor. "Your wife won't deliver until July 2," the doctor told him.

The labor pains continued through the afternoon and evening. About 1 A.M. on June 19, the doctor examined her. "This baby isn't coming before July 2," he said.

However, the pains became more frequent and severe. Again the doctor was urged to come. He refused, once more saying the baby was not due for nearly a week.

Now the woman felt the delivery beginning. Her husband went to the doctor and begged him to come. The doctor refused, and added: "I'm not going to have anything more to do with the case."

In panic, the charge continues, the husband drove to a town thirteen miles distant trying to find another doctor. While he was out, the woman had the baby—alone, and with nothing done to relieve the pain. For more than an hour, until a doctor returned with her husband, she remained attached to the baby by the umbilical cord.

Abandonment can also take place if a physician incautiously relegates a patient to the administrative machinery of a hospital or other institution. Dr. Frank B. Berry, assistant secretary of defense in charge of health and medical affairs has condemned this tendency of some doctors: "Every doctor must always accept decision and personal responsibility and owes it to his patient to treat him as he would like to have himself or a member of his family treated. Whether it be for simple vaccination or major surgery, he should ensure that every safeguard possible has been provided and not leave it to the enfolding arms of the organization."

In a case of organizational buck-passing cited by Dr. Berry, a sixteen-year-old boy underwent a tonsillectomy. The nurse in charge looked at him and then went to lunch. When she came back he was dead of respiratory failure. The anesthetist said that he took no responsibility for the patient after handing him over to the nursing staff. The coroner's comment: "I would have thought the common-sense view was that the person responsible for making a person unconscious should have been responsible for him until unconsciousness wore off." In a similar allegation resulting in a verdict for the plaintiff:

A five-year-old Minnesota boy was abandoned to hospital routine by a doctor treating the boy's broken leg. "Discharge the boy and allow him to go home," the doctor told a nurse. But he neglected to note the order in the boy's chart, and the nurse did not carry out the oral instructions.

This took place on the last day of June. On the first day of July, a new rotation of interns and residents came into the boy's ward. None were aware that he should have been discharged. Nor, since he was listed as having an attending physician, did any of the house staffers feel responsible for him.

For nearly two weeks, the boy did not get proper medical attention. Only a phone call from his parents alerted the doctor to the fact that he was still in the hospital. By this time, the boy's leg had been in traction long enough to cause severe pressure sores and loss of circulation. The ulcer and dead tissue exposed tendons on his foot and left a raw area two and a half inches in diameter. Skin grafts and other surgery were required over the next year. In the end the foot sustained permanent disability of 40 percent.

Letting the patient slip into the care of an unqualified person is another form of abandonment. A malpractice suit was successfully prosecuted from a charge that went as follows: During an office visit, a Tennessee doctor prescribed an antibiotic for 22-month-old Kevin, who suffered from a mild throat inflammation. Within an hour after taking the medication the child had a sharp reaction, apparently from a drug allergy. Kevin's mother rushed him back to the doctor's office. The doctor was out, but over the phone his office assistant repeated what the mother had told her of the boy's condition. By now Kevin was unconscious and breathing heavily.

"How does he look to you?" the doctor asked.

"About the same as when he was here earlier," the woman replied.

"In that case I'll have my lunch before coming back to the office."

Kevin was left in the care of the receptionist, who lacked even first-aid training. After about half an hour, the unconscious child vomited while lying on his back. With the receptionist looking on, Kevin's mother picked him up. A physician or nurse would guard against holding the child upright, for this position causes vomit to drain into the lungs. The receptionist also did not know to turn Kevin on his stomach and use her finger or a syringe to extract the vomit from his mouth. As she watched, the boy's breathing grew faint and his lips became blue.

She had the presence of mind to call the doctor and describe to him what was happening. Normal procedure would be for the doctor to give emergency instructions over the phone so that help could begin at once. Instead, this doctor made a dash for the office. Before he got there, Kevin had choked to death.

Patients are further abandoned through faulty postoperative care. The Principles of Medical Ethics state that a physician "having undertaken the care of a patient may not neglect him." A persistent group of offenders are found among "itinerant surgeons." These doctors travel to distant areas, perform the surgery, and leave the patient in the charge of another physician.

The Board of Regents of the American College of Surgeons condemns the practice, for it often leaves delicate postoperative care in the hands of a physician who "by training and experience is not fully qualified to undertake it." Itinerant surgery also is often a method of fee splitting. The itinerant surgeon gets the case, and the referring doctor gets the fee for the postoperative work.

Except where the patient's life would be endangered if he were moved, the College of Surgeons prefers that the surgery be performed at a hospital where the surgeon can supervise the aftercare. The Regents have voted to discipline members who, through itinerant surgery, engage in a practice which "subordinates the welfare of a patient to the surgeon's personal advantage or profit." The A.C.S.'s blanket ban on itinerant surgery has been challenged in respect to patients who cannot afford to travel to the nearest surgeon's hospital. But even medical leaders who feel the A.C.S. is hypercritical agree that itinerant surgeons should not perform an operation unless they are confident that the patient will get adequate aftercare.

Some surgeons keep too busy to give postoperative patients proper attention. One doctor used to remove tonsils and adenoids with record speed and would schedule a number of T & As a day. One morning he operated on a ten-year-old girl. Shortly after the operation she began to hemorrhage. But the doctor was already in another operating room with another patient. He could not come to the girl immediately, and she died.

When the case came to court, the surgeon sought to excuse himself by saying that he was busy doing another operation. "I must have operated on about twelve children that morning," he said in court. The jury found against him, feeling that the girl's postoperative need should have been "reasonably anticipated."

After the patient leaves the hospital, a surgeon is obligated to exercise the same care in performing necessary treatments as he did during the actual operation. This entails frequent examinations to keep post-surgical developments under supervision. Courts have ruled that a surgeon cannot abandon a patient to the accidents of random healing. According to the charge in one suit:

A woman suffering a prolapsed uterus underwent a hysterectomy. When she was discharged from the hospital, her surgeon told her, "Come to my office for a checkup at the end of six weeks."

During this interval the doctor did not examine the site of the operation. Only after the woman came to him a month and a half after the surgery did he discover that the hysterectomy had healed abnormally. Her vagina had grown together and was almost entirely closed.

"We probably could have avoided this," the woman's husband testified the surgeon later admitted. "If I'd examined her sooner I would have seen it."

PART V

Negligence and
Incompetence

IN ASSAULT AND abandonment cases, the physician's skills are seldom at issue—merely that he wrongfully proceeded or equally wrongfully
withheld his services. But in cases of incompetence and negligence the
doctor's skills *are* seriously in question. A significant number of physicians
fall below the prevailing standard of performance. They are unqualified
for the services they attempt, or their carelessness causes injury to the patient.

15
The Toll of Ignorance

A TWENTY-FIVE-YEAR-OLD MAN with a high school diploma was looking around Detroit for a profitable line of work. He hit upon the practice of medicine.

To prepare himself he read a few medical books and sat in on some medical school lectures. By putting on a white coat he was able to walk into hospitals and observe surgical procedures. After a month or so of study he bought the practice of a deceased physician and hung out his shingle.

He specialized in internal medicine and treated patients for diabetes and diseases of the heart and lungs. He wrote about twenty prescriptions daily. For four years his practice flourished, and he earned more than $100,000. By the time he was caught he was grossing over $1,000 a week.

The deception might never have come to light had he not applied for medical malpractice insurance. In a routine check, the insurance company learned that he had not been to medical school and did not have a license to practice medicine. The company informed the authorities, and his patients had to find a new doctor. This case illustrates a critical reason for medical discipline: Patients often cannot judge a physician's competence.

The public needs protection not only from medical impostors but also from grossly negligent M.D.s. Some laymen posing as physicians are not noticeably less capable than, apparently, one M.D. against whom the following was alleged in court: He claimed he specialized in the treatment of diseases of the rectum. But before surgery for the relief of an anal fissure, he failed to take the routine precaution of ordering the patient an enema. He operated with dirty instruments. On at least one occasion, he failed to complete an uncomplicated rectal operation but sent the patient home as if he had. His license was ultimately revoked for incompetence.

Enforcement of a high standard of medical competence is not helped by existing licensing laws. In most states, the mere possession of a medical license legally entitles a physician to perform any medical procedures, however unqualified he may actually be. One retired G.P. in his eighties is nearly blind and has long since lost touch with medicine. But he has kept up his medical license by paying an annual registration fee. He is amused at the fact that he can legally do brain surgery.

181

With such carte blanche, most physicians are restrained mainly by their conscience and judgment as to what procedures they will attempt. The threat of a malpractice suit gives a doctor added incentive to stay in his medical depth. Should that retired G.P. try his hand at brain surgery it could cost him a great deal of money. If he were sued for negligence, he would most likely lose on the ground that he fell below the level of acceptable practice.

Malpractice litigation is not wholly effective as a protection against incompetence. For one thing, it is after the fact. A lawsuit can be brought only after damage to a patient is already done. For the patient already injured, curbing the defendant is largely academic. Moreover, it is questionable how much an unqualified physician is actually deterred by fear of suit. His license will be unaffected whatever the malpractice verdict. Even physicians who have been scathingly denounced by the courts for gross negligence are still in practice.

Furthermore, the courts do not generally enforce a high caliber of medicine. They benefit incompetents as well as all other physicians through a by and large lenient interpretation of acceptable standards of skill. The first rule of negligence law is that the physician is in no way expected to guarantee a good result. In 1897 William Howard Taft, then a U.S. Circuit Court judge, expressed the classic affirmation of this doctrine: "If . . . a failure to cure were held to be evidence, however slight, of negligence on the part of the physician or surgeon causing the bad result, few would be courageous enough to practice the healing art, for they would have to assume financial liability for nearly all the ills the flesh is heir to."

Taft thus recognized that in medicine things happen that the physician is not to blame for. A doctor may make the usual allergy checks, but the patient's taking of a heretofore harmless aspirin tablet can cause death from an unrevealed hypersensitivity. An orthopedist exercises great skill in setting a fracture; yet particles of bone marrow can enter the patient's bloodstream and fatally block the heart. An anesthesiologist may take every normal precaution. Even so, the administration of a general anesthetic carries a 1 in 5,000 risk that the patient will unforeseeably die.

"Medicine is indeed a hazardous profession," writes Dr. Joseph F. Sadusk, Jr., an authority in medical law, "and the yearly advances in the diagnosis and treatment of disease, despite the overall benefit to mankind, burden the physician with the danger of serious and irreparable damage to the patient in spite of the utmost care."

The traditional judicial view of the physician-patient relationship is that the patient ultimately bears the consequences of his illness. The problem is his, and he seeks the physician's aid in combating it. The doctor for his part represents by implication that he possesses the ordinary skill and learning common to local physicians in the same field of practice.

Courts will clear a doctor of negligence if he meets merely the *lowest* acceptable standard of performance. Here the courts are more lenient with doctors than most other defendants. Ordinarily, in setting the grade of performance required of the "average man," the courts apply the yardstick of the average *prudent* man. "This is 'up the scale' from the average," observes William J. Curran, director of Boston University's Law-Medicine Research Institute and a member of the Harvard Law School faculty. "Yet for professionals we seem to be satisfied with average or minimum acceptable conduct." Curran adds that "just in case even this standard is considered too high," most courts further weight the scales of justice in favor of the doctor by considering where he practices. He is required to exercise only that skill ordinarily possessed in his or a similar community.

Most negligence verdicts turn on whether the defendant met this modest standard in his alleged act of malpractice. The standard the defendant is held to is likely to be still further reduced, shrunken on the basis of testimony by sympathetic local colleagues. (See Chapter 23, "Conspirators in Silence.") Some courts grant the defendant so much freedom of judgment that if he can produce *any* defensible authority for his act he will be held not negligent.

Thus many doctors escape legal liability for negligence even though they attempt procedures beyond their competence and continue to act in excess of their qualifications. "Unfortunately," says an official of the American College of Surgeons, "some doctors—either to save face or to make more money—will refuse to accept their limitations. They do not call for help when it is needed. They undertake procedures for which they are not trained."

Dr. Paul R. Hawley of the College of Surgeons once declared that no one has a "moral right" to undertake any procedure if he is not competent to deal with "any situation he may encounter." Dr. Hawley suggested that physicians apply a kind of Golden Rule to the procedures they attempt: If they would not do it unto themselves, they should not do it unto a patient.

Except in an emergency, there is little need for a physician to treat a condition he is not competent to handle. Isolation, formerly the excuse for low-caliber rural medicine, has ended with the development of high-speed highway travel. Many medium-sized cities have become centers of first-rate skills and facilities. Virtually every member of the population thus has specialty services within less than a two-hour drive. "In this day of rapid transportation and communication," one court has said, "there appears to be no reason why enlightened medicine with much of its improved practices and facilities should not be available to all."

There is, however, at least one reason: The doctor who is incompetent for a procedure often does not refer the patient to a qualified man.

OVER THEIR HEADS

"No one five years out of medical school is competent to practice medicine on the basis of only what he learned in medical school and in his hospital internship."

So said Dr. Roger I. Lee, former chairman of the board of the A.M.A. and a president of the American College of Physicians. But according to an estimate of the American Academy of General Practice, no more than 20 percent of practicing G.P.s take any kind of continuing education. A significant number of specialists similarly continue to practice largely the medicine they originally learned.

Not unusual is one doctor who was a top student in medical school. From his internship he went into the wartime Army Medical Corps. There he was conscientious about staying abreast of medicine. He resolved that he would still keep up with medical changes after he set up practice in civilian life.

But almost from the day he hung out his shingle he was busy. Between his general practice and his family and social commitments, he has found almost no time to take postgraduate study. Dr. Mahlon Delp, chairman of the Advisory Committee on Continuing Medical Education, has said that the "original attainments of the medical student must be constantly renewed and replenished."

Yet the doctor in question has lost the sharp edge of his interest in medicine. The A.M.A. annual meeting, with its extensive scientific program, has been held in his city several times. He has not been to the recent ones. His knowledge of drugs comes chiefly from pharmaceutical detailmen, the salesmen who visit him to promote the prescribing of their company's products. He cannot remember the last medical text he bought. He finds all but the most general medical journals increasingly difficult to read.

Mentally this doctor is isolated from much of today's medical progress. To visit his office is to step back medically in time. His knowledge has increased little in twenty or more years, and he has grown rusty at that. This doctor is affable and he works long hours. Nonetheless he has become a medical Rip Van Winkle.

A woman who had an enlarging abdomen charges she came to one such doctor. Continues her allegation: To see if she were pregnant, he relied on the traditional digital examination. After feeling her uterus with his fingers, he assured her, "You're going to have a baby." Months later the patient underwent an operation for the removal of a uterine cyst. By this time it had grown to over two pounds and made surgery difficult.

The woman contends that this doctor was negligent by being behind the times in his methods. To corroborate pregnancy, she maintains, he should have used a rabbit test, an accurate procedure that had long since become standard. An appeals court reversed a judgment for the doctor and ordered a new trial on the question of negligence. Observed the court: "The physician must have due regard for the advances in medical and surgical science."

Conversely, a suit against another physician charges that he overestimated his ability to perform a relatively new diagnostic procedure. The doctor was visited by a man who suffered from thrombophlebitis, a circulatory obstruction, in the lower calf of his left leg. According to the patient's complaint: The doctor advised an aortogram, which entails the surgical injection of a dye into the aorta for x-ray studies of blood vessels. Because an aortogram is hazardous, it is generally done by a specialist skilled in translumbar aortography. Even then, other procedures are often tried first, with the aortogram done only as a last resort. Details of the charge go on:

This doctor was inexperienced in aortography. He neglected to take elementary precautions against an adverse reaction. Physicians trained in the field ordinarily take preoperative x-rays and perform allergy tests. This doctor merely anesthetized his patient and with no safeguards began injecting him with a six-inch needle.

Good practice calls for first inserting an empty needle, then with suction checking if the blood vessel has actually been penetrated. This doctor went in directly with the dye. Despite perhaps a dozen tries, he never found the aorta. Instead he injected the dye into the patient's spinal cavity, spinal column, and bloodstream. In the process, the doctor ruptured the blood vessels around the man's spinal cord.

When the patient regained consciousness, he was suffering excruciating pain in the lower part of his body. His bladder was paralyzed and he was unable to urinate. "What's wrong?" the patient asked.

"Don't worry," said the doctor. "This didn't happen because of the aortogram and it isn't serious." The doctor did nothing to diagnose or treat the condition.

Seventy-two hours after the operation the patient was in critical condition. He could not move his body or control any organs or limbs from his midsection to his toes. A permanent paralysis was setting in, but the doctor failed to call in specialists who might help arrest the injury. Without referring the patient to another physician, the doctor withdrew from the case.

The patient thus stranded is now a permanent invalid. Both his legs are paralyzed and he has no control over his bladder and bowels. He suffers from extreme arthritis. The continuous pain he is in cannot be relieved with drugs.

The treatment of fractures is an area in which some doctors are especially likely to exceed their limitations. Broken bones are common and are often repaired by G.P.s and general surgeons. But simple fractures can cause complex problems warranting the care of an orthopedist. Yet nonorthopedists have continued treating unsuccessful fracture repairs long after the patient should have been referred to a specialist.

An unqualified physician may merely apply a cast where an orthopedist would perform surgery. In one case involving complicated fractures, x-rays showed a man had broken both the tibia and fibula, the bones of the lower leg. Without consulting an orthopedist, the doctor simply applied a plaster cast and told the man to stay in bed for a month.

After the doctor took more x-rays, he assured the patient, "Your recovery is proceeding satisfactorily. A good callus is forming and you're coming along fine."

"But," complained the patient, "my leg hurts and feels sore."

The doctor applied an electric heating pad. "Don't worry," he said. "You're doing fine."

For over a month the patient found that standing on the leg was extremely painful. The doctor took another x-ray. Again he told the man, "The fractures are coming along fine."

Unsatisfied, the patient consulted another doctor. From x-rays, he found that the broken ends of the tibia were not united, and very little callus was forming. Prompt surgery, he told the patient, was the only way of correcting this condition to avoid a permanent deformity.

"HALF THE OPERATIONS"

During an operation for an abdominal hernia, a surgeon accidentally cut the patient's large intestine. Thus begins the charge in a lawsuit, which proceeds as follows: He sewed the patient up without repairing the cut. "I may have nicked an intestine," the doctor said. "Don't worry about it." But instead of healing, the incision was pouring forth fluid. The discharge worsened, soaking the gauze dressing. A week after the operation, the nurse noted on the patient's hospital chart: "Much draining with appearance of feces."

Without examining the dressings and without performing corrective surgery or calling in a consultant, the charge continues, the doctor let the patient go home. Some days later, during an office visit, the doctor saw that the drainage was so persistent that the stomach band holding the dressings was too soiled to keep the gauze in place. The doctor directed his nurse to wrap a cloth strip around the patient's abdomen. This kept the dressings in close contact with the skin. The dressings were soaked with the drainage, which was made up largely of digestive juices. Already, from constant exposure to these acids, the skin around the incision was raw and inflamed. The doctor damaged the tissue still further. He placed a large piece of adhesive tape directly over the wound.

For weeks the condition worsened. The doctor readmitted the patient to the hospital. But he did not add to the treatment. "You're going to have to do something," the patient had told him.

Now, according to the allegation, the doctor made a confession. It is asserted that he admitted to the patient: "I don't know what to do."

Dr. Paul Hawley, of the American College of Surgeons once said: "One half of the surgical operations in the United States are performed by doctors who are untrained, or inadequately trained, to undertake surgery." The doctors he was speaking of are for the most part general practitioners who have received little training in surgery.

A battle rages continually within the medical profession as to what, if any, surgical privileges G.P.s should be allowed in hospitals. Some hospitals classify surgery as major or minor and allow G.P.s to do only minor surgery. But, declare most surgical specialists, minor surgery simply does not exist. "All surgical procedures are hazardous," Dr. Joseph Sadusk has said. "All operations are serious and carry with them an irreducible number of complications."

As an example of minor surgery that might turn out to be major, Dr. Robert S. Myers cites the removal of a mole on the leg. Sometimes the mole proves to be a malignant melanoma, a cancerous growth that defies the capabilities of most G.P.-surgeons. While administrative assistant of the American College of Surgeons, Dr. Myers recommended abolishing the major/minor classification of surgery, saying it was "based on the erroneous assumption that surgery comes in certain sizes, like pajamas." Dr. Myers adds: "All surgery should be considered of major significance, and the physician permitted to do surgery should be qualified by training, experience and ability."

Even the commonest surgical procedures—appendectomies, hernia repairs, gallbladder operations—can be risky. Because these operations are usually simple, they are often the surgical stock in trade of G.P.s. But experienced only with the routine conditions, the nonspecialist often cannot handle the inevitable unusual case. One G.P. used to say, "Any fool can take out an appendix." Then, during an appendectomy, he could not find it. He searched inside the patient for two hours. Finally he sent for the help of a surgeon. "A physician should accept only such cases as are well within his ability to handle," the medicolegal authority Dr. Louis J. Regan has said, "and he must thereafter give such care as the case requires."

One distinguished surgeon has said that at least half his practice consists of attempts to correct the bad results of surgery by untrained doctors. Even surgical specialists sometimes go beyond their competence. Board-certified surgeons generally have unlimited hospital privileges in their specialty—a urologist may perform any procedure in urology, an ophthalmologist any eye surgery, and so on. Dr. Charles V. Letourneau, a hospital consultant, argues that such blanket privileges invite surgeons to do work beyond their qualifications.

"It has been noted that some board-certified surgeons fail to keep up to date with the latest developments," Dr. Letourneau has remarked. Furthermore, he says, some surgeons dedicate a lifetime to perfecting one or two operations in a particular region of the body. "It is travesty for a surgeon untrained in such operations to attempt them."

One surgeon in California lost a negligence suit that charged he went beyond his training in claiming he could treat severe burns, although he was not certified by the American Board of Plastic Surgeons and had never treated a third-degree burn case. The following were details of the plaintiff's allegations: Six-year-old Alan (not his real name) suffered extreme burns while playing Superman. His mother took him to the emergency room of a small proprietary hospital. Alan was admitted in serious condition. Eighteen percent of his body was charred. There were third-degree burns on the right side on his face, on his right arm, and on more than half his chest and back.

Infection is the cardinal problem and main cause of death in burn cases. A mild burn can grow in severity as a result of infection, and a burn patient is so vulnerable that he can become infected merely by a person's exhaling in his room. Thus, burn patients should be placed in isolation where no one may enter except under sterile conditions. But. Dr. Black (as we'll call the chief surgeon of the hospital) had Alan placed in an open ward with nine other beds.

Specialists in the treatment of burns agree that every three or four days dressings on burns should be changed and antibiotics applied. Dr. Black changed Alan's dressings only once every twelve days. Plastic surgeons ordinarily try to start skin grafts within two weeks of the accident. An early skin graft reduces the possibility of scars, prevents infection, and has a better chance of a "take." If skin grafts are delayed, a thick layer of scar tissue will form and contractures—abnormal shortening and distortion of tissues—will develop.

But Dr. Black did not perform any skin grafts for over a month. By that time, contracture was already setting in and scar tissue had begun to form. Dr. Black performed only one graft in the fifty-three days that Alan was under his care. It covered merely one percent of the third-degree burn area. Instead of splitting the grafted skin as thin as possible—the accepted procedure—Dr. Black took "full-thickness" skin from Alan's uninjured right thigh. Plastic surgeons call this procedure "passé and unacceptable." Dr. Black placed the skin in small pieces on Alan's right wrist, three fingers of his left hand, and the inner surface of his right elbow. Plastic surgeons later testified that these pieces were "very small postage stamp affairs." The pieces were not large enough and not the right shape to prevent contractures, and they resulted in incomplete takes. A plastic surgeon described the graft on the elbow as "quite inadequate."

In removing the skin from Alan's thigh, Dr. Black caused a further injury, itself similar to a third-degree burn. After fifty-three days under

Dr. Black's care, Alan's third-degree burn area had increased to cover 25 percent of his body. The boy's father recalls: "There was no skin on him."

At last Alan was transferred to a hospital where he could receive competent care. When plastic surgeons began to treat the boy he was suffering from infection. Both hands were disabled by contractures; he had deep scar tissue over much of his body. He needed to undergo six corrective operations. Doctors believe more will be necessary as he grows. Despite the extensive repair work, plastic surgeons feel that Alan will always suffer a deformed right hand and grotesque scarring.

CHARGES OF CONCEALMENT

In 1932, while operating on a woman, a South Dakota doctor allegedly broke a surgical needle in her back. The woman charges he neglected to remove the fragment or mention the accident to her or her family.

Nearly twenty-one years later, after the embedded fragment caused the woman discomfort, it was discovered and removed. The woman brought a malpractice action against the surgeon. He argued that his state's two-year statute of limitations had long since run out and hence he was legally safe from suit.

The trial judge agreed with the doctor and dismissed the suit. An appeals court later ordered a trial to afford the patient the opportunity to prove fraudulent concealment on the doctor's part, ruling that the statute of limitations would be suspended if the doctor fraudulently concealed the injury and the patient could reasonably be expected to discover it. The trial court's verdict, however, shows why some doctors are tempted to conceal their errors. Statutes of limitations are designed to eliminate fraudulent and stale claims that would otherwise constitute a sword over the doctor's head. They operate against those who "sleep on their rights."

But on some malpractice victims the statutes of limitations work a hardship. In only five states does the limiting period begin when the patient learns of the injury (or, using common sense, should have discovered it). In most states an adult must bring suit within two years following the treatment. Otherwise he may be disqualified from suing despite his unawareness of his injury.

Thus after suffering possible negligence at the hands of a physician a patient may not learn of it if the doctor, through his silence, hopes to avoid suit. A successful negligence suit was brought by a Michigan laborer suffering an inability to urinate. According to his allegations: A doctor inserted into the patient's urinary tract a tube with a steel-capped needlelike attachment called a filiform. This device was intended to relieve a constriction in the tract and allow urine to pass unobstructed.

When the doctor removed the tube, he found that a length of the filiform had broken off inside the patient. But he said nothing about the breakage. Nor did he take any steps to remove it. The patient was in pain and continued to experience difficulty urinating. He found relief only after consulting a university hospital, where doctors discovered the fragment in his bladder and removed it.

Where an error is obvious, some doctors attempt to conceal its seriousness. In one suit, the allegation is as follows: A California physician gave an injection for the treatment of shingles. Fifteen minutes later, the patient felt a burning sensation in his left arm. His thumb and three fingers of his hand became numb and partially paralyzed.

The doctor looked at the hand and said: "I want to have you examined by another doctor." He called in his associate. The patient testifies the two physicians "just kind of shook their heads and didn't know."

"Come back in about a month," he says the first doctor told him. Now, some weeks later, the doctor again examined the patient's hand. "There isn't much we can do about it," he asserts the doctor said. "It will take about a year. The nerves will grow the thickness of a hair each week. In about a year you'll see improvement."

The patient charges he waited out the year without finding any improvement. Indeed, the disability and deformity worsened. When he returned to the doctor at the year's end, he was informed that the paralysis in his left hand was permanent.

"The only thing we can do is call the insurance company and try to get him a settlement," he says the doctor remarked to his associate. But no compensation for the patient was arranged. The state has a one-year statute of limitations for malpractice actions.

When the patient sued, the trial court entered a summary judgment for the doctors, ruling that the patient was barred from filing suit because the year had run out. On appeal, however, a higher court found that the doctors were not entitled to a summary judgment and that it was triable whether they had misrepresented the seriousness of the injury by treating it casually and speaking of the likelihood of its being cured. Thus, the court ruled, the statute of limitations in this case conceivably did not start until the patient discovered the permanence of his injury.

This decision is one of several that help stop the clock if the doctor attempts fraudulent concealment. "Fraud is repugnant wherever encountered," the Supreme Court of South Dakota has said. But not all the injustices a patient may suffer under a statute of limitations are thus resolved. Courts are reluctant to allow implied exceptions extending the time limits on malpractice suits. Moreover, the burden is on the patient to prove that the doctor fraudulently concealed the injury.

Some doctors not only say nothing to a patient about an error. Despite the continued hazard it may present, they try to keep the patient from finding out about it. This in part was alleged in a suit brought by an Englishwoman, here called Cynthia Densen. While living in this country, she underwent the removal of a breast because of cancer. In sewing her up, the surgeon left a sponge in the muscle of her armpit. This in itself is not necessarily negligent, for Mrs. Densen was going into shock. Speed in getting her off the operating table was justified, even if it meant omitting the sponge count. The allegation continues:

About two months after the operation, Mrs. Densen came to the surgeon for an examination. Her wound was still draining. A notation the doctor made in his records shows he recognized the "possibility of a foreign body in this wound." He added: "X-rays should be obtained."

Mrs. Densen was returning to England in two days. The doctor so far had not knowingly committed negligence. But now he held back from Mrs. Densen the possibility that an object remained inside her. Nor did he x-ray the wound area.

On the day of her departure, Mrs. Densen stopped at the surgeon's office. He gave her a letter for her physician in England. Supposedly an abstract of the patient's case, the letter contained technical details of Mrs. Densen's treatment and condition. But it also contained this deviation from the surgeon's notes: "The prognosis is very excellent and we do not believe that x-ray treatment is indicated."

On the boat for England, Mrs. Densen became feverish. Her wound was draining and painful. Despite the letter from the surgeon, doctors in England decided that x-rays were called for. The film revealed an opaque shadow in the region of the right underarm. Mrs. Densen entered a hospital, where the surgical sponge was removed.

If the original surgeon had acted on his suspicions weeks before, removing the sponge most likely would have been a relatively uncomplicated procedure requiring a short convalescence. As it was, it took half a year for Mrs. Densen to recover from the infection caused by the sponge and from the operation required to remove it. In the malpractice suit growing out of the surgeon's failure to reveal to Mrs. Densen the possibility that she retained a sponge, the trial court commented: "It is unthinkable that a competent surgeon, having a suspicion as to the existence of a foreign body left in the operative wound by him, would permit a patient to leave the country without at least advising the patient of his suspicions."

16
Where Physicians Blunder

In the medicolegal text *Doctor and Patient and the Law*, Dr. Louis J. Regan lists over a hundred grounds for malpractice actions. Some causes of suit are rare—for example, a doctor carried contagion or subjected the patient to involuntary experimentation. This chapter discusses types of negligence that occur almost every day.

Diagnosis is the beginning of medical treatment and the origin of about 10 percent of all medical malpractice suits. One classic case of improper diagnosis involves Boston doctors who removed a man's right kidney. He died almost instantly. The doctors had neglected to notice a birth defect: The patient had only the one kidney. Another lapse in observation occurred in Binghamton, New York. A physician told a jury in a drunken driving case that he had examined the defendant and found him intoxicated. "His eyes were bloodshot, his pupils unresponsive to light," the doctor explained. What the doctor did not notice was that the man had a glass eye.

Such mistakes illustrate "observer error," a major cause of faulty diagnosis. One of the pitfalls medical students are cautioned to guard against is their own bias, which may lead them to see a condition for other than what it is. The obstetrician Dr. Alan F. Guttmacher tells that for years he warned mothers-to-be against riding horseback. It would be harmful to their pregnancy, he said. He had no objections, however, to pregnant women playing tennis. A colleague of Dr. Guttmacher's, on the other hand, allowed horseback riding but forbade tennis. One day the two doctors compared notes and realized why each thought a particular activity was dangerous. Dr. Guttmacher could barely stay on a horse. His colleague played a terrible game of tennis.

One project aimed at classifying schoolchildren according to physiological type ended surprisingly. The data that developed showed that the category a child was placed in was determined not so much by the objective measurements of the child's build as by the doctor's subjective interpretation. Preconceptions thus obstruct diagnosis. "Observer differences exist in the accuracy of measurements of height and weight, the interpretation of the electrocardiogram, and the interpretation of various sorts of x-rays," Dr. H. N. Robson, a medical editor, has written.

Disagreement may prevail not only between different doctors. The same physician may interpret the same finding in conflicting ways on encountering it at different times. "Thus," Dr. Robson adds, "we find our notion of clinical accuracy . . . draining off into a kind of amorphous gray."

At one hospital a study of more than a thousand autopsies has shown that fully 6 percent of the cases had been "clinically misdiagnosed." The study team reported that at least 28 percent of the patients had pertinent signs and symptoms that the doctor "conveniently" ignored, apparently because the findings did not fit a preconceived diagnosis. For example, five patients had unexplained pain, five hemorrhaged, four had unaccounted-for fever. Other patients suffered shock, breathing difficulties, an enlarged spleen. If these signs and symptoms had been taken into account, the study team observed, they would have helped draw a more accurate diagnostic picture and would have made possible more beneficial therapy. But, concludes the study report, in several cases "there was a prejudiced viewpoint or blind spot on the part of the doctor in charge."

Laboratory studies are an essential adjunct of diagnosis, and many misdiagnoses occur because doctors fail to do necessary tests. At the aforementioned hospital, routine tests on admission include a blood count, urinalysis, and chest x-rays. Postmortems showed that not all patients received even this minimum workup. The study team reported that one in eight of the patients incorrectly diagnosed would have almost surely received proper care had merely these routine tests been performed.

In some cases of diagnostic negligence, the laboratory report is available but ignored. While examining a woman who was menstruating heavily, one doctor thought he felt a fibroid tumor in her uterus. He took a hemoglobin test, using a kit with which he matched a sample of her blood to a printed spectrum of shades of red. This method can give only a rough estimate and has long been outmoded by more precise techniques. Trusting the rough test as final, however, the doctor told the woman that her hemoglobin count was low and that she needed to have her uterus removed.

At the hospital, an accurate blood study was performed as part of the admission routine. It showed a normal hemoglobin, and thus no indication for a hysterectomy. But the doctor neglected to look at the lab report before he operated. While performing the hysterectomy he inadvertently cut a ureter, the duct that carries urine from the kidney to the bladder. The kidney could not be saved.

The extracted uterus went to the hospital laboratory for analysis. There the hospital pathologist found it normal. He reported that the woman had lost a kidney in an operation that had no justification in the first place.

Diagnostic negligence can occur where the patient should be kept under surveillance because he is likely to develop some pathological condition. The law considers a doctor negligent if he fails to keep watch through proper tests. In one successful malpractice suit, the jury found that a Virginia pediatrician failed to make needed follow-up studies while caring for a newborn girl who was in danger of a reaction from a blood incompatibility. The infant's blood was Rh-positive, her mother's was Rh-negative. During the trial, witnesses for the patient related the following account:

Tests during pregnancy showed that mother and child had incompatible blood and that a dangerous interreaction was taking place. The mother's condition became so severe that labor was prematurely induced. The hazard in cases like this is that the fetus's Rh-positive cells may filter through the placenta into the mother's bloodstream. The alien cells cause the mother to develop antibodies which destroy them. The antibodies also circulate back through the placenta and attack blood cells in the unborn infant. To eliminate the dead cells from the bloodstream, the child's liver produces excessive amounts of bile. Bile can destroy brain tissue, and the overall condition, erythroblastosis fetalis, often leads to brain damage in the newborn. If detected in time, the condition can generally be corrected through an exchange transfusion in which the baby's blood is replaced with healthy blood.

Now, fifty hours after the infant girl was born, she developed jaundice. This is a symptom of erythroblastosis, but it is also a development common in normal newborns. The pediatrician took no special measures, for he relied on tests made a few hours after the child's birth. But these tests were obviously in error—for example, they reported that the child's blood was Rh-negative. A general rule in medicine is that when laboratory tests are inconsistent or contradict the doctor's own finding, the tests should be rerun. However, this pediatrician proceeded on the basis of the erroneous tests and diagnosed the jaundice as benign. Despite further evidence that the baby's jaundice was pathological, he ordered no new tests. He ignored the jaundice and sent the baby home. He did not see her again for three weeks.

Within a week, the infant had a convulsion, a strong symptom of brain damage. Over the months, the jaundice remained and the child had additional seizures, once in the presence of the doctor. Only after nine months, when the mother consulted a neurologist, did she learn that her baby was a hopelessly brain-damaged cripple.

"WHY DIDN'T YOU BRING HER SOONER?"

In negligent diagnosis, a doctor's failure to realize the seriousness of a patient's condition can mean the difference between life and death. The parents of a two-year-old New York girl took her to the hospital, where a doctor found that she had a temperature of 104.2 degrees. She had a fast pulse, enlarged and inflamed tonsils, red throat, running nose, respiratory distress, and abnormal sounds in her chest. Further, a chest x-ray showed an inflammation in the right lower lobe of the lung. The large number of white corpuscles in the child's blood indicated an infection. Continues the plaintiff's evidence in a wrongful-death suit the family won:

The examining physician reported the girl was looking ill to a "mild degree." He did not yet have the results of a throat culture, which would have helped define her condition. Nevertheless, he informed her parents that she was not ill enough to be hospitalized.

At home, the child's condition grew worse, and her family doctor sent her back to the hospital. There she died of staphylococcal pneumonia, the condition ultimately revealed by the throat culture. A surgeon who attended the child informed her parents of her death. "Why didn't you bring her sooner?" he asked them. "I might have been able to save her."

One type of diagnostic procedure, the x-ray, has become so standard that failure to use it may be tantamount to negligence. One court has ruled: "The use of the x-ray as an aid to diagnosis in cases of fracture or other indicated cases is a matter of common knowledge, and the failure to make use thereof in such a case amounts to a failure to use . . . care and diligence."

X-rays are especially called for following falls of elderly people, for the brittle bones of the elderly easily break and quickly degenerate. In one allegation of a failure to take x-rays, a seventy-year-old Pennsylvanian had slipped and fallen in his home. "I heard a crunch in my hip, right where it hurts now," he says he told his family doctor. The doctor, he testifies, merely gave him an injection to ease the pain, and recommended bed rest and massage. His charge goes on:

The pain grew more intense. Eleven days after the fall, the right leg turned outward and became completely paralyzed. At the family's insistence, the elderly man was admitted to a hospital. Here he received his first x-ray. It showed a severe fracture in the right hip, now complicated by large areas of dead tissue. Three operations were needed to set the break. It is asserted that the disability and disfigurement were never relieved.

Diagnostic tests are sometimes performed in a manner so careless as to injure the patient. Illustrative is the successful suit, upheld on appeal, of a six-year-old girl who entered a hospital for a kidney examination. A dye was needed to see the kidneys under x-ray. But the strong concentration the doctors employed was, in the literature of the manufacturer, "not recommended for routine use" and "should be reserved for difficult cases." According to court findings, the following ensued:

The dye was injected into the girl's right hand. Immediately the hand started burning and swelling. For adverse reactions, the manufacturer's literature accompanying the dye recommended diluting the dye at once with a commonly used chemical dispersing agent. Instead, the doctors applied hot compresses to the hand and sent the child home.

That evening she was back at the hospital, her hand blistering and painful. Again she was given mild treatment and sent home. Several days later, her mother noticed that the girl was unable to close her hand. The dye had contracted the tendons of the knuckles, causing the fingers to extend rigidly.

In an attempt to loosen the tendons, the hand was placed in traction, and the girl underwent frequent physiotherapy. Despite these measures, she remained unable to bend her fingers.

A year and a half after the accident, doctors performed an operation on the hand, but improved it only slightly. The hand was still disabled and had not grown normally. It was smaller than the other hand.

WORSE THAN THE DISEASE

Therapeutics is the branch of medical science that deals with the application of remedies. Some three out of four medical malpractice suits spring from questions concerning therapeutic technique. While negligence law does not require physicians to guarantee a cure, the doctor is expected to exercise a reasonable degree of care and use methods that ordinarily meet at least a minimum standard of effectiveness. Some negligence cases are marked by the doctor's failing to do this and thereby producing in the patient a condition worse than the original disease.

The transfusion of blood is among the common procedures where negligence occurs. Some 2,500 Americans die every year from mistakes in transfusions, and blood transfusion accidents alone account for about one percent of all medical malpractice charges. Dr. Lester J. Unger, director of the blood bank of New York University-Bellevue Medical Center, says: "Every bottle of blood is a bottle of dynamite." Dr. Jacob Geiger, chief of the blood bank at New York's Lenox Hill Hospital, has warned physicians against taking transfusions for granted. "So many things can go wrong in the laboratory or at the bedside, Dr. Geiger has said. "Certainly, the blood transfusion technique has improved enormously in recent years. Perhaps for that very reason doctors tend to forget the tremendous medical and legal hazards of blood transfusions."

Such dangers have been impressed upon physicians by what has come to be known as the "$150,000 blood transfusion," the result of a series of errors at a suburban New York hospital. Here is the case as unfolded in the trial and court findings:

A twenty-five-year-old mother of two children—one four months old, the other sixteen months old—was undergoing delicate surgery for a kidney obstruction. In the middle of the operation, a nurse came in with a bottle of blood, which she gave to the anesthetist. The blood was intended for another patient, who had been operated on earlier in the day.

Without checking the label on the bottle—which gave the name of the other patient, his blood type, and the name of his doctor—the anesthetist said to the operating surgeon: "Doctor, I have blood ready for this lady. Shall I give it?"

At this point, the surgeon might have become suspicious. According to hospital procedure, no blood should have come to him without his written order. Indeed, he had been a founder of the hospital's blood bank and had instituted this rule. Now, lawyers contended at the trial growing out of this incident, he should have said, "Blood? What blood? I didn't order any blood." However, he *had* ordered blood—for a recent operation on the same woman. The blood had not been used. Now, even though he had not asked for it, he assumed the bottle was being brought to him again.

Therefore overlooking the irregularity, he replied, "Yes. Give it to her."

The woman, whose own blood type was O-positive, received a transfution of B-positive blood. Within ten hours, she was dead.

Suit was brought against the surgeon and other parties. The jury found against them and voted a verdict of $150,000. While the trial judge reduced the amount to $135,000—on appeal it was settled for $90,000—the case is a landmark. The judgment is thought to be the highest in a medical malpractice suit resulting from the death of a nonworking housewife. One reason the judgment is so large: This is perhaps the first case in which the court allowed expert testimony on the dollar value of a mother's life.

Although the woman had no measurable income or earning capacity, the trial judge reasoned that her death would cause her husband to suffer unusual expenses in bringing up their two small children. The director of a social-work agency testified that the father would need to employ a nurse-governess, a housekeeper, and baby-sitters—all jobs a mother would routinely perform. According to the social worker's formula, the salaries of those mother-substitutes—plus such miscellany as advertising for them, paying social security tax on their earnings, and securing professional guidance—would cost at least $119,000 over twenty years.

Burns account for about 8 percent of all medical malpractice suits. Applying heat to promote circulation is a home remedy so effective that it has a place in the hospital. Despite its simplicity, it requires care. One Florida case illustrates what can happen if doctors overlook the dangers of too much heat. One such allegation, accepted in the trial court and upheld on appeal:

Jessica Lynn (we'll call her) was delivered by cesarean section. She was small, but otherwise normal. About an hour and a half after she was born, Jessica Lynn's left arm turned chalk white, indicating a circulatory obstruction. The doctor who had delivered her wrapped hot towels around her hand and arm. The child began to wail. Instead of being just above body temperature, the towels were steaming hot. A nurse said the water was "as hot as you could get out of the faucet." Still, the doctor told the nurses he wanted the towels even hotter. "I want them steaming hot," he said.

A few minutes after the towels were first applied, color started to return to the baby's hand and arm. The doctor continued to apply the steaming towels, changing them every two minutes. After about fifteen minutes, he directed the nurses to change the towels every ten minutes, and left.

The baby's forearm now appeared normal. But at 12:30 P.M., about three hours after the start of treatment, a blister formed near the baby's wrist. At 2:30 the blister was sufficiently bad for the head nurse to call the doctor and report it. He ordered Vaseline strips applied to it. "Continue the hot towel treatment," he told her. The blister grew. When the doctor returned to the hospital at 5 P.M., he ordered the towel treatment stopped.

Subsequently, the physician told Jessica Lynn's mother: "It's just a slight burn and you won't have anything to worry about."

But the baby's hand and arm had been wrapped in steaming towels for seven and a half hours, despite increasing evidence of burns. Moreover, no special care was given to the baby's tiny thumb and fingers, which would heat more than the arm. Jessica Lynn suffered extensive injury to her left arm and hand. The baby was taken to a surgeon. He found that the application of the extreme heat had resulted in gangrene. The baby's fingers and thumb sloughed off.

Negligence in x-ray therapy is another major cause of burns. Improperly used x-rays can lead to cancerous degeneration of the skin. Other skin damage from x-rays may include atrophy, ulcers, the blockage of blood vessels. The excessive use of x-rays has caused bone deformities in growing children.

Because x-raying can result in such severe damage to tissue, it is ordinarily used only after less hazardous remedies have failed. In some cases of negligence, the doctor uses x-rays to treat minor conditions that would respond well to safer therapy. A man in Illinois consulted a doctor because of a wart on the ball of his left foot. Most doctors attempt to treat such warts by first applying ointment or acid or by removing them surgically in a brief office procedure. In the negligence suit the patient later filed and won, he charged that this doctor exposed the wart right off to x-rays. The following was alleged:

The patient was placed on a table with the sole of his foot toward the x-ray machine. The doctor started the machine. Either the voltage was too high or the machine was left on too long, for the patient suffered adverse effects.

Three weeks after the treatment, his foot was sore. The treated area began to peel off. Ordinarily only the wart would fall away, but now layer after layer of tissue disintegrated. The bones became visible in the wound. A doctor who visited the patient at home recalled: "He was sitting in a chair. The flesh between the big toe and the second toe was gone and the bones were exposed. The ball of the foot and the surrounding structures in the toes were inflamed."

The foot continued to deteriorate. It could not be salvaged and was amputated.

ERRORS IN MEDICATION

The woman was suffering from mumps. She was given a penicillin injection by her doctor. Almost at once she began to feel much worse. She became convulsive, then went into shock. Less than twenty minutes after receiving the injection, she was dead.

The negligence suit charging the above postulated that the woman had been allergic to penicillin. Moreover, it was charged, the injection was unjustified. Penicillin is generally considered useless for treating mumps.

Negligence in administering drugs is "alarmingly common," says George F. Archambault, chief pharmacist of the Public Health Service. Archambault has found that medication mistakes are the leading cause of injuries to hospital patients. Among the commonest accidents associated with the administering of drugs is the breaking of a hypodermic needle in the patient. A needle's breaking does not necessarily signify the doctor's negligence; faulty manufacturing, for example, may have caused the needle to be defective. But some physicians are lax in replacing worn needles. Witnesses testified in court to the following:

Over a fourteen-month period, one doctor gave more than a thousand injections. He used a mere dozen needles, averaging over eighty shots per needle. Good medical practice allows each needle to be used only about five times. One day in mid-injection a needle that had been rendered brittle from over-use broke, becoming lodged in a patient's right buttock.

"Hold still," the doctor said. He probed deeply, but failed to locate the broken tip. The patient was x-rayed, then underwent surgery to remove the missing fragment. The operation was unsuccessful, for the tip lay hidden in tissue. Doctors now brought in a metal detector to locate the fragment. At last it was removed, in another operation.

Irritating an already inflamed blood vessel is another frequent error in injections. In giving injections, physicians are expected to develop a "feel" for the needle. Even though the needle is out of sight in the patient, doctors can generally direct it through a knowledge of anatomy combined with established techniques for injecting different regions of tissue. In some cases of negligence the doctor releases the syringe in the wrong spot and causes a circulatory obstruction. According to one allegation in a successful suit:

A four-year-old southern boy got a penicillin injection for an earache. The shot was given in Mike's left buttock. Almost at once the boy complained of pain in his left leg and foot. That evening, worried by Mike's worsening condition, his mother called the doctor. He responded by having a prescription sent from a drugstore. The mother called again. "He's getting worse," she reported.

The doctor agreed to see the boy. After the examination he assured the mother. "It's only a mild reaction to the penicillin shot. Use hot packs and elevate his feet."

Over the next two days Mike's toes turned blue. The tissues died, and gangrene set in. Mike was put in a hospital. There his toes were removed. He underwent four operations to complete the necessary amputations and skin grafts.

Medical detective work put the blame on the penicillin shot. Instead of being injected into the large muscle of Mike's buttock, the oil-penicillin mixture was thrust into an artery. This mass of oil fluid blocked circulation in the blood vessel much as grease can obstruct a pipe.

WRONG PRESCRIPTIONS

Drug therapy often causes injury because the patient receives the wrong dosage.

Taking the wrong bottle off the shelf is a basic medical error. A fourteen-year-old girl was admitted to a hospital with acute appendicitis. In preparation for emergency surgery, she received a salt solution intravenously. Less than two hours later she was dead, her blood disintegrated from too much salt in her bloodstream. She should have received a 2 percent sodium chloride solution. What the doctor actually administered was a solution of 20 percent. He had not looked carefully at the label.

Overdoses also result from negligence in writing a prescription. Doctors are cautioned to always mark on the prescription blank that a medicine is intended for a child. Adult doses of some medicines can be disastrous if taken by youngsters.

After diagnosing a ten-month-old child's illness as bronchitis, a doctor wrote a prescription for one suppository of the drug aminophylline every four hours. But he neglected to say on the prescription that it was for an infant. The pharmacist filled the prescription from a container whose label warned that children should get no more than one suppository every 24 hours. Since there was no indication that the patient was a child, the druggist in this Washington, D.C., store did not check with the doctor.

The overdose led to destruction of the infant's nervous system. The child has no hope of ever walking or talking, and has lost nearly all sight, hearing and coordination.

For allergic patients, any dose of an allergenic drug is hazardous. A doctor is responsible for making sure the patient suffers no drug allergy, for in a sensitive patient a pharmaceutical can produce a devastating reaction. For example, the effects charged in this case:

During an idle moment, a Kansas office worker was fixing her sunglasses when a lens broke and cut her finger. She was sent to the emergency ward of a nearby hospital. After the wound was cleaned and sutured, a doctor on duty prepared to give her an injection of tetanus antitoxin (TAT). Because she had never had a TAT shot before, she was given a skin test on her upper right arm to see if she was sensitive to horse serum, the fluid in which the antitoxin is transmitted.

Most doctors wait ten to thirty minutes to determine the results of the sensitivity test. This doctor, however, injected 1,500 units of TAT into the patient almost immediately. By the time the woman reached her car, the test area on her arm was showing a severe positive reaction. The spot became red and puffy, and grew in size from a nickel to a half dollar. Soon her muscles were aching and she was suffering a fever and a rash over her body.

Two weeks later she was still ill. A roaring started up in her ears. She made a trip to the Mayo Clinic for diagnosis. There she learned she had lost more than half her hearing, a result of her sensitivity to horse serum. The patient has also suffered a marked personality change. Formerly vivacious, she had been good at meeting people. Now, deaf and distracted, she can hold only a factory job at which she earns only about half her former pay.

Patients often know that they are allergic to specific drugs. One such patient has charged that he repeatedly warned of his sensitivity but his cries were lost as error compounded error in a Philadelphia hospital's routine. The court record of a negligence suit resolved in his favor tells the following story:

This patient, a construction worker, was operating a compressed-air hammer when a nail ricocheted, entering his lower right leg and breaking a bone. A police car took him to the hospital. As soon as he got there, he warned a nurse in the receiving ward: "Don't give me any penicillin. I'm highly allergic to it."

From his wallet he took a note from his family doctor, who had discovered the allergy during a recent illness. The note cautioned that under no circumstances was the patient ever to receive penicillin. The nurse reported this to an intern. The receiving ward personnel were thus alerted to the patient's sensitivity.

Surgery was needed to repair the leg. On duty in the hospital were two doctors who now took over the case. One doctor was a resident physician taking postgraduate work in surgery. The other was a privately practicing surgeon who taught in the hospital's training program. In this capacity, he was expected to supervise any surgery the resident might perform.

Both doctors (it was charged) committed a series of omissions. Neither asked the receiving-ward staff what they had learned of the patient's condition and medical history. Nor did either physician order a penicillin-sensitivity test, a routine precaution. Further, the resident had the patient's history taken by a junior assistant not yet out of medical school. After delegating away this essential step in preoperative procedure, the resident failed to check whether the history had been fully recorded. The supervising surgeon did not detect this lapse, for he neglected to see if a presurgical history and physical examination had been recorded at all. He merely gave his okay for the resident to perform the surgery.

Because of these lapses, neither doctor was alert to a mistake the medical student made while taking the patient's history. The patient, ever mindful of his allergy, was protesting so much against the use of penicillin that the nurses considered him a pest. During the history-taking, he told the medical student of his sensitivity. He also showed the student the family doctor's note of warning.

But, evidently from inexperience, the student did not make a note of the allergy. The chart, accompanying the patient onto the operating floor, thus bore no allergy warning. After putting the cast on the patient's leg, the resident followed standard procedure and ordered that the patient receive 600,000 units of penicillin every four hours.

That night the patient got two shots of the drug. Early in the morning he got a third. He was about to get a fourth, but his objections were so vehement that they reached the ears of the supervising surgeon. The doctor ordered a change to another antibiotic.

Four days later, the patient was discharged from the hospital. He appeared to be making a good recovery. But after two days at home, he broke out in a rash. The next morning he suffered a stroke, resulting in paralysis of the right arm and partial blindness in the right eye.

Another result of the brain damage is a severe mental illness. The patient now suffers from paranoia. While some allergists may challenge the connection, the defense in the ensuing court case did not dispute that the patient's condition was caused by the penicillin. A person who has followed the case said: "His delusions of persecution would not be surprising considering how he fought getting the drug."

UNHEEDED WARNINGS

The more powerful a drug is in combating disease, the more potent its effects are likely to be on other systems of the body. To tell doctors what a drug might do wrong and when it should be avoided, pharmaceutical manufacturers enclose brochures detailing major side effects and contraindications.

Physicians generally believe that pharmaceutical houses overstate a product's virtues and understate its limitations. Careful doctors therefore proceed even more cautiously than the manufacturer's brochure suggests. They take warnings very seriously, especially if they have never used the drug before. However, as held by a jury and affirmed by the courts:

One New Jersey G.P. who failed to heed such warnings was treating a man of forty-eight, hospitalized because of kidney disease. For possible therapy there were at least fifty antibiotics on the market. One of the four most dangerous was neomycin, a drug used mainly for external, relatively safe applications like dressings and ointments. The manufacturer warned that injections of neomycin should be attempted only after safer drugs have failed.

Neomycin is especially to be avoided in kidney disease, the manufacturer cautioned. A kidney malfunction keeps the body from excreting the drug, permitting it to build up to levels that damage the nerves for hearing. The manufacturer's brochure warned: "The benefits that may be derived from . . . neomycin therapy should be weighed against the possible development of deafness." The same warning appeared on the package containing the drug and on the wrapper surrounding the package.

This G.P. had no experience with the drug. Although he consulted with an internist and a urologist, he did not discuss the use of neomycin. Nonetheless, he gave this patient larger doses over a longer period than would have been safe even for someone with healthy kidneys.

As the manufacturer warned, the patient began to lose his hearing. Soon he was totally deaf, unable to engage in conversation and able to receive communications only in writing. In addition, he developed tinnitus. A sufferer from this nerve disorder hears constant noises. Sitting in a silent room, this patient would be bedeviled by the bursting of bombs, cricket chirpings, whistles, distant rumblings. He would try to sleep— and suddenly would be jolted awake by a blast of wind. Then he would lie awake, enveloped by noise.

He described his condition: "My God, I have been so nervous that I shake all over. My poor wife has to keep writing all day to me." His condition is incurable.

17

... And Surgeons Go Astray

ONE THURSDAY in October a woman we'll name Mrs. Emily Joy awoke in a hospital room after an ear operation. She looked in a mirror at her face. Thus was launched a celebrated lawsuit that has helped define how and where surgeons may be negligent.

The law recognizes that surgery is an "experimental science" always accompanied by some hazard. Despite reasonable precautions, a danger of cardiac arrest or shock generally remains. Hemorrhaging threatens. Infections are possible. The patient may unavoidably develop a fistula—an abnormal passageway, as between the bladder and vagina after a hysterectomy—and this will lead to complications.

The unavoidable hazards of surgery have created one of the grayest areas in law. On one hand, despite the bad results in the foregoing cases, it is unlikely that any of the surgeons would be held negligent, for an unfavorable outcome alone is not ordinarily proof of malpractice. "No inference of negligence arises solely because the result of the operation is something that rarely occurs," one court has ruled. How, then, in the absence of medical witnesses, may an injured patient show that a surgeon has been negligent?

The case of Mrs. Joy has helped determine the kinds of circumstances that may reasonably lead a jury to conclude that a surgeon was negligent. On looking in the mirror, the courts have held, Mrs. Joy saw that the left side of her face was crooked and paralyzed. Her left eye remained constantly open. She was drooling uncontrollably.

"Something went wrong," she was told by the surgeon, whom we'll call Dr. Curley. "You might be all right in a day or two."

But when she was discharged a week later, her facial condition had worsened. Her left eye continuously watered. Gradually it became sunken into her head. Her nose felt always blocked, and her voice sounded as if she were suffering a heavy cold. Her lips were dry and still. The left side of her tongue was numb.

Subsequent surgery revealed that during the ear operation Dr. Curley had severed the facial nerve, which extends from the brain to the cheek, mouth, and eye. A jury found Curley negligent. Severing a nerve of itself does not prove negligence. But in upholding the verdict against Curley the California Supreme Court reasoned that this nerve could not be severed without great external force. At the point where it was cut it was encased in bone much harder, one doctor testified, than the lead sheath around a cable.

The court found additional evidence of negligence in the fact that such an accident is extremely rare. Three physicians testified that they had performed a total of 1,630 similar operations without severing a facial nerve. Further, a colleague testifying for Dr. Curley explained that a surgeon may "get disoriented"—which, the court said, is "in itself a form of negligence." Lastly, the court found that Dr. Curley had not exercised one of the standard safeguards against injury to facial nerves. He did not tell the nurse-anesthetist to watch the patient's face for twitching. The fact that medical men recognize such safeguards, commented the court, implies that the accident would not happen if all the safeguards are observed.

Other common acts of surgical negligence include cutting the wrong tissue, doing an improper job of sewing up, and failing to respond to postoperative warning signs. All these errors, one suit alleges, occurred in the course of a single gallbladder surgery. The gallbladder is a storage place for bile (also called gall), which is produced by the liver and used in the digestion of fats in the small intestine. If chemicals in the stored bile solidify to form gallstones, the gallbladder often needs to be removed. In this operation it is essential to tie off the bile duct, which leads from the liver to the gallbladder. But the main bile passage—from the liver to the small intestine—must remain intact to prevent bile from escaping into the abdomen.

A woman suffering from gallstones underwent removal of her gallbladder. Instead of the usual uneventful recovery, she developed a fever. Her stomach became distended, and she was unable to retain food. For ten days she had no bowel movement and was racked with pain. These abnormalities would warn most surgeons that an accident had occurred during surgery. Her doctor, however, did not explore the need for a repair. He discharged her from the hospital.

Within two weeks, she was readmitted in critical condition. Her doctor called in a consultant, who drained large amounts of fluid from her abdomen. It showed the presence of bile. If bile enters the abdominal cavity, it inflames all organs it reaches. Unless prompt action is taken, the resulting peritonitis will lead to death.

The woman was too weak for an exploratory operation. She dismissed her doctor and engaged a surgeon of considerable skill. He built up her strength for a month, continuing to drain her abdominal bile. Then he did exploratory surgery. He found that the passage leading from the liver to the intestine—which should have been kept intact—had been severed. The loose ends of this duct were still separated. One end was partly tied off as if it were the bile duct.

Surgeons know that a primary need in this type of operation is to expose and identify the gallbladder and the various ducts. The woman's original doctor had evidently not done this and in confusion had cut and tied off the wrong tubes, causing bile to pour into the abdominal cavity. The second surgeon was able to repair much of the damage. But for eight months the woman needed to have a drainage tube protruding from her abdomen.

"NOTHING LIKE THAT GROWS IN PEOPLE"

A foreign object is occasionally left inside the patient's body. These cases constitute about 9 percent of all medical malpractice suits.

• The G.I. had a stomach operation in an Army hospital. After his discharge from the service, he underwent another operation. In his abdomen doctors found a towel 30 inches long by 18 inches wide. It was marked "Medical Department, U.S. Army."

• Immediately after an appendectomy, a woman felt sharp jabbing pains in the region of the incision. This pain continued for five years. It disappeared entirely after doctors discovered and removed a needle from the woman's pelvis.

• While cleaning the incision from a scrotal repair, a young man found deep in the wound a white rubber tube. It had been meant to extend from the scrotum as a drain, but it had slipped into the body. Now, because the wound had not drained properly, it was infected. The left testicle had to be removed.

• A surgical clamp was left inside a housewife during a gallbladder operation. Her condition deteriorated, complicating the surgery performed to remove the clamp. From the effects of the second operation, the woman died.

A foreign body may be left in the patient not because of the surgeon's carelessness but because of his good judgment. In a Kentucky suit, often cited as the "Humphrey case," the patient on the operating table was responding poorly and faced the danger of spreading infection to other tissues. Dr. Humphrey, the surgeon, followed the safest course. He closed the wound as soon as possible, electing to reoperate later to search out fragments of a broken needle.

A distinguishing feature of this case is that Dr. Humphrey knew that alien material was being left in the patient. He acted judiciously in not prolonging the operation and in thereafter taking care that no injury developed from the foreign matter. He was thus cleared of any hint of negligence.

This is quite different from the typical foreign-body case. The courts hold surgeons responsible for taking out of a patient all objects not intended to be left in. If a foreign body remains, judges usually expect the surgeon to explain away a presumption of negligence. The prevailing feeling has been expressed by one court which reversed a directed verdict for the defendant and ordered a new trial in a case alleging a left-behind sponge: "Why was a foreign substance left . . . which the operating surgeon should have removed? It was for him to acquit himself of the negligence in respect to it. The sponge escaped his observation. Why? Was it so hidden and concealed that reasonable care on his part would not have disclosed it, or were conditions such that . . . further exploration by him for sponges would have endangered the safety of the patient? In a word, did he do all that reasonable care and skill would require? Except as one or the other of these questions can be answered affirmatively . . . the law will presume to the contrary, and attribute the unfortunate consequences to his contributory negligence."

Thus two North Dakota surgeons were found negligent after they left a 6½-inch forceps in a woman's abdomen during a gallbladder operation. The scissorslike instrument pierced the patient's large intestine. The doctors cited the Humphrey case in their defense. But the court declared: "There is no analogy whatever between the Humphrey case and this one."

According to the opinion, the surgeons did not realize the forceps were inside the woman. Her condition did not warrant leaving the instrument inside her. The surgeons did not act promptly to get the forceps out. Corrective surgery was performed only after her bowel was pierced, some fourteen months after the original operation.

A reasonable inference of negligence was found in another foreign-body case. For two years after an abdominal operation, it was charged, a woman suffered excruciating pain in the area of the incision. Finally, the same doctor reopened the woman's abdomen. In her large intestine he found a souvenir of the previous operation: a cloth sack about ten inches wide by eighteen inches long.

On the witness stand, the surgeon admitted that the woman could not have swallowed the sack. But, he claimed, she could have inserted it into her rectum. The woman emphatically denied this, protesting that it was not only unlikely but biologically impossible. The sack would need to travel some four feet against the muscular motion of the intestine and lodge itself in a ball. In reversing a directed verdict for the doctor and ordering a new trial, the court concluded that in the absence of expert testimony the doctor's contention appeared to border on the ridiculous.

Considerable spans of time and mysterious symptoms often characterize foreign-body cases. The charge in a suit brought by one woman who underwent surgery to correct the position of her uterus: After the operation she had nagging pains an inch or two above the bottom of her spine. She now was operated on for removal of her coccyx, the bone at the base of the vertebral column. The back pains persisted, at least as bad as ever. Eighteen years after the original surgery, doctors diagnosed a cyst in the patient's right ovary. They operated, and removed a growth the size of an orange. In it was a piece of foreign matter about one-and-a-half inches long, a half-inch wide, and an eighth of an inch thick. One of the surgeons who removed it said it was most likely a piece of rubber glove or rubber tube. The pathologist who analyzed the material thought it might be a piece of surgical sponge. In any event, he said, "It was a foreign body. . . . Nothing like that grows in people." For the first time since the uterine operation, the woman's back pains were gone.

Foreign-body cases are sometimes complicated by inadequate post-operative care, as was alleged in this negligence suit decided in the patient's favor: After a tonsillectomy, a Utah woman suffered trouble with her throat. Painful ulcerated areas developed. Over the next three years she consulted a dozen doctors and dentists to try to find out what was wrong.

One doctor suggested that she might be suffering from cancer. To determine whether this was the cause of the ulcers, the woman submitted to a biopsy. Embedded as much as three-quarters of an inch in the biopsy tissue were threads of gauze.

During the tonsillectomy the surgeon had evidently left a gauze sponge in the tonsil depression. Why hadn't it been discovered? The surgeon did not see the patient again until a month after the operation. By that time, scar tissue had formed over the area.

The commonest cause of foreign-body negligence is the relaxing of operating-room safeguards. One hospital requires that before sewing up the patient the surgeon count the sponges to see that all that had been used were removed from the incision. Ordinarily the count is made by the scrub nurse, who assists at the surgeon's side, and is double-checked by the circulating nurse, who serves the surgeon as general helper and messenger. But one day, according to the allegation in a successful suit, the following slip-up occurred:

A surgeon in Tennessee was operating on an eighteen-day-old girl suffering from pyloric stenosis, a constriction of the opening between the stomach and small intestine. Just before the sponge count was to begin, the surgeon sent the circulating nurse of the operating room for supplies. He made no other arrangements to verify the scrub nurse's count. When told by her that all the sponges were accounted for, he sewed the baby up.

About a month after the operation, the baby's abdomen became distended. She had not moved her bowels for two days. From tests and x-rays, doctors discovered that a sponge had been left inside her. When doctors performed another operation to remove this four-by-four-inch pack of gauze, they found it had caused the small intestine to become gangrenous. Two thirds of the baby's small intestine had to be removed, leaving her with a gross deficiency for her digestion and growth.

ANESTHETIC ERRORS

Anesthesia is another major area of operating-room negligence. Exactly who should bear responsibility for anesthetic accidents is the subject of a doctor-versus-doctor dispute still being thrashed out in the courts.

In general, the "captain of the ship" doctrine makes the surgeon at least jointly responsible for the acts of all personnel under his direction. The surgeon would thus share liability for negligence by a nurse-anesthetist or other lay hospital employee furnished for his assistance. But if the anesthetic is given by a fellow M.D., a specialist in anesthesiology, court decisions have varied as to whether the surgeon or the anesthesiologist, or both, must stand liable for anesthetic errors. In many jurisdictions, the anesthesiologist is regarded as the surgeon's subordinate, making the surgeon in part responsible for any negligence. Increasingly, however, the anesthesiologist is a co-captain to whom the surgeon can delegate full responsibility for the anesthesia. During a cesarean section, for example, an accident in spinal anesthesia resulted in the mother's legs becoming paralyzed. The obstetrician was cleared of negligence, while the anesthesiologist was held liable.

One type of negligence in anesthesia is marked by misplacement of the breathing apparatus. Sometimes this lapse is compounded by failure to keep the patient under proper surveillance, as is alleged in this suit: A fifty-five-year-old farmer lay on the operating table, anesthetized for ear surgery. Doctors and nurses moved about the room, preparing for the operation. But, the suit charges, no one checked the patient's blood pressure or his pulse and breathing. His abdomen became unnaturally distended. He began to turn blue from oxygen deprivation.

What had gone wrong? In addition to administering the anesthetic, anesthesiologists generally are responsible for maintaining the patient's respiration. Often this entails transmitting oxygen to the lungs through a tube set in the patient's windpipe. But the anesthesiologist in this case had allegedly inserted the tube into the patient's esophagus, which lies behind the windpipe and oxygen was pumped into the stomach instead of reaching the lungs and circulatory system.

Thus deprived of oxygen, the allegation continues, the patient suffered irreparable brain damage. Now he is almost totally blind. He is unable to speak coherently. He cannot control any part of his body. He must be fed and bathed. He will be in this condition for an estimated nineteen years, until he dies.

Dislodging teeth is another hazard springing from faulty insertion of an oxygen tube into the windpipe. According to the charge in one suit: The day before an ulcer operation, a woman was examined by the anesthesiologist, a female. The anesthesiologist looked at the woman's teeth because, in the doctor's words, it is "routine . . . to be sure that they have their teeth. If they have a plate, take it out." The doctor assumed that the woman had all her own teeth, and thought it would be insulting to ask. Said the doctor afterward: "I got the impression . . . that the teeth were all right [and] didn't dream those two front teeth were false." The complaint goes on:

After the woman was anesthetized, the doctor inserted an oxygen tube into the patient's larynx. As she did so, she heard a faint noise like the cracking of glass. Part of a tooth fell into the doctor's hand. The rest of that tooth, and another tooth, had disappeared.

For weeks after the operation, the woman had a cough. X-rays were taken. They revealed two teeth lodged in a bronchial tube. The teeth were later removed by a surgeon.

Selection of an anesthetic is ordinarily meticulous because of the possibility of an adverse reaction. To avoid injuring the patient, surgeons are advised to learn if he had had difficulty with an anesthetic during previous surgery. Before undergoing a tonsillectomy, one patient warned that an operation on him had once been abandoned. "I stopped breathing shortly after being put under general anesthesia," he told the surgeon. But the surgeon failed to note this on the patient's chart or bring the information to the attention of the anesthesiologist.

A moment after the anesthesiologist began administering the anesthetic, the patient went into cardiac arrest. Although revived, he suffered brain damage. In court, the surgeon was found negligent. The jury deemed inadequate his excuse for not mentioning the patient's earlier problem with anesthesia. The surgeon told them: "I didn't think it significant in view of modern advances in anesthesiology."

The courts tend to regard anesthesia as especially dangerous when administered to a patient in weak physical condition. It is considered particularly hazardous to give ether to someone who has a bad cold, since the anesthetic is likely to cause severe distress in the already-inflamed respiratory system. One court suit suggesting the need for extra caution:

A baby girl was admitted to a hospital for surgery to correct feet deformities. She was sickly and poorly nourished, weighing only sixteen pounds at two years. The operation had already been delayed for two months because the child had an upper respiratory infection. She was still suffering from it.

Despite the child's poor condition, it was decided to go ahead. As ether was being administered, the little girl died.

MOTHERS AND BABIES

The obstetrician-gynecologist is the surgical specialist a family is most likely to have dealings with. About four million babies are born in this country each year, and there are few enough accidents along the birth route for obstetrician-gynecologists to term obstetrics a "happy specialty." In obstetrics cases, the physician is legally responsible for the care of the mother throughout the pregnancy, delivery, and postpartum period. He has a further obligation to exercise skill and care in delivering a healthy child.

Faulty diagnosis of pregnancy is a major cause of action in obstetrics cases. One woman has charged the following in a suit: She sought a gynecologist's help for abdominal discomfort. On a hunch she asked him: "Am I pregnant?"

"No," he replied. "You have a tumor and it must come out."

During the surgery to remove the tumor, the woman's husband waited outside the operating room. Finally the doctor appeared and assertedly informed him that she had actually been at least three months pregnant. "This is a terrible thing I have done," the husband testifies the doctor went on. "I should have made some other tests."

Failing to take proper precautions in an abnormal pregnancy is another cause of wrongful prenatal deaths. Diabetic mothers tend to produce abnormally large infants. Because oversized babies have a reduced chance of survival, it is standard practice to keep close watch on the development of the fetus and deliver by cesarean section before the baby gets too large.

Conversely, trying to force delivery may also be an act of negligence. The allegation in one bizarre suit proceeds as follows: A doctor stopped by the rural home of a woman whose delivery he thought near. The woman, already the mother of four, told the doctor: "I'm not having labor pains, and my water hasn't broken."

The doctor gave her a pill. "Maybe this will bring on the time," he said. They waited, but her condition remained unchanged. The doctor put her to sleep with chloroform. He reached inside her apparently in an effort to get hold of the baby. Then he inserted his forceps and pulled for some five minutes.

The woman began bleeding. The doctor now took off his shoes and got onto the bed. He braced his feet against the patient's thighs. For about 30 minutes he pulled at the forceps.

"You're killing the baby!" the doctor was warned.

He said nothing, but continued pushing his feet against the inside of the woman's legs and yanking at the fetus. At last the husband interceded. "I want to get my wife to a hospital."

The doctor got up from the bloody bed. "Do what you want to," he told the husband. "I'm through." Four hours later, at the hospital, the wife expelled the corpse of the baby. It was bruised from head to foot. The mother was also injured. Said a physician who examined her: "I've never seen anyone butchered up like that."

A physician who undertakes a delivery is legally responsible for the newborn until another doctor takes over its care. In some instances of negligence the doctor takes inadequate care of the baby after it has been safely delivered. One little girl has been described as "just vegetable matter" as a result of an obstetrician's alleged negligence in a delivery room. Mrs. Ellis, as we'll call the girl's mother, had delivered without anesthesia and thus was awake As she charged in a suit decided in her favor, she was a helpless witness to what followed.

About three minutes after birth, the baby was normal and pink and squalling healthily. "Is she perfect?" Mrs. Ellis asked.

"She looks and sounds it," replied Dr. Terhune, the name we'll give the obstetrician in charge of the delivery.

She sure has a healthy set of lungs," added another physician, an assistant. "If all babies were born like this we doctors would have no trouble."

"Let's get the afterbirth," said Dr. Terhune. He placed the naked child on a table alongside the mother.

Mrs. Ellis grew concerned over how cold the delivery room was. On this frigid January afternoon the room seemed unheated. Even the nurses complained of the cold. One was wearing a coat. Two others wore sweaters.

The baby lay on the table for some five minutes. She stopped crying. "It's so quiet," Mrs. Ellis said. "Is everything all right?"

A nurse turned toward the baby. The infant had turned a deep blue-black. "Doctor," she called. Dr. Terhune joined her at the table. They placed the baby in a bassinet, then applied a resuscitator.

"You're using oxygen," cried Mrs. Ellis. "What happened to my baby?"

Dr. Terhune spoke: "Oh, you mothers that won't take anything when you have your babies. You know when something happens the minute it happens. Well, I don't know what happened to your baby. But she is not turning nice and pink again the way she ought to."

"I'm not going to stay nice and pink either," Mrs. Ellis replied. "It's freezing cold in here."

The doctor returned to administering the oxygen to the baby. An airlock incubator, equipped with an oxygen tank and measuring gauge, was in the delivery room for his use. With this late-model device, he could automatically control an even flow of oxygen and count on its being retained in the airtight enclosure. Instead, Dr. Terhune employed a relatively primitive method of resuscitation. He held a funnel-like oxygen outlet to the infant's face. To estimate the rate of oxygen flow, the doctor counted the bubbles passing through a water chamber. As the baby moved her head in struggling, the oxygen escaped from the funnel.

The infant screamed.

"You might as well know," Dr. Terhune announced. "This baby absolutely will not live. She has a congenital malformed heart."

The doctor has proved wrong on both counts: The baby has lived, and no heart defect has been found. After administering oxygen for some forty-five minutes, Dr. Terhune instructed a nurse to take the child upstairs to the nursery. Then he went to the telephone and called his house.

"I'm coming home now," he said into the phone. "I want to get started before the five o'clock traffic."

Mrs. Ellis, overhearing him, expressed surprise. "You aren't going home? Aren't you going up to see the baby?"

"I deliver them," replied the doctor. "I don't take care of them. I'll call you a pediatrician."

He left the hospital for the day without giving any instructions regarding the care of the infant. As a result, the baby got no attention other than what hospital routine provided. Her temperature was not taken until three days later—on the occasion of her going on the critical list.

The exposure the child suffered in the cold delivery room had evidently caused her to go into shock. This produced the oxygen deficiency shown by her turning blue. Had oxygen been properly applied with the use of the airlock incubator, the brain might have survived the interval of deprivation.

But the child's brain and nervous system have degenerated irretrievably. She is blind, deaf, and unable to speak. She has no sense of touch. Nor has she muscular control. She is subject to twitching and convulsive seizures.

A final area of negligence in obstetrics is connected with substandard care in circumcisions. According to the allegation in one suit: A healthy baby boy was routinely circumcised in a hospital when he was two days old. Soon thereafter a black spot developed at the tip of his penis. It was gangrene, the result of the circumcision or its aftercare.

The spot was noted without being diagnosed. None of the doctors who saw it called in a pediatrician or urologist who might recognize the condition and treat it. The doctor who performed the circumcision routinely discharged the child from the hospital.

When the black spot continued to grow, the parents took the child to the hospital emergency room. It was a Saturday. Rather than summon any of the specialists on call, the doctor at the emergency room told the parents to return during normal clinic hours Monday. All Saturday the black spot spread. On Sunday the parents brought the baby back to the emergency room. The new doctor on duty also told them to wait until regular clinic hours on Monday.

As the day passed, the black spot grew larger. On Monday, the parents finally saw the proper specialists. By this time there was no course left but to amputate the forepart of the penis.

PART VI

Mental Illness

THE INCOMPETENCE of some doctors is associated with mental derangement. They include the sex offenders, the narcotic addicts, and the senile. They constitute the gravest problem in medical discipline—physicians who are too emotionally disturbed to practice competently, yet extremely difficult to remove from practice.

18

THE MENTALLY ILL:
"Our Biggest Problem"

"OUR BIGGEST PROBLEM is in dealing with physicians who are mental cases." So one state medical society has reported to the A.M.A. Medical Disciplinary Committee. From its investigation, the committee has concluded that mental illness among physicians is a widespread disciplinary problem. Among the terms used by disciplinary officials to describe individual physicians who are currently in practice: "mentally unbalanced," "severely disturbed," "deranged," "irrational," "alcoholic," "senile," "psychotic."

Studies show that physicians have the highest suicide rate of perhaps any occupational group, a barometer of mental illness. More than one in every fifty male doctors takes his own life, nearly two hundred times the rate for the general population.

Suicide accounts for 6 percent of all doctors' deaths under age sixty-five, the same rate as death from lung cancer. Seven out of eight doctor suicides are under age fifty. They "destroy themselves when they would be expected to be most socially productive," one team of investigators has observed.

What accounts for the high rate of physician suicide? "The principal reason is certainly the availability of poisonous drugs," the *British Medical Journal* has written. "The doctor has no need to invent an excuse to get them; he has them ready at hand, ready when the melancholy comes. For another man a fit may pass before he gets them, but the doctor has only to go to the cupboard.

"Almost all doctors who kill themselves use drugs—far more than other people who commit suicide. And the doctor bent on killing himself is not likely to misjudge the necessary dose."

A study in Oregon has shown that six of eight physician suicides used poison (the other two shot themselves). The researchers who performed the study for the University of Oregon Medical School hypothesize that many personality traits that characterize a good physician are also traits that predispose him to depression, a malaise frequently leading to suicide and other forms of aberrant behavior. Among these traits are careful con-

217

trol of emotional expression, compulsive attention to details, and great conscientiousness. While ordinarily laudable in themselves, these traits are often found in persons prone to feelings of hopelessness and inadequacy.

The susceptibility to severe depression is increased by the physician's need to defer for long periods of time his normal impulses toward gratification. The Oregon researchers have noted that the extensive training required of physicians "may result in a series of short-term gratifications followed by long-term privation or loss. The graduating college senior may feel great for the short time until he becomes a lowly freshman medical student. The graduating medical student at last has 'arrived' until he begins his internship. After completing his residency the doctor is often depressed by the fact that his fantasies of material and social reward are undercut by the realities of professional competition and economics. Since the growth of wish-fulfilling fantasies is often proportional to the extent of the deprivation (the starving man dreams of filet mignon, not hamburger) it may be found that the most thoroughly trained and skillful doctor becomes depressed."

If in addition the doctor suffers financial losses, or has a disappointing family life, or undergoes a decline in physical health, the balance may be tipped toward severe depressive illness. Mild symptoms may include cynicism, irritability, a compulsion to overwork. (The cantankerous, hardworking doctor beloved in medical folklore has many of the earmarks of a depressive case.) The Oregon Medical School researchers have observed that depressed physicians—"fearing further loss of self-esteem"—are loath to seek psychiatric help. Often they compound their problems by attempting self-medication, and (see the next chapter) addiction to narcotics is far commoner among physicians than among the population in general.

SEX OFFENSES

Severely depressed physicians are sometimes guilty of "sexual indiscretion," the Oregon Medical School researchers note. Sex offenses by physicians, while extremely rare, are the manifestation of mental illness perhaps most disturbing to other doctors.

Self-restraint in sexual matters is fundamental to the practice of medicine. Without a monastically asexual approach to patients, the profession could hardly function or enjoy the confidence of the public, for the intimacy of the doctor-patient relationship and the relative powerlessness of the patient are conditions suggestive of seduction. Indeed, the physician himself is likely to be the target of a seductive patient. There is a type of disturbed female who acts out her problem partly by making overtures to doctors. Often she poses a "double bind" situation: If the doctor says no, he feels guilty about rejecting her. If he says yes, he feels guilty about accepting.

From early in medical training, physicians thus learn to repress any

sexual urge they may have toward patients. The Hippocratic Oath specifically prohibits "lasciviousness," and a ban on sexual contact with patients is axiomatic to every ethical code. Enforcement is rigorous. In
Queens, New York, a woman was kissed by her doctor during an office
visit. She complained to the county medical society, which called him on
the carpet. "It was merely a paternal gesture," he protested. "After all,
I'm seventy-one years old." Nonetheless the society gave him a sharp
reprimand.

By exercising such strictness, a local medical community gives notice
that it will not tolerate any kind of sexual molestation. Many societies
feel that to be more lenient would be to invite behavior like that attributed to a Texas physician who offered female patients a treatment he
called "pelvic massage." When one local housewife visited him for an
examination, he allegedly manipulated his hands and fingers in and
around her genital organs, telling her: "This is good for your health."

The woman filed a complaint against him, claiming that his massage
was actually a deliberate manipulation of her clitoris to sexually excite
her. At the trial, where his license was canceled, her charge was echoed
by seven other women.

A psychiatrist testified at the trial that it is important to suspend the
license of such offenders. "It is almost impossible to obtain a cure," he
told the court. "Under stress, under some driving need to refrain, they
will refrain for periods. But inevitably they repeat their misdeed."

Such a pattern of recurrence has been charged against another physician. According to the complaint against him: He purported to treat
women for backache, nervousness, and headache by massaging their bare
backs. He would have the patient disrobe and lie on a table. No nurse
or other attendant would be present.

Thus alone with a woman patient, the allegation continues, the doctor
turned out the lights and began massaging the woman's back, slowly
pulling her toward him. Becoming sexually aroused, he forced his penis
into the woman's face, neck, and thigh. This he was accused of doing
with at least seven women.

Because of the patient's vulnerability to sexual assault, medical jurisprudence has evolved the "sleeping woman" doctrine. This ruling calls it
rape if intercourse occurs by surprise or without the patient's knowledge
or consent. The ruling originates in a Missouri case in which a woman
visited a physician for a vaginal examination. The examining position
makes it difficult for the patient to see in any circumstance. But, embarrassed, this woman closed her eyes and covered them with one arm.
Under this further cover, the doctor allegedly completed a sexual penetration.

In court, he fought the rape charge. Not only did he deny sexual assault, but he claimed that the law defined rape as "forcibly ravishing"

a woman, whereas he had used no force. Nonsense, replied the court: "If it is rape under our statutes for a man to have illicit sexual connection with a woman while she is asleep and incapable of consenting, . . . we are unable to see why it is not also rape for a man to have improper sexual connection with a woman by accomplishing penetration by surprise, when she is awake but utterly unaware of his intention."

The sleeping-woman doctrine also applies to protect patients from rape in which the act occurs during the course of the medical treatment. At sixteen, a high school coed in California had a history of sexual promiscuity. In an effort to be helped, she started seeing a psychiatrist. The doctor, a jury found, took advantage of her emotional disorder. On his office couch, he had sexual intercourse with her. The offense earned him a jail term for statutory rape.

Some physician-rapists have been convicted of drugging their victims. In one case, the prosecution portrayed the following sequence of events: A twenty-one-year-old mother who was bothered by chest pains went to a physician for an x-ray. She found the doctor alone in his office.

"Remove your clothes and put on this examination robe," he told her. He gave her an injection. "This will cut the mucus in your throat," he said. Then he had her take a capsule. "To quiet your nerves."

Within minutes, the young woman became lightheaded. Her feet felt glued to the floor, her body felt as if it were swaying.

"Close your eyes," the doctor told her. "Now try to touch your nose with your fingers."

She could not perform this act of coordination. Satisfied that she was thoroughly sedated, the doctor undressed. With the woman too drugged to fight him off, he raped her.

"I did that to bring up your blood pressure," he said afterward. He tried to kiss her as she was leaving. "What's the matter, honey?" he asked. "Didn't you like that?"

The doctor, however, had overestimated the degree of sedation induced by the drug. The woman recalled what had gone on. By the time she got home, she was hysterical. A neighbor took her to the police station, where she told her story.

"Does he want you to come back?" a police officer asked.

She nodded. "On Monday."

The police outfitted her with a portable recording machine and told her what to say. As the machine picked up every word, the doctor recounted the events of the previous visit. Despite his denials of the charge, the evidence helped a California court convict him of rape.

Another doctor, in Oklahoma, denied the charges against him but was convicted of not only drugging his victim but of assaulting her in her own bed. According to the state's evidence against him: The doctor gave the woman injections of Nembutal, which produces reactions ranging from mild drowsiness to complete unconsciousness depending largely on the individual. The doctor thus first made sure that an intended victim was susceptible to the drug.

In one case, a housewife visited him because of a severe sinus headache. To relieve the headache, he gave her a shot of a mild pain-reliever. He noted that when she got up, she almost fell, suggesting marked sensitivity to sedatives. He gave her a shot of Nembutal. She was so weakened by this, he observed, that her husband had to carry her to the car.

That evening the doctor presented himself at the couple's home. He examined the woman, then told the husband: "I'm going to phone a prescription into a drugstore. I want you to pick it up right away." Other drugstores were in the neighborhood, but the husband was sent to a pharmacy that would require a trip of over half an hour.

As the husband was leaving, the doctor gave the woman yet another Nembutal injection. Almost immediately, she passed out. When she came to, she saw the doctor naked and turning her onto her back. Without a word he got into the bed. She was coldly conscious of what was taking place, but was paralyzed and unable to resist. When her husband returned home, he found the doctor with his shirt off. "It's hot," the doctor told him.

The next day the doctor called the woman. "I've been wondering if you suffered any unusual nightmares during the night."

"You know what happened as well as I do," she said.

"Now, now," he replied. "You know I wouldn't do anything like that to you."

IMPAIRED PERFORMANCE

A Wisconsin surgeon was found on psychiatric examination to be "paranoid" and "under severe stress." "Some of his acts appeared to be irrational," a psychiatrist told the court. The surgeon had been evading his income tax by filing fraudulent returns. After being convicted on four counts, he was sentenced to a year's imprisonment and fined $15,000. Then, seeking to arrange an escape, he allegedly tried to bribe an officer of the court. For this he got an additional fine of $5,000 and five years more in prison.

Almost inevitably, profound emotional disturbance impairs the doctor's medical functioning. Dr. R. C. Derbyshire of the Federation of State Medical Boards has reported that mental illness in physicians is often bound up with alcoholism. At first the condition may be manifested only by a tendency to be slipshod. Later the doctor may be guilty of errors in judgment which he can still rationalize. His social drinking increases. He becomes unavailable for emergencies. "His deterioration proceeds gradually and all too often his true situation is detected only after a major disaster has occurred," Dr. Derbyshire has said. "How much simpler this problem would be if our surgeon, early in his illness, would appear in the operating room obviously intoxicated. Embarrassing as this might be, the problem could be met squarely before a disaster occurs."

In California, a physician's emotional problems first showed up in his erratic private life. Witnesses asserted the following: After a long series of domestic upheavals, he left his wife and fled with their six children to Mexico. He divorced his wife there and married a former employee. Later he divorced her, then remarried her.

In the meantime, kidnaping charges were lodged against him for taking his children without authority. In a courtroom, he cursed at the judge and struck a bailiff, earning himself a contempt order.

The doctor had long been aberrant in his professional performance. At his former hospital in California, he had repeated disagreements with the staff. When other physicians offered suggestions, he became enraged. After many disputes, the other doctors concluded he was seriously ill.

For the protection of patients, they denied him use of the hospital facilities. He then opened his own "clinic," an ill-equipped building that was never licensed. Despite inadequacies in facilities and staff, he used it to perform major surgery.

After leaving Mexico, he entered into practice in Alabama, only afterward applying for a license. At a hearing, the Alabama Board of Medical Examiners asked him about his background. "None of your business," he replied. The board checked with some of his former colleagues who, according to the court's opinion, called him "a mental case, a psychopath."

The Alabama board denied his application for a license. But he *was* entitled to return to California and, still duly licensed, re-enter practice.

Mental illness interfered with the medical performance of another physician, whom we'll call Dr. Hannah Kowalski. She was born in Poland and got her medical training at a German university. On coming to the United States she served a seven-month internship at a hospital in Chicago. Her work was rated "not entirely satisfactory." She then served as an assistant junior resident at another Chicago hospital. After her year's contract expired, she was denied reappointment. Her work was rated fair to poor.

Considering her unqualified to care for patients, a university hospital in Detroit gave her a job as a researcher. The chairman of the department found Dr. Kowalski "completely unreliable." He felt she was psychopathic and advised her to enter an institution for psychiatric treatment.

Meanwhile Dr. Kowalski was applying for a license to practice medicine in Illinois. Her department at the Detroit hospital expressed its collective opinion that she should not be granted a license. Nonetheless, Illinois granted her a license on the basis of her grade on a written examination.

While in Detroit, Dr. Kowalski did not take her department chairman's advice about entering an institution. Within two years, however, she was a patient in an Illinois sanitarium. Her presenting complaint; narcotic addiction. In the six months after leaving the sanitarium, she wrote for herself no fewer than sixty-two narcotics prescriptions.

While under the influence of narcotics, Dr. Kowalski caused a serious automobile accident. She was held in jail overnight, so confused that two physicians who examined her recommended that she be committed to a state hospital for psychiatric treatment. The judge sent her home, but revoked her driver's license.

Just three days later, driving recklessly and without a license, she was in another car accident. Injured, she was taken to a hospital, where she remained for almost a year. She was given the narcotic Demerol daily. Totally addicted, she threatened suicide if it was withheld. Two psychiatrists who examined her urged her to enter the state mental hospital.

Despite, or because of, her derangement, Dr. Kowalski had refused to seek psychiatric help. Because she repeatedly violated narcotics statutes by prescribing drugs for her own use, Illinois revoked her medical license. However, she has persisted in trying to become licensed in other states.

One attempt occurred in North Dakota. She presented her credentials to the physician who was serving as administrative officer of the state board. "North Dakota has various steps necessary for a foreign-trained physician to obtain licensure," he told her.

She became agitated. "I demand a temporary license at once," she said.

Citing board procedure, the other doctor refused. This prompted Dr. Kowalski to launch a campaign of vilification against him. She made abusive phone calls to him, wrote defamatory letters about him to his U.S. senator and to the governor, even got in touch with his patients.

A hearing was scheduled on her application. The board prepared for it by investigating her background. After the evidence was presented, Dr. Kowalski's attorney declined to press further for a license for his client. "It would only be embarrassing," he told the board.

Another physician, again a woman, is charged with being a chronic bad-check passer. According to testimony about her: Dr. Gloria Guinn (pseudonym) roams the country, taking jobs or practicing without a license for a few weeks or months, then moving on. She was a fugitive from justice in New York on a bad-check charge. Once, in seeking a Louisiana license, she sent the medical examining board a ninety-dollar check for her application fee. The check bounced.

Dr. Guinn applied for a license in Ohio and is remembered for her bizarre behavior. "She acted peculiarly to say the least," a member of the Ohio board recalls. "In fact I do not believe she is *compos mentis*. While here, she carried with her her diploma of graduation, lived in a trailer court and gave free medical advice as well as complaining against other physicians in the neighborhood."

While in New York, Dr. Guinn got a job through a personnel agency. Her employer, an upstate medical group, found her services "*very, very* unsatisfactory." The physician who heads the group has said he thinks Dr. Guinn "very unstable mentally and emotionally."

"I've had complaints about her from patients as well as from other physicians," he recalls. He suggested that the personnel agency not recommend her again.

Subsequently, Dr. Guinn went to work at a hospital in Washington State. In less than two weeks she was fired. "Her mental and physical development were far ahead of emotional maturity, and we couldn't wait for the two to get together," the hospital director has said. "She was incompatible with both staff and patients, and extremely irregular in hours of service. We question her training and experience because of her unsatisfactory performance."

Dr. Guinn's application for a Louisiana license offers an interesting sidelight on the looseness with which state boards grant medical licenses. The board decided to overlook the fact that it had received a bad check from her and was about to give her a license. An investigation was prompted only by a phone call that New York authorities chanced to make to Louisiana in an effort to track her down.

In outward appearance, an emotionally upset doctor may, of course, seem thoroughly normal, especially to a patient preoccupied with his own illness. Sally Benson is an astute observer who writes for the *New Yorker* magazine and whose books include *Junior Miss* and *Meet Me in St. Louis.* But even so perceptive a person as Miss Benson fell prey to such a physician.

She told a grand jury this story of her treatment by the doctor: Feeling ill after a shopping trip, Miss Benson tried to get medical help. Her own doctor was out, so she called in a physician whose name she got from the Los Angeles County Medical Association's referral service. He appeared to be a calm, competent young man. After examining Miss Benson, he gave her an injection of what he smilingly called "miracle medicine." The only thing about him that might have raised an eyebrow was his car. He made house calls in a Rolls-Royce.

He returned the next day to give another injection. Miss Benson questioned him about her condition. She had long suffered from a calcium deficiency and back ailments. Now the doctor told her: "You have cancer of the spine."

Soon he was making three or more visits a day to give her injections of his miracle medicine. While the shots gave Miss Benson considerable relief, she could not help noticing that the doctor's behavior was becoming increasingly erratic. He brought her weird wire figures—"his hobby," he told her. Whispering and looking about, he confided suspicions of a Communist conspiracy against him.

After a few months, Miss Benson discovered that the miracle medicine was actually codeine. The doctor had systematically made her a codeine addict, bringing her to a point where she could not do without him or the drug. The shots continued for about a year and cost about $30,000. At last, Miss Benson steeled herself, dismissed the doctor and went through the anguish of kicking the habit.

Miss Benson brought the case to the attention of the Narcotics Bureau. A year later, on the testimony of sixteen witnesses, the doctor was indicted by a grand jury for a number of narcotics violations. He responded by firing off telegrams and pamphlets to news media charging that he was the victim of a Communist frame-up. Among the persons he presented his case to were the governor of California, Queen Elizabeth of Britain, and one President.

Then the doctor had a rough, loud fight with his wife. He accused her too of being a Communist agent. The police arrested him on charges of battery and disturbing the peace. From jail he was committed to a mental institution. Subsequently he was sentenced for narcotics convictions, and his license was taken away.

DOCTORS WHO GET IN TROUBLE

Dr. Robert Mayo Tenery, a past president of the Texas Medical Association, calls one type of emotionally disturbed physician "pathologically unethical."

During his service on the Texas society's ethics committee, Dr. Tenery came across many doctors who suffer severe character disorders. He has concluded that the lay public must be protected from such physicians— for they have a "completely warped" attitude toward others, "cannot be rehabilitated," and "use every loophole they can find in current disciplinary procedure." Dr. Tenery adds: "The only treatment is radical amputation from the profession."

The physician who gets in trouble often has deeply rooted personality problems. Dr. Richard H. Blum, a psychologist, has found in a study for the California Medical Association that the doctor who repeatedly gets sued for malpractice usually is a far cry from the mistreated hero of medical legend. According to Dr. Blum, the suit-prone doctor is not a kindly, conscientious practitioner who has made only a few slight human errors and then is undeservedly stripped of his public reputation, his professional standing and his fortune. Instead, Blum finds that the suit-prone doctor has little love or respect for his patients. And his past record is dotted with examples of substandard medical practice.

From his studies, Blum has drawn personality profiles comparing frequently sued doctors with doctors who have never been sued. Among the points of contrast: Suit-prone physicians have more interest in money matters. They are more likely to own side businesses; they are less likely to be troubled by the fact that they must ask a fee for the medical care they provide. Suit-prone doctors also attach less importance to keeping medical records, although good records are essential to patient care. Suit-prone doctors are less ready to admit they cannot handle a case. They seldom call in consultants.

Indeed, the typical suit-prone doctor is generally mistrustful of other physicians. He has an exaggerated dislike for psychiatrists in particular. So great is the suit-prone doctor's disdain for psychiatrists that rather than call one in he often exceeds his competence in attempting to treat mental illness.

Where other physicians let off steam, suit-prone doctors swallow their feelings. They tend to see life in terms of black and white—flatly approving or disapproving of large numbers of things and people, with relatively little acknowledgment of reality's shades of gray.

Equally awry is the suit-prone doctor's conception of his patients. He is likely to view patients as emotionally immature, backward, stupid, and incapable of common sense.

In general the suit-prone doctor sees himself as the severe, all-knowing Victorian father—which he thinks his patients want him to be. Suit-prone doctors have yet another self-delusion. Despite the high frequency with which they are sued for malpractice, they are under the impression that their relations with patients are unusually good.

In another survey for the California Medical Association, Dr. Blum closely compared the attending physicians of two hospitals. At one hospital the doctors have an abnormally high rate of malpractice charges filed against them. At the other the staff has a suit rate extremely low. To physicians at each hospital, Dr. Blum administered a series of personality tests.

Hospital malpractice is generally thought to be a product of administrative deficiencies, which often stem from defects in the medical staff. Blum's results bear this out. In particular, he found, the much-sued doctors show severe personal maladjustment. Their character disorders prevent them—and thus the institution that depends on them—from working well.

Self-control is essential to the individual physician's medical performance. Blum finds seldom-sued doctors as a group are more patient and thorough. By contrast, physicians on the often-sued staff tend to be more impulsive, excitable, irritable, and self-centered. Doctors who are relatively free of suits tend to be energetic and enterprising. On the much-sued staff, physicians lean to the apathetic and to being constricted in thought and action.

Character disorders on the frequently sued medical staff are strongly suggested by the difficulty the physicians have in becoming cooperating members of a social environment. Dr. Blum administered a standard personality test, the California Psychological Inventory, to doctors at both institutions. To a marked extent, physicians on the rarely sued staff were revealed as conscientious and responsible, as honest, obliging, and steady. By contrast, on the staff often accused of malpractice, doctors showed up as undependable and deceitful.

SENILITY

Senility, the deterioration of body and mind in old age, is the price many pay for living long. The once-light step becomes slow and unsure. Formerly steady hands tremble. Reality mingles with illusion.

When a doctor's fingers and mind begin to slip, it is time for him to stop treating patients. Many elderly physicians, however, continue in practice even after they become too impaired to give good care. Dr. James F. Regan, a California disciplinary official, calls older physicians by far the greatest problem medicine has in respect to mental incompetence. In a typical instance of a senile doctor's going downhill, notes Dr. Regan, the change at first is imperceptible to all but the most astute observers. A surgeon becomes slower and gets careless. He is not able to perform delicate techniques owing to less acute vision and less manual dexterity. Assistants note his forgetfulness. His surgery becomes bloodier. His patients are not followed as carefully. His records are less accurate. Evidence of poor judgment appears. The number of postoperative complications increases.

Some well-known surgeons, when they have been retired by their group, will go elsewhere and continue to practice, Dr. Regan adds. If their own hospital curtails their privileges, they go to smaller institutions where they continue to do progressively poorer work.

Sometimes a doctor's senility is accompanied by visible signs of deterioration. After visiting the office of a Kentucky doctor who had been practicing nearly fifty years, a mother wrote her local newspaper: "The office was so filthy dirty that I couldn't believe my eyes. Medicine bottles black with dust were everywhere. A table was stacked with junk.

"He told me the baby should have a shot of penicillin, and he took a tube and needle from this junky table, rinsed it off with water, and started to give her a shot. At this time I was able to recover from the shock of this filth in the doctor's office, and I picked up my baby and walked out. . . . I suggest that something be done about this, as he is a menace to the public."

The aging process impairs not only a doctor's skill but also his evaluation of his abilities. "Like a driver with alcohol in him, he may think he's hell on wheels," an East Coast surgeon has said. "Actually he ought to be flagged off the road." To prove he is as good as ever the senile physician frequently begins to take shortcuts and will go to great lengths to justify his reluctance to perform a long operation. The incompetent elderly internist misses diagnoses that would have been obvious to him in earlier years.

The great problem is often, Who is going to tell this patriarch of the local profession that he is slipping? The staffs of many hospitals are strewn with the wrecks of friendships broken after a younger man was frank in dealing with an aged colleague. "I tell my colleagues that I want them to give it to me straight when I start slipping," an aging Minnesota orthopedist says. "I hope to God they do, because otherwise I probably won't know myself."

But even a stinging rebuke from colleagues may fail to convince the senile doctor. One seventy-four-year-old G.P. was suspended from his hospital staff because he was not giving patients an acceptable level of care. He continued to treat patients in his office. Every time he came across a symptom he could not account for, he diagnosed "aluminum-pot poisoning," an invention of his wandering mind.

Unless precautions are taken, a physician's mental decline may end in tragedy. The mind of a sixty-six year-old gastroenterologist began to cloud so that he could not keep his patients straight. He kept getting the patients and their charts confused. Only an alert hospital staff, constantly unscrambling charts and identifying the patients, averted disaster.

Eventually this hospital limited the doctor's privileges. This staff recognized the impracticality of trying to always look over a senile doctor's shoulder.

The only solution is to keep the senile doctor from attempting patient care. The alternative can be fatal. In Arizona, an eighty-four-year-old doctor was visited by an eighteen-year-old boy who complained of pains in his abdomen. The doctor's diagnosis: "Bad stomachache." It was actually appendicitis. Untreated, the boy died of peritonitis that developed when the appendix burst.

19
THE NARCOTIC ADDICTS:
Doctor's Disease

ADDICTION TO NARCOTICS is an occupational disease of physicians. One percent of all M.D.s, more than 2,500 physicians, are addicted to the use of drugs. Medicine's addiction rate is from 30 to 100 times greater than that of the population at large. About 15 percent of all the nation's known narcotic addicts are physicians. Moreover, Dr. Solomon Garb, of the Cornell University Medical College, has concluded that the rate of addiction among doctors is on the rise.

At most major facilities for addict rehabilitation, there are generally enough physicians present as patients to constitute a sizable medical sub-community. At the U.S. Public Health Service Hospital in Lexington, Kentucky, a week rarely passes without one or more physicians being admitted to the institution for cure of the habit. At the Menninger psychiatric center in Topeka, Kansas, doctors comprise almost half of all the narcotic addicts admitted for treatment.

Much of the disciplinary activity of medical societies and state licensing boards deals with addicted doctors. In some areas, addiction poses the profession's largest single disciplinary problem. During one recent month, state boards reported twenty-three disciplinary actions. Fully five concerned narcotic addicts.

The pattern of physician addiction would hardly be recognized by most readers familiar with the life of the "street addict." Charles Winick, director of research of the American Social Health Association, has sketched some of the broad areas of difference, based on interviews with ninety-three physicians with histories of addiction.

The most obvious difference, Winick has found, is that the physician begins to use drugs at about the age the typical addict "matures out" of the habit. The street addict typically begins drug use in adolescence. The physician begins in his late thirties and afterward, when he is established in his community and profession.

The street addict takes heroin, while the typical physician-addict takes pharmaceutical preparations. The physician can get a pure quality of his drug; the street addict gets a diluted drug, and often starts with marijuana, which though nonaddictive produces a "high." It is a rare physician who has ever smoked marijuana.

The physician is usually discovered by the indirect evidence from his narcotic prescriptions; the street addict is usually arrested because he has narcotics in his possession or has been observed making an illegal purchase. Paying for drugs is no problem to physicians—in contrast to the typical addict, who must steal to support his habit. Aside from the fact that physicians are financially able to pay for the drugs, prices of pharmaceutical narcotics are extremely low (about a nickel for a 50-milligram tablet of Demerol).

Most nonphysician addicts associate with other addicts, forming a subculture that revolves around drug use and drug-users' jargon. By contrast, physicians almost never associate with other physician-addicts or do so unknowingly. In the street subculture of drug use, addicts are likely to have been introduced to narcotics by a contemporary. The physician, being a solitary addict, virtually never recruits a colleague.

For all the points of difference, however, the physician and the street addict have in common that life is dominated by a craving for the high induced by narcotics. This point of similarity disturbs many physicians, especially after they have come in contact with street addicts as patients or as fellow patients in narcotics hospitals. A typical reaction to such contact is: "I feel so degraded when I realize I'm like those people."

TRAP DOOR INTO HELL

At one large eastern hospital no fewer than five doctors became addicts almost simultaneously. Two have died tragically. One has addicted his wife.

"Why are these disciples of Hippocrates, false to their oath of healing and preserving life, bent upon destroying themselves?" asked Dr. Herbert C. Modlin, of the Menninger Foundation, at a meeting of the American Psychiatric Association. Dr. Modlin is seeking the answer to one of the strangest paradoxes of medicine: that physicians take narcotics in the face of their knowledge of the devastating effects of addiction.

A major contributing factor, Dr. Modlin and other investigators find, is the ready access doctors have to narcotics. A layman who is a potential addict either must buy drugs through an underworld connection or have them prescribed illegally. A doctor who succumbs to the temptation to use narcotics has merely to go to his medicine bag.

Most particularly, doctors are in easy reach of Demerol (the sedative meperidine marketed by the Breon and Winthrop pharmaceutical companies). Demerol is ordinarily used to prevent or relieve severe pain and to reduce the amount of anesthetic needed for surgery. It takes effect rapidly, produces an almost unsurpassed sense of elation, then wears off reasonably quickly. "It gives a quick trip," addicts say.

For physician-addicts Demerol is inexpensive, effective, and widely available. Demerol is seductive in other ways as well: A physician might not dream of taking heroin, which smacks of the gutter. But he attaches no such stigma to the Demerol in his drug cabinet. Also, despite warnings in manufacturer's literature and in the medical press, a surprising number of physicians tell themselves they are unlikely to become addicted to Demerol and that addiction to Demerol poses no great problems.

In this they could not be more wrong. Demerol is quicker to addict to—and harder to shake—than morphine, methadone, codeine, or virtually any other narcotic the doctor is likely to encounter. Moreover, like all narcotics, Demerol makes the addict dependent on larger and larger doses, causes greater and greater impairment of his professional performance, and increasingly strains his relations with family, patients, and friends.

The physician-addict problem is largely a Demerol problem. An estimated 90 percent of all doctor-addicts are on Demerol. Each year, authorities believe, well over 250 new physicians take Demerol injections or tablets and slip into addiction. This number of new addicts is equal to the total graduating classes of three average-sized medical schools. At least 25 additional doctors a year start on other narcotics, most often morphine.

Specialists in the study of addiction speak of "potential addicts," persons who by psychological makeup are vulnerable to the narcotic habit. Without an exposure to narcotics, this potential may never ripen, and the latent addict will remain a non-user. Thus the first encounter with drugs is a critical step in any pattern of addiction. What, then, prompts physicians to reach out for the narcotics they have so close at hand?

Fatigue from the rigors of practice often spurs the doctor's first use of narcotics. Typically a potential addict loses sleep several nights. He receives yet another call—and feels he cannot make it without a "stimulant" to keep him going. Commonly he takes a dose of Demerol and makes his call. Finding a great relief he repeats it, infrequently at first and then more often, until he slides into addiction.

One California physician was tired and tense from a daily grind that included postgraduate study and a research project. He tried taking barbiturates. But ordinary sleeping pills were little help.

One night he experimented with Demerol. He swooned off into a sound sleep and woke refreshed in the morning. Like most addicts, he spent much of the day musing over his drug-induced rapture. Few nights passed thereafter without his taking increasing dosage of the drug. His drain on his hospital's Demerol supply became so great that he fell under suspicion. The hospital dismissed him. He set up practice in a small town but continued taking drugs. His practice failed. In ensuing years he has drifted in and out of institutions.

A doctor in an eastern city who slipped into the narcotics habit through fatigue tells his own story: "Going night and day, I would come home so tired and tense that sleep was impossible." He began taking Nembutal capsules, but they took too long to work. To speed things up he filled a syringe with Nembutal and slipped it into his vein. "Before I hit the bed I was asleep. Impossible as this may sound, I thought it was smart. Just look at all the time I saved getting to sleep. Imagine a doctor thinking like that!"

One evening he came home tired out. His back was aching. His feet were sore and swollen. But he had promised his fifteen-year-old daughter he would take her roller-skating. He was sure he wouldn't be able to put on a pair of skates if he didn't do something for the pain. Surreptitiously he went into the bedroom, took a vial of Demerol from his bag, and gave himself a shot.

"I went skating and felt swell; in fact, I never had a better time. That started me off. I had found an escape from my pain and fatigue. But I little realized that I was falling through a trap door into hell."

Many addicts don't so much fall through the trap door as float through it on a tide of alcohol. A heavy drinker may be too hung over to carry on his practice the day after a spree. He may hit upon the idea of taking a narcotic to relieve the headache and nausea of his hangover. Soon he is likely to find himself drinking less but taking the drug more. By this slow substitution of one addiction for another, he becomes addicted to drugs.

For some doctors, the first continued use of a narcotic occurs under the imprimatur of scientific research. The dean of a midwestern medical school was a prominent researcher who took an active role in his experimental work. While studying pain-killing agents, he made tests on himself. He did this repeatedly. Before long he realized he was now using the experiment as an excuse to take the drugs.

Despite this realization he continued. Several times he tried to kick the habit but each time fell back. At last, he committed himself to the Public Health Service Hospital at Lexington.

The physician suffering from a chronic painful disease may find that a narcotic will dull the pain enough to allow him to get through his day much more easily. Before he realizes what has happened, he is chained. One doctor in Indiana who had a severe arthritic condition found that Dolophine, a methadone product, would relieve his pain. To get sufficient quantities, he began to write prescriptions for it in the name of patients.

Law enforcement agents check on unusually heavy prescribers of narcotics. The quantity of this doctor's orders for Dolophine put a red flag next to his name at the local Narcotics Bureau office. When agents inquired, the doctor admitted: "I've got a narcotic problem." A court found him addicted to narcotics to such a degree as to render him unfit to practice. It revoked his license.

To avoid detection by the Narcotics Bureau, doctor-addicts often resort to ruses to conceal the doses they need. After an addict has built up his tolerance to drugs so that relatively inconspicuous quantities no longer satisfy his need, much of his day is spent on stratagems to hide his intake. Some doctor-addicts spend a great deal of time forging narcotics records. They report drugs as lost, stolen, and spilled. In a not uncommon trick, one doctor prescribed Demerol for a woman with terminal cancer, then gave her distilled water, keeping the full dose for himself.

WHO BECOMES ADDICTED?

"We always find a serious emotional disorder in the background which leads to addiction," says Dr. Harris Isbell, director of the Public Health Service Hospital at Lexington.

Contrary to the popular notion of addiction, the drug alone does not make an addict. Widespread belief has it that an addict remains on drugs because withdrawal is unbearably painful. But authorities have learned that withdrawal resembles the distress caused by influenza. The symptoms last for a day or so and, while very unpleasant, are hardly insurmountable.

Many patients become addicted to medications or sedatives given in connection with illnesses or surgery. Not having the addict's "predisposing personality," the great majority follow the usual pattern: They put up with the misery of withdrawal for the necessary interval. Then, cured of both illness and addiction, they return to normal life unburdened by any craving for the drug.

By contrast, an emotionally disturbed individual may continue with an excessive yearning for the euphoria the drug induces. So it is with physicians for whom addiction is one symptom of an already disordered personality.

Dr. Herbert Modlin of the Menninger Foundation reports that the emotional disturbances that physician-addicts suffer are severe and progressive. Almost all physician-addicts whom Dr. Modlin has studied have had unsatisfactory relationships with their patients. They are generally disappointed in the practice of medicine, often because they started out with grandiose expectations. In marriage, they are generally the dependent partner. About three out of four have difficulties related to sex. Through narcotics, Dr. Modlin concludes, these physicians obtain some temporary relief from the anxieties, disappointments, and frustrations that otherwise threaten to overwhelm them.

A study by Dr. James H. Wall, at the Westchester Division of New York Hospital, shows that the outstanding personality trait of addicted physicians is "sensitive tendermindedness." Physician-addicts, Dr. Wall finds, tend toward hypochondria. They are likely to tire easily and be unable to stand life when the going gets rough.

Fully three out of five of the doctor-addicts seen at the hospital have traits commonly found in the psychopathic personality. They are immature, irresponsible, and unreliable. Typically, they feel inadequate and are unable to stick to a task. Most of the other physician-addicts seen at the hospital are neurotics with long histories of tension. Generally they have long suffered from headaches and insomnia, and have fallen prey to periods of depression and muscular weakness.

Once on drugs, doctors tend to withdraw from family and friends. This is a marked symptom even in formerly outgoing personalities who had gone to great trouble to cultivate grace and charm. This inability to relate, this neglect of loved ones and family for years is often masked by an apparent dedication to medicine.

Even before becoming addicted, the doctor may disguise his problem by seeming extremely conscientious. Actually he often is merely frittering away time to avoid coming to grips with life. While presumably working, a potential addict may sit and talk for hours with a gossipy patient. Or he may personally attend to tasks that could be as easily delegated.

According to the New York Hospital study, most doctor-addicts avoid sex and lack the ability to have good sexual relationships. Many marry women who are much older. As husbands they give and get little satisfaction from their marriages and home life. Often they refuse to have children.

In spite of these emotional abnormalities most doctor-addicts are brilliant in intellectual spheres and have given many years of satisfactory service in the profession. But the tendency to feel alone, inadequate, and undisciplined leads them to falter. Potential addicts incline to be accident-prone. By doing and saying things that provoke hostility, they tend to appear in a bad light with superiors and associates. As a relief from such constant emotional short-circuiting, the typical doctor-addict welcomes the feeling of oblivion through drugs.

To psychiatrists, the doctor-addict's slow self-destruction and lack of interest in sex and family suggest a death drive. Many doctor-addicts see this trend in themselves and feel helpless to counteract it. Indeed, four of the physician-addicts who were at New York Hospital took their lives within five years after leaving treatment.

Even without contributing to a suicide, the use of narcotics leads a doctor to run down physically. The typical addict, having lost touch with the realities of taking care of himself, is in poor physical condition. One physician showed up at a New York State narcotics hospital with bleeding stomach ulcers. The drugs he used masked the signs and symptoms of the ulcers, and the hospital staff failed to recognize that he was in extremis. He died within three days.

Once a doctor recedes into narcotic addiction, what are his prospects for finding his way out? Follow-up studies reveal they are far from good: Three out of four doctor-addicts fail in their attempt to be cured.

Generally the habit persists despite repeated attempts at rehabilitation. A doctor who becomes addicted is likely to seek a cure in a private sanitarium. After a few months he kicks the habit. But he returns to his practice prematurely. The same emotional pressures that drove him to narcotics in the first place now start him up again.

Thus doctor-addicts relapse time and again. Typical is the California physician-addict who was placed on probation for three years by the board of medical examiners. He was counseled and allowed to return to practice in slow stages, at first without the temptation of a narcotics permit. Finally, his permit was restored and he was taken off probation. Only eight months later he resumed taking narcotics.

Sometimes a doctor's own addiction impels him to write drug prescriptions for other addicts. One Washington, D.C., doctor had been writing Dolophine prescriptions for twenty-one addicts. When picked up by the police, the doctor voluntarily surrendered his narcotics stamp for a year. He asked to be sent to the Public Health Service Hospital at Lexington for treatment of his addiction.

When the year was up, the doctor reregistered for his narcotic stamp. He again issued prescriptions to addicts. After being caught, he once more voluntarily surrendered his narcotics stamp, this time for five years. But before long he was writing prescriptions for addicts again, even though he had no narcotics permit. When the law caught up with him, the doctor pleaded guilty and was sentenced to prison for up to two years. The court recommended that he be sent to an institution for treatment of narcotic addiction.

Over half the physicians interviewed by Charles Winick of the American Social Health Association have stopped drug use and then reverted at least once—one doctor after nineteen years of abstinence. The circumstances of reversion vary, and the physicians do not seem able to explain it. One doctor has told Winick: "I got into a taxi to go to the hospital for an operation. Suddenly, as if it were another person inside me, I stopped the taxi at a pharmacy and got a shot."

Another tried a ranch "cure" for three months. He "felt great" there, he recalled. But he took drugs within an hour after his return to his office. Yet another physician was succeeding well in abstaining from drugs. Because of previous offenses the doctor came under investigation by an official agency, which was seeking to check on his present behavior. Now, when any lapse could not help but be uncovered, the doctor reverted.

ONE ADDICT'S TALE

Charles Kay (pseudonym) was born in 1924 in a small town in the South. His father, a doctor, had a heart condition and for many years was addicted to morphine.

Charles was the youngest of three boys. During World War II, the oldest was killed in action. The middle son, a sufferer of severe depression, committed suicide at age twenty-seven. Charles was in the Navy for seventeen months. "I had a lot of time to think," he recalls. "I decided I wanted to study veterinary medicine or dentistry."

After his discharge, he tried to thumb a ride to Atlanta to go into dentistry school there. No ride came along. So, with characteristic flightiness of mind, he decided to go to his state university.

There he was told that if he got a B in one year of science he could be admitted to medical school. That decided him to be a physician.

His grades in college and medical school were unexceptional. The reason he gives: "I could have done better if I hadn't had such headaches."

Charles—now Dr. Kay—served a one-year internship, then set up a general practice in a very small town. Two years later the Bureau of Narcotics began to be suspicious of him. In less than six months he had bought 3,000 Demerol tablets and 195 Demerol injection doses.

When confronted, Dr. Kay admitted: "I've taken all the Demerol myself. I use them to relieve migraine headaches." He attributed the headaches to tension. "I took the only drug that would relieve me, and I became addicted."

A month after committing himself to a hospital, he was discharged as cured. But only four days after he left the hospital he ordered 24 hypodermic doses and 100 tablets of Demerol. A narcotics agent paid Dr. Kay another visit. The doctor surrendered the remaining drugs, along with his order forms and narcotics stamp. He was no longer permitted to order or prescribe narcotics. But he was still practicing medicine.

For four years Bureau of Narcotics agents kept a careful watch on him. Evidence began to accumulate that he was getting narcotics illegally and was connected with a narcotics ring. One day he confirmed the agents' suspicions: He entered a hospital as a result of overusing narcotics, barbiturates, and alcohol.

"Drug addiction and alcoholism" was the diagnosis entered on his chart. The examining psychiatrist added: "A constitutional psychopath, completely unstable, unpredictable, and unreliable. He is not completely truthful, but stretches the truth to fit the picture he wants to present."

Dr. Kay left the hospital and resumed treating patients. The state licensing board, after getting complaints about his addiction and unreliability, held a hearing on his case and revoked his license. Leading citizens in his community protested. "He is the only physician we have," they told the board. "We need him."

The board acceded to the community's request and restored Dr. Kay to practice. Within three months, the board found that he had violated the terms of his probation. Finding this too much to ignore, the board revoked his license.

Now thirty-six years old, Dr. Kay entered a mental institution. This time he responded to treatment. He successfully worked on the staff of a state mental hospital, and his license was reinstated (without a narcotics stamp).

"DON'T TOUCH ME!"

"The addicted physician is his own worst enemy," a psychiatrist has said. "Also his patient's."

There is a grave enough hazard if a doctor is under the influence of alcohol. One suit alleges the following: A surgeon removed urinary bladder stones that were troubling a patient. Following routine, he inserted through the patient's penis a catheter, a tight-fitting tube for postoperative draining of the bladder.

The operation was uneventful. But some days later the catheter stopped draining. In response to a call, the doctor came to the hospital—reeling drunk, the patient claims. The doctor entered the patient's room. Suddenly it dawned on the patient that he was helpless, that no one else was in the room and the doctor was planning to remove the catheter.

"Don't," the patient pleaded. "Don't touch me!"

The doctor stumbled forward. Removing a catheter is a delicate procedure, but the doctor tugged on the tube. Then, unsteady on his feet, he tripped. Instead of relaxing his grip, he tore the catheter from the patient's body. This caused internal hemorrhaging and damage to the patient's genital area that made emergency surgery necessary.

One surgeon was heavily addicted to amphetamines—"pep pills" which charged him up during the day—and to barbiturates, which he took in massive quantities to get some sleep at night. He would have hallucinations, walking about his hospital holding conversations with himself or invisible companions. Alternating with his high good humor were fits of paranoid delusion. He yelled at a nurse for supposedly not following his orders. During one tantrum, he pushed a nurse against a door, injuring her. He got the nickname "Knife-Happy" because of his blatantly needless surgery. Finally he removed both breasts from a woman, then left town for two days and nights without arranging for another doctor to look in on her. After a five-minute hearing, he was suspended from the hospital.

Use of drugs can reduce the level of a physician's performance to near zero. Witnesses related the following to the state licensing board: One evening in a Connecticut suburb a Demerol addict we'll call Dr. Bailin was found by his wife lying on their bedroom floor. He was stuporous and turning blue. His breathing was labored. Froth foamed from the corners of his mouth. His eyes were rolling. A needle was still stuck in his arm.

Mrs. Bailin recognized that he had taken an overdose. She called a physician friend. He pulled Bailin out of the coma.

"Go to a hospital," the friend urged. "Detoxify."

"No," Bailin replied. "No. I don't want to."

About a month later, Dr. Bailin took another overdose. In his pajamas he fell unconscious on the dining room floor, again frothing at the mouth and cyanotic. Mrs. Bailin tried to reach their friend but failed. Desperate, she called in another doctor, an acquaintance who lived nearby.

"He needs an ambulance," this doctor told her.

The wife shook her head. "My husband wouldn't like that at all."

"You're making a mistake," the doctor said. "But I'll do what I can."

He slapped Bailin's face to bring him around. Slowly Bailin's breathing grew regular. His color became normal. At last his eyelids fluttered and he regained consciousness. His first words to his rescuer: "Leave this house at once."

Bailin continued to maintain an active practice. One woman who wasn't feeling well went to him for treatment. While she was telling him her symptoms, he dozed off. The office nurse shook him awake. In a few minutes he fell into a stupor again. Once more the nurse roused him. After this happened several more times, the woman left. Her complaint was instrumental in the investigation that led to the suspension of his license.

This woman was perhaps lucky that the doctor was too groggy to treat her. A woman in San Francisco was not so fortunate with a surgeon who, state board records show, later admitted being addicted to methadone. She came to him for repair of a prolapsed uterus, which entails restoring the uterus to its normal position. No organs are ordinarily removed in this operation. But, the woman charged in a successful negligence suit:

The doctor performed the surgery while under the influence of methadone. The drug adversely affects reflexes and judgment. As a result, the surgeon proceeded to perform the wrong operation. Without the woman's consent, he removed the uterus and her one remaining fallopian tube and ovary, all of which were normal.

Further, befogged by the drug the doctor inadvertently cut a hole between the woman's vagina and rectum, so that gas and fecal matter escaped through the vaginal opening. Despite additional surgery, the damage to the vagina has left the woman permanently unable to have sexual intercourse.

PART VII

Opposition to Discipline

In view of the hazards posed by offenders, why is there no strong push for disciplinary reform? Many physicians feel persecuted by the lay community, a misperception that leads them to oppose stronger controls. The canons of medical ethics do little to bring about regulation—for while humanitarian in part, they are largely guild-type rules with a business purpose. The medicolegal nightmare of rising malpractice judgments adds to physicians' feelings of harassment, promoting mutual protection and the so-called conspiracy of silence. The effect, as detailed here, has been resistance by the organized profession to sensible measures for reform.

20
False Alarm

AT AN A.M.A. meeting in December 1958 the Board of Trustees established the A.M.A. Medical Disciplinary Committee. "The A.M.A. has become aware that someway, somehow, medicine should have something to say about the behavior of its practitioners," explained Dr. Raymond M. McKeown, an A.M.A. trustee and chairman of the new committee. "Those of us who have tried to bring about changes among the three to five percent of colleagues who are disreputable frequently lost out." Added another committee member: "The three to five percent often force us to live with their behavior instead of our guiding them."

Thus began the most exhaustive study of medical discipline ever undertaken in this country. The committee held four regional meetings, attended by representatives of 27 state medical associations and 24 state licensing boards. It analyzed questionnaires returned by 37 state boards and 38 state medical societies. Committee staff interviewed officials of 15 medical societies and 15 licensing boards. The committee also met with other groups concerned with discipline: the National Association of Blue Shield Plans, the Health Insurance Council, the Association of Casualty and Surety Underwriters.

At last satisfied that the study was "most comprehensive and most factual," the committee submitted its findings in June 1961 to the A.M.A. Board of Trustees and House of Delegates. The two-volume report was greeted as a stunning piece of work. In scope and importance, it promised to do for medical discipline what the Flexner report did for medical education.

There—on hundreds of pages of observations and exhibits—was evidence of the disciplinary weaknesses in medical licensing laws, in medical societies, in hospitals. Now needed was action by the A.M.A. to begin putting the committee's recommended reforms into effect.

Yet as of today not one of the committee's major proposals has been implemented. Nor has the profession begun any other meaningful program of reform.

"PARANOIA IS RAMPANT"

The organized profession's reluctance to improve discipline bodes ill not only for reform within medical societies. Licensing laws also are unlikely to be strengthened.

241

State legislatures seldom enact statutes affecting medicine without the concurrence of the state medical society. In an address before a medical audience, Governor Ernest F. Hollings, of South Carolina, summed up the attitude of most state governments: "The profession must agree in overwhelming majority to the regulation. . . . [Otherwise] the mere introduction of a bill to secure medical discipline will never succeed." Significantly, the most extensive revisions of medical discipline laws in recent years—in Washington and California—were drawn up with the help of the state medical societies. Without such support from the profession, the prospects for licensing reform are tantamount to nil.

Yet, outside of a handful of physicians, the cause of medical discipline has virtually no constituency. On one hand, vigorous organizations defend the interests of general practitioners and of members of every specialty in medicine. Physicians who practice in groups have associations of their own. So also do doctors who are in various fields of employment. Practitioners in small states have a powerful lobbying group in Aces and Deuces, a banding-together at A.M.A. meetings of one- and two-member delegations. There is even an organization—the American Medical Women's Association—that labors in behalf of the 5 percent of physicians who are female.

Nowhere is comparable pressure exerted for the advancement of medical discipline. Activity occurs mainly among a few leaders of the Federation of State Medical Boards. Some medical society and hospital officials call for stronger controls, and a vocal minority of critics are on medical school faculties. By and large, their combined power to bring about disciplinary reform has proved extremely limited.

The profession's general resistance to disciplinary reform thus presents an obstacle extremely hard to surmount. But over and beyond the individual physician's distaste for matters relating to discipline, what accounts for such reluctance? Why do doctors who themselves are honorable and competent so refuse to support improvements whose need is well documented?

Much of the answer lies in the feeling many private practitioners have of being threatened by the lay community. A large number of physicians sincerely believe that the house of medicine is a fortress under siege—surrounded by hostile patients, aggressive unions, dictatorial government agencies, domineering insurance companies. This sense of being "intruded upon" and "interfered with" by laymen and their instrumentalities is implicit in many a private practitioner's perceptions of himself and the world around him. Trained to act on his own initiative, he resents being "pushed around." Oriented toward autonomy, he is often frustrated by his inability to have the full control he would like.

In an attempt to explain medicine's conservatism, a psychiatrist-member of the A.M.A. Council on Mental Health said of the practicing profession: "Paranoia is rampant, insecurity is rife." Professor Herman M. Somers of Princeton University, a specialist in the politics and economics of health insurance and social legislation, speaks of the "tension between medicine and the lay community" that arises from doctors' feeling that their territory is being increasingly poached on. In recent years there has been no labor or government health measure that has not provoked an angry outcry from a large segment of the profession. Still more recently, hospitals and private insurance companies have been attacked by private practitioners as impinging on the doctor's freedom.

Physicians in private practice are correct in sensing that they are no longer as free as they once might have been. But the restrictions on them are generally minimal and unavoidable. To the extent that regulation exists, it demonstrates that health services are no longer the nearly exclusive domain of the private practitioner. Rather, health care has become a social institution—indeed a $15.5-billion-a-year industry—of which the private practice of medicine is but one part.

While physicians are the most important figures in health care, they are under increasing pressure to share initiative with health insurers and government officials. This is a direct result of the scientific advances that make medicine more effective as a prolonger of life and curer of ills. In a nutshell: Medicine now offers a better product—and people want it.

But the fruits of medical progress are often more expensive than most people can afford. Open-heart surgery—not long ago impossible but now reasonably common—requires special equipment, specially trained personnel, and a lengthy hospital stay. The patient may come out good as new, but his care is likely to cost several thousand dollars. A tremendous consumer demand has therefore arisen not only for the more efficacious medical services now available but also for ways to help pay for them.

One major answer is health insurance, including medical cooperatives and union health plans. But private health insurance is feasible only for those who can pay the premiums: the employed and their families. It is not for the impoverished—especially high-risk groups like the elderly and the disabled—for whom premium costs would be out of sight. For indigent people Medicare, Medicaid, and other government programs have evolved and are almost certain to expand.

These third parties reserve the right to set minimum standards for what they pay for. Ergo, many doctors complain of "interference" and "intrusion." Such protests are often out of focus, for third parties are not outsiders but have a vested interest in what the doctor does. Third parties, of course, are not above reproach. Genuine abuses by insurance clerks and petty bureaucrats, however rare, arm those doctors who blast all health plans. But as Dr. Milton I. Roemer, a professor of public health at the University of California at Los Angeles, observes: "Freedom is a many-splendored thing and our social order abounds with examples of trading one form for another. . . . We are continually restricting the individual doctor's freedom to do as he pleases in favor of a compulsion to meet certain scientific standards that are designed to save the lives of patients." Physicians who accept the idea that third parties have a justifiable interest in patient care can usually redirect their fire and make sound objections to particular instances of unfairness and heavy-handedness.

The growth of these other forces in medicine is as inexorable as the advance of medical progress. Nonetheless, physicians widely resent incursions into what they regard as their bailiwick. "Would you advise your son to enter medicine?" is a conversational topic popular among physicians. A layman listening in is likely to be surprised at how many doctors argue no, they would advise a son to stay away from medicine. A major reason is that medicine is being "taken over."

Thus an individual physician is likely to grant that medicine's disciplinary problem is an embarrassment. Chances are he will agree it warrants clearing up. But he is also likely to say, "Not now"—for he has an allergy to controls. Moreover, he fears that efforts to improve discipline will divide and weaken an already beleaguered profession. Domestic reform is the first casualty of war. So also, this doctor, in the struggle he perceives with the laity, is loath to expose what he feels is a soft underbelly.

The don't-rock-the-boat attitude of many physicians is illustrated by this incident: At a National Association of Science Writers meeting, Dr. Robert S. Myers of the American College of Surgeons said that half the operations in the United States are performed by doctors unqualified to do surgery and that the A.M.A. has done little about either this or fee splitting. Shortly thereafter, Dr. Edward R. Annis—subsequently elected A.M.A. president—wrote in his column that "such intramural dissension can only harm all doctors."

A graphic representation of the nightmare that many doctors share has been published in a political cartoon aimed at arousing the 19,500 recipients of the *Pennsylvania Medical Society Newsletter*. The message it carries is repeated over and over in the medical press—and doctors read little else. Depicted here (see opposite page) is the evil figure of socialism, the captive physician, the gullible public, the threat of control.

BLURRED IMAGE

The profession's concern over its relations with the lay community is reflected in gloom-tinged writings about medicine's "image." *Current Medicine for Attorneys*, a journal edited by physicians, has told its readers, "The 'image' organized medicine tries to present to the public and the actuality of the situation . . . are quite far apart." The Michigan Board of Registration in Medicine has sent out a questionnaire asking about "The 'Bad' Public Image of the Medical Profession." Dr. E. C. Swanson's report of the results is called "Blurring of the Image." The

Reprinted by permission of the State Publishing Company; from "Socialists' Plans for Control of the USA," *The State Labor News*, Columbus, Ohio.

Rocky Mountain Medical Journal has printed an article on medicine's public relations entitled ". . . How Sick Is Our Image?"

The public relations concept of "image" is an oversimplification to begin with. Medicine's relationship with the public is highly complex. It cannot with any accuracy be characterized as merely this or that, for there are too many currents, crosscurrents, and countercurrents all at play at once. Every article like the *New York Times Magazine*'s "The Doctor's Image Is Sickly" therefore suffers from tunnel vision. Another article with an equally narrow focus can with equal accuracy reaffirm the public's high opinion of physicians. In a special issue, "The Crisis in American Medicine," the editors of *Harper's* demonstrated the paradox in two sentences: "Most people agree that American medicine is the best in the world," and "Millions of people are bitterly dissatisfied with the medical care they are getting."

Two such contrasting statements can both be true because neither the profession nor the public is monolithic. Far from being a uniform mass, the world of medicine wears as many faces as there are physicians and patients in it. Any layman's opinion of medicine is subject to an infinity of variables—including what doctors he knows, which institutions he is exposed to, what his expectations are.

Moreover, many people react to the subject of health care with considerable emotion. Whereas a person may be neutral toward lawyers and indifferent about clergymen, he is likely to feel strongly about doctors. Responses to public opinion surveys reflect this emotionalism. Replies tend to be inconsistent, often immoderate.

For example, the University of Chicago's National Opinion Research Center has found that the public thinks so well of physicians as to rank them second in occupational prestige, after U.S. Supreme Court justices. At the same time, Harvard sociologists William A. Gamson and Howard Schuman have determined that laymen who rank physicians highest in prestige are also likely to be the ones most hostile to the medical profession. Six out of ten persons who placed doctors first, second, or third in prestige also felt that "if you go to two doctors, you'll probably get two opposite kinds of advice." Four out of ten felt that when it comes to colds, headaches, and a great many other illnesses, the neighborhood druggist "probably knows as much as the highest-priced doctor." Over three out of ten felt that doctors "know a whole lot less about medicine than they let on" and that doctors "have more money and prestige than they actually deserve."

Sociologist Alfred McClung Lee of Brooklyn College has observed that any group that has reached the "intimate and trusted status" achieved by the medical profession is subject to feelings of both "gratitude and high expectations on the one hand and of distrust and rejection on the other." Physicians, in their malaise with respect to laymen, often mark only the unfavorable public-opinion reports and take no comfort from favorable findings that are at least as valid. Doctors thus feel depressed after reading reports of how medical fees arouse patients' antagonism. In one such study, Elmo Roper concluded that one American in three believes that doctors "generally get too highly paid for the services they provide." Well-to-do persons picked out plumbers as the people who overcharge them most, with doctors in second place. The poor said they are gouged most by doctors, with landlords a close second.

After conducting a survey for Blue Shield, interviewers reported they had uncovered "a startling degree of anger, accusation, and indictment of the medical profession." Typical comments from respondents were: "Doctors aren't 'dedicated' to anything except profit." "They're misusing and abusing the coverage we're paying for." "They participate in Blue Shield only for their own profit."

Nor are doctors cheered by some opinions of their services. Dr. Daniel Funkenstein, a psychiatrist, interviewed forty-four Harvard seniors who decided not to go to medical school despite their premedical studies. Most of the students said they changed their plans because the typical physician was "cold and cynical" or a "second-class scientist." During Dr. Dwight H. Murray's term as A.M.A. president, he received stacks of letters from laymen. In his departing address he reported that most of the correspondents complained of their inability to get a doctor when needed, especially at night, on weekends and holidays. A study by the National Opinion Research Center asked people how much interest doctors took in their patients as compared with thirty years ago. Fully a third of the respondents replied "a little less" or "much less." *Parade* magazine polled readers on their opinion of the medical profession. Nearly one out of three said they were disappointed in today's doctor.

MYTHS IN MEDICINE

Unless carefully qualified, reports like these help perpetuate what Mac F. Cahal, executive director of the American Academy of General Practice, calls "false assumptions that have long gone unchallenged in the folklore of medicine." Let us now pick apart some of the myths many doctors treat as gospel:

Authoritative studies show much less hostility on the part of the public than many physicians believe. In a study sponsored by the A.A.G.P., the Opinion Research Corporation of Princeton, New Jersey, tested a number of suppositions that support medicine's sense of being under siege. A statement of what many doctors think and fear might go as follows: "Patients are unhappy with medical care. They believe that the old-fashioned family doctor was the best ever, that doctors don't care about people anymore. This is because people don't want competent doctoring: They just want to be comforted—they want the doctor to play

God. Patients also think doctors are all money mad. The public just doesn't understand what the physician is up against."

Point for point, the Opinion Research Corporation found that in general the opposite is true. According to the O.R.C. study: People always want improvement but basically are satisfied with American medicine. Far from being overly sentimental about the past, most patients believe that today's doctors are better than ever. The strongest impression people have of their physicians is that they take a personal interest in each patient. The public's outstanding demand of medicine is for competence. Omniscience on the part of physicians and other unrealistic demands are held by only a small minority of patients, the average patient being aware of the limitations of modern science. Typically, people feel that physicians' services are the fairest priced of all medical expenses. The public has a remarkably clear idea of the physician's life, his rewards, and his problems.

Among the most prevalent of the myths held by doctors is that the patient is naïve about what constitutes good medical care. Of course, few laymen can tell an antigen from an antibody from an antibiotic. Nonetheless, studies show that patients are remarkably tough-minded about the care they receive. While a patient may not be able to tell if this surgery is well performed or that EKG properly read, he feels he is able to judge the end product: how well he comes out. The Opinion Research Corporation study for the A.A.G.P. contains this statement:

"Some physicians comfort themselves, when under criticism, by pointing out the incompetence of the public to judge diagnosis or treatment. However, the responsibility for entering into a relationship with one doctor or another does rest with the patient. He has to form some opinion of the effectiveness of what is being done. Accurate or not, the patient has a duty to himself and his family to decide on the competence of the doctor."

Mac Cahal, of the A.A.G.P., believes that many doctors will find it a "somewhat surprising revelation" that people apparently buy medical care as they buy a commodity. When a patient evaluates a physician, he thinks of pragmatic results before any other consideration. The A.A.G.P. survey asked patients to rank items that would be most important to them if they were to decide on a doctor today. Foremost, replied nearly two thirds of the patients, the doctor should do "absolutely everything to make one well again."

A related myth holds that patients are unfair in their demands on doctors. Physicians widely believe that laymen expect them to perform feats of medical magic while surpassing the saintliness of an Albert Schweitzer. Every doctor has had overdemanding patients who expect physicians to act like minor deities. But studies show that these querulous souls are irritating out of proportion to their numbers. Surveys on physician-patient relations demonstrate that laymen by and large are reasonable about what they want from doctors.

According to preferences expressed in the A.A.G.P. study, laymen wish the doctor to be thorough and patient in explaining his diagnosis and treatment. The A.A.G.P. respondents gave these other expectations in this order: The doctor should be up to date in his diagnosis and treatment. He should live up to the special trust placed in him. He should know how to get along with the patient and his family. He should give full value for what he charges.

Nor would most doctors quarrel with the traits that weigh most heavily with patients. "What do you like most about doctors?" patients were asked in a survey carried out for the A.M.A. by Ben Gaffin & Associates of Chicago. The most-desired qualities, patients volunteered, were: Friendliness, personality, manner (mentioned by 30 percent). Personal interest, sympathy, kindness (19 percent). Competence, intelligence (18 percent). The fact that doctors heal and cure (13 percent). Sincerity, dedication (13 percent). Frankness, honesty (10 percent).

Conversely, patients were asked, "What don't you like so well about most doctors?" Their charges and interest in money, replied 13 percent. Don't take time, hurry you too much (9 percent). Impersonal, cold (9 percent). Not frank, speak half-truths, dishonest (9 percent). Unavailable, won't come, can't be reached (6 percent).

Psychologist Ernest Dichter, a pioneer in the application of motivational research to business, was engaged by the California Medical Association to explore laymen's emotional expectations in the doctor-patient relationship. Dr. Dichter conducted lengthy interviews among physicians and patients of the Oakland area. His report was called, in a preface by association spokesmen, the "most valuable public relations document that has yet been presented to medicine."

Dichter's basic finding was that patients are eminently sensible in their desires. They want a "personal physician"—a doctor who diagnoses and treats the whole person, who reveals to his patients a warm and friendly interest in them as people, and to whom patients can come for help in any problem relating to mental as well as physical health. This doctor would be a general manager of medicine. He would refer patients to specialists as needed, but would always serve as the coordinator and overall supervisor of the patient's care.

Many individual G.P.s, internists, and pediatricians already meet most of the specifications of the personal physician. The most successful ones, Dichter determined, also encourage the patient to become an active and informed participant in the treatment, rather than merely a passive recipient of care, for patients wish to take part in their therapy.

When a physician fulfills these criteria, Dichter concluded, his patients are generally satisfied, often enthusiastic about him. As a further result, money is almost never a problem between doctor and patient. The physician feels all right about charging a fee. The patient pays as a matter of course.

Medical Economics similarly surveyed a cross section of patients. The magazine found the greatest source of patients' dissatisfaction to be over-busyness on the part of physicians—as manifested by crowded waiting rooms, long waits, rushed visits. Patients especially resent what smacks of assembly-line medicine when they feel the doctor's hectic schedule results not from any local shortage in medical manpower but from his trying to build a bigger practice than he can handle.

Impersonal care, often a side effect of overbusyness, causes many patients to switch doctors, *Medical Economics* found. Common are complaints like: "I felt I was just another patient." "He could never remember my name." "He disregards personal feelings."

Medical mistakes, real and imagined, are also high on the list of patients' complaints. Patients often complain of too many pills, too many shots, too many stays in the hospital. There are innumerable tales of negligence: misdiagnoses, improper therapy, faulty follow-up care.

Fees too are a leading area of friction. Patients welcome the going rate and speak approvingly of the doctor whose charges are "in line." By the same token, patients object when doctors scale up fees for higher-income people or charge the usual fee for a shorter-than-usual visit. Patients generally like the doctor to initiate the discussion about fees and tell right off what a procedure will cost.

As seen from these surveys, what patients want can be summed up as good medicine at a fair price. In addition, the doctor is judged according to three other criteria. These are: (1) *Availability*. His willingness to make house calls, his promptness in phoning back, his availability for appointments. (2) *Unhurried attention to details*. If he is busy, he doesn't show it. He takes his time and does a careful job. (3) *Compassion*. His sympathy for the patient as a suffering human being, his concern for the patient as an individual rather than as merely another collection of symptoms.

US VERSUS THEM

Another myth held by doctors is that physician-patient conflict is a new phenomenon. This disturbs some present-day doctors, who sense an unprecedented crisis. Actually, an us-versus-them relationship with laymen is part of the history of medicine. It is an incidental but illuminating parallel that primitive healers—witch doctors in Africa, medicine men among American Indians—are jealous of their prerogatives. They band together, excluding outsiders from their private councils. In Chaucer's England, a fourteenth-century code of physicians' conduct warned: "Avoid the company or friendship of laymen. They make a habit of mocking doctors."

Medical historian Donald E. Konold has found that most early efforts by physicians to improve doctor-patient relations took the form of pressures to force the patient into a subordinate position. In this country around 1900 there were frequent demands by doctors that patients overlook their errors, on the grounds that the doctor always did his best and no one could avoid a few slips. Dr. J. A. Cox of Wheeling, West Virginia, whose *Practical Paragraphs for Patients and Physicians* reached a large readership, wanted patients to have nothing short of blind devotion for their doctors. "Unless your faith remains steadfast in failure as well as in success," he instructed them, "it is not worthy of the name. You should believe that, come what may, no other doctor could have done so well as yours."

Many of today's doctors romanticize a period of medical history that has been idealized in the widely reproduced painting by Sir Luke Fildes. The room in the painting bespeaks poverty. Lying on a pillow supported in humble fashion by two chairs is a little girl, desperately ill. Her father stands by helpless, trusting. Her mother is at a table, face buried as she weeps with grief and fear. Beside the girl sits the doctor. His clothes are rumpled, his head bowed. He will keep his solemn vigil until the crisis passes or until death claims the child. No matter, he will leave with the knowledge that he has the affection and devotion of the family. (*Mad Magazine* spoofed such pictures in a satire of a pharmaceutical company's "Great Moments in Medicine" advertising series. A similar scene—depicting great shock, grief, and fear—bore the title "The Doctor Presents His Bill.")

By contrast, today's doctor often feels unappreciated and longs for days gone by when, like Luke Fildes' doctor, he would be loved and respected by patients. The reality, however, is that that day exists more in fancy than in fact. "Medicine's public relations were never as glorious as they are sometimes made out to have been," Dr. Jacob J. Feldman, a biostatistician at the Harvard School of Public Health, has said. "There is evidence that many people were aware in the past that doctors' healing abilities were at best severely limited and their ethics were not beyond reproach."

Lay skepticism about physicians crackles through the ages. The fourteenth-century Italian poet Petrarch warned the ailing Pope Clement VI: "I know that your bedside is beleaguered by doctors and naturally this fills me with fear." Charles Dickens attributed Oliver Twist's uneventful birth to the fact that no physicians were around to kill him with their wisdom.

In December 1793 the citizens of Philadelphia assembled at the statehouse and voted their thanks to the committeemen who had superintended the city during an epidemic that year. A motion was then made to thank the physicians of the city for their services. The motion was not seconded.

In 1922, respondents to a public-opinion study described physicians as "rapacious," "arrogant," "pompous," "inconsiderate." This, observes Dr. Jacob Feldman, was at a time when today's doctors believe the medical profession was "accorded nothing but deification by a grateful populace."

CURRENT ATTITUDES

What do today's Americans think of the medical profession? The answer most frequently offered by authorities is derived from the study conducted for the A.M.A. by Ben Gaffin & Associates.

The Gaffin organization interviewed 3,000 members of the general public. In addition, Gaffin spoke to 100 members of each of five special groups that are unusually knowledgeable about physicians and can influence public attitudes about the profession. These special respondents are journalists, lawyers, pharmacists, nurses, and medical society executives.

Gaffin's conclusions are: People almost universally like and respect their own doctor. Physicians as a group are less well thought of, but attitudes toward doctors are far more favorable than unfavorable.

To explain this, Gaffin has theorized that people's attitudes toward their own doctors are based on their own personal experience, but their attitudes toward doctors in general must necessarily be based upon hearsay. A corollary of this is that bad news is more likely to get reported than good news, and so secondhand information would tend to be negative.

Biostatistician Jacob Feldman believes furthermore that patients unconsciously stack the deck in favor of their *own* doctor. "People are drawn to believe that they are using the 'right' doctor," Dr. Feldman says. "Clearly, it would not be very pleasant to view oneself as having the 'wrong' doctor and still keep using him." Thus patients are predisposed toward liking their own physician but not necessarily doctors at large.

Whatever the dynamics, physicians stand high in the esteem of the patients they see. When asked, "Do you like your own doctor as a person?" 96 percent of the Gaffin respondents gave an unequivocal yes. Only 1 percent said no. In regard to specific attributes, 99 percent believe their doctor is "very capable"; 87 percent think their doctor has "enough personal interest" in patients; 81 percent are satisfied that their doctor gives as much time as patients would like.

The strong affection the typical patient feels for his physician was shown in another way. Gaffin interviewers challenged each respondent with complaints frequently voiced about the medical profession. In most cases, the respondents defended their own physician, denying that such charges applied to him. A common complaint about doctors is that they think they are better than other people. Fully 9 out of 10 Gaffin respondents denied that this was true of *their* doctor; and 8 out of 10 denied that he is not frank enough in discussing illnesses, or that he keeps patients waiting longer than necessary. Are doctors hard to reach for emergency calls? Not *my* doctor, said 3 out of 4.

In another vote of confidence, only 1 person in 8 feels his doctor's charges have gone up too fast. As few as 1 in 17 believes his doctor should be more dedicated. A mere 1 in 20 thinks his doctor ever operates unnecessarily.

Patients are less affirmative when they consider doctors as a group. At least 85 percent feel that their own doctor has one or more virtues—such as sympathy, competence, honesty—that the profession as a whole lacks. The physician at large is uniformly thought to give less time, have less personal interest, and be less frank than the patient's own doctor.

But even with these reservations, the profession as a whole is held in high regard. There is only one ground on which as many as half the Gaffin respondents specifically faulted the profession: 51 percent feel that most physicians are hard to reach for emergency calls.

In only three other areas did 40 percent or more of the interviewees believe that most physicians need improvement: 43 percent feel that doctors charge too much. Another 43 percent believe doctors have the idea they are always right. Some 41 percent are of the opinion that doctors keep people with appointments waiting longer than necessary.

Aside from these expressions of disapproval, physicians can be cheered that over 9 out 10 patients interviewed by Gaffin are satisfied that most doctors are very capable. Some 7 out of 10 believe that most doctors are as dedicated to serving mankind as they should be.

The Opinion Research Corporation survey for the American Academy of General Practice has also produced evidence that people are generally satisfied with their medical service. Again, the patients are shown to think better of their own doctor than of the profession at large. By a three to one margin, the patient's own physician was judged more likely than the average doctor to be sincerely dedicated to his work, to try to prevent illness as well as cure it, to be completely ethical in his dealings. Even so, most people express strong approval when asked: "In general, what do you think of the doctors who have treated you or your family in the past?" Fully two out of three volunteered such comments as "Excellent," "Good," "Fine man," "Splendid physician." Patients were also asked, "Would you say the quality of medical treatment available to you or your family is good, average, or poor?" Seventy-five percent replied "Good." Only 4 percent said "Poor."

So much for the conflict with the public that many physicians perceive. On the whole, doctors exaggerate the degree to which the profession and the laity are at odds. Conversely, they underestimate the high esteem they are held in, especially as individuals by patients they personally see.

Any number of programs have been put forward to improve the relations between the public and the profession as a whole. Many medical societies have at least nominal services to make physicians available twenty-four hours a day. Routinely, societies work with community agencies on health-related projects. Some, recognizing the value of continuing care by one doctor, are promoting the concept of the personal physician. An increasing number are helping members make their practices more efficient in the hope that the doctor will give patients better service with less waiting.

Revising disciplinary procedures would be another effort directed to the needs of the public. It is questionable if even a genuine battle with the lay community would justify the profession's resistance to disciplinary reform. But the battle cry that many physicians hear is largely a false alarm. Public-opinion studies show that at worst there are only spotty areas of friction.

Ironically, some of these sore points derive from the organized profession's tolerance of wrongdoers in its ranks. The A.A.G.P. study found that only 18 percent of the public think the average doctor is completely ethical in his dealings. After surveying 1,200 persons, *Parade* magazine summed up these conclusions: "Today's honest, capable doctor truly deserves what he earns. But there is a mounting belief by the public that the so-called 'few' rotten apples in the doctor barrel are increasing in number. . . . Doctors must police their own ranks more carefully and remove rather than protect the incompetent and dishonest practitioner."

THE TREADMILL

Besides feeling threatened by the lay community, an individual physician often suffers a sense of personal precariousness.

Few physicians are sorry they are in medicine. The clinical satisfactions of successful diagnosis and therapy, the interesting and challenging work, the privileges enjoyed by doctors—none has its equal in any other field. But it is a rare private practitioner who is not greatly dissatisfied with some parts of his practice. Clinical satisfaction—the mainstay of most doctors—wanes with the frustration of trying to keep up with the flood of scientific literature. No doctor can read all he feels he should. Yet to throw away a pile of unread journals is almost sure to produce a twinge of guilt.

Doctors often speak of being on a treadmill. Boredom is a constant problem to many physicians. The same types of cases, often not clinically interesting to begin with, arise too frequently to sustain enthusiasm. Paperwork in medical offices is increasingly becoming an avalanche. Belden Menkus, editor of *Records Management Journal,* estimates that every patient generates at least two and a half pieces of paperwork: health insurance reports, billing slips, letters to employers, and so forth. Each is a dull chore, an irritant to the doctor.

The physician who sees himself on a treadmill is likely to also feel financially insecure. It is a commonplace that doctors handle money poorly. This is attested to by members of the Society of Professional Business Consultants, an organization of management consultants who specialize in serving physicians. A former president of the society has observed of his clients: "They don't realize how out of line their spending habits are in proportion to their true income. Our first problem is usually to get a doctor to stop up the hole in his pocket." The typical private practitioner nets around $30,000 a year before taxes. But as medical management consultants have found, the doctor often spends to the hilt. Despite conspicuous signs of good living, few doctors put aside enough to get rich or even be adequately insured.

The journal *Massachusetts Physician* has warned doctors against "living in a pink cloud" by misreading their true incomes. A doctor who has an inflated idea of what he can spend is "going to pay sassy all along the line. . . . Hospitals and other charities will clamor for handouts. His family will eat and dress at [overblown] standards, and his children will go to expensive schools. . . . When the physician wishes to retire—or has to—[he will find] there has been too little put aside." If the Cadillac-owning physician is a cliché of our culture, his real-life counterpart is the impoverished medical widow.

"Insecurity is the fear of having to lower your standard of living," a New York radiologist has observed. Although this doctor drives an imported sports car and his wife a new sedan, and he lives opposite Central Park, and he sends his children to private school, he is also able to say, "I haven't got a dime."

Maintaining an unrealistic scale of living leads to a common syndrome that is demonstrated by a suburban gastroenterologist in his early forties. Few if any of his patients have any inkling of the depressing merry-go-round this doctor is on. His family spending combined with his income-tax bracket require him to net some $30,000 from his practice merely to meet household expenses. In addition, he must also spend about $20,000 on practice expenses—the private practitioner's normal overhead of 40 percent of his gross. Thus merely to make ends meet he must take in from his practice roughly $50,000 a year. Taking into account vacation and other time away from his practice, he must gross over $1,000 a week—or about $200 a day.

The fact is, he manages to do this. But at considerable expense. He seldom works less than 60 hours a week, sometimes more than 70. Because of his crowded schedule, he believes that his professional development has been arrested. When he began practice he took time to do original work in his field. Ten years ago he regretfully gave that up, and now he feels he devotes too little time even to his professional reading.

He seldom reads for enjoyment, a loss he greets with a pang because he has an interest in contemporary fiction. He completes perhaps one novel a year. His magazine reading is confined to glancing over publications he subscribes to for his reception room. He keeps up with the outside world mainly through television. While he welcomes this nontaxing form of entertainment when he is tired, he recognizes that much that is important is left out of the TV diet. For example, he wishes he knew more in depth about international crises. He knows there are subtleties unexplored on the television screen. But he simply hasn't the time to explore the subject on his own.

Nor has he the strength. Bushed a great part of the day, he keeps going mainly on nervous energy. His routine has taken its toll on his family life. He is home far less than he would like, and much of his time at home is spent merely unwinding from a hectic day. During this interval, he is uncommunicative, often snappish and morose.

He realizes that his relationship with his wife and children has suffered because of his outside pressures. To what extent he is a stranger in his own home he is not prepared to contemplate. Like many men who wish they were closer to their families, he does not stint on their pleasures. He does not dwell on the fact that these expenditures make it that much more difficult for him to get off the treadmill.

This doctor is more introspective than most of his colleagues. He recognizes that he has fallen into something of a trap. At the same time, he can justify nearly all his expenses in the light of his income and his tastes. His house does not seem excessively large, his cars are medium priced, his furnishings are not elaborate. Where does the money go? He wishes he knew.

His pattern of life is so ingrained that it is difficult to break out of despite his resolutions that he "must do something." For this doctor to reorganize his life, it may well take a crisis—an illness, a sudden inability to continue at his present pace. Such an emergency is precisely what he and many private practitioners like him fear most. A store can stay open without its owner being present. A company can continue an employee on salary. But without a physician's direct participation, a medical practice cannot long survive.

Since practitioners characteristically run through so much of their current income, many are in a poor position to retire or undergo a period of disability. Doctors labor in the shadow of a coronary. A wry joke among them is that they often have less security than patients they treat on charity.

21
The Medicolegal Nightmare

THE DOCTOR'S SENSE of insecurity is not eased by the fact that every patient is a potential plaintiff in a malpractice suit. For growing numbers of physicians, the first principle of patient care is "Don't get sued."

Since the dawn of medicine physicians have been liable for malpractice. This general heading takes in acts of negligence, abandonment, and assault. Less often, it also includes such other offenses as breach of contract, breach of privacy, and improper commitment to a mental institution.

At one time the doctor's malpractice picture was even bleaker than now. The Code of the Babylonian king Hammurabi, promulgated around 2000 B.C., provided that if a physician operated on a wound and the patient died, the doctor's hand was to be cut off. The first recorded malpractice action occurred in 1374. One J. Mort, an English surgeon, allegedly maimed a wounded hand through negligent treatment. The court dismissed the case on procedural grounds but indicated that if Mort had not been diligent and had not done his best "it is . . . right that he should be culpable."

The first reported American suit was in 1794. A Connecticut physician named Guthrey performed a mastectomy on a Mrs. Cross. Three hours later she died. Her husband brought suit, alleging that Dr. Guthrey had removed the breast "in the most unskillful, ignorant and cruel manner." A jury found Guthrey guilty and fined him the then-substantial sum of forty pounds.

A later case in Illinois is distinguished by the fact that the attorney for the defendant physician was Abraham Lincoln. The suit alleged an improperly treated wrist fracture leading to a permanent deformity. Lincoln lost the case. In 1860, the year he was elected President, the verdict against his client was upheld. The judgment against the doctor amounted to $700. Most of today's physicians would say "Amen!" to a verdict of only a few hundred dollars, for malpractice awards have risen so dramatically that professional liability and the avoidance thereof is an obsession with many doctors as well as a cause of their feeling oppressed.

$50 MILLION A YEAR

Judgments and settlements in malpractice cases now total some $50 million a year. The size of judgments and the direction of court decisions are largely what make physicians and their insurers nervous, rather than any breathtaking increase in the number of suits. Nationwide, following a sharp rise in the nineteen forties and early fifties, the frequency with which suits are filed appears to be leveling off. A 1963 A.M.A. survey determined that 18.8 percent of actively practicing physicians had been sued at least once for malpractice. There was "no substantial increase" over the 18.6 figure five years earlier. An A.M.A. opinion poll found that only about 30 percent of doctors thought malpractice claims were becoming more frequent. By contrast, 40 percent felt that the incidence of claims had not increased in the past five years. An additional 6 percent believed there had actually been a decrease.

Contrary to the national trend, an individual doctor may find suits coming thicker and faster, depending on where he practices and on his specialty. Malpractice litigation is heaviest in California, where some one in four physicians have been sued. Other states marked by a high incidence of claims are New York, Minnesota, Oregon, and Alaska. By contrast, claims are a relatively minor problem to doctors in North and South Carolina, Pennsylvania, Maryland, and Alabama. Individual cities show similar variations. Physicians and insurers describe the situation as generally calm in Philadelphia, Pittsburgh, Kansas City, and Baltimore, but "shocking" and "intolerable" in New York, San Francisco, Los Angeles, Chicago, and Washington, D.C.

Even states with relatively few malpractice suits experience judgments in six figures. A rough measure of the steady increase in awards has been the rise in premiums for malpractice insurance. (Throughout this chapter, "award" is used in its legal sense—a verdict or judgment by a court to compensate a plaintiff for damages.) Between 1955 and 1965 malpractice rates doubled. If trends in awards continue, rates would double again over the next ten years. In just five years in the 1960s rates for some categories of physicians tripled. Some of these increases point up how not only the doctor's locale but also his premium ratings affect his chances of being sued.

In Iowa, where there is little malpractice litigation, internists—who generally are a low-risk group—can pay under $85 a year for $100,000/$300,-000 policy. (This covers up to $100,000 for each claim and up to $300,000 for all claims filed within the year). A high-risk surgical specialist, like a urologist, in Iowa may pay a bit over $300 for the same coverage. In extremely litigious parts of California, internists pay some $250 and urologists $850. Between the Iowa internist and the California urologist there is a tenfold spread in premiums for identical coverage. For some high-risk specialties, anesthesiology and therapeutic radiology among them, some insurers refuse to write any policies at all.

Because malpractice awards are going up and up, many authorities see more million-dollar verdicts in the offing. Physicians are being widely advised to increase their malpractice coverage to $500,000/$1,000,000. The former typical policy, $5,000/$15,000, has gone the way of the dodo. At one time doctors believed they would be wise to carry only small malpractice insurance policies. "If we carry a policy of only a thousand dollars or so," it was reasoned, "no patient or his lawyer would be foolish enough to sue us for more."

This belief was permanently dispelled when a doctor was sued for allegedly botching plastic surgery. The doctor carried malpractice coverage of only a few thousand dollars. The jury found he had been negligent and awarded his badly scarred patient a judgment of $115,000. The doctor lost his life savings, his home and his car, and finally had to sell his practice. The malpractice premium is now one bill no private practitioner forgets to pay, and some doctors borrow against their life insurance rather than let their malpractice coverage lapse.

Multimillion-dollar *claims* are already quite common. In Bethesda, Maryland, a nine-year-old girl allegedly suffered faulty surveillance at the naval hospital following the exploratory insertion of a tube into her heart. Her father is charging that she suffered heart stoppage that destroyed her brain and reduced her to the state of a vegetable. He is asking damages of $3,000,000. In Baltimore a physician is being sued for $4,500,000 for an accident that occurred during a circumcision. In Buffalo, New York, a patient is asking $5,000,000 for injuries allegedly caused by a sex-transformation operation.

The inevitability of million-dollar malpractice verdicts was seen in the rising through the 1960s of the upper limit of malpractice awards. A judgment of $334,000 (reduced on retrial) was awarded to a woman who charged that she was administered a drug in excessive doses and without proper precautions. The drug allegedly crippled her body's capacity to manufacture red blood cells, resulting in severe aplastic anemia. Male hormone treatments then supposedly caused her to grow a beard.

Some $400,000 was awarded a California boy who is now totally paralyzed, a result of brain damage. Physicians were slow to restore his heart after it stopped while he was receiving anesthesia for surgery to correct crossed eyes. Damages of $650,000 were granted a former aeronautical engineer in New Jersey who is paralyzed from the chest down. His spinal cord was severed during a lung operation.

In California an infant was brought to a proprietary hospital with a fractured skull. According to the allegation: A pediatrician failed to order transfusions immediately in spite of extremely strong indications. A neurosurgeon failed to diagnose a brain hemorrhage. A vascular surgeon failed to administer drugs to keep the child's blood from coagulating and causing dangerous obstructions. The infant suffered permanent brain damage and lost both feet. A jury found the doctors had been negligent and awarded the child $700,000.

Then, in 1967, there were not one but at least three malpractice decisions of over a million dollars. In Covina, California, a nursing instructor with four children suffered paralysis of her arms and legs as the result of an operation to correct a spinal cord problem. Her orthopedist was charged with negligence. The associate surgeon was alleged to have neglected a phone call regarding her paralysis, and a radiologist allegedly overlooked an obvious abnormality. The jury verdict plus settlement brought the total award to $1,238,514. In San Francisco a truck driver underwent surgery on his back. He remained unconscious for several weeks. When he awoke he was found to have the mentality of a three-year-old. There was testimony that a nurse had terminated oxygen only thirty minutes after surgery, and for six hours after surgery no doctor looked in on him. The patient was awarded $1,400,000. In Miami, a woman entered a hospital for varicose veins and hemorrhoids. Two days after surgery she slipped into a coma and has since been paralyzed from the neck down. She asserts that the condition was caused by an excessive dosage of painkilling drugs, which her doctors sometimes prescribed by phone. The judgment in the case was for $1,500,000.

These verdicts may ultimately be brought under a million dollars on appeal to higher courts. The largest malpractice judgment thus far awarded to a patient and upheld on appeal, although later settled for less, has gone to a man who began having attacks of breathing difficulty while serving in the Navy during World War II. The man—here called Andrew David Michaelson—went for treatment to the naval hospital at St. Albans, New York. There, doctors took x-rays of his sinuses, injecting a radioactive contrast dye called Umbrathor to make them visible on x-ray film. X-rays showed a rounded shadow in the left antrum (chamber), apparently a polyp requiring minimal treatment. The allegation continues:

A year later, after his discharge from the service, Michaelson went to the Veterans Administration clinic in Philadelphia for treatment of his sinus trouble. X-rays now showed the presence of an opaque substance in the left antrum. Over the next ten years, clinic doctors took more x-rays, always noting the substance in the left antrum. But no doctors cleared out the sinuses or ascertained what the substance was.

Michaelson continued going to the clinic, complaining increasingly of burning in the nose and throat, and discharge of blood and pus. Although doctors saw him many times, none consulted the original x-ray records in his file. These would have shown that the opaque substance was the radioactive dye that had been injected into the sinuses and had never been removed.

By the time the trouble was finally diagnosed, the retention of the dye had caused cancer. Michaelson underwent radical surgery. His left eye was removed, as was much of the left part of his face, including the left palate and jawbone.

Michaelson now must wear an eyepatch. Strain on his one eye has forced him to give up reading for pleasure. An instrument is attached to his remaining teeth to assist in speaking and eating. His left cheek and upper lip droop. At mealtime he must lift his lip with his hand to place food in his mouth. He is unable to control drooling and the emission of food particles and mucus from his nose and mouth. He is self-conscious of his appearance and has withdrawn even from his own children.

Michaelson was a thirty-six-year-old attorney at the time of the operation. His disfigurement and impaired speech and sight have forced him to curtail his law career. "Far beyond any economic loss and the ending of hopes for advancement in his chosen profession are the dreadful limitations he has suffered in the enjoyment of his everyday life."

So wrote Judge Abraham Freedman of the U.S. District Court in Philadelphia. Judge Freedman found that the physicians at the Veterans Administration clinic had been negligent in failing to remove the substance from Michaelson's antrum. Even if unidentified, Judge Freedman noted, the substance should have been regarded as an irritant that warranted cleaning out.

Moreover, the judge observed, one V.A. doctor actually saw on Michaelson's original x-ray record that he had received Umbrathor which had not been removed. The doctor specifically noted this on the record—but failed to inform the treating physician. The reason he gave was that he was reviewing Michaelson's record for pension, not treatment, purposes.

After computing the extent of the V.A. doctors' negligence and their injury to Michaelson, Judge Freedman awarded him the record total of $725,000 (later settled for $525,000 plus $65,625 attorney's fees).

PATIENTS VERSUS DOCTORS

It is ironic that malpractice actions are looming as a larger threat at a time when most doctors are practicing ever better medicine.

But medicine's growing efficacy is accompanied by increasing specialization. More doctors are tending to see patients only for limited, specialized services. Such care is often impersonal, if not anonymous and cold. And deficient rapport between physician and patient sets the stage for a malpractice suit.

Authorities on malpractice litigation agree that a physician who enjoys a good relationship with his patients is fairly safe from suit, even if he makes a slip. "Patients frequently forgive the accidents of medicine when they are fully informed and fairly treated," says Howard Hassard, executive director and general counsel of the California Medical Association.

"A patient who knows that his doctor is really interested in his welfare and is trying hard rarely sues."

The same slip may send the patient to his lawyer if he is angry or suspicious. The New York State Malpractice Insurance and Defense Board has made a study of claims arising from secondary causes, where there were stimuli in addition to the physician's alleged act of malpractice. In one in five such cases, the board reports, the final decision to sue is prompted by the physician's "callousness" or "lack of frankness." In their book *Trial of Medical Malpractice Cases*, Dr. Harold Williams, a physician-lawyer, and Professor David W. Louisell, of the University of California Law School, hold that malpractice actions differ from most other personal injury cases in the strength and pervasiveness of emotional elements. Frequently, malpractice suits seem to be "more or less independent of the physical injury itself."

Thus whether suit is brought may hinge as much on the doctor's politeness as his medical skill. In *Doctor and Patient and the Law*, Dr. Louis J. Regan tells of a physician who was setting a young man's broken arm. The patient's family asked the doctor some questions. Incensed, he shouted: "Just leave this to me. I know what I am doing." The fracture healed less than perfectly, and the family used the poor result as a reason to sue.

Patients often become angered enough to claim malpractice if they feel a doctor is overzealous in trying to collect his fee. The New York State Malpractice and Defense Board reports that in 23 percent of cases with secondary causes the doctor first sues for payment. The patient then countersues charging malpractice.

One California patient and his physician had a poor relationship from the time the doctor first set a fracture in the patient's lower leg. Pressure sores developed under the cast. The patient protested that he could not reach the doctor when he needed him, and that the doctor was constantly criticizing "unreasonable complaints." At last he discharged the doctor, paying him $150 for his services.

Other physicians thought this a fair fee. But the doctor demanded more and sued to collect. In retaliation, the patient filed a cross-complaint for malpractice.

The A.M.A. Committee on Medicolegal Problems has found that a suit against a physician by a patient of long standing is unusual. The great majority of malpractice claims are lodged against doctors whom the patient knows only from the treatment in question. Physicians are thus often reminded that a warm, continuing association with patients is the strongest deterrent to malpractice claims. Through professional channels doctors are urged to be tactful, show interest, act courteously, follow the Golden Rule.

But many doctors feel that such advice, although well-intentioned, is gratuitous. The American College of Surgeons *Bulletin* has commented:

"A wise and experienced surgeon said not long ago: 'The doctor who is loved by his patients is never sued.'

"As practical advice today, many doctors will protest, this is poppy-cock. Under modern conditions of specialty practice, they ask, how can one possibly be 'loved' by patients—in the way that the old-fashioned family doctor was loved?"

No doctor, it is reasoned, sets out to have a poor relationship with patients. Rather, the realities of present-day medicine make it more and more difficult to develop the sort of rapport that effectively deters suits. Most specialists treat only specific conditions, seldom the whole patient. They see the patient only for a brief period, perhaps surrounding an operation, or else infrequently over long intervals, as in follow-up care for a chronic condition.

Moreover, by training and temperament, many doctors are far more interested in the science of medicine than in the people it serves. While the doctor who is a scientist first and a physician second may realize that he is chilly or awkward with patients, he is likely to turn his mind to what he feels is more important: keeping up with his specialty. In addition, doctors often feel too harassed to engage in the delicate art of patient relations. Keeping one's temper is deemed hard enough—and even this is becoming ever more difficult as the physician shortage worsens, as doctors have more demands upon their time.

A private practitioner may thus be aware of the human-relations causes of malpractice suits. But he also may feel helpless to do anything about them.

Doctors are especially hard put to deter patients who for emotional reasons are suit-prone. In a study for the California Medical Association, psychologist Richard H. Blum has characterized the patient who is most likely to sue as a mild neurotic who wants to have a child-to-father relationship with his doctor. Such patients tend to have "patently unrealistic attitudes toward doctors and medicine." They expect miracle cures and hold it against the doctor if recovery is slow.

A typical suit-prone patient is ambivalent about physicians. He feels all doctors charge too much and he has consulted with chiropractors, yet he sees doctors twice as often as the norm. The suit-prone patient is likely to move from address to address more often than average. He is more likely to suffer from insomnia and worry about constipation.

Dr. Blum feels his findings draw a composite portrait of an immature, dependent personality. In bringing a malpractice suit such persons "are not opportunists selfishly seeking personal gain by dishonest or immoral means," Blum concludes. Rather, they are people who chiefly resent "Father's" failure to cure them. By suing, says Blum, they seek to punish "Father" not so much for his lack of medical skill as for his neglect of their emotional problems.

In trying to avoid malpractice suits, the doctor must also contend with outright frauds. Every physician knows the story of the doctor who encountered a patient in a wheelchair. "What's the matter with you?" the doctor asked. "I told you you were cured."

"Yes," replied the patient. "But my lawyer says I'm permanently disabled."

Malpractice claims are sometimes concocted by patients who deliberately infect wounds, who turn examining tables on top of themselves, who willfully ignore the doctor's orders—all to build a case against a blameless physician. Healthy patients take to their beds for years to prove paralysis. To substantiate charges that the doctor failed to diagnose a fracture, patients who never had one produce borrowed x-rays of friends who actually did. Women attempt to frame doctors with charges of sexual assault. Men claim impotence from treatments that have had absolutely no effect on their sexual performance. Impotence is a hard charge to disprove since the chief witness is usually the man's wife. Legend has it that at least one such plaintiff became a father in midsuit.

Still other patients the doctor must deal with can most charitably be described as irrational. One woman accused a surgeon of deceiving her about an operation six months earlier. He was supposed to have removed an open safety pin from her stomach. But now she was suffering the same symptoms, and x-rays revealed her stomach contained an open safety pin.

She was so convincing that a second physician supported her claim. However, a comparison with the surgeon's original x-rays showed that the pins were different. The woman was a pin swallower. She was eventually committed to a mental hospital—but not before she had brought charges against yet another innocent doctor.

THE LIABILITY REVOLUTION

Plaintiffs sometimes badger innocent physicians by naming in a suit every doctor remotely connected with a case, even every doctor in the community. Such abuse of the right to sue is cited by physicians and insurers who argue that 90 percent of all malpractice claims have no justification. At the opposite extreme, some plaintiffs' attorneys say that even with the charlatans and cranks 90 percent of all malpractice claimants *do* have a bona fide grievance even if it cannot be proved in court.

A number of emerging legal doctrines are now making it easier for patients to prove malpractice and so sue doctors successfully. This liability revolution is a good thing, say plaintiffs' attorneys. They maintain that legal rules governing the trial of medical malpractice suits have long been weighted in favor of the doctor, making it difficult for the abused patient to get justice. "After long years, the small, frantic voice of the patient is heard in the land," says Lou Ashe, a San Francisco trial lawyer.

All this, of course, is expensive to the doctor and his insurer. Physicians and the lawyers who defend them argue that recent court cases are coming perilously close to saying that the doctor ought to be financially liable for unsuccessful treatment whether he has been negligent or not. They complain the trend is making it harder for him to protect himself against unjustified claims. "The average medical practitioner cannot afford to underwrite and guarantee and pay for every bad result that may occur," warns R. Crawford Morris, a Cleveland attorney specializing in malpractice defense.

Doctors and insurers are furthermore worried over a new development affecting the entire field of personal injury claims, of which medical malpractice is a part: The courts are showing a growing feeling that a person ought somehow to be compensated for an injury regardless of who is to blame. This attitude, implicit in many recent decisions, represents a legal philosophy that is spearheading what is sometimes called the Age of Absolute Liability.

Edward J. Bloustein, a philosopher who teaches at the New York University School of Law, is a leading advocate of overhauling malpractice and other personal injury law. "The whole notion of fault as the primary condition of liability just doesn't make sense anymore," he declares. "We used to view an individual's injury as his problem—a misfortune which the one at fault and his family should help to alleviate, but not a problem for society to be concerned about. But now we are beginning to view an individual loss as a society loss—that this man's services are lost to society if he is injured." And so, says Professor Bloustein, through the courts society is compensating those who are injured.

Already, one of the highest personal injury compensations on record has sprung from a questionable connection between the defendant and the plaintiff's injury. At a Baltimore and Ohio Railroad yard in Cleveland a fifty-three-year-old yard helper was standing near a pool of stagnant water. He felt a sting at the back of his left thigh, just above the knee. A moment later he saw a large insect fall from his trouser leg.

The area of the bite gradually came to resemble a boil. Later, similar lesions appeared on his arms, legs, neck, and chest. The condition was diagnosed as pyoderma gangrenosum, a progressive ulceration of the skin. The sores deepened to expose blood vessels, tendons, nerves, underlying muscle sheaths. It became necessary to amputate both legs.

The patient brought a negligence suit against the B. & O. Medical witnesses challenged each other over whether or not an insect bite could cause pyoderma gangrenosum. Opposing entomologists argued over whether the biting insect was a water bug and whether water bugs inhabited pools in the railroad yard. Most fundamental was the question of whether the railroad was liable for the bite of the insect.

A Cleveland jury voted the plaintiff damages of $625,000, holding that the railroad-owned pool of stagnant water brought about the patient's illness and amputations. The verdict was ultimately affirmed by the U.S. Supreme Court, but that hardly laid the matter to rest. Because of the broad implications stretching the limits of liability, intense interest in the case continues in medical circles. "Bizarre," said Dr. Isadore Kaplan, the B. & O.'s medical director, of the jury finding. The Cleveland Academy of Medicine has attacked the verdict in an editorial.

Attorneys representing physicians often speak of such new, broader rules of liability as the law's being "perverted by sympathy." Edwin J. Holman of the A.M.A. Law Department has protested as "unconscionable situations" and a "travesty upon the law" such verdicts as $115,000 for scars on the breast of a fifty-year-old woman and $105,000 for the loss of toes on one foot, with no reduction in earning capacity. Physicians regard it as ominous that more and more six-figure judgments are being brought in against defendants who are only distantly connected with an accident—for the benefit of plaintiffs whose injuries will not necessarily keep them from enjoying a reasonably normal life.

In Brooklyn, for example, the cable on a passing tow truck snapped and the car in tow, now loose, crushed against a young man. A jury held at fault the *city*, on the ground that a hole in the street jolted the truck, causing the cable to break. The young man lost his left leg. In compensation, the jury awarded him $400,000.

Doctors and defense lawyers say such cases exhibit a growing social welfare approach to personal injury claims. One of the most vehement attacks on the "recent effervescence of litigation directed against doctors" has appeared in a law-review article that decries the feeling by patients "that if anything goes wrong someone should be made to recompense them by the payment of damages. This attitude gives rise to hundreds of unfounded or ill-founded claims, virtually blackmailing actions in that it is cheaper to buy off the small ones by a small payment than to fight the case and win. Every bump and bruise and fight and scratch seems now to be thought to justify its quota of compensation, and this mental attitude tends to lead to a legal claim being brought every time there is a real or imagined complaint in respect of medical treatment."

Most physicians feel particularly under a gun. In general, as medical knowledge increases, the legal standard of skill and care becomes more rigorous. The higher the medical level rises, the higher also rises the doctor's legal duty. While doctors may feel this sliding scale is inevitable, they worry that medicine's increasing efficacy is leading the public to go further—to believe that poor results are necessarily the product of carelessness, even though the misfortune was not the doctor's fault. Leaders of the profession feel that the standard being set by many juries is unreasonable. Juries, it is argued, are starting to expect the impossible: that doctors should guarantee perfection.

"The public still recognizes that *certain* ills are incurable," Bernard D.

Hirsh, head of the A.M.A. Law Department, has said. "But in those areas in which cures are normally obtained, many patients immediately blame the doctor if the results are not entirely what they expected. Too many patients think that the doctor can guarantee results, a feeling which, unfortunately, some doctors encourage and other doctors fail to correct."

TOWARD SEVEN FIGURES

Malpractice awards are being swept upward in an overall trend that is raising judgments in every area of personal injury litigation.

J. Victor Hurd, chairman of the Continental Insurance Companies, has contended that the "welfare concept" of compensating injured people has so been adopted by juries that neither the insurance industry nor the public at large (which pays the premium) can continue much longer to afford the steadily increasing awards. Despite such protests, the higher awards do not necessarily represent an abuse, for until recently personal injury awards were marked by their modesty. Judicial interpretation of liability has long tended to protect perpetrators rather than victims, and many deaths and disabilities have resulted in awards of a mere few hundred dollars, often of zero.

Even today, some state laws are stacked against the victim seeking compensation. In Pennsylvania, for example, a defendant who has been found guilty of negligence can enjoy great wealth, ride around in a new limousine, live in a mansion. Yet he may not be required to pay a penny to a victim crippled by his carelessness. If a negligent party sees an adverse judgment coming, with a minimum of discretion virtually all he need do is put his assets jointly in his wife's name. Then, under Pennsylvania's joint-tenancy law, they may not be attached to satisfy a judgment against him as an individual. While he may be liable for fraudulent conversion, chances of proving this are remote—and Pennsylvania is often called the "debtor's paradise." In California, by contrast, the plaintiff almost certainly could collect, for a court judgment equals a lien even if property is jointly held.

Historically, patients have stood only a shade better than a 50-50 chance of collecting on a malpractice claim. A 1958 A.M.A. analysis of claims processed through to completion shows that of 100 claims filed by patients, some 18 were dropped, 35 were settled by the insurance company, and 47 went on to court. Some 7 of these suits were withdrawn before trial, 11 were settled out of court, 5 were decided in favor of the patient, and 24 were decided for the physician. In all, 51 percent of the patients received money.

Today's judicial trends are not only improving the patient's chances of winning a suit. They also are spurring larger settlement offers from insurance carriers. The companies often assume that if a claim reaches a jury it is likely to cost far more.

In one such case, a forty-nine-year-old mother of twins entered a Bronx, New York, operating room for a vaginal repair. Six doctors were present. For reasons none could explain the woman's heart stopped, evidently for a long period, while she was anesthetized. She suffered permanent brain damage, leaving her unable to walk, bathe, or dress without help. Today still, she speaks haltingly and without intelligence.

Her family filed malpractice charges against the physicians and hospital. The defendants elected to fight, only to hear the woman's attorney ask each prospective juror, "Can you conceive of anyone's suffering being worth a million dollars?" He eliminated all those who answered no.

Then the defendants watched their case fall to pieces. None of the four anesthesiologists who had been in the operating room would admit to administering the anesthesia. On the witness stand, the senior surgeon was asked what he did when the operation ran into trouble. He testified, "I tore my hair out."

After nearly three weeks of unflattering testimony, the defendants and their insurers decided that they had better not risk the jury. They came to terms with the woman's attorneys for $317,000—the record out-of-court settlement in a malpractice case.

Plaintiff's lawyers defend rising awards as long overdue. Melvin M. Belli, the San Francisco claimant's attorney, has said: "The most expensive unit of our entire economy is not the wheel, nor the hoist, nor the pulley, but man himself. . . . We pay higher prices than ever for Cadillacs and aluminum buildings and hunting rifles and new airplanes. . . . We are just beginning to pay adequate amounts for human bodies."

Some judges are likewise left cold by complaints about increasing verdicts. The late New York Supreme Court Justice Walter R. Hart challenged whether damage awards can be "excessive" if "human lives and wrecked bodies" are involved. He adds: "Prize bulls have [sold] for $200,000 and a champion race horse for $700,000." Continuing this reasoning, plaintiff's attorneys often ask: What figure begins to pay for a destroyed face, a lost limb, a life of paralysis? How much is an eye or a hand worth to *you?* What value would you place on your pain, your life? How many dollars would compensate you for a wife or child killed by negligence? Imagine a hundred thousand, even five hundred thousand dollars on a table before you. Would you reach for it if first your leg had to be torn off?

This combination of emotion and reason, of sympathy and logic, of evolving law and changing attitudes, has led to what insurers consider their industry's Black Friday. A seven-year-old boy, whom we'll call Arthur Wald, had been walking on 34th Street in Manhattan when he was struck by a large metal sign falling from the roof of a candy shop. The sign left Arthur more dead than alive. It broke his back, cut open his skull to the brain, and left him completely without muscle power. Although he further suffered a collapse of the right lung, he managed to pull through. Now, six years later at the age of thirteen, he was totally paralyzed. He was strapped in braces and confined to a wheelchair, with no voluntary control of his bowel and bladder, and no sensation of touching and feeling other than numbness.

On Friday, September 27, 1963, Arthur's case against the candy chain came to a close. In a summation that has become a classic of its type, attorney Jacob D. Fuchsberg pointed out that Arthur had no hope for rehabilitation and was condemned to being cared for all his life. With blackboard and chalk, Fuchsberg estimated how much it would cost for lifetime help, how much medical expenses would amount to, how much Arthur would have earned if he could have led a normal life. Fuchsberg also sought to put in dollars the price of Arthur's pain, his embarrassment, his loss of the enjoyments of ordinary living.

The damages itemized on the blackboard added up to some two million dollars. After deliberating six hours, the jury returned the nation's first million-dollar negligence verdict—$1,000,000 for Arthur plus $100,000 to his father in compensation for services and suffering.

Insurance companies regarded this as a portent of seven-figure verdicts to come. Within months, a seventeen-year-old New Jersey boy who was paralyzed after an accident in the school gymnasium won $1,215,140 from the school board. Shortly thereafter, in Illinois, the heirs of a real-estate developer killed in a plane crash won an award of $2,000,000 against an airline and an airplane manufacturer. With million-dollar medical malpractice verdicts now a reality, physicians and their insurers look with dread to the first *multi*million-dollar judgment.

EXPANDING GROUNDS

To prove a medical negligence charge, a patient ordinarily needs to establish that the doctor had a duty to act with reasonable care toward the patient, that he did not, and that because he did not injuries were suffered. For lack of such proof, many malpractice suits are thrown out of court.

Now physicians are increasingly uncomfortable over an expansion of the grounds for suit. In many jurisdictions, it seems to many as though doctors are being held strictly accountable. This broadening of liability has been done not by legislatures but by the judiciary, and the setting of precedents favoring patients reflects changing attitudes on some benches.

Dr. Franklin J. Evans, a physician-lawyer and a professor at the University of Miami Law School, has warned doctors: "This judge-made law has been directed toward strict liability . . . almost to the point where the doctor has been made the insurer [of a good result]." Most legal authorities, however, are quick to reassure physicians that these rulings affect only a minority of cases. They are not a wholesale reversal of the favored position the law has generally granted physicians in malpractice suits. The judicial benefits the doctor still enjoys have been summed up by one judge sitting on a malpractice case: "Malpractice is hard to prove. The physician has all the advantage. . . . Physicians . . . are loath to testify a fellow craftsman has been negligent. . . . The physician is not an insurer of health. He undertakes only for the standard of skill possessed generally by others practicing in his field, and for the care they would give in similar circumstances. He must have latitude for play of reasonable judgment, and this includes room for not too obvious or gross errors according to the prevailing practice of his craft."

But despite such expressions of assurance, doctors see a sharp diminishment in their protection from suit. As a result of recent rulings, physicians widely fear that a patient need not even prove existence of an injury to make his malpractice charge stick. Several cases have established the precedent that a plaintiff can collect damages merely for a state of mind. Where formerly a physical injury of some sort was needed to sustain a malpractice suit, "mental anguish" now is enough.

There need not even be physical contact. In New York a medical laboratory reported that a patient's sperm analysis showed his sperm count so low as to constitute sterility. Later it was discovered that an error had been made; the sperm count was normal. The patient sued the lab for mental suffering, pain, and anguish resulting from his belief that he was sterile. In the course of this litigation, the court cited the new rule that physicians and their insurers lament: "Freedom from mental disturbance is now a protected interest in this state."

This ruling raises the possibility that an act by a physician could be held to constitute malpractice if it produces anxiety in the patient. The first state-of-mind suit was brought by a New York City housewife who was burned by x-rays while being treated by radiologists for bursitis in her right shoulder. A dermatologist who treated the burn routinely suggested that she have her shoulder checked every six months. "That burn might become cancerous," he explained.

The woman sued the radiologists for negligence, charging that not only had they burned her but they also had caused her to suffer cancerophobia, the morbid fear of developing cancer. "We are not making any claim that this person is going to sustain cancer," her attorney told the court. "We are going on a neurosis." A psychiatrist attested to her dread of cancer and testified that she might have permanent symptoms of anxiety.

The jury voted an award of $25,000. In this landmark judgment, only $10,000 was for the burn. The larger sum of $15,000 was to compensate her for her cancerophobia. The New York Court of Appeals, upholding the award, ruled that a "wrongdoer is liable for the ultimate result" of his mistake, even though the damage may be mental rather than physical. A strong dissenting opinion argued otherwise. Expressing the apprehension held by many physicians, the dissenting judge warned that the decision introduces into the law a new field of damages affording "countless opportunities for fraudulent unverifiable claims."

"It is small wonder that many physicians were suffering 'mental anguish' of their own," Dr. Franklin Evans has remarked. Malpractice losses are further rising because of new evidence rules that many doctors deem medically questionable or unfounded. Physicians often complain that the courts are not only writing new law but are also rewriting medicine, making assumptions that science regards as speculative at best. "The 'rule of sympathy' is gradually replacing scientific tenets and medical opinions are falling gradually into disrepute," protests Dr. Evans. "In effect, medicine no longer need be called upon to evaluate and to opinionate on medical problems; the laity, the lawyers, and the courts have taken it upon themselves to usurp the practice of medicine."

The conflict of legal versus medical evidence has recently been dramatized by cases in which large judgments have been awarded despite considerable challenging on grounds of medical fact. In Queens, New York, a fifty-three-year-old toolmaker watched as a passing car went out of control, roared across his lawn and headed toward where he was standing. The car veered into a pole at the last moment. But forty-five minutes later the toolmaker, unscratched, died of a heart attack. His widow charged that the attack was the result of shock and fright, and she sought damages against the owner of the car.

Doctors point out that they cannot be sure when fright—or any severe emotional shock—has actually brought on a fatal heart attack. Yet at a hearing a court ruled that the toolmaker was literally frightened to death. Despite physicians' cautioning that the medical evidence was doubtful, a Queens Supreme Court judge awarded the widow $740,000.

Physicians sometimes feel that a judge knows even less about the development of unborn infants than he does about the heart. Thus doctors are disturbed by recent decisions extending the physician's liability into the area of prenatal injuries. A fetus is now considered to have the legal right to begin life unimpaired by physical or mental defects. It may sue after birth and recover damages for an injury it received in the womb due to alleged negligence. If it is miscarried or born dead, suit may be brought in its behalf.

On this extension of liability, a Washington State doctor was ordered to pay $89,000 in damages for injuries suffered by a child before he was born. The child was born with cerebral palsy. The Washington Supreme Court, supported by plaintiff's medical witnesses, held that the disease could have been caused by a prenatal oxygen deficiency resulting from the doctor's failure to treat the mother's anemia. To deny the doctor's responsibility in this case, the court said, "would do reverence to an outmoded, timeworn fiction" that a fetus has no legal rights.

Physicians who must use hospital facilities and staff are especially worried about the expanding doctrine of respondeat superior, "the master must answer." Doctors have long been liable for negligence by their own employees: by, say, an office nurse who gives a harmful injection through carelessness. The doctor controlled her acts and she was acting for him, and so he comes under the respondeat superior rule.

The hospital presents a gray area—for who is responsible for the acts of residents and interns? They are hospital employees, but they often work under the attending physician. He is expected to train them, but he also gets the benefit of their services. Is he therefore also liable for their negligence?

Depending on the degree of control he has over them, the courts are increasingly answering yes. This is part of a general trend in negligence law to spread the liability. Where the hospital alone or one physician alone was formerly deemed the liable party, now joint responsibility is likely to be divided among the hospital and the physicians on the case. Doctors often feel this is unfair, since they are being held personally liable for acts over which they argue they have no real control.

In a precedent-setting case, an obstetrician followed hospital delivery-room routine to the letter. While he completed a cesarean section on the mother, he had an intern take over care of the newborn. Out of his sight, the suit charged, the intern administered silver nitrate solution into the baby's eyes. This powerful germ killer, used to prevent blindness, is ordinarily given by the drop and flushed out immediately. The inexperienced intern allegedly poured the substance into the little girl's eyes. Burns developed and one eye had to be removed.

The obstetrician, occupied with sewing up the mother, had no opportunity to alter the course of events. But the court reversed a nonsuit in his favor and made a jury question of whether he had the power—and the obligation—to give the intern orders. Thus the possibility was raised that he was personally liable for the intern's error.

Physicians find this responsibility for hospital staff members oppressive. In the eyes of the law the relationship between a private practitioner and an intern or resident may be that of a master and his servant. But physicians know that in reality the relationship can be extremely tenuous, for house staffers exercise considerable independence.

In one Pennsylvania case a resident in anesthesiology gave a faulty injection of Pentothol, causing an obstruction in blood circulation and subsequently requiring amputation of the patient's left arm. No other doctor was present when the resident gave the injection, and the patient had not yet entered the operating room. Although the chief anesthesiologist learned that the patient's arm had been injured and should be treated immediately, he went ahead with the operation. For two hours neither he nor anyone else told the surgeon of the accident. Nonetheless the surgeon was judged to have overall responsibility for the case and was held co-liable for the $75,000 verdict.

THE THING SPEAKS FOR ITSELF

The expanding doctrine that is most worrisome for physicians is that of res ipsa loquitur, "the thing speaks for itself."

As applied in most malpractice cases, this doctrine implies that some injuries patients receive are in themselves such overpowering evidence of negligence that a patient does not need medical witnesses to prove his case. If the judge agrees with the patient's attorney that the injury "speaks for itself," it is up to the doctor to prove that his negligence is not to blame for it. In effect, res ipsa shifts to the doctor the burden of defending himself, where previously the burden was on the patient to prove the doctor at fault.

Lawyers point out that the defendant's bearing the burden of proof is not unfair or even very unusual under the law, especially not in the many accident cases in which res ipsa is applied. Even in criminal cases, where the prosecution by tradition must prove guilt beyond the shadow of a doubt, the burden of proof can shift to the defendant—for example, if he claims self-defense or insanity as his defense. Despite the frequent use of res ipsa in other areas of the law, physicians widely feel put upon by its being applied to malpractice cases. An ominous note in the *Journal of the Medical Society of the State of Alabama* expresses the prevailing view in medicine: "You are no longer innocent until proved guilty, but you are deemed guilty until you prove yourself innocent."

Actually, res ipsa is merely a way the courts have of expediting a case by responding to apparent facts. It does not guarantee a plaintiff's victory. The defendant physician is entitled to explain away the charge of negligence. If he demonstrates that he acted with reasonable skill despite the bad result, the judge may throw the patient's case out of court. At a minimum, the judge may withdraw res ipsa and put the burden of proof back on the patient. John H. Tovey, a malpractice lawyer who frequently counsels physicians, calls res ipsa the "most inflated malpractice threat." Tovey estimates that in only seventy cases a year are patients successful in their use of res ipsa, less than half the cases in which it is attempted. "It's time doctors learned a few facts about the one threat that's less menacing than they think," Tovey has said.

Res ipsa can be traced back to a case occurring in Liverpool in 1863. A pedestrian, Mr. Byrne, was walking on the sidewalk when he was struck on the head by a barrel of flour falling from a storeroom window. At the trial, Mr. Byrne's attorney—the jurist Sir Frederick Pollock—first expressed the doctrine of res ipsa loquitur. Said Baron Pollock: (1) The barrel was in the exclusive control of the owner of the property. (2) Barrels do not fall from windows unless they have been negligently placed. (3) It is the duty of persons who keep barrels to take care that they do not roll out.

Since this case, res ipsa has been routinely applied in train wrecks, plane crashes, and the like. While there is often no way of knowing whether a company or employee was negligent, it is assumed that such accidents do not happen unless negligence is present. In Mississippi a decaying human toe was found in a package of chewing tobacco by a consumer who developed ptomaine poisoning from it. In the lawsuit that followed, a judge restated the res ipsa principle: "We can imagine no reason why, with ordinary care, human toes could not be left out of chewing tobacco, and if toes are found in chewing tobacco, it seems to us that somebody has been very careless."

In medical malpractice cases, res ipsa can be invoked if the plaintiff's attorney convinces the trial judge that three conditions are met: The injury did not arise from the patient's willful action. The injury sprang from a situation under the doctor's exclusive control. And the injury would not ordinarily occur without negligence. The first application of res ipsa to medical malpractice occurred in 1916 in California, the state where the doctrine continues to have its widest application. A woman was burned on the leg while she was still anesthetized from an appendectomy. The shape of the burned area strongly suggested that a scalding bed warmer had been placed next to her leg. Though none of the persons who treated her would admit putting the bed warmer near her, the woman was able to prove her case. The Supreme Court ruled: "Negligence like almost any other fact can be proved by circumstantial evidence."

Res ipsa has been applied most often in cases in which objects have been left in surgical patients: sponges, rubber drains, needles, gauze, hemostats, scalpels, towels. The foreign bodies in res ipsa cases could stock a small hospital. In 1944 res ipsa as a doctrine for medical malpractice suits gained great impetus. A patient named Ybarra awoke from an appendectomy to find that his right shoulder was paralyzed. His case was thrown out of court for lack of witnesses.

On appeal, the Supreme Court of California found for him. The court stated that when a patient receives unusual injuries while unconscious or under treatment, all those defendants who might have caused the injury can be expected to be called on to prove they were not negligent. Then the court went on to strongly defend the use of res ipsa in some malpractice cases: "Without the aid of the doctrine a patient who received permanent injuries of a serious character, obviously the result of someone's negligence, would be entirely unable to recover unless the doctors and nurses in attendance voluntarily chose to disclose the identity of the negligent person and the facts establishing liability."

The Ybarra decision provided a precedent for applying res ipsa that has been cited by courts in every geographical region of the country. Res ipsa has also spread because of the reluctance of physicians to testify against one another. The doctrine presupposes that some results of negligence are so obvious that no expert testimony is needed to establish carelessness.

In many cases res ipsa is the only way the patient can get around the unavailability of medical witnesses. Recognizing this, courts often apply res ipsa as a means of restoring equity to the patient. One court recalled how this has come about: "Gradually the courts awoke to the so-called 'conspiracy of silence.' No matter how lacking in skill or how negligent the medical man might be, it was almost impossible to get other medical men to testify adversely to him. . . . Not only would the guilty person thereby escape from civil liability for the wrong he had done, but his professional colleagues would take no steps to insure that the same results would not again occur at his hands. . . . [These facts] forced the courts to attempt to equalize the situation."

EFFECTS OF THE NIGHTMARE

"Throughout the medical profession there is a growing fear that any doctor can be branded as negligent even though he is not negligent." So one effect of the physician's malpractice nightmare has been summed up by Dr. Joseph F. Sadusk, Jr., who has conducted much medico-legal research.

Protecting oneself against suits amounts to a major preoccupation among physicians. At medical conventions and medical society meetings, tens of thousands of doctors have seen two of the most popular films in medicine. These have nothing to do with clinical science but have been prepared by the A.M.A. and the American Bar Association. One film, *The Doctor Defendant*, presents cases of physicians involved in malpractice claims, with advice on how to avoid such situations. The other, *The Medical Witness*, outlines the proper conduct of the testifying doctor.

Just as plaintiffs' attorneys hold seminars on how to beat the doctor in court, so the A.M.A. conducts regular medicolegal forums on how to avoid suit. Some seven out of eight medical students are introduced to the ins and outs of medical jurisprudence as part of their medical school curriculum. Their instruction continues at hospital meetings and through the hundreds of articles medical journals run on the subject each year. Malpractice insurers unceasingly remind doctors to stay within their field of competence, get the patient's consent, call in consultants, keep good records—the better to avoid a malpractice charge. "If the specter of a suit is raised," malpractice carriers advise in sum, "say nothing and call your insurer."

There is evidence that doctors suffer more from anxiety over what might happen in a suit than they do from an actual verdict. Broadly speaking, the doctor who sustains a malpractice claim suffers little material damage to his practice or reputation. In response to an A.M.A. survey, some three out of five executives of state medical societies said the effect of claims and suits on a doctor's professional standing was "very little" or "none." Over three out of four executives who gave an answer said effects of a suit were "not at all lengthy—a matter of months or weeks."

In a study for the Yale University School of Law, Dr. Robert L. Wyckoff interviewed fifty-eight members of the Connecticut State Medical Society who had been sued for malpractice. Dr. Wyckoff, a physician-lawyer, found that not one of the former defendants felt he had been permanently hurt, professionally or socially, as a result of the suit. Even where publicity was greatest, the damage was apparently fleeting. No doctor needed to relocate. None suffered a long-lasting or sizable loss of patients. The most measurable adverse effect came at the hands of insurance carriers. A few doctors had to pay higher premiums. Two were dropped by their insurer.

While dollars-and-cents effects may generally be relatively mild, in individual cases they are extremely severe. Physicians' finances have been laid waste by malpractice judgments far in excess of their insurance. Doctors who go bankrupt can lose even their offices and equipment. Merely replying to the claim and attending trial can cost the physician-defendant thousands of dollars in lost time. Bernard Hirsh of the A.M.A. Law Department has observed: "A lawsuit is a serious matter irrespective of the fact that the doctor wins. There's a certain stigma that attaches to a malpractice claim even if it does turn out to be unfounded."

Probably worst for most physician-defendants are the emotional effects of a suit. The anxiety doctors feel about being sued is real, and so also is the ordeal that accompanies actual litigation. A physician is seldom able to take a suit in stride in the way that lawyers and businessmen often can, especially not with a six- or seven-figure verdict hanging over his head. The much-feared first suit is jarring in many ways. A physician who was sued for the first time in a long career tells how the experience affected him. "It was devastating," he recalls. "For two months after the suit was filed, I couldn't sleep. I completely lost confidence in myself. The list of charges seemed to be a record of nearly every medical mistake possible. I kept asking myself, 'Could I have been so wrong? Is it really possible to see ten thousand patients and never make a mistake and then fall flat on my face with the ten thousand and first.'"

A physician who is present at his trial must sit silent as his professional abilities are examined in microscopic detail. One former malpractice defendant has recalled that he felt like a specimen insect with a pin through his middle. The physician in court will hear his training, his skill, his motives put in the worst possible light. But however maligned he feels, he may say nothing until he takes the witness stand. Then he is in for a corrosive cross-examination by the plaintiff's attorney. And though he is angered by the opposing lawyer's sarcasm and offended by his insinuations, he must reflect naught but patience and good will at the risk of antagonizing the jury.

Throughout the trial, the doctor may be caught in the glare of unfamiliar and extremely unwelcome publicity. Unsympathetic reporters and sensational accounts of the trial have permanently soured many doctors on the press. The physician is likely to fear that all the accusations against him are being believed by his patients and colleagues. He may become self-conscious enough to disbelieve people who express commiseration and equally mistrust those who say nothing.

A malpractice trial is bound to be the most trying experience in a doctor's life, and the days he spends on the witness stand may be nearly unendurable. For some doctor-defendants the anxiety has an aftermath. Dr. Robert Wyckoff reports that, in a sizable minority of cases, a malpractice suit poisons the physician's attitude toward his patients and practice. One pediatrician told Dr. Wyckoff of being more lawsuit-conscious than ever before. "I'm very cautious now about telephone calls. I always have a nurse on the extension listening in as a witness." While extreme, this reaction is only a shade more elaborate than another doctor's. "I find myself making two diagnoses," this physician says. "What's wrong with the patient? And: Will he sue?"

ON THE PLUS SIDE

Because of the doctor's fear of being sued, patients are getting medical care that in some respects is better and in others is worse.

Medical Economics has asked 500 doctors what net effect they think the growing threat of malpractice suits is having on patients' welfare. Results of the survey show that only one doctor in five thinks the malpractice threat is inhibiting good medicine. Twice as many believe the quality of medicine has actually improved.

On the plus side, doctors are forced to be more thorough. The individual physician is mindful of the suit that might result if he slips up. Where physicians work together—in hospitals, groups, partnerships—there is often an organized effort to use better methods, spurred on by the fear of litigation. The new accountability that hospitals have to the courts has hastened the development of cardiac resuscitation teams to revive patients suffering heart stoppage. A big impetus to making instrument and sponge counts after surgery has been given by the courts' applying the doctrine of res ipsa loquitur to cases in which objects have been left in patients. With hospitals now liable for accidental injuries to patients, new attention is given to safety in the selection of materials and equipment.

More than half of the general practitioners replying to the *Medical Economics* survey say that the malpractice threat is making them keep more detailed records and order more x-rays. Doctors in general tend to be more cautious in administering therapy. Rather than give advice over the telephone, they are more likely to insist that a patient come into the office—a burden to both the patient and the doctor in most cases, but one that assures more accurate diagnosis and treatment.

Similarly, physicians are less prone to allow automatic refills on prescriptions. Doctors have learned that to write "refill p.r.n." ("pro re nata," according to circumstances) on a prescription is to risk the patient's continuing the wrong medication, even deliberately taking a suicidal overdose. Under the onus of liability, doctors are thus becoming more exacting in their follow-up care—requiring patients to come in more frequently, supervising a case more closely.

Doctors are furthermore exercising more caution in the procedures they attempt. Dr. Earl Barth, while president of the American College of Radiologists, said: "One good effect of the malpractice threat is that it's helping limit x-ray therapy to trained therapists." Throughout medicine, physicians are being stimulated to confine themselves to services for which they are fully qualified.

Consultations are more in order, with the result that a patient is likely to be referred to an appropriate specialist faster. Many physicians have simply withdrawn from fields in which they feel shaky. Even where G.P.s could retain hospital surgical privileges, great numbers have given up surgery largely because of the difficulty they would have defending themselves in a suit.

Malpractice suits thus constitute a preventive device, helping to upgrade standards of care. Once sued, physicians and hospitals generally take great pains to avoid making the same mistake twice. Among those who have never been sued, an intense amount of effort is devoted to not making that mistake even once. Lawyers like to tell the story of the doctor-defendant who was charged with a serious misdiagnosis. He contended that he had to do all his own diagnostic work because the nearest specialists were too far away.

"Do you still do all your own diagnosing," he was asked in court.

"No," he replied. "I send a lot of patients fifty miles to the medical center."

"When did you start doing that?"

"The day I got this subpoena."

THE PATIENT PAYS

At the same time, the malpractice threat is costing patients a lot of money. Some of it represents the unavoidable costs of higher-quality care. For safety's sake, an increasing number of doubtful cases are being hospitalized—which translates directly into higher hospital and insurance costs. Similarily, to pin down a diagnosis, the doctor is ever more likely to recommend a beneficial consultation and additional worthwhile lab tests—despite the added expense to the patient.

But such carefulness can reach a point of diminishing returns. The patient may be called on to continue paying while the doctor seeks to dot the last *i* and cross the last *t*. Out of overcaution, physicians increasingly give treatments of marginal value immediately, even though the patient would be better off if nature were first allowed to take its course. Thus many patients suffering from colds get—and pay for—penicillin to prevent complications, although complications may be only a remote possibility. A child with an insect bite may receive an antihistamine injection, whereas an ice cube and calamine lotion would bring relief just as well.

Illustrative of excessive medical treatment is the case of a young man who woke up one morning with a stiff neck. His family doctor gave him treatments with a diathermy machine, costing $18 for three visits. The stiff neck lasted five days. Some months later he again developed a stiff neck. This time, on his boss's recommendation, he went to a specialist in physical medicine. He received ultrasonic treatments, injections of procaine, applications of low-temperature vapor, and massages lasting a half-hour each. This cost him a total of $120. The stiff neck lasted five days. The following summer he and his wife were on a vacation when once more he came down with a stiff neck. The owner of their hotel lent him a heating pad. This cost him nothing. The stiff neck lasted five days.

"Malpractice suits are [making] . . . the cost of illness . . . almost prohibitive, because of the numerous laboratory tests, x-ray pictures, and consultations they make necessary for the protection of the doctor," Dr. Miley B. Wesson, a past president of the American Urological Association, has written. At the patient's expense, many physicians order more extensive lab work than is actually needed for making or confirming a diagnosis. Their eye is toward demonstrating, if need be, that they were not negligent.

So it is with x-rays. "Many unnecessary procedures in the field of roentgenology are performed daily throughout the United States in order to avoid a subsequent lawsuit," Dr. William F. Mitty, Jr., a surgeon, has said. "Surgeons are ordering x-rays primarily to avoid legal problems and complications rather than to exercise good clinical judgment."

How the malpractice threat can inflate diagnostic costs is illustrated by what sometimes happens after, say, a housewife hits her head on a kitchen-cabinet door and gets shooting pains across her forehead. In a less litigious day, the doctor would have told her over the phone: "Of course you've got a headache. You just banged your head. Take two aspirins, lie down with a cold compress, and call me if it's not better in an hour." In all but a minuscule number of cases, this approach would prove right, and the episode would end.

Now, a substantial number of physicians are unwilling to take even that slight a risk of failing to spot a brain injury. Today's doctor may therefore order the patient in for skull x-rays, for it is prudent to check for a fracture. Just to be safe, the doctor might also have an electroencephalogram performed. Driving him on is not only good medicine but also the fear of a lawyer's voice pressing him, "Is it not good practice to perform electroencephalographic examinations on patients with head injuries? What made you decide not to have an EEG performed on the late Mrs. Jones?"

On the off chance that there might be a blood clot in the brain, the doctor may have Mrs. Jones stay in the hospital overnight for observation. A hospital admission necessitates history and physical examination and a battery of laboratory tests. It is a relief to all concerned when all the tests are negative and Mrs. Jones goes home. Meanwhile there has been a frightened Jones family, now faced with over $100 in medical and hospital bills.

MORE THAN DOLLARS

The cost is measured in more than dollars when the threat hurts patient care.

In his study of former malpractice defendants, Dr. Robert Wyckoff found the "most distressing aspect of the malpractice menace" to be that "doctors who have been burned tend to stop doing valuable procedures." Hundreds of physicians told the *Medical Economics* survey on malpractice effects that the fear of suits is causing them to shy away from many risky but clinically desirable procedures. These doctors regret that they are thus practicing poorer medicine.

"There are physicians today who are *afraid* to use certain proved, useful diagnostic procedures," says Dr. Louis Regan. "Why? Because there's one chance in a thousand that the procedure might harm a patient—and that one chance has resulted in a disproportionate number of malpractice suits." Dr. Albert G. Clark, a San Francisco surgeon, has remarked: "There is no doubt that patients are being turned away, referred to other doctors, or sent out of state by physicians afraid to attempt procedures involving a certain degree of risk." In New York State Supreme Court, judicial notice has been given to the reluctance of physicians to engage in certain procedures. Justice Jacob Markowitz has cautioned: "Neither a physician nor a hospital should be deterred from the exercise of sound medical judgment with respect to necessary treatment merely by threat of possible legal action."

But deterred physicians are. At a hospital affiliated with the Stanford University Medical School, Martin Salgo—a fifty-five-year-old San Franciscan suffering pains and poor circulation in his legs—was diagnosed as having a blockage in the aorta, the large artery carrying blood from the heart to branch arteries in the legs. With Salgo's consent, physicians sought to trace the obstruction by means of aortography, a procedure in which an opaque fluid is surgically injected into the aorta and then x-rayed.

Salgo's x-rays, read while he lay anesthetized, showed the aorta to be blocked just below the vessels leading to the kidneys. The procedure seemed to go normally. But when Salgo awoke the next morning he was unable to move from the waist down. His legs, bladder, and bowels were completely paralyzed.

In the ensuing malpractice suit, the trial judge applied the doctrine of res ipsa loquitur, ruling that Salgo's paralysis was grounds for the jury to infer the defendants' negligence. The jury awarded Salgo $250,000. Though the judgment was reversed on appeal and a new trial ordered, the case of Salgo versus Stanford has cut a wide swath among physicians.

Aortography is a preferred technique when patients suffer poor circulation with apparent blockage to the leg. But largely because of the Salgo case, many physicians are loath to recommend aortography. The judge's application of res ipsa plus the jury's quarter-million-dollar award has convinced them that the procedure is too risky.

The courts have long recognized that medicine is not an exact science, just as the human body is not a perfectly understood machine. "Even with the greatest of care untoward results do occur in surgical and medical procedures," the California District Court of Appeal has written. Indeed, physicians add, virtually every service in medicine has some element of risk. Dr. David B. Allman, a past-president of the A.M.A., has predicted that as doctors grow ever more fearful of being sued, they "will have a tendency to omit highly successful but slightly dangerous medical procedures."

Already many radiologists elect to do no radiation therapy because they skate on thicker ice if they do diagnostic work only. Often radiotherapists seek to keep risks to a minimum by referring away conditions such as benign tumors that may also be treated surgically, although radiotherapy would be the technique of choice. In some conditions the preferred diagnostic or therapeutic technique entails catheterization of blood vessels, the insertion of a fine tube into the circulatory system. Because of complications that occur in a small percentage of patients, internists often decline to risk it.

Surgeons frequently hesitate to do preventive surgery if they lack the patient's consent. Thus a surgeon operating for another condition in the abdomen may see an apparently diseased appendix. Even though it would benefit the patient not to undergo another anesthesia and operation, the surgeon is likely to leave the appendix in rather than risk suit over an unauthorized appendectomy.

Large numbers of emotionally disturbed patients are finding it increasingly difficult to hold on to their doctors. Where formerly a physician would be reluctant to cast adrift patients who are uncooperative or excessively demanding, he may now regard them as suit-prone. Such patients are labeled DYNAMITE in many medical offices and are excused as quickly as possible.

The field of anesthesiology well shows how the medicolegal threat has wrought changes of doubtful medical value. When the anesthetic halothane first appeared, it seemed an answer to the anesthesiologist's dream. Its induction is smooth and rapid, and it produces few side effects. However, though one of the safest anesthetics, it got bad headlines.

After long and successful use, halothane was involved in a freak outbreak of operating-room explosions, largely the result of faulty methods and equipment. The public became unfavorably aware of halothane. Now many anesthesiologists, fearing that juries would find negligence in their use of this "dangerous" anesthetic, have abandoned it for less satisfactory methods.

Spinal anesthesia has met a similar fate. Anesthesiologists regard anesthetizing the spinal cord as one of the safest methods they know. But the possibility of nerve injury from the spinal needle has received an enormous amount of publicity. Moreover, courts have applied res ipsa to cases of paralysis resulting from spinals. Thus the technique is avoided by many physicians and is forbidden by some hospitals, even when it would be the method of choice.

So much for the physician's medicolegal nightmare and its profound effects on doctors and patients and medicine. "If a physician must become increasingly apprehensive of legal suits," the *Journal of the A.M.A.* has concluded, "his own aggressive instincts will inevitably in some measure overcome his humanitarian and professional motivation. Such a doctor will be inclined to give too much time to protecting himself and less to the care of his patient."

22
Rules of the Guild

IN THE YEAR 1363, the world was in disarray following the siege of the Black Death. To help restore order, the church under Pope Urban V issued an edict requiring every artisan in Christendom to join a guild.

The guilds, which developed throughout the Middle Ages, were associations combining religious and professional functions with the regulation of a craft. Each guild held a monopoly on its trade. Each had the right to control the work and behavior of its members.

Physicians belonged to professional fraternities comparable to guilds. These governed the individual practitioner's relations with colleagues and patients. One code of medical ethics in medieval England instructed physicians: "Do not look lecherously on the patient's wife, daughters, or maid-servants, or kiss them, or fondle their breasts, or whisper to them in corners. Such conduct distracts the physician's mind from his work." The present-day Royal College of Physicians evolved from such regulatory associations.

Medieval physicians were aristocratically inclined and thought surgery a menial, technical branch of medicine. Physicians came to disdain surgery altogether after the church in 1272 forbade clerics to shed blood in any form. The gap was filled by barbers, who had some experience with minor surgical skills. In addition to cutting hair and trimming beards, barbers had long pulled teeth and opened abscesses. Now barbers, under aegis of the Barber-Surgeons' Guild, moved into major surgery.

The surgical needs of battlefield casualties spurred the growth of a separate group, military surgeons. As a means of protecting their craft interests, London practitioners formed the Guild of Military Surgeons. Subsequently, barber-surgeons and military surgeons united. From the resulting guild decended the present Royal College of Surgeons.

With the settlement of America, the influence of both Royal Colleges was carried across the Atlantic. The background to American medical developments is thus provided by the guilds of Britain—with their emphasis on the business life of the doctor as well as on his humanitarianism. Early guild philosophy still prevails in many of the rules governing American medical societies. Some of these are detrimental to the patient. Some contribute to the disciplinary weakness of the profession.

THE ANATOMY OF ETHICS

"The principal objective of the medical profession is to render services to humanity." Thus the A.M.A.'s Principles of Medical Ethics sets forth the profession's humanitarian ideal.

While much of medical ethics does in fact rest on high ideals, the word "ethics" as used in regulating medicine operates in its more general dictionary sense, being merely the bylaws—good and bad—that guide a group. Medical societies often overlook the distinction and speak of whatever is ethical as being necessarily virtuous. The humorist Irvin S. Cobb came close to the true meaning of medical ethics when he said, "Anything doctors do in a mass is ethical."

There are at least three categories of bylaws governing medical societies. One, the best known, is aimed at humanitarianism—the deep concern for the patient's well-being, the "full measure of devotion" that the A.M.A. Principles require. Other ethics are actually rules of etiquette, setting forth how doctors should behave toward one another as colleagues and competitors. A third type of ethic is economic, protecting the profession's financial interests.

Much the same areas of self-interest exist today as in May 1847, when some 250 physicians met in Philadelphia to found the American Medical Association. "From slumbers too long indulged, the profession has at length awoke," intoned the association's first president, Dr. Nathan Chapman of the University of Pennsylvania. While the A.M.A. owed its origins to an effort to reform medical education, it quickly moved into other matters.

A committee headed by Dr. Isaac Hays was formed to draft a code of ethics. Dr. Hays studied existing state society codes and found that to a considerable extent they echoed the phrases of Dr. Thomas Percival, an English physician of a half-century before. Dr. Hays and his colleagues decided to carry on the Percival tradition. "Believing that language so often examined and adopted must possess the greatest of merits . . . the committee carefully preserved the words of Percival," Hays reported.

Many ethical principles still current were first codified by Percival. This general practitioner of Manchester, not far from Liverpool, became interested in the deportment of physicians while he was on the staff of the renowned Manchester Infirmary. In 1792 he drafted the "Scheme of Professional Conduct" that became the Infirmary code. When one of his sons began training for medical practice, Percival—"with the tenderest impulses of paternal love"—embarked on writing a "little Manual of Medical Ethics" for the young man's guidance. It was published in 1803. Almost at once it became the standard code for practitioners in Britain and America.

Percival urged doctors to show consideration for the patient, tailoring his message to the harshness of his era. He implored physicians to change their bloody aprons and wash their instruments between operations. Female patients should be treated with "delicacy. To . . . sport with their feelings is cruelty."

The bulk of Percival's manual of ethics was concerned with maintaining an orderly market for the profession. Doctors should not indulge in "rivalship or jealousy," he wrote. In Talmudic detail he set ground rules for the delicate problem of consultations. If several doctors are present, "the junior physician should deliver his opinion first, and his brethren afterwards in succession, according to progressive seniority." When surgeons and physicians consult on the same case, the surgeons—lower in rank than physicians—should deliver their opinions first. Thus rule of seniority was intended to preserve protocol, which might otherwise be liable to "troublesome interruptions by new settlers."

Similarly, Percival advised on fees, which he called "pecuniary acknowledgments." While "avaricious rapacity" is to be deplored, he wrote, money is nonetheless important to the physician. "Wealth, rank and independence, with all the benefits resulting from them, are the primary ends which [the physician] holds in view, and they are interesting, wise and laudable." Percival counseled the medical men of every town to fix "some general rule . . . relative to . . . pecuniary acknowledgments." Percival suggested that a wealthy physician refrain from giving advice without charging. It would be an "injury to his professional brethren" if he dispensed with a fee that another physician might claim.

Taking a leaf from Percival, the fledgling A.M.A. adopted a code of ethics that stressed the doctor's livelihood as well as the patient's well-being. The code paid homage to the humanitarian obligations of the physician. He "should not only be ever ready to obey the calls of the sick, but his mind ought also to be imbued with the greatness of his mission."

But, even more than Percival's manual, the A.M.A.'s National Code of Medical Ethics was concerned with guild principles. Of the original code's fifty subsections, a mere seven deal with the obligations of physicians to patients. By contrast, fully twenty-eight cover the duties of physicians to each other. Ten others specify the *patient's* obligations to physicians.

Patients should send for the doctor in the morning instead of "during the hours devoted to meals or sleep," the code declared. The patient should obey instructions without permitting "his own crude opinions" to interfere. Above all, he should be grateful for the services rendered him by his physician—"for these are of such a character that no mere pecuniary acknowledgment can repay or cancel them."

The original A.M.A. code stood for half a century. Since 1903 it has undergone eight revisions. The most recent, in June 1957, produced the present terse Principles of Medical Ethics--ten statements plus a preamble, totaling under five hundred words. Amplifying the Principles are detailed opinions and reports of the A.M.A. Judicial Council and a large number of resolutions passed by the House of Delegates and Board of Trustees. There are also many modifications by state and county medical societies.

While the language of the present rules of ethics is more modern, the self-concern of the guild is still evident. An early version of the A.M.A. code declared that "these principles are primarily for the good of the public." Suggestively, in 1953 this statement was omitted.

INCONSISTENCY

Portions of the Principles of Medical Ethics suggest that the code has the universality of the Ten Commandments. According to one annotation written by the Judicial Council: "There is but one code of ethics for all, be they group, clinic or individual and be they great and prominent or small and unknown."

In practice, however, there is considerable inconsistency in what is permissible in different locales. Each local society can interpret ethics as it chooses, and an activity prohibited in one area may be encouraged in another.

For example, recent civil rights activity has prompted some state medical societies to declare it unethical to discriminate because of race. By contrast, the Medical Society of North Carolina censured the Mecklenburg County society in Charlotte for admitting Negro members. Local prejudices in the guise of ethics can take an even more extreme form. In Georgia during Reconstruction, a physician was expelled from his medical society, ostensibly for no longer being a "gentleman of respectable social position." His offense: He posted bond for Negroes.

Local inconsistencies also occur in matters pertaining to economics. The profession has long frowned on a doctor's seeking patients through advertising, solicitation, or personal publicity. The first A.M.A. code held it "derogatory to the dignity of the profession" to resort to "public advertisements." This stricture was intended to separate honorable practitioners from the quack majority, many of whom huckstered shamelessly. Banishing solicitation also keeps competitiveness within limits. Few doctors have a taste for salesmanship. The majority thus prefer that merchandising not be a factor in the medical marketplace.

In stating anew the traditional ban on "self-laudation," the A.M.A. Judicial Council has said the "most worthy and effective advertisement . . . is . . . a well-merited reputation for professional ability and fidelity." The degree to which the prohibition is enforced, however, depends on the local medical society.

In some communities a doctor must clear all public announcements with a society committee. A physician who gets his name in the papers does so at considerable risk. As a result of rigorous local prohibitions, doctors can become so shy of the press that newspaper reporters have trouble verifying if an accident victim is dead or alive.

The wisdom of this stringency is open to question. Physicians in such communities are often reluctant to speak in public even about medical advances that would do honor to the profession. "Fear of indictment by one's colleagues as a 'publicity seeker' has been a major obstacle to comfortable communication between the physician and his lay-public," says Dr. Clyde E. Stanfield, of the Colorado State Medical Society public relations committee. Dr. Stanfield adds that the resulting silence "doubtless has contributed to the 'secret society' label imputed to . . . medicine."

Moreover, while wholesale commercialism would almost certainly lower the tone of the profession, it is questionable if occasional publicity really gives a physician a measurable competitive edge. Dr. James R. Fox received over $22,000 worth of personal publicity during eight years of radio and television broadcasting for the Minnesota State Medical Association. During that time, a mere six listeners called for appointments.

At the opposite extreme are societies whose members are permitted to advertise in local newspapers. The gradations of what is and is not allowed are extremely fine. In one New Jersey county, only the physician's name, address, and phone number may be listed in the classified telephone directory. Any additional information is condemned as unethical advertising. Across the county line, the medical society advises members to list their office hours as well. Some county societies forbid any mention of the doctor's field of practice. Other societies urge members to list their specialty, even notice of board certification.

What a society decides is ethical often depends on the makeup of the membership. G.P.s generally like the patient to be referred through them. Specialists have no objection if the patient comes directly himself, without first going through a G.P. If specialists prevail over a society, specialties may be listed in the phone book to help the patient pick the doctor for his case. If G.P.s predominate, specialties are unlikely to be listed.

PATIENT STEALING

Just as the present code of ethics prohibits patient hunting through advertising and publicity, so also it forbids "patient stealing."

Except in emergencies, a doctor may not treat a patient who is under another physician's care unless the original physician "has relinquished the case or has been formally dismissed." Doctors often cover for one another, and a patient seen by a substitute "should be returned . . . as soon as possible" to his regular physician. A physician who receives a patient on referral is expected to send him back to the referring doctor after the consultation or service is completed.

These rules can promote the orderly administration of medical treatment. If one doctor manages a patient's care during an illness, the patient is less likely to suffer conflicts of opinion and duplications of service. In a long-term or complicated case, chaos would result if every physician who saw the patient treated him as exclusively his own.

But the ethical ban on patient stealing is also used to restrain competition. While in many communities physicians will accept any patient who comes to them, where the ban is rigorously observed it can do the patient more harm than good. Physicians often express the notion that doctors own their patients and that patients are commodities. A doctor may say accusingly to a colleague: "That patient belonged to me but you kept him." This attitude can obstruct the patient who wishes to switch from one doctor to another.

In one case, a small boy was running a high temperature. His mother called her regular pediatrician. The doctor refused to make a house call, but his secretary arranged for another pediatrician to come.

The boy's parents liked the young doctor who made the call. They felt he gave better service and was "more modern" than their regular man. Some weeks later, the child had a minor complaint. He was brought to the new doctor's office. But the young man refused to treat him because the child was "the patient of another doctor."

In a small southern city, such overstrict adherence to protocol possibly cost a patient his life. Here is the allegation put forth in a suit by the patient's family: At about one o'clock one morning, forty-six-year-old Clyde Flint (names in this account are disguised) was brought to a hospital after having been shot in the neck. The bullet had punctured his windpipe. Now in critical condition, he was suffering from shock and having great difficulty breathing. An immediate danger was that air would penetrate the raw walls of the bullet hole and cause damaging air pockets in his body.

The first physician called was Dr. Barton, a surgeon. Witnesses later testified that Barton, smelling of alcohol, staggered about the hospital red-eyed and thick-tongued. Barton assertedly spent only a little time with Flint. To help the patient out of shock, Barton had a laboratory technician called from home to prepare a blood transfusion. The doctor also ordered preparations made for surgical insertion of a tube into Flint's windpipe, which would help him breathe.

Without administering the transfusion or inserting the tube (the complaint continues), Dr. Barton went home. "I'm going to change my clothes," he told the hospital supervisor. "Call me if the patient's condition gets worse." Standard practice calls for a doctor to stay with a patient in Flint's condition or arrange for a replacement. Barton did neither.

Flint's son Dave found his father strangling and thrashing about. Dave asked a nurse to call Dr. Miles, a physician he knew. Miles came almost at once. He found Flint bubbling blood from the mouth and suffering pockets of air under the skin and in the neck and chest.

Miles was informed of Dr. Barton's visit. He paused, then told the Flint family: "If he's Dr. Barton's patient, I can't take charge. As a matter of professional ethics, you'll have to call Dr. Barton and get him to release the patient."

A nurse phoned Barton at home. "Let me speak to Dr. Miles," Barton said.

"The patient's dying," Miles told him. "Something has to be done."

Barton spat out a string of curses. "You're a louse to steal my patient," he said. He hung up.

Dave Flint rang him back. "My father's dying," he pleaded. "Will you please let Dr. Miles take care of him."

Barton now swore at Dave. At last he said: "Okay. You pay me fifty dollars right now and I'll release your father."

Dave, who had no money with him, begged Barton to wait a few hours until the banks opened. Finally Barton agreed that Dr. Miles could take the case. All this delayed treatment at least forty minutes.

Flint was taken to an operating room. While he was on the table his heart stopped. His chest was opened and his heart massaged, but it did not respond. His death was caused by the large amount of air that had gotten into his blood, causing a bubblelike blockage around his heart.

ECONOMIC WARFARE

In 1857 a Dr. Gray of Buffalo, New York, was expelled from the Erie County Medical Society for charging below the society's schedule of minimum fees. The doctor sued and was reinstated. The courts ruled that enforcing minimum rates was unrelated to the society's avowed purpose of furthering "true science and . . . the healing art."

A century later, a Los Angeles physician alleged the same sort of economic pressure from a medical society. Although the society would officially give him no reason for refusing him membership, the doctor asserted it was because he would not charge more than three dollars for an office visit. In a $2,500,000 damage suit, he charged the society with restraint of trade, claiming that medical societies "have combined to fix rates which may be charged as minimum rates to the public for medical treatment."

Such incidents have made it customary to note the similarities between medical societies and labor unions. The A.M.A. itself has argued that it should be exempt from the Sherman Antitrust Act for the same reasons labor unions are. While the courts rejected the argument, A.F.L.-C.I.O. officials often wish that they had the solidarity and influence of the A.M.A. Medical societies sometimes adopt the terminology of unions. They speak of "boycotting" government health plans and engaging in "collective bargaining" over fees and services. Dr. Herbert Ratner, of the Stritch School of Medicine of Loyola University, has accused the A.M.A. of confusing a professional concern for the learnedness and ethical conduct of its members with "'union concerns'—that is, matters of self-interest, working conditions, fees, and the like."

Some of the A.M.A.'s economic "ethics" risk running afoul of the law. The A.M.A. is principally an organization of private practitioners. Its positions have long favored private practice as opposed to employment by hospitals and other third parties. The A.M.A. has urged that radiologists and other physicians who provide hospital services bill separately from the hospital. Thus a hospital patient who has x-rays would get two bills: one from the hospital, the other from the radiologist. If the radiologist allows his services to be part of the hospital bill, the A.M.A. argues, he would be acting as an employee of the hospital instead of as an independent practitioner.

Hospitals, on the other hand, often insist on rendering the patient one bill for all the services received at the hospital, itemizing on it the radiologist's fee. This, hospitals argue, allows bookkeeping control over the complex financial arrangements often made with physicians over division of revenues, maximum earnings, payment for use of hospital facilities. If a physician insists on billing separately contrary to hospital policy, the institution is unlikely to renew his contract.

To strengthen the hand of such doctors, a resolution was presented to the A.M.A. House of Delegates calling for a boycott of the hospital. The resolution would declare it unethical to "displace a hospital-based physician who is attempting to practice separate billing when said displacement is primarily designed to circumvent separate billing." Thus if a hospital does not renew a radiologist's contract because he insists upon billing separately, any other radiologist who takes over the post could be found unethical. By being unable to get a successor, the hospital would presumably be forced to allow the first radiologist to bill separately.

In returning the resolution to the House of Delegates, the committee that had considered it recommended that it be referred to the Board of Trustees for further study because of "as yet unsolved legal issues." The A.M.A. Law Department commented that the resolution states a policy in terms of ethics, "which involves significant exposure to possible legal involvement." A.M.A. lawyers feared that the resolution would expose medical societies to damage claims by persons alleging economic injury and to criminal suit under antitrust and monopoly laws.

Despite these warnings, the House of Delegates adopted the resolution. Once it was passed, the only way medical societies could avoid its legal consequences was to not implement it. In a remarkable action counter to its own House of Delegates, the Board of Trustees sent a letter to every state medical society urging that the resolution be set aside. "Physicians cannot avoid legal consequences of certain actions merely by categorizing them as 'ethical' or 'unethical,'" the board wrote. "To describe an ethical principle . . . does not preclude a court or jury from determining . . . that its purpose or effect is the unreasonable restraint of trade."

The profession frequently exerts economic pressures in the name of ethics. Dr. Jonathan Barker (pseudonym), an anesthesiologist, was employed by a Seattle hospital. He received a salary and percentage rather than a fee for each service. Privately practicing anesthesiologists charged that Dr. Barker was unethical in lending himself to the "corporate practice of medicine" by the hospital. Dr. Barker was excluded from membership in the local medical society and in the Washington State Society of Anesthesiologists. By extension he lost his membership in the American Society of Anesthesiologists, the specialty's leading organization.

Dr. Barker and his family were also subjected to social pressure. A colleague described the Barkers' situation: "He was warned not to take the job, but he took it nevertheless. So the anesthetists boycotted him and would have nothing to do with him, socially or professionally. Furthermore, they enlisted the aid of their wives to do the same to his wife."

Dr. Barker countered by filing a court complaint charging the Washington State Society of Anesthesiologists and the King County (Seattle) Medical Society with collusion to prevent him and any other specialist from rendering services of any type on salary in any hospital. Further, he asserted, the societies conspired "to damage or ruin the professional reputation of any specialist who accepted such salaried employment, through the practice of social and professional ostracism and other means." Such pressure was put on him, Dr. Barker said, because private anesthesiologists were attempting to "exploit their patients" by charging more than the same services would cost if performed by a salaried anesthesiologist.

Before Dr. Barker's suit came to trial, he changed his financial arrangement with the hospital so that he would be salaried only for administrative, teaching, and supervisory duties. For administering anesthesia he would bill patients directly, in effect becoming a private practitioner.

In exchange for his coming to terms, the medical societies allowed Dr. Barker to be a member.

ENFORCING THE STATUS QUO

Medical societies employ ethics as a means of enforcing the economic status quo. The *Yale Law Journal* has noted that "organized medicine has conveyed veiled threats to doctors participating in disapproved plans by outspoken condemnation of such plans in ethical terms. . . . The doctor . . . is tried and judged by his fellow physicians who may have an economic interest in proscribing his allegedly offensive conduct."

Medical ethics as an economic weapon has been widely used against closed-panel health insurance plans. Under these plans, an organization employs specified physicians (the "closed" panel) to treat its members. Closed-panel plans can present formidable competition to individual practitioners in a community. To combat the plan, medical societies in the name of ethics often invoke requirements that can be met only by physicians in private practice. It is generally held unethical, for example, to restrict the patient's "free choice of physician." This automatically proscribes closed panels since a limited number of physicians provide services for the plan.

Medical societies have waged war on health plans since their inception.

In 1929 Dr. Michael Shadid set up the nation's first medical cooperative, the Community Hospital-Clinic at Elk City, Oklahoma. The co-op owned a hospital staffed by salaried physicians and offered its members nearly complete medical coverage.

Dr. Shadid's local medical society first tried to talk him out of going ahead with the plan. Then it tried to expel him. When that failed, the society disbanded and reorganized without him. In addition the county and state medical societies sought to have Dr. Shadid's license revoked.

For twenty years the medical society harassed the co-op, denying membership to doctors who participated in it. Finally, the clinic sued the society for $300,000, charging restraint of trade. The society settled out of court and agreed to accept clinic doctors.

Several other health plans sprang up during the Depression. The A.M.A.'s response was a resolution asserting that "no third party must be permitted to come between the patient and his physician in any medical relation." Since then, medical societies opposing health plans have had the backing of an A.M.A. principle of ethics.

Sometimes the mere threat of expulsion has been sufficient to discourage doctors from participating in an incipient prepayment plan. In Williston, North Dakota, such threats allegedly resulted in staff shortages that inhibited the development of the Farmers Union Medical Service.

Often explusion is more than a threat. In Los Angeles, the Ross-Loos Clinic established a program of comprehensive medical care for employees of the city Department of Water and Power for a premium of two dollars a month. The Los Angeles County Medical Association tried to stop the plan by expelling many doctors who participated. Among them was a former society president. The clinic doctors appealed to the A.M.A. Judicial Council. They were reinstated only because of procedural defects in the local society's action.

Physicians participating in the Civic Medical Center, a prepayment plan in Chicago, were denied membership in the Chicago Medical Society. The society ostensibly refused to allow the doctors to join because the group had advertised during its first ten months of practice. But eleven years after the group stopped advertising, no doctor on its staff was a member of the medical society. In Arkansas, the entire Logan County Medical Society was expelled from the state society. The local society allegedly was dominated by physicians participating in a disapproved medical plan.

Physicians who are denied membership in a medical society are often kept from practicing in hospitals as well. In Tampa, Florida, a physician was furnishing services under contract to a health plan. He was denied membership in the Hillsborough County Medical Society. Subsequently he was barred from the local hospital because he was not a member of the society.

In Seattle, the Group Health Cooperative of Puget Sound was organized to give prepaid medical and hospital service to members of several granges, unions, and consumer cooperatives. The co-op did not have a hospital of its own, so its twenty salaried physicians had to use the facilities of local hospitals for treating member patients.

The King County Medical Society intervened to make this impossible. It labeled the co-op's staff "unethical" and expelled participating physicians. The hospitals in turn refused them staff privileges, even emergency surgical facilities. At one hospital, medical society members threatened to remove their patients if a co-op doctor were granted surgical privileges —although 100 beds were then empty.

Several co-op doctors were denied specialty board certification requiring society membership. Thus harassed, the cooperative sued the medical society. The Washington Supreme Court decided in favor of the cooperative and condemned the tactics of the society. Said the court: "There can be no question but that the purpose of the combination . . . is to preempt and control all contract practice of medicine."

Organized medicine got a comeuppance because of tactics aimed at killing the Group Health Association of Washington, D.C. At first, the District of Columbia Medical Society merely urged the seven participating physicians to quit. They refused. Next the society sent its members a list of organizations approved for their participation. Omitted was the Group Health Association.

The seven doctors still refused to give up their positions. The medical society expelled them on the grounds that they unethically disposed of their services under conditions that "interfere with reasonable competition among physicians in the community." Medical society members abruptly stopped sending these doctors referrals. The society prevailed on most hospitals in the area to deny these doctors privileges. A medical society official said: "I personally raised the question and forced the issue of compelling wavering or undecided hospitals to deny courtesy privileges to staff members of G.H.A."

In one case, a G.H.A. doctor had a woman anesthetized when he was told he could not have access to the operating room. He argued with the hospital director for four hours to no avail. Finally, he had to move the woman to another hospital. A G.H.A. patient with acute appendicitis was informed at a hospital that not only would his own doctor not be permitted to operate on him, but he would have to go elsewhere unless he agreed to withdraw from the program.

Because of such maneuvers the G.H.A. was on its last legs. Then the situation came to the attention of Thurman Arnold, chief of the Antitrust Division of the Department of Justice. From evidence Arnold's investigators collected, the A.M.A. and the District of Columbia Medical Society were indicted for violation of the Sherman Antitrust Act. The case was fought through the lower courts. When it came to the U.S. Supreme Court the Justices unanimously found the A.M.A. and the local medical society guilty of criminal conspiracy. This, said the court, was a "concerted criminal action to prevent the people from developing new methods of serving their needs."

"WE BURIED DR. JOE"

In the war against closed-panel plans medical societies sometimes misapply the ethical ban on solicitation. Societies have ruled that just as advertising is unethical for a physician, so also it is unethical for a medical plan.

Through this prohibition, the New York State Medical Society has tried to curb the growth of one of the state's largest closed-panel programs, the Health Insurance Plan of Greater New York. With H.I.P. as its primary target, the society introduced before the A.M.A. a resolution to make it unethical for any doctor to practice in a closed-panel plan that solicited patients. New York delegates asked that the A.M.A. code of ethics include the statement that "advertising should be understood to be unethical if it was aimed at getting patients for a panel of physicians of a medical care plan, company or other organization."

Dr. George Baehr, a founder of H.I.P., objected that the plan needed to advertise to survive. "Prohibiting advertising by a health insurance plan like H.I.P. is designed to prevent it from informing the public of its existence and of its premium rates, benefits and methods of operation," Dr. Baehr said. "In this manner, it would prevent the public from knowing about and joining a nonprofit voluntary insurance plan which is authorized by law."

The courts tend to support the health plans. The Washington State Supreme Court upheld the right to advertise of the Group Health Cooperative of Puget Sound, saying it could find no objection from "the standpoint of professional ethics or general public interest."

The official position of the A.M.A. has been equivocal. The House of Delegates turned down the New York resolution. In a ruling on a similar question, the Judicial Council sanctioned solicitation of subscribers as "necessary to the success of medical insurance plans." In general, the A.M.A. has avoided stands that would risk another antitrust conviction. The association was cautious after the New York State and Queens County medical societies found one H.I.P. doctor guilty of violating medical ethics because he associated with a plan that advertised. The doctor "directly benefited by solicitation of patients," the Queens medical society charged. On appeal, the Judicial Council reversed the judgment, observing that the doctor did not engage in self-laudation and under state law H.I.P. may legally advertise. At the same time, the Judicial Council has forbidden "the solicitation of patients . . . by medical groups" even though some groups offer prepaid medical insurance.

H.I.P. doctors frequently experience economic and professional discrimination from local societies. One H.I.P. doctor recalls a part-time H.I.P. surgeon who was forced out of the plan by pressure from colleagues: "They said they wouldn't refer any more surgery to him unless he quit."

In Staten Island, a borough of New York City, the medical community has been in opposition to the plan since it started. A past president of H.I.P., Dr. David Barr, has said that many doctors on the island "still resist introduction of anything that can disturb or modify their vested interest."

Doctors at the island's three voluntary hospitals greeted the plan by making it difficult for H.I.P. physicians to get staff privileges. The few H.I.P. doctors who could admit patients were greatly overburdened. But non-H.I.P. physicians at these hospitals blocked the appointment of additional H.I.P. doctors. At least nine applicants were told they would be able to join the staff at once if only they resigned from the plan.

When two H.I.P. doctors—a surgeon and an obstetrician—sought courtesy privileges at the three hospitals, application procedures made their acceptance virtually impossible. Dr. Herbert S. King, medical director of the Staten Island H.I.P. group, has described the techniques used to exclude these physicians: One hospital required two letters of recommendation—from members of its own medical board. "We learned these letters under no circumstances would be provided for the new surgeon or the new obstetrician. . . . This technique proved so successful that not a single [H.I.P.] physician was admitted to that hospital from that time on."

Two days after the second hospital received the applications of the H.I.P. doctors, it announced a policy of limiting courtesy privileges because of a shortage of beds. The third hospital simply failed to act on the applications.

The patients of H.I.P. physicians thus excluded also suffered. Patients who needed hospitalization often could not see their doctor in the hospital.

H.I.P.'s situation worsened with the death of Dr. Joseph Garabedian. Dr. Garabedian was the only H.I.P. obstetrician who had privileges at an island hospital. He thus delivered all the plan's babies, a colossal strain for a man suffering from severe ulcers. After his death, expectant mothers could not be delivered by any obstetrician who had seen them through pregnancy. They would present themselves at a hospital and would be delivered by whichever doctor was on duty. H.I.P. took a full-page advertisement, an open letter to all three hospitals. It ran in part:

"We buried Dr. Joe Garabedian yesterday. It was known to you and to us for a long time that Dr. Garabedian cheerfully carried his heavy professional burden in spite of the recurrent illness which finally resulted in his death. . . .

"A qualified obstetrician applied to your staffs so that he might act as Dr. Garabedian's assistant. He was not accepted by any hospital in this county . . . and was forced to leave. . . . You can no longer give Dr. Garabedian the help he so sorely needed, and which you withheld from him. But . . . you can resolve to accept the applications, when you receive them, of the TWO obstetricians who will be needed to do Dr. Garabedian's job."

The letter caught the attention of State Senator George R. Metcalf, who arranged a public hearing on the issue before the Joint Legislative Committee on Health Insurance Plans. After the hearing, the Senator concluded that H.I.P. physicians were systematically being denied hospital privileges. He called a meeting of H.I.P. and the hospitals. With corrective legislation in the offing, five more H.I.P. doctors were appointed to Staten Island hospital staffs.

Since then, the state has passed a law forbidding hospitals to discriminate against physicians because of participation in plans like H.I.P. On Staten Island all H.I.P. doctors have been granted courtesy privileges. These are sometimes called "discourtesy privileges." While they allow the essential privilege of admitting patients, they are not full staff appointments. Such doctors do not have hospital rank or responsibilities. They cannot take part in hospital teaching programs. Nor are they included in many other hospital activities that provide professional advancement and satisfaction.

OBSTRUCTION TO DISCIPLINE

To most minds, codes of ethics suggest yardsticks of virtue, rules for enforcing a superior standard of behavior. Many of the ethics governing medical societies do, of course, reflect the profession's ideals of service to humanity. It is a failure not in ethics but in administration that enforcement of these high principles is lax.

At the same time, other bylaws of medicine run counter to idealism, indeed actually obstruct discipline. In the name of medical ethics, incompetent and dishonest physicians have been supported by medical societies while doctors who seek to better serve the public have been cast out and reviled.

For many years, some of the most consistently bad medicine in this country was practiced in impoverished mining areas. The coal fields of Colorado, Illinois, Kentucky, Pennsylvania were considered backwaters of American medicine. The miner's lot was made even grimmer by the level of medical care he was likely to receive from "check-off" doctors—practitioners who were paid so much a month from deductions out of miners' wages.

Check-off doctors were chosen not for their competence but for their availability, often because they were willing to work for low fees. At some mining camps, the check-off was a form of patronage. Physicians vied for the favor of local mining officials, sometimes to the extent of paying kickbacks. Once a doctor was established on a check-off, he had a virtual monopoly on medical care for the miners whose deductions he received.

Few check-off doctors were specialists, but many were reluctant to refer away cases they could not treat properly. Hospitals were generally substandard and unaccredited, with few controls over staff members' performance. In discussions of surgery performed by check-off G.P.s, the word "butchery" frequently appears. An investigation revealed that twenty-nine out of fifty-four major operations were mistakes caused by improper diagnosis. In some mining areas, infant mortality and the death rate for mothers were double the national average. Physical rehabilitation was almost unknown. Many injured miners were left crippled although rehabilitation services would have restored them to reasonably normal lives.

Nor were all check-off doctors careful to accept only as many patients as they could personally see. "A lot of these men were much too busy, and they'd hire assistants," recalls Dr. Charles B. Stacey of Harlan, Kentucky, who started practice as a mining-camp physician. "Sometimes these assistants were men who'd been kicked out of medical school, or who had never been to medical school. The only excuse for having them was that they were working in desolate country where no one else wanted to go."

The check-off system in coal fields gave way as a result of a landmark strike settlement negotiated by John L. Lewis. Henceforth the coal companies would pay the United Mine Workers Welfare and Retirement Fund a royalty on each ton of coal coming out of the mines. With this financing, the U.M.W. Fund set up a comprehensive medical care program in forty-five states for a million miners and their families.

The guiding spirit of the $60-million-a-year medical program has been Dr. Warren F. Draper, formerly Deputy Surgeon General of the U.S. Public Health Service and general in charge of Army health services during World War II. In his early days as the fund's executive medical officer, Dr. Draper planned that all services would be provided by local physicians, preferably by the beneficiary's regular doctor. The fund would do little more than pay the bills, enabling former check-off physicians to charge individual fees for services they performed.

After several years' trial this was proved unworkable. "Too many doctors have been soaking the plan," Dr. Draper told an audience of physicians. He reported evidence of "unnecessary surgery performed by . . . physicians who know better but want the money." One series of medical audits showed that over half the appendectomies paid for by the fund were unnecessary. One doctor performed eleven appendectomies, of which only three were justified. A physician billed the fund for removing the same woman's appendix five times.

Medical audits disclosed physicians attempting services beyond their competence. The audits uncovered doctors "who know they are not qualified for certain work but will attempt almost anything in order to retain the fee." Dr. Draper's comment: "The results are often gruesome."

The fund embarked on a campaign to bring quality medical care to all its beneficiaries. In some regions that lacked adequate hospitals, the fund built medical centers. These institutions, each meeting accreditation standards, had full-time staffs of board-certified specialists who supervised the work of local private practitioners. Throughout the coal district the fund weeded out wrongdoers from its lists of physicians eligible for fund payments. G.P.s remaining on the lists were expected to stay within the limits of their competence and refer patients to specialists when necessary. The participating specialists were largely board-certified men selected on the basis of training and performance.

The fund is widely credited for doing for coal-region medical care what the Tennessee Valley Authority has done for rural electrification. Each of the fund hospitals has served as a community hospital, upgrading the health services of its entire region. The availability of fund fees attracts specialists to areas that formerly could not have supported them. In the Cumberland Valley in Kentucky the number of board-certified specialists jumped from a handful to over thirty in less than five years. The standards of medical practice have risen correspondingly. Where there was not one accredited hospital in the valley, there now are about a dozen.

The quality of surgery has risen. Hospital supervision by specialists has upgraded the performance of G.P.s. Infant mortality and the maternal death rate have dropped to about the national average. Miners disabled by long-neglected injuries have been sent to rehabilitation centers at fund expense.

How do some of the local medical societies regard the fund? They attack it as unethical.

Medical societies make an ethical doctrine of the phrase "free choice of physician." Superficially, "free choice" is hard to argue against, for no reasonable person would dispute that a patient should have the right to select the doctor who will treat him. Medical societies, however, employ the phrase in conjuring up a fantasy in black and white. On one hand, a patient with free choice is supposedly treated only by a physician whom he chooses on the basis of knowledge and trust. Without free choice, the patient presumably is ordered into the hands of a stranger of dubious qualifications and questionable character.

The reality is that free choice is scarcely a consideration to most patients. In many medical situations, free choice is neither expected nor feasible. In hospitals, the patient may never even learn the names of the physicians he is assigned to. When one doctor refers a patient to another, it is the referring physician, and not the patient, who generally does the choosing.

Within broader limits, free choice comes as a matter of course. Outside of prisons and the armed forces, virtually no system of medical care can force an unwilling patient to be treated by a specific doctor. Indeed, government health programs like Medicare and Medicaid specifically guarantee patients the right to select and switch doctors. Private health plans that limit beneficiaries to a panel of physicians generally permit the patient to choose whichever participating doctor he prefers. By the same token, beneficiaries implicitly accept a proviso. In the words of a health plan administrator: "The patient as a free citizen can, of course, go to any doctor he wishes. But he shouldn't expect us to pay for any doctor but those we certify."

Thus, insofar as patients are concerned, free choice is a false issue. As a principle of medical ethics, it is intended not so much to safeguard the patient as to protect the private practitioner who fears a health plan will exclude him from payment or limit the services he can perform. An official of a closed-panel plan has said: "To many doctors, the ethic of 'free choice of physician' really means 'free rein of physician.'"

The flag of free choice was raised by medical societies after the U.M.W. Fund warned it would drop offending practitioners from its list of participating physicians. To correct disciplinary problems, the fund urged medical societies to police their ranks, but met with little success. Appealing to some societies for the correction of gross violations proved to be a "tedious, wearing and generally unsatisfactory process that we should dread to repeat," Dr. Draper later reported. In one state, the local head of the Mine Workers program, a physician, told Dr. Draper the state society was reluctant to act against offenders because coal-area doctors "although not of high quality are probably no worse than in other sections of the state." Also, said the fund official, the society feared that other medical organizations and health programs "would tend to take the same action," and that private patients might learn of the disciplinary measures.

Dr. Draper asked the A.M.A. to "focus the attention of state and local medical societies upon . . . what is in the best interests of the patient, in contrast to what is in the best interests of the physician." Draper also called on the A.M.A. to "take disciplinary action against members of the profession who make the practice of medicine a racket for personal gain."

At an A.M.A. convention, a number of physicians argued in favor of the fund's position. Dr. Robert L. Novy, former head of Michigan's Blue Shield plan, said: "Some of the United Mine Workers' criticism of abuses can be substantiated chapter and verse. At least 3 percent of the profession would be guilty. We're all aware of this 3 percent who bring discredit on the medical profession. But too often we don't do enough to discipline our own members." Other doctors observed the irony of making free choice an issue, since few patients have ever had less free choice than miners tied to check-off physicians.

The House of Delegates rejected a suggestion by Dr. Novy that the A.M.A. take self-disciplining measures that would give medicine "clean hands." Instead, the delegates reaffirmed a resolution that condemned "the current attitude and methods of operation of the U.M.W. as tending to lower the quality and availability of medical and hospital care." The delegates called for a "broad educational program" to inform the general public—with special attention to U.M.W. members—about "the benefits to be derived from preservation of the American right to freedom of choice of physicians and hospitals."

In some local societies, free choice quickly won out over discipline as a principle of medical ethics. Little action has been taken against practitioners whose abuses were reported by the fund. Yet physicians who participate in the fund—and thus possess some degree of certification of their skill and honesty—have been widely cast into the role of pariahs.

The Illinois State Medical Society has informed doctors that "it does not look with favor" upon any member who cooperates with the U.M.W. Fund. In Pennsylvania the state medical society changed its code to declare unethical any doctor who "participates in . . . any medical plan which denies its beneficiaries the right of free choice of physician."

The Colorado State Medical Society has proclaimed a rule of ethics admittedly aimed at forcing the fund to open its lists to all physicians. Any doctor who "aids and abets the operation of a medical plan which denies its beneficiaries free choice of physician" would be considered unethical and subject to discipline. In one town a surgeon and an internist treating fund patients claimed they were denied membership in the Las Animas County Medical Society on the basis of this rule. They brought suit on the grounds that the denial of membership kept them off the staff of the area's only hospital and prevented them from getting specialty board certification.

In Kentucky the state medical society helped push through the state legislature a bill that would have required the U.M.W. Fund to permit any physician to participate. Only the governor's refusal to sign the legislation kept it from becoming law. At the state society's convention, a resolution was introduced declaring ineligible for state society membership any doctor working with the fund. Another resolution would have abolished appeals machinery for doctors who are denied or suspended from county society membership.

Had either resolution passed, there would have been little redress for physicians barred from local societies because of being associated with the fund. In one county, for example, the exclusion of seventeen fund physicians was voted by the society's eight members, thereby keeping out two thirds of the doctors in the county. The society did, however, welcome three ex officio members who were not even M.D.s.

23
Conspirators in Silence

THE FIFTY-SIX-YEAR-OLD WIFE of Edwin Price (pseudonym) was suffering from low-back pain. Doctors in a Boston hospital put her in a full-body cast. Five weeks later she was dead. Hospital officials admitted to Price that her death was the result of an accidental blocking of the pulmonary artery. But, they contended, there had been no negligence of any kind.

Price, a patent attorney in his sixties, was certain doctors in the case had been negligent. But when he attempted to bring suit, he could not find a physician to testify in his behalf. He charged that the doctors he approached were "covering up" for their colleagues.

Price concluded that the only way he could get expert medical testimony was to become an expert himself. He took undergraduate premedical courses, then attended a medical school and worked at a hospital.

From his medical training and research in medical texts, Price amassed ten filing cabinets of material to back up the case he brought to court. "As the testimony shows," he says, "my trial attorney—who obtained much of his medical instruction from me—knew more about the medicine involved than the defendant doctors themselves."

He won a judgment against two of the doctors. A week later a judge threw out the verdict and ordered a new trial. The chief reason was that a medical witness testifying for Price "did not have the surgical experience which he testified he did have." It was not until some fifteen years after his wife's death that Edwin Price finally won the court battle. The two doctors were found guilty of negligence and ordered to pay Price $10,000.

Few plaintiffs claiming malpractice can go to such lengths when they cannot find a doctor who will testify against a colleague. They thus are walled in by the so-called conspiracy of silence. In many communities this is yet another abuse in the ethics guiding relations between doctors. While there has been a slow increase in the number of physicians who will testify, the problem is largely unremedied.

The A.M.A. officially denies that medical societies discourage physicians from testifying against colleagues. George E. Hall, of the A.M.A. Bureau of Legal Medicine and Legislation, declared that "there is no policy or principle of ethics of the medical profession which can be cited as justification by any physician for refusing to act as a witness." At the same time, the A.M.A. does not discourage silence. To quote Hall: "The individual physician must determine in his own mind and conscience whether or not he will act as a witness."

Medical ethics generally prohibit physicians from airing a colleague's wrongdoing before the laity. In "embarrassing situations," a set of A.M.A. principles has stated, "a physician should seek a personal interview with his fellow." The code adds that physicians should refrain from making a colleague's errors a matter of public knowledge. "Questions of conduct should be considered first before proper medical tribunals in executive session."

One effect of such strictures is that physicians feel advised to gloss over one another's substandard treatment. An A.M.A.-sponsored survey shows that 58 percent of physicians believe that most doctors try to hide other doctors' mistakes. In a nationwide survey 85 percent of physicians said they would not tell a patient he had been injured by another doctor's error. Physicians who feel this way point to findings that a large number of suits are precipitated by doctors' criticizing one another's work to patients. Physicians thus relish a story reported by J. Joseph Herbert, legal counsel for the Michigan State Medical Society. A woman called on a prominent Detroit physician and asked him to examine an abdominal burn caused by an electric-cautery instrument.

"What doctor did that to you?" he asked. "You could sue and collect for a burn like that. Who was the physician?"

"Why," replied the woman, "you were."

The woman followed the doctor's advice and sued. She received damages of $4,500.

At a roundtable discussion on medical ethics sponsored by a medical journal, the question was raised as to what a doctor should say and do if he finds that a patient will need to undergo surgery to correct a colleague's mistake. The physician who was the first panelist to reply advised: "He should discuss the problem with the previous physician and not with the patient. In the patient's presence, he shouldn't even raise his eyebrow over what he's found. Thereafter, it's up to the physician who first treated the patient to see that he gets the necessary repairs."

The panelists agreed that the present doctor should alert the patient to the injury only if the colleague is not eager to repair the damage. Most courts feel this advice runs counter to the law. While the doctor need not say who was to blame, the courts obligate him to inform the patient of the injury right off. Legally, it is irrelevant that a suit against the colleague may result.

Most medical societies consider a doctor unethical if he implicates a colleague. Should the patient ask if the previous physician made a mistake, societies advise the doctor to reply: "I don't know. I wasn't there." In Delaware, the state medical society has gone further. A statute it supported, now on the books, provides that if a doctor encourages a malpractice suit, his license can be revoked.

THE MISSING MEDICAL WITNESS

Suppose a pedestrian is struck by a car speeding through a red light. The rules of safe driving fall within the common knowledge of the ordinary layman. Thus the injured pedestrian on bringing suit rarely needs an expert witness to help prove the driver was negligent.

By contrast, a patient who has been injured by a negligent physician is at a disadvantage when it comes to proving malpractice. To meet the law's requirements for establishing negligence, the patient must show that the doctor's care fell below the standard of medicine practiced in the community. For this the patient needs at least one qualified physician to furnish expert medical testimony.

Without a medical witness the patient's case may die on the vine, no matter how flagrant the negligence may be. What is the likelihood that this miscarriage of justice will occur? "Let's assume that the patient's suit is meritorious," Dr. David S. Rubsamen, a physician-lawyer, has said. "Can he win? Even today, in many states, the answer is more probably no than yes. Why? Because, traditional law requires that the patient-plaintiff bring forth a medical witness to support his case . . . And often the patient-plaintiff, even if his suit has merit, is unable to find a competent physician willing to testify for him, and against a fellow physician."

The problem is not only of silence but often of manipulation of the facts. One of the more forceful discussions of physicians protecting one another appears in *Trial of Medical Malpractice Cases*, a standard work on medical jurisprudence. The authors, Dr. Harold Williams, a physician-lawyer, and Professor David W. Louisell of the University of California Law School observe: "Clearly there is a general reluctance of physicians to testify to facts or to give opinions which likely will involve their brethren in legal liability or professional embarrassment growing out of alleged malpractice. . . . The reluctance has been so general and notorious as to be equivalent in a practical sense to a concert of purpose and action. Moreover, courts, lawyers, and the public have seen the consequences of this reluctance result in miscarriage of justice in certain fact situations as to which the conclusion of malpractice, even of gross negligence, is rationally inescapable. Sometimes the picture is compounded by serious suspicion that the defendant's experts have blinded themselves to the realities, even to the point of wilful misrepresentations or perjury."

Dr. Williams and Professor Louisell cite a large number of cases in which they hold that medical witnesses gave highly challengeable support to defendant colleagues. In a suit involving a permanent impairment of arm motion, physicians told the court that a colleague's three-week delay in repairing a fractured shoulder blade caused no harm. In another case, a doctor on the witness stand refused to admit that a blood count is a standard procedure when appendicitis is suspected. In a third case, an orthopedist testified that a colleague had done everything possible in repairing a child's broken arm; yet for weeks the defendant had failed to notice that the arm had a second fracture.

One lawyer recalls a family doctor who came to a house call drunk and failed to recognize a boy's abdominal pains as the obvious symptom of appendicitis. He prescribed enemas and cathartics instead of advising against them. The boy died of a burst appendix. The family could not find a doctor who would testify to the standards for care of appendicitis. Yet five doctors took the stand in behalf of the defendant. The head of a university hospital told the court that the doctor had followed "good practice."

The injustices posed by such medical testimony have raised protests in legal circles. Early judicial notice of the problem was taken in 1903, when a court commented on a medical malpractice case: "We cannot overlook the well-known fact that in actions of this kind it is always difficult to obtain professional testimony." Some present-day judges echo the same sentiments. In one appeal, a majority of the California Supreme Court held that evidence was insufficient to establish a doctor's negligence. But, in a much-cited dissent, Justice Jesse Carter observed: "Anyone familiar with cases of this character knows that the so-called ethical practitioner will not testify on behalf of a plaintiff regardless of the merits of the plaintiff's case. . . . Physicians who are members of medical societies flock to the defense of their fellow member." In Louisiana, a federal court trial judge decried the reluctance of physicians to testify against eminent doctors. The judge noted that "the plaintiffs' case here founders before it begins on the rock of self-interest."

Countless plaintiffs' attorneys have found themselves up against the same wall of silence. At a meeting of the National Association of Claimants Compensation Attorneys, the 500 delegates passed a resolution urging the medical profession to permit individual physicians to testify in open court against doctors charged with malpractice. One delegate denounced an "organized conspiracy in the medical profession to stifle any attempt to provide justice for the victim of malpractice."

Lewis Lercara, an attorney in Oakland, California, recalls many such experiences when he worked for a law firm specializing in defending doctors charged with malpractice. "Frequently negligence on the part of the doctor was clearly apparent. When leaders of the medical profession were called in for consultation as experts, they would emphatically state that the negligence was so serious that it was almost criminal. Yet they would show interest only in how the case could be successfully defended."

When a case got to court, Lercara says, no expert witness would testify for the patient. But the doctors Lercara had spoken to would rally around their colleague. On the witness stand, they would make such statements as "Everything he did seems to have been proper." Or "Some doctors do things one way, and some do them another. It's impossible to say which is preferable."

"After five years I couldn't take this any longer," Lercara recalls. "I became an attorney for the patients."

PRESSURES AGAINST TESTIFYING

Only a rare physician can testify with impunity against a colleague.

Some can do so because of their prominence in the profession. In California, a former A.M.A. president helped win a $100,000 verdict against a colleague. Other doctors help patients' lawyers sub rosa. In surgical malpractice cases, an anesthetist will often interpret the hospital chart for attorney Alfred Julien of White Plains, New York, Julien says he must provide an "adequate fee, plus a promise not to use his name in the case."

Still other physicians fill the gap caused by their colleagues' silence and make a lucrative full-time specialty of testifying in court for plaintiffs. One New York City orthopedist dictates the script attorneys should follow in questioning him. He charges $150 plus expenses for a court appearance, makes a number of appearances a day, and is booked months in advance.

In many communities a doctor who decides out of conscience to testify for the patient does so at professional peril. Justice Jesse Carter describes such a physician as a "lone wolf or heroic soul, who for the sake of truth and justice has the courage to run the risk of ostracism by his fellow practitioners." According to one nationwide survey, only about 7 percent would agree to testify to a colleague's negligence. This is a reflection of the pressures exerted on doctors to keep silent.

Threats are seldom necessary. A great deal of mutual sympathy prevents physicians from testifying against each other. Doctors recognize that under certain circumstances even a careful physician, taking all reasonable precautions, can miss a diagnosis or experience unsuccessful therapy. A doctor, looking at a defendant in a malpractice suit, often cannot help thinking, "There but for the grace of God go I." One such instance was alleged in the course of a successful negligence suit: A physician promised to testify that an orthopedist was negligent in repairing a two-year-old's broken arm. An unhealed circulatory obstruction left the child's arm paralyzed. The doctor called this the "grossest case of malpractice" he had ever seen. Shortly before the trial, he was visited by the orthopedist, who explained that he carried no malpractice insurance. The other man agreed to drop out of the case. (The patient nonetheless went on to win.)

In all but the largest communities, doctors are likely to either know each other or be linked through mutual friends. Testifying against a colleague is generally regarded as an unthinkable breach of etiquette. "It's worse than sleeping with the man's wife," one doctor has commented.

On purely social grounds, a physician will be disinclined to bear witness against a nodding acquaintance much less a golf partner or close associate. Besides making an enemy of the defendant, a plaintiff's witness is likely to alienate the defendant's friends as well. He opens himself up to snubs. He risks losing referrals. He is likely to become fair game for other doctors' attacks on him.

In extreme cases, the local medical community may take reprisals normally used against doctors found guilty of criminal acts. For many types of appointments, physicians require letters of recommendation from their local medical society. Societies furnish these routinely even if the doctor is only a nominal member who merely pays his dues. But if the physician has testified against a colleague, the recommendation may be withheld. Or if addressed to another doctor, it may go out with mention of the applicant's testimony—a clear way to put the applicant in bad odor. One physician who testified against a colleague wound up losing his job as county health officer.

Hospitals often grant privileges for a year at a time on the recommendation of the medical staff. Ordinarily, reappointment is automatic—a committee reports that all current privileges should be extended, and the staff accepts the motion unanimously. A staff member who has been a plaintiff's witness may, however, prompt a charade. In an effort to sidestep a conspiracy charge, the committee is likely to hold a hearing into each staff member's qualifications. To no one's surprise, all the physicians at the hospital will be found to merit their privileges—except the one who testified against another doctor.

The possibility that such reprisals will be taken is often enough to discourage a physician from testifying. Similarly, there is a widespread belief among doctors that testifying for the plaintiff may void the physician's malpractice insurance coverage. For a long time malpractice carriers stifled testimony by including a clause voiding a doctor's policy if he took the witness stand against another practitioner. An American Bar Association committee protested this proviso as an "indefensible attempt to suppress evidence." Not only is it unenforceable, the A.B.A. committee reported, but "it might be deemed to be in contempt of court."

Largely because of A.B.A. attacks on such clauses, insurance companies have deleted them. The clauses were probably worthless to begin with. Samuel Polsky, director of the Philadelphia Medico-Legal Institute, has theorized: "It would seem so clearly against public policy that there would appear to be no real problem in voiding the restrictive clause, even if a modern insurance carrier were so ill-advised as to insert it in its policies, or attempt to enforce it, or refuse to abandon it."

Thus a physician need have little worry that his malpractice insurance will be canceled if he testifies. Nonetheless, malpractice carriers continue to imply that this will happen. In a California courtroom a physician testifying for the patient recalled: "We had one case in Stockton a little while ago—twenty-seven doctors in Stockton, and the poor little boy that lost his arm, they couldn't get one doctor to say a good word for him, not one doctor. They were all told if they testified their insurance would be cut off."

The "man with a briefcase" is a menacing figure in medical lore. One way to nip a malpractice suit in the bud is to get a nonsuit declared because the plaintiff lacks a medical witness. If a physician agrees to testify for a plantiff, he may be visited by a man with a briefcase, a representative of his malpractice insurance company. In the briefcase is the insurance company's copy of the doctor's malpractice policy. The smooth stranger, the powerful company that can pluck the doctor's policy out of its vast files, the veiled threat of discontinuance—all add up to a powerfully persuasive tactic. One doctor was crossing his state by train to testify for a patient. The man with a briefcase visited him in his compartment. By the time the doctor reached his destination, he had changed his mind. A nonsuit was declared.

Insurance companies often call on all the physicians treating a patient involved in a malpractice claim. The company advises them to avoid all discussions with the plaintiff's counsel, even though none of them are connected with the suit. The patient's attorney thus may find doctors are not willing to talk to him even about the patient's present condition.

One way malpractice carriers secure such cooperation is by keeping doctors on edge over their own likelihood of being sued. While some threat of suit is real, insurance companies tend to overblow it in their publicity to physicians. They obscure a finding by the A.M.A. Law Department that the risk rate of malpractice claims to patient-visits is actually extremely low: Only 37 claims arise in 100,000 patient-visits. "It is important . . . that the legal risks for physicians not be exaggerated," the Law Department has cautioned. Nonetheless, malpractice carriers exploit the physician's terror over being sued. One attorney who has been chairman of the Malpractice Committee of the International Association of Insurance Counsel tells his colleagues: "In lecturing to the M.D.s, I have always emphasized the need for mutual cooperation on the theory that if the M.D.s do not hang together they will most assuredly hang separately."

One lawsuit has charged that through falsehoods and coercion a malpractice carrier prevailed upon a doctor to betray a patient's confidence. According to the allegation: The patient was at a hospital recovering from successful back surgery when his bed collapsed. The patient was thrown to the floor. Claiming an injury, he brought suit against the hospital.

Despite his grievance against the hospital, the patient was thoroughly satisfied with his surgeon and continued seeing him, with no thought of bringing him into the suit. It happened that the hospital's insurer also wrote malpractice coverage for the doctor. The hospital's attorney (the patient's charge continues) wanted to see the patient's current medical records, which were confidential but might contain information the hospital could use against the patient. At the attorney's suggestion the company sent an investigator to the doctor's office.

"This patient intends to sue you," the agent lied. "I'm investigating the claim. What records do you have on his case?"

The doctor gave him the patient's chart. The company passed it on to the hospital's attorney. Meanwhile, the insurance carrier strongly hinted to the doctor that he would do well to treat the patient no further. Thus intimidated, the doctor resigned from the case.

"INTIMIDATED BY SUGGESTIONS AND THREATS"

The greatest obstacles to a malpractice plaintiff's finding a medical witness are likely to be erected by the local medical society.

In a midwestern city, an eighteen-year-old girl charged the following in a suit: She found a doctor's advertisement in the classified telephone directory under "Plastics." It featured before and after nose-repair pictures. Seeking a prettier nose, the girl went to him for surgery. She was gravely disappointed in the result and became increasingly depressed over her appearance. In part because of psychiatric injuries, a suit was instituted against the doctor.

The doctor, who was in his seventies, was already held in low esteem by the local medical society. There had already been some twenty suits filed against him for medical malpractice. He was so great a liability that no malpractice carrier would give him insurance.

But when the girl's lawyer asked the medical society's help in locating a witness to testify for her, the society refused. It was up to each plastic surgeon whether he wished to testify, society officials said. No expert witness was willing to come forward and the girl lost her case.

Her psychiatric condition worsened. Wielding a gun, she made an attempt on the doctor's life. Thereafter she was institutionalized.

Meanwhile, the doctor continued his substandard surgery. While under the influence of a narcotic, he attempted surgery on a woman. She died. The next week, while he was again unable to function because of drugs, another woman died under his knife. He was indicted for manslaughter. With his age as a consideration, he was allowed to plead guilty to narcotic violations. Then he too entered a mental institution.

Some officers of medical societies do not merely refuse to cooperate in finding a medical witness. They actively try to keep a prospective witness from testifying. In Pennsylvania, the following was alleged in court: The mother of five young children died after an abdominal operation that resulted in peritonitis, a severe inflammation of the abdominal cavity. Her husband brought a suit (ultimately unsuccessful) against her two doctors.

charging that they had mistaken a pregnancy for an abscess and were negligent in their surgery.

Word got around that a doctor who had examined the woman shortly before she died was planning to testify for the husband. A physician in the community who was an officer of the Pennsylvania Medical Association sought to stop the witness. Using state society stationery and identifying himself with his official title, he wrote a letter. It was to a prominent doctor who knew the witness and it asked this doctor to try to talk the witness into "withdrawing his support from the opposing side." The other man refused to interfere. Eventually the letter came to the attention of the husband.

The husband's attorney charged that the society officer had attempted to obstruct justice. On the witness stand the doctor told the court that his position with the Pennsylvania Medical Association entitled him to try to stop the plaintiff's witness from testifying.

"I was a councilor and trustee having certain prerogatives to act on my own," he said.

"Did you have the authority to write such a letter?" asked the attorney.

"Yes."

"From whom?"

"As a councilor I have such authority, to do as I see fit in an individual case."

Melvin M. Belli, the San Francisco plaintiffs' attorney who is called the King of Torts, recalls a neurosurgeon who endured a great deal of harassment from his medical society colleagues. Belli's client, a young Navy wife, developed paralysis following childbirth. The neurosurgeon she consulted agreed to testify to malpractice.

Just before the case came to trial, the doctor was summoned to a meeting of his medical society. For two hours he was, in his words, "examined, cross-examined, and persuaded." His colleagues urged him not to break the "ground rules" (their words) by testifying. "They not only were unperturbed about the plight of the paralyzed young woman," comments Belli, "they were actually conspiring to defraud her of a judgment."

The session made the neurosurgeon determined to testify. At the trial, a doctor who had been at the meeting was called as a witness to impugn the surgeon's testimony. He told the court the neurosurgeon had been "acting strangely" for the past six months. In fact, he added, the surgeon may have become psychotic.

On cross-examination, Belli lessened the impact of this testimony by bringing out that, only the day before, the witness had referred a patient for a spinal tap to the doctor whose sanity he now professed to doubt.

More often than not, medical societies succeed in keeping prospective witnesses from testifying. The pressure can be exerted even across state lines. The details of one such allegation: A patient died after being given anesthesia. In the ensuing malpractice suit, the attorney for the patient's family presented the evidence to two doctors who practiced in Spokane, Washington. They agreed to testify that the patient had received substandard treatment.

As late as the afternoon before they were to appear, the charge goes on, both doctors assured the family's attorney they would be in court the following morning as scheduled. But that night the attorney received a call from one of the doctors. He would not be in court the next day, he said. Early the next morning, the other doctor called. He, too, would not be present. The timing was extremely detrimental to the patient, for the trial had already begun. Caught short, the attorney was unable to find other expert witnesses in time. A nonsuit was declared.

Both doctors told the attorney they had been "importuned" by officers and members of the Spokane Medical Society and by agents of their malpractice insurance company not to testify for the plaintiff. They were "intimidated by suggestions and threats" and warned that their "professional relations with the society and the insurers and their practice would be damaged" if they became witnesses.

The attorney filed a motion for a new trial, citing "a campaign of coercion" consisting of "threats of withdrawal of professional patronage and professional reprisals." In granting the new trial, the court commented: "If true, it is hard to conceive of conduct more damaging to the medical profession."

In Los Angeles, a woman's malpractice suit was almost sabotaged by misrepresentations by physicians. Mrs. Clarice Burton (names in this account are disguised) brought suit against Dr. Earl Irving for failing to x-ray her hip after a fall. Mrs. Burton approached nine physicians, all members of the Los Angeles County Medical Association, and asked them if they would testify in her behalf. All nine refused. One told her that if he testified his malpractice insurance would be canceled and his membership in the medical society would be jeopardized. Another said he would not testify because "the practice of doctors appearing for plaintiffs was frowned upon." A doctor who had treated Mrs. Burton said: "You had a pretty rough time. But I could not testify against another doctor."

Mrs. Burton's attorney told the lawyer for Dr. Irving that he was having trouble finding a medical witness. Irving's lawyer replied: "You will never get a doctor to testify against another doctor. No doctor would dare do it." At last Mrs. Burton was forced to resort to a special procedure whereby the court would appoint a disinterested medical witness to testify as an expert. One of her own doctors had warned her that if the expert were a member of the Los Angeles County Medical Association, he "cannot testify for you against another doctor."

Now following the procedure for finding a witness, the judge called the Los Angeles medical society. He told the society he was hearing a malpractice case and wished the name of an impartial physician who would be willing to testify. He specified that the doctor should be "unknown to any of the parties or the attorneys."

Four days later the medical society submitted the name of Dr. Lee Rogers. The judge asked Dr. Irving, the defendant, if he knew Dr. Rogers. Irving said no. Then the judge told Dr. Rogers he was hearing a malpractice case and wanted to "obtain a physician . . . wholly disinterested and unrelated" to any of the parties. The judge gave their names and asked Dr. Rogers if he knew any of them. Rogers too said no.

Thus appointed as an unprejudiced witness, Dr. Rogers advised Mrs. Burton to confide in him and had her bring him all the x-rays and records relating to her case. She asked Rogers several times if he knew the defendant. "No," he replied, "I never heard of him."

"Have you ever been on the same hospital staff as Dr. Irving?" she asked.

"No," he said, "I have never been on the staff of a hospital with him."

When Dr. Rogers got on the witness stand, he testified that on the basis of his findings Dr. Irving was innocent of any negligence in treating Mrs. Burton. What is more, he added, his examination showed that Mrs. Burton had sustained a second fall which she did not mention and in fact denied. Largely as a result of Rogers' testimony, Mrs. Burton lost the case.

In a retrial, Rogers appeared as a witness for Irving. It developed that they had known each other for over fifteen years. For most of that time, they had been on the staff of the same hospital.

"I met him there, sure," Rogers admitted under oath. He also admitted that although he knew Irving he told the judge he did not. The court noted that the medical society had recommended a witness who scarcely was as "unknown" and "disinterested" as the judge had specified.

Subsequently Mrs. Burton succeeded in locating a physician to testify in her behalf. She proved her case and was awarded $37,000.

Physicians who fear that their medical society will oust them if they criticize a colleague can point to at least one medical witness to whom this happened. The doctor testified in a judicial proceeding that did not even involve malpractice.

In the Oakland, California, area the Industrial Accident Commission was adjudicating whether a steelworker had died from natural causes or from an on-the-job injury. One doctor's autopsy report concluded that death was from natural causes. This would have prevented the widow from receiving compensation benefits from the commission.

At the widow's request another physician, whom we'll call Dr. Stone, prepared a report giving his impressions. He expressed the opinion that the steelworker's death "was caused directly by the injury." In the course of setting forth his reasons, he analyzed the autopsy report and the qualifications of Dr. Farrell (not his real name), the physician who wrote it.

Stone described Farrell as a pathologist "who is not a certified pathologist, and who has rendered a very inexpert report." Farrell was a "rather inept and inexpert individual," Stone wrote. "A more experienced pathologist would have examined the heart a little more thoroughly."

The commission treated Dr. Stone's report as written testimony and subsequently made an award in the widow's favor. A copy of the Stone report came to Dr. Farrell's attention. Nearly two years after it was written, Farrell brought it before the local medical association, charging Dr. Stone with unethical behavior. Specifically Stone was accused of violating a section of the A.M.A. Principles of Medical Ethics that declares: "When a physician does succeed another physician in charge of a case, he should not disparage by comment or insinuation the one who preceded him."

The local association found Dr. Stone guilty and expelled him. The verdict was upheld by the state medical society, then reaffirmed by the A.M.A. Judicial Council. Dr. Stone turned to the courts. The first court ruled against him. On appeal, the California District Court found in his favor on the disparagement charge. It ordered the society to set aside the penalty for this supposed violation and ordered his penalty redetermined solely on the basis of another charge.

Of broad significance is the court's declaration that it would not permit a medical society, in the name of medical ethics, to inhibit a doctor's testimony through threats of expulsion should he "disparage" another doctor: "With such a threat facing him, he must weigh carefully and well his every utterance lest through some slip of the tongue he 'insinuate' something about another physician which his medical society may, perchance, deem disparaging and, as such, just cause for censure, suspension, or expulsion. It is inconceivable that the law could tolerate the holding of such a sword of Damocles over any medical witness in any judicial proceeding."

ROADBLOCKS IN THE COURT

Many courts help obstruct the malpractice plaintiff by making a medical witness an absolute necessity. This requirement is to a large degree unparalleled in other types of litigation. Professor Robert M. Markus, of the Cleveland-Marshall Law School, has remarked: "While experts frequently do testify as to the standard of care in other fields of negligence law, there is not the same blind insistence that the standard can only be proved by expert testimony." Indeed, in some nonmedical negligence cases courts rule that the standard of care is a matter that should be left to the jury.

By contrast, in one typical malpractice case, the judge instructed the jurors to base their judgment solely on medical testimony: "You are not permitted to set up arbitrarily a standard of your own" in determining whether the sued doctor fulfilled the duties imposed on him by law. Rather, "the standards . . . were set up by the learning, skill and care ordinarily possessed and practiced by others of the same profession in good standing, in the same locality, at the same time." In establishing the standard of care in a particular community, the jurors were told to rely on the testimony of local physicians only.

This "community rule" was originally intended to protect rural physicians who did their best despite their isolation. Today the rule presents a major obstacle to patients, since it is local physicians who are least likely to testify against a colleague. Outside doctors who would testify for the plaintiff are often disqualified under the community rule. Not being from the community, they could not show familiarity with the treatments usually employed in this particular locale.

In terms of actual medical practice, the community rule bears little relationship to reality: There is a *national* uniformity of medical standards; the practice of good medicine is essentially the same in Maine and in Hawaii, in small towns and in big cities. Doctors go to similar medical schools with comparably high standards set by a national organization, the Association of American Medical Colleges. Physicians, wherever in the country they practice, read the same nationally distributed medical texts and journals. The certification requirements of all nineteen specialty boards are nationally uniform.

A few courts are starting to recognize this, but it is still noteworthy when physicians who practice in Chicago are permitted to testify for a plaintiff in Florida, or when a San Francisco doctor is qualified as an expert witness in Utah. In Baltimore, a distinguished physician from Philadelphia sought to testify for the patient in a malpractice case. The defendant protested under the community rule. The court ruled in the patient's favor: "We fail to see how there could be any substantial variance between the proper surgical standards in two sophisticated eastern cities such as Philadelphia and Baltimore which are less than 110 miles apart."

While more decisions are reflecting such reasoning, some courts continue to require the plaintiff's witness to practice in the identical community as the defendant. In one case, doctors from Los Angeles were not allowed to testify as to medical standards in adjacent Long Beach. The court ruled, "There may be something peculiar in the practice of one community that is not followed in the other and, unless the proposed doctor witness can assure us this peculiarity doesn't exist, he cannot testify." This, later reversed, was ruled even though physicians in these indistinguishable, contiguous communities belong to the same medical societies, often have privileges at the same hospital, and even treat many of the same patients.

The courts also are often rigorous in deciding which doctors are qualified by schooling and experience to testify in a particular case. In some medical specialties, the patient's chances of getting to trial are especially hampered by the unavailability of medical witnesses. Where courts are unyielding on specialty qualifications, attorneys will not even attempt to prosecute a claim. An official of the American Trial Lawyers Association has said: "I generally won't take a case if I need expert witnesses in urology, pediatrics, plastic surgery or anesthesiology. I just can't find witnesses in these specialties."

Despite the unavailability of such witnesses, the trial judge may disqualify physicians who can show considerable experience. A mother was suing a doctor for negligence in the death of her nineteen-year-old son, who had suffered a head injury. She located a physician who was willing to testify in her behalf. For almost thirty years he had served as autopsy surgeon in the coroner's office. During that time he had personally performed 35,000 to 40,000 autopsies, of which at least 5,000 were on persons who had died of head injuries. He had often conferred with doctors at county hospitals on head injury cases, and he had become familiar with the practice adopted by reputable physicians in the treatment of traumatic injuries to the head and brain.

Yet the trial court disqualified him as a witness. Although his knowledge of head injuries was expert, the judge wanted a doctor who operated on living patients. As a result of this disqualification, the plaintiff's evidence was held insufficient to establish negligence.

In a partial attempt to help the patient get a fair trial, some courts in recent years have allowed medical books to be submitted as evidence in the absence of a medical expert. The Massachusetts Legislature has passed a statute that a medical publication may be admitted in evidence at "the discretion of the court." Theoretically, a patient who can produce an authoritative book will not suffer because he lacks a medical witness. In fact, however, the Massachusetts statute is often of no value to the patient.

This was shown in the case of a twenty-year-old student who was admitted to a hospital early one morning with appendicitis. He was given a spinal anesthetic at 7:50 A.M. Blood pressure readings were supposed to be taken at five-minute intervals. But no readings were taken at either 8:05 or 8:10. The anesthetist-nurse testified that although she was then present in the operating room she was not required to take any readings until she went on duty at 8:15.

At that time, she discovered that "there wasn't any blood pressure as far as I could hear." Still, she did not give the alarm. She thought something might be wrong with her blood-pressure apparatus. By the time she took the patient's blood pressure a second time, it was 8:20. The young man's heart had stopped.

Doctors hurriedly performed an open-heart massage. The boy survived, but his brain was damaged during the minutes his heart was not supplying it with oxygen. He will have to be cared for as long as he lives.

Attorneys were unable to find a doctor who would testify as a witness, so they offered two books as evidence to sustain their case. One was a book on cardiology. The other was a standard work in the field of anesthesiology. The judge admitted the book on cardiology because it was written by Dr. Paul Dudley White, known for treating President Eisenhower's heart condition.

The other book, however, was rejected and thus the case was lost. The anesthesiologist admitted that he had read it and that it was by an "authority on anesthesia." But, reasoned the judge, the authority was an Englishman. The requirement is that the standard of care be proved for the community and its vicinity. "That certainly doesn't include England," he said.

The plaintiff in malpractice cases cannot count on finding a sympathetic figure on the bench. In the preceding case the judge interrupted the plaintiff attorney's opening statement with the question, "Don't you think you can shorten this up?" The attorney announced his intention of using a book as evidence. "I don't think it's fair to put in things like that," the judge commented. When the attorney sought to establish authority of the anesthesiology text, the judge stopped him: "Go ahead and get through with this." At the end of the trial he said of the young man's mother: "The thought occurred to me that perhaps instead of suing these people for half a million dollars, she ought to get down on her knees and thank God." Heart massage is a standard resuscitation measure learned early in medical training, yet the judge berated the woman for not appreciating a "miracle."

Besides the chancy use of medical textbooks, the plaintiff who cannot find a medical witness has only a few ways to introduce expert testimony. All are feeble. Plaintiff's attorneys sometimes put the defendant doctor on the stand and ask him about the standards of care in his community. Hoping he will admit his error, the attorney then asks him how he deviated from these standards in this case.

This tactic often worked when it was new. Around the time doctor-defendants were first being hauled to the stand by the opposition, defense counsel Walter G. Murphy observed: "The poor fellow is usually so startled by this unexpected development that he can almost be guaranteed either to bare his soul or to make some unforgivable blunder." Now defendants are generally prepared for this by their counsel and avoid making revealing remarks.

In the absence of expert witnesses, plaintiff's attorneys sometimes serve an unwilling medical expert with a lay subpoena. Occasionally they summon all the doctors in the community. The physician cannot refuse to accept the subpoena. Once on the stand, however, he can refuse to give expert testimony. In some cases, the doctor can be urged into testifying on a medical question. More often, he will avoid the issue by replying, "I would have to do some studying to answer that."

THROWN OUT OF COURT

For lack of a medical witness, countless malpractice cases do not even get to a jury.

Thus thrown out of court was the case of a forty-five-year-old school teacher who had entered a hospital for a possible stomach cancer. In a gastroscopy, a flexible tube about three feet long is gently inserted into the esophagus, the passage leading to the stomach. It has a light at the end so the doctor can see into the stomach's interior.

The woman was given anesthesia and a drug to relax the muscles of her esophagus and stomach. The doctor started to pass the tube down the esophagus. It went with ease until it encountered an obstruction, probably a constriction resulting from the natural tendency of the esophagus to repel a foreign object.

The doctor says he then applied "gentle pressure" to pass the tube further. Immediately, the woman seemed in distress. Her right eye began to swell. Her neck and cheeks distended with gas.

"Her esophagus is punctured," the doctor said to the nurses. He removed the tube and hurried the woman to the surgical ward. There, doctors found a hole over an inch wide.

Semiconscious, the drugged woman heard a nurse ask her if she wanted the services of a priest. "If you come out of this," said another nurse, "we will celebrate."

To repair the tear in the wall of the esophagus, the doctors cut open the patient's chest and removed a rib. When the woman awoke, she learned that she had received forty-five stitches and now had a disfiguring scar on her chest. She was also greeted by a large number of doctor bills.

The woman sued, charging that the doctor had mismanaged the gastroscopy. But she could not locate a medical expert who would tell the court that esophaguses are not ordinarily ripped during gastroscopies. The court declared a nonsuit which was affirmed on appeal. A dissenting appellate judge argued that the matter should at least have reached the jury. "Should not a jury determine whether a 'gentle' pressure could tear and rip cartilage, muscle and membranes?" he asked. "Was it not more like a heavy pressure?"

Even if a jury finds for the plaintiff, an appellate court may reverse the verdict if medical testimony is deemed inadequate. A young man in his early twenties we'll call Allen Tanner was suffering from manic-depressive psychosis and had been committed to a state mental institution. Among the treatments given to him were wet packs. According to a suit he filed:

A doctor ordered that Tanner be tightly bound in wet sheets. For six hours he lay immobile. As the sheets began to dry they constricted, painfully enclosing one of Tanner's arms. He complained, but when the sheets were dry he was tied up in another wet pack. This again interfered with his blood circulation.

When the second pack was removed, Tanner's arms were swollen and numb. His hands had puffed to twice their normal size. But he was swathed in sheets once more and placed in a tub of hot water for five hours.

When the sheets were removed, Tanner's hands were scarcely recognizable as hands. "His hands were swollen two and a half times their normal size, and resembled two raw steaks," a hospital staff member who saw them recalls. "There were blisters in the center of both palms, about the size of a half-dollar, and other blisters over his hands and fingers."

A doctor took an ordinary pen knife from his pocket. Without sterilizing it, he cut into the blisters. A judge commenting on the case said about the doctor's use of an unsterilized pen knife: "Every school child is taught the necessity for hygiene, every housewife knows the absolute need for cleanliness in handling all items used in feeding her infants or caring for a sick one at home."

Infection set in. The young man was racked with pains "like electrical current going through, like my fingers were going to be drawn up." His fingers began to curl permanently toward the palm. Before Tanner entered the hospital his hands were normal—indeed, dextrous enough for him to work as a piano tuner and carpenter. When he left the hospital they were clawlike and had lost at least 60 percent of their functioning.

Tanner had a doctor testify as an expert on administering wet packs, and a verdict was returned in his favor. The compensation was a relatively modest $5,000, but the defendants appealed. The Pennsylvania appellate court overturned the verdict, ruling that Tanner's expert did not show there had been a "deviation from proper practices."

A dissenting judge expressed his "moral indignation" at so strict a requirement. He said of the defendant doctors: "Through indolence, indifference, and outright carelessness they practically wrecked the chances for gainful employment of a young man, who, already groping in the darkness of mental illness, was then . . . deprived of . . . his hands."

A celebrated case in which lack of medical testimony denied a plaintiff compensation began after the birth of a child. A large mass remained in the upper part of the mother's abdomen. A few hours later it shifted to the lower part of her pelvic cavity. The woman's suffering became intense.

Her condition was diagnosed as "inflammatious tumor, locked bowels and gas on the stomach." The mass continued to bulge from her body. Although she was hospitalized for eleven days, no x-rays were taken. This was a small hospital owned by a surgeon. At the time the woman was admitted, her husband was required to sign a promissory note to the hospital and doctors before they would treat her. Her sole treatment throughout her stay consisted of enemas and compresses.

The woman's condition worsened. She was sent home from the hospital with the doctors' instructions to continue her treatment. A week later, she was taken in agony to another hospital. Emergency surgery disclosed the cause of her difficulty. She should have delivered twins. Her uterus had ruptured, and the second fetus had slipped into the abdomen. The mass of festering tissue had remained inside her for twenty-five days.

She died the following week. Her husband, left with three young children, brought suit against the hospital, its surgeon-owner, and the physician who had performed the delivery.

But he was unable to persuade the doctors at the second hospital to testify to what they discovered. Because he lacked medical witnesses, the trial court directed a verdict for the defendant. The husband appealed.

The appellate court was highly critical of the physicians in the case. In a decision notable for its anger, the court castigated physicians at the first hospital for not having taken the x-rays that would have revealed the woman's condition. Though doctors there failed to x-ray the patient, the court declared, they "promptly made an x-ray" of the husband's "pocketbook and assets [and] succeeded in getting a good exposure." Ordering a new trial, the court observed: "It is clear from the record that appellants were handicapped during the trial by the reluctance of physicians to testify with reference to the mistakes of other doctors. . . . There were eleven prominent doctors listed on the [second] hospital's stationery . . . and from none of them was a sound ever heard."

At the retrial, the husband again could not obtain the medical testimony necessary to establish malpractice. Moreover, colleagues testified in support of the defendant doctors and hospital. With no medical evidence to the contrary, the jury returned a verdict for the defendants. This time, on appeal, it was sustained.

TAMPERING WITH THE RECORD

Ordinarily, medical records are sacrosanct. Accurate reporting is one of the first essentials taught in medical training. It is a habit that remains with most doctors for life, for the notations in a patient's chart can be of life-and-death importance. In hospitals, patient care is the product of many complex parts and fragmented personnel. Records can spell the difference between cure and chaos.

Tampering with the record is regarded in medicine much as altering the books is in banking. However, in malpractice suits the same urge that leads doctors to give false testimony sometimes prompts physicians to corrupt medical records. Melvin Belli has said: "I have had to learn to deal only with the original records. Photostatic copies do not reveal alterations."

Belli tells of a case in which a man was hospitalized for abdominal surgery. He was found to have type A blood, and he was given two correct transfusions. "Then," recalls Belli, "through sheer carelessness, a doctor who didn't even bother to read the label on the blood bottle gave him a type B transfusion." The incompatible blood caused the patient to go into shock. He was rushed to an artificial kidney in a hospital several miles away. But it was too late to save him.

There was no question that incompatible blood had been administered, Belli continues. "But when I examined the hospital records I noticed they had been clumsily altered. One nurse, confronted with evidence that she had made the changes, accused a doctor of having directed her to do so. She was in tears as she testified."

Doctors on hospital staffs sometimes try to conceal mistakes by suppressing hospital records. Aaron J. Broder, president of the New York State Association of Trial Lawyers, cites the case of a woman who was found dead on the floor of her hospital room. At the ensuing malpractice trial, the plaintiff's attorney learned that the last six days of the patient's chart had mysteriously disappeared.

With strong words fired from either side, legal battles are sometimes fought over whether physicians covered up for each other. In one of the malpractice allegations coming closest to charging a literal conspiracy, a trial court found that "hospital records were altered, doctored, or tailored so as to present a defense." A higher court overruled this decision, and the case continues to intrigue medicolegal authorities. A thirty-three-year-old woman went into labor one morning shortly after breakfast. She went to the hospital, where an obstetrician examined her and found the unborn child in distress. The woman was immediately prepared for delivery. Then, according to the subsequent complaint:

The doctor instructed the nurse-anesthetist to place the woman under an inhalator mask. A large percentage of deaths in anesthesia occur in patients who have just eaten. Unless precautions are taken, the food may be coughed up into the tightly sealed face mask. With each breath, the vomit would then be inhaled, clogging the respiratory passages. However (the allegation continued), neither the doctor nor the nurse asked the woman when she had last eaten. It was less than two hours since her breakfast.

Minutes after the baby was born, the woman gave several gasps. The nurse pulled the mask from the patient's face. Large amounts of vomit were coming from her mouth. She was dead.

Entries in hospital records showed that the birth occurred at 9:55 A.M. and that the woman died nine minutes later, at 10:04. That afternoon, an autopsy found large amounts of vomit in the woman's breathing passages and in her lungs. As the cause of death, it was listed on the autopsy report and death certificate that she had choked after inhaling stomach contents. These documents were signed by an assistant medical examiner of the city, and they were damaging as evidence, for they suggested that safeguards had not been taken for a patient who had recently eaten.

A malpractice suit was brought against the doctor, nurse, and hospital. Thereafter a revised death certificate was filed with the Board of Health. Signed by the same assistant medical examiner, it changed the cause of death to "amniotic fluid embolism." This is a blockage in circulation that results if the bloodstream is penetrated by droplets from the fetal water sac.

Presented as a cause of death, this diagnosis was greeted skeptically. There have been fewer than fifty known deaths throughout the world from amniotic fluid embolism. For the condition to arise, there needs to be a rip at the point where the mother and fetus are linked. No such rupture was found in this patient.

Amniotic fluid embolism causes death within two minutes after the infant is born. This represents the interval between when the tear occurs and when the blockage would be fatal. Some of the hospital records now showed that the time of the birth had been changed to 10:02. This would be two minutes before the mother's death, fitting a diagnosis of amniotic fluid embolism.

Judge Louis L. Friedman of the New York State Supreme Court, who reported these findings, concluded as follows: Members of the hospital staff had sought to change the record to substantiate amniotic fluid embolism as the cause of death. They might have succeeded if some records had not been beyond their reach. Thus it finally could be shown that death resulted from improper administration of anesthesia and the failure to take usual precautions.

The judge further concluded that the assistant medical examiner collaborated by signing the amended death certificate to report a false diagnosis. He was also implicated in alterations made in records pertaining to the case at the Health Department and the Medical Examiner's Office. Judge Friedman attributed his participation to "his personal friendship with the hospital personnel."

In the courtroom the defendants projected onto a screen microscopic slides, purporting that these came from the patient and showed amniotic fluid embolism. The assistant medical examiner testified that he had performed a microscopic examination disclosing amniotic fluid embolism. There was testimony noted by Judge Friedman that this was virtually impossible, that under the hospital's strict procedure he could not have done any such examination.

An appellate court reversed Judge Friedman's findings as an "erroneous misconception of the proof in the record," and the jury absolved the hospital and the nurse-anesthetist of any liability (upheld by the appellate court). On the other hand, the jury rejected the contention that death was caused by amniotic fluid embolism and found against the obstetrician to the tune of $60,000.

Thus the outcome of this litigation is muddy. But its significance lies outside itself: Many people find it easy to believe—wrongly so, in the eyes of the law—that a conspiracy actually occurred. And the fact that such suspicion persists is one of the tragic effects of medicine's conspiracy of silence.

24
Resistance to Reform

"WE ALL SHUDDER at the thought of displaying our dirty linen for public view. However, until this problem is called to the attention of all physicians, and all physicians exercise their moral responsibility, we cannot hope to solve our dilemma."

Thus has an editorial in the *Omaha-Douglas County Medical Society Bulletin* urged reforms in medical discipline. Other voices in medicine have similarly called for an end to keeping the problem under wraps. "We know there is some soiled linen in our medical closet," Dr. Bentley P. Colcock of Boston's Lahey Clinic has written. "However, we prefer not to talk about it. . . . This is where we are wrong." While Dr. George F. Lull was secretary and general manager of the A.M.A., he said of offenses by physicians: "We should not hide these things. They must be brought into the open."

Dr. Stanley R. Truman, a former president of the American Academy of General Practice, headed an A.M.A. committee investigating fee splitting and other abuses. He has criticized his colleagues for keeping medicine's problems from public view. "The medical profession is not a priesthood within whose ranks . . . behavior and methods are to be kept secret. . . . We doctors have been a little too lackadaisical about some of the hidden sins of our colleagues."

Dr. David B. Allman, a past-president of the A.M.A., has warned that if "individual physicians do not keep medicine's house in order, outside organizations—like hospitals or government—will do it for us. . . . Our first responsibility is to our patients, and not to ourselves."

The *Federation Bulletin* has called on doctors to heed the critics of medical discipline who hold that "many physicians do have human frailties and . . . their shortcomings are of sufficient importance to cause serious difficulties among a small but important part of the profession. They are also concerned over the fact that they are likely to cause grave damage to a significant number of patients each year. They believe in facing the problem squarely by bringing it out into the open in an effort to remedy the situation."

But medical leaders who engage in self-criticism are few and far between. The medical educator Dr. Alan Gregg once said: "We doctors resemble dictators in alternating between complete disregard of criticism and exquisite sensitiveness to it." As a whole the profession has been reluctant to discuss its bad apples, even to admit that the problem exists.

An example of this defensiveness has arisen in connection with fee splitting. A *Saturday Evening Post* article said merely that, among many other areas in the country, "fee splitting is said to be widespread in certain West Coast cities." Although no individual city was named, the San Francisco Medical Society took this as an attack. The society protested "emphatically . . . there are no illegal and unethical medical and surgical practices in existence in this city."

This is a challengeable statement because medical discipline is weak in San Francisco as elsewhere. In addition, the society objected to articles of this type on the grounds that "they destroy the confidence of patients in honest, ethical family physicians."

An editorial in a local paper, the *Call Bulletin,* replied that by the same logic no fraudulent banker or corrupt judge ever should be exposed because it might "destroy the confidence" of the public in banks or the judicial system. "Doctors are human and subject to imperfections just like the rest of us," the *Call Bulletin* added. "And if a condition arises which calls for exposure, then it ought to be exposed."

However well founded a criticism may be, if made by a layman it is likely to meet a broad front of opposition. Lois Hoffman, as editor of the medical journal *RISS* (for Residents, Interns, Senior Students), wrote an article about the problems of medical licensure. Authorities in the field reviewed the article and commented that it was accurate and fair. After publication, some members of the Federation of State Medical Boards took a public position deriding Mrs. Hoffman's findings. The *Federation Bulletin* rose to defend the factualism of Mrs. Hoffman's article and condemn the attack on it: "We have heard some of our members express considerable indignation over her remarks even though many of her statements have been repeatedly expressed at some of our own meetings."

Many doctors frown upon criticism even from other members of the profession. Dr. Thomas Percival, in his eighteenth-century *Manual of Medical Ethics,* wrote that in speaking of colleagues a physician should avoid "all general charges against their selfishness or improbity." Percival would have belonged to a school of thought described by the *Federation Bulletin* as holding that "at least 99 percent of physicians are paragons of virtue. Members of this school believe that the extremely small numbers of physicians who are likely to get into trouble should be ignored or at least the dirt should be swept under the rug and not mentioned." As if to illustrate this way of thinking, a Tennessee physician has said: "Our disciplinary system is O.K. . . . It's better to let a few men keep on practicing poor medicine than to open the door to acrimonious and destructive judging of skill."

Efforts to bring a problem out of hiding are often viewed as an attack on a noble profession, even an act of treachery. A South Carolina doctor expresses this defensiveness in a letter to a medical magazine: "I feel there is entirely too much kicking of the medical profession by the doctors themselves. I feel there is no profession that deserves so much praise as do the doctors."

When Dr. Louis Lasagna, a pathologist at Johns Hopkins Medical School, criticized some policies of the A.M.A. in his book *The Doctors' Dilemmas,* one medical reviewer did not dispute Dr. Lasagna's accuracy. But he did object to Dr. Lasagna's making negative comments about medicine's foremost organization. "Whether or not the statements are true," the reviewer wrote, "they seem in questionable taste and we can only conclude that he is eager to join the large number of people who are constantly trying to denigrate an honorable profession."

TWO MEN WHO SPOKE OUT

Among the outspoken critics of unethical practices among physicians has been Dr. Loyal Davis, a Regent of the College of Surgeons, professor of surgery at Northwestern University Medical School and chief of surgery at one of Chicago's top hospitals. Dr. Davis, along with other representatives of the American College of Surgeons, met with members of the press to discuss the evils of fee splitting. In the course of the meeting, Dr. Davis said: "There is no question but that fee splitting is on the increase in Chicago and surrounding areas."

Theoretically, colleagues should have universally applauded Dr. Davis, for the A.M.A. Principles of Medical Ethics call on physicians to "expose, without fear or favor, incompetent or corrupt, dishonest or unethical conduct on the part of members of the profession." Instead, Dr. Davis was castigated. Some 150 members of the Chicago Medical Society signed petitions charging him with making statements for personal publicity advantages, releasing misleading information, and making statements detrimental to the entire medical profession. The doctors called upon the society to investigate and expel Dr. Davis. Advised of the charges against him, Dr. Davis was summoned to appear before the society's Committee on Ethical Relations to defend himself.

Dr. Davis received wide public support. Editorials called the investigation an "ill-timed and unwise attack." Said the *Chicago Daily News:* "The ouster effort seems to be a sanctimonious attempt to silence a critic without bothering to refute his charges. The energy would be much better spent in combatting the evil of which Dr. Davis complains."

At the hearing, no effort was made to dispute the accuracy of Dr. Davis's statement. As a matter of fact, fee splitting was so prevalent in the area that at the time some members of the society were trying to rewrite the ethics code to make kickbacks permissible. In this topsy-turvy setting, the Committee on Ethical Relations voted to find Dr. Davis guilty of "unethical conduct."

Final approval of the report against Dr. Davis was to come at the next meeting of the Society's Council. The Council approved the report but then in the outcry tabled it. A month later the Council, by a small majority, rescinded approval. Charges against Dr. Davis were finally dropped. But the Council did pass a resolution deploring use of the public press in fighting unethical practices.

The American College of Surgeons defended Dr. Davis for speaking out against fee splitting. In a statement to the press, the College said: "A small minority of the medical profession chooses to circumvent its moral and ethical responsibilities and strongly resents any action which calls the attention of the public and the profession to its wrongdoing. This group desires to keep the knowledge of these unethical practices from the public and to silence all doctors of good will who decry conduct which is prejudicial to the best care of the sick. Professional men . . . should welcome the opportunity to profit from criticism. It is inconceivable that the medical profession as a whole can be injured by exposing and weeding out those relatively few who violate, or evade, the high traditions of the medical profession."

At least as outspoken as Dr. Davis was Dr. Paul R. Hawley, and he too incurred the hostility of many of his colleagues. In World War II, Dr. Hawley, a major general, was chief surgeon of the European Theater of Operations. When General of the Army Omar N. Bradley became chief of the Veterans Administration, he called on Dr. Hawley to reorganize V.A. medical services, then known as "the backwash of American medicine"—a morass of neglected patients, underpaid staff, and inadequate equipment. By initiating a medical corps modeled after the U.S. Public Health Service, Hawley accomplished what has been hailed as a medical miracle. One year Hawley threatened to quit unless Congress came through with an appropriation. The V.A. got the money.

After a period as chief executive officer of the Blue Cross and Blue Shield Commission, during which he was a forceful proponent of health insurance, Dr. Hawley became director of the American College of Surgeons. He had long complained of medicine's laxity of self-discipline. "Had organized medicine devoted half as much energy toward kicking out the rascals as protecting them," he once told a group of doctors, "there would be no more danger of government control of medicine than there is now of government control of the clergy."

One winter day while director of the A.C.S., Dr. Hawley talked with an editor of U.S. News & World Report. Believing he was simply filling in the background for a writer unfamiliar with medicine, Dr. Hawley spoke candidly about fee splitting, unnecessary surgery, and surgical incompetence. A few days later Dr. Hawley left on a business trip to South America. During his absence, *U.S. News* submitted for review a transcript of the conversation. A staff assistant of Dr. Hawley's checked it for possible transcribing errors and sent it back, not realizing that *U.S. News* was planning to carry it word for word as an article.

Thus was published Dr. Hawley's comment that half the surgery in the United States is performed by doctors who are "untrained, or inadequately trained, to undertake surgery." Another charge that attracted much attention was: "The sin that is killing the practice of medicine—in all its specialties—is greed." By the time Dr. Hawley returned to this country he was the focus of a medical furor.

"Bull-in-the-china-shop tactics . . . ill-tempered accusations . . . churlish invective," protested an editorial in *Northwest Medicine.* "Ill-advised, unfounded, false, misleading and vitriolic," charged the American Academy of General Practice. Said the president of the A.A.G.P., Dr. R. B. Robins: "Dr. Hawley has taken advantage of exceptions to condemn the whole medical profession. At least, that's what the average person . . . would conclude."

Dr. Hawley had his defenders. Robert M. Cunningham, Jr., editor of the journal *The Modern Hospital,* rejoindered: "The average person who concluded that Dr. Hawley condemned the whole medical profession must have read the article with his eyes closed."

Hawley, in fact, stressed that "the great majority of hospitals are as clean as a hound's tooth" and "never in the history of the world has medical care been anywhere near as good as it is in this country today!"

Delegates to the A.M.A. House of Delegates introduced eleven resolutions condemning Dr. Hawley. Among other things, the resolutions charged Dr. Hawley with making "misstatements, distortions of fact, unfounded and uncorroborated charges . . . individual and collective self-laudation of grandiose proportions and scurrilous and derogatory remarks." Included in the resolutions were motions to censure Dr. Hawley.

The resolutions were referred to the Reference Committee on Legislation and Public Relations, which heard testimony on them. At the hearing Dr. Hawley challenged the committee: "Is it the intent here to abridge free speech? Is no one to speak up against evil unless he first is approved by organized medicine? I will continue to raise my voice. Doctors are citizens as well as doctors. Their responsibility to the public transcends their loyalty to the medical profession."

The committee recommended that no action be taken on any of the resolutions, and so Dr. Hawley escaped censure. However, the House of Delegates adopted a statement formulated by the committee. This reaffirmed the long-standing belief that "Destructive critical comments serve no useful purpose," and "The method evolved for dealing with the problems of unethical conduct . . . is still the best."

"OUR LIBERTY WILL CRUMBLE"

Dr. William L. Baughn of Anderson, Indiana, is a past-president of the American Association of Physicians and Surgeons, an organization so ultraconservative that it has accused the A.M.A. of being dominated by left-wingers.

If Dr. Baughn had his way in a hospital he would abolish all the audit, tissue, and utilization committees. He would do away with the Joint Commission on Accreditation of Hospitals. His reasoning: "Our professional and personal liberty will crumble just as surely under 'self-policing' as it would under Government regulation."

Dr. Baughn is more extreme an individualist than most physicians, but he illustrates how many doctors and medical bodies resist regulation. In the name of freedom and liberty, the profession has often preserved anarchy. Nowhere more so than in the field of medical discipline.

Even so elementary and benign an institution as the local medical society grievance committee generally has trouble becoming established and accepted among doctors. The A.M.A. recurrently urges local societies to establish grievance committees and make existing ones more effective. Success is minimal, in large part because society members have no wish to come under additional regulation.

"Our grievance committee was originally founded with a great deal of resistance from the member-physicians," recalls the executive secretary of one county medical society. The members "felt that this was simply inviting trouble from patients who presumed that they have a complaint." They also feared that the committee might turn into a runaway grand jury. Some opponents started calling the proposed committee an Inquisition and would say, "I'm against the Inquisition, aren't you?" The grievance committee was formed over a decade ago, but the first rule of holding any society together is not to anger a large bloc of members. The committee is kept largely inactive, and the society does not publicize its existence. Patients must find out by word-of-mouth that a facility for handling complaints against physicians does in fact exist.

Doctors often show the same kind of resistance to disciplinary controls in hospitals. Dr. Edward H. Daseler, formerly an investigator for the American College of Surgeons, tells of his frustration in trying to set up a tissue committee in a new hospital: "Response was lukewarm," he recalls. Although all the doctors he spoke to agreed that a committee was badly needed to curb unnecessary and unskillful surgery, they refused to take part in its establishment. "They feared that participation in such a venture might harm their own practices."

At the first meeting of the surgery department, a doctor moved that a tissue committee be established. "This created quite a stir," says Dr. Daseler. One of the surgeons said that although he realized a great deal of unnecessary surgery was performed in this hospital, "still the relations between members of the profession had always been peaceful and pleasant." Rather than introduce a controversy, the motion was shelved.

Official word came to the hospital that a functioning tissue committee was a requirement for accreditation. Simultaneously, a new pathologist told the staff that more than half the appendices, tubes, ovaries, and uteri removed at the hospital showed no evidence of disease. This finding was repeated over several months. At last, after nine months of bickering, the hospital formed a tissue committee.

The committee met only once before a new chief of staff was elected. His first major act was to disband it. The pathologist was told to temper his reports by using nonspecific jargon like "acute catarrhal appendicitis" rather than saying the appendix was normal.

At another hospital, the pathologist told Dr. Daseler of evidence of much unneeded surgery. But, complained the pathologist, the tissue committee was of no use whatever because of the presence on it of one of the worst offenders. The pathologist devised a plan to reactivate the committee by having two ethically practicing surgeons appointed to it.

Three months later, the pathologist did a turnabout. He reported to the staff on the "excellence" of the surgery performed at the hospital. In closing, he recommended that the tissue committee be disbanded since he could see no logical reason for having such a watchdog in this hospital. Comments Dr. Daseler: "Powerful pressures must have been brought to bear on him" because of the competition between this and another hospital to fill their beds.

Efforts to reform medical licensing laws are similarly resisted. There is wide mistrust of state legislators, and many officials of medical societies and medical licensing boards fear that initiating corrective legislation would open a Pandora's box. In one state, the board reports that it is reluctant to attempt to amend the licensing law because of the fear that chiropractors would try to make their practices legal. The executive secretary of another board says: "We are afraid to touch our medical practice act. We have bad legislators in this state and if we were to open up the law for changes, we would be opening it up for a lot of bad changes."

Thus legislative reforms die on the vine. In New York State legislation was introduced to suspend the medical licenses of doctors afflicted with mental disease. But the bill met opposition among physicians. One prominent doctor, later president of the New York County Medical Society, suggested that such a law should also cover politicians. Without support from the profession, the bill was shelved.

PROTECTING THE PROFITEERS

Some 10,500 physicians (a conservative estimate) own pharmacies or have stock in small drug companies.

Unavoidably, many of these doctor-owners are tempted to subordinate the patient's welfare to their own financial gain. Leaders in medical discipline agree that physicians should be barred from owning pharmacies and drug companies. The *Federation Bulletin* condemns doctor-owners as being "driven by profit motive either to increase their incomes or to help pay the mortgages on their office buildings."

No correction is possible without the support of the A.M.A. But the A.M.A.'s position has been weak and inconsistent. For a long while the Principles of Medical Ethics prohibited doctors from owning pharmacies, drug companies, or similar businesses—unequivocally stating: "An ethical physician does not engage in barter or trade in the appliances, devices or remedies prescribed for patients, but limits the source of his professional income to professional services rendered."

Then, at a convention in 1955, the House of Delegates yielded to lobbying by doctor-proprietors. The House ruled it permissible for a doctor to own a pharmacy. Physicians could now ethically "supply drugs, remedies or appliances as long as there is no exploitation of the patient." In 1957, the language was further modified: "Drugs, remedies or appliances may be dispensed by the physician provided it is in the best interest of the patient." The House also sanctioned investments by physicians in pharmaceutical companies. Its reasoning: The doctor as a private citizen has a right to invest in any company he cares to.

For the next five years there were frequent complaints from the public of doctors profiteering through pharmacies and drug companies. Late in 1962, the Judicial Council—medicine's Jimminy Cricket—recommended that the A.M.A. adopt an unequivocal position at least against doctor ownership of pharmaceutical companies. Many doctor-owners objected, and the matter was shelved "for further study and report."

In 1963 the House of Delegates voted it unethical for a physician to have a "financial interest in a drug repackaging company" or to "own stock in a pharmaceutical company which he can control." The A.M.A. has told the public and Congress that this should effectively keep doctors from owning drug companies. But the new prohibition has a loophole. It condemns doctor ownership only of *repackaging* companies. To sidestep this, some doctor-owned companies have set up a small manufacturing branch. Moreover, the prohibition is generally unenforced, and many doctor-owners ignore it and continue as before.

The Judicial Council has recommended many times that the A.M.A. take a strong stand against physician control of drugstores. Each time the council has made the recommendation to the House of Delegates, it has been defeated. After one defeat, Dr. Arnold O. Swenson, chairman of the A.M.A. Investigating Jury, charged that those delegates who had approved of doctor-ownership had "dollar signs in their eyes."

Among the thousands of doctors who own pharmacies are a number who help make A.M.A. policy and hold high office in medical organizations. At least one has been an A.M.A. president. One of the attractions of medical group practice is the opportunity to have a pharmacy in the group building. Profits from a group-owned drugstore can be so large that group members often consider it unthinkable to sell off a prize source of income.

To curb prescription profiteering, the states of Washington, California, Maryland, and North Dakota have laws restricting doctor-ownership of pharmacies. Antimonopoly legislation, introduced by Senator Philip Hart of Michigan, has gone before Congress. The Hart Bill would prohibit physician ownership of drug companies and pharmacies. The A.M.A. has attacked the bill on the ground that it would encroach on physicians' liberty. An editorial in the *A.M.A. News* has said: "Tradition has shown that the physician must be free to exercise the proper judgment and medication for each of his patients. To do so requires freedom from unnecessary restraints in the practice of medicine. Passage of the Hart legislation will only serve to curtail this freedom."

Senator Hart, after completing an investigation that revealed widespread exploitation in prescription writing, criticized the A.M.A. for not taking a stand against doctor-owned pharmacies and drug companies. "The public," he said, "would benefit greatly if the American Medical Association worked as hard to stop these practices as it has to block Medicare."

THE SHAME OF THE A.M.A.

One of the simplest and most easily implemented of the A.M.A. Medical Disciplinary Committee's recommendations calls for state licensing boards and state medical societies to report all major disciplinary actions to a central file at A.M.A. headquarters. This clearinghouse of information would remedy the current fragmentation of disciplinary activity. It would help societies and boards spot repeat offenders, especially newcomers in flight from previous communities.

When this recommendation was introduced before the A.M.A. House of Delegates, speakers documented the need for the reform. Nonetheless, the proposal met intense opposition. At a hearing on the measure, one doctor charged that it was a "usurpation of state's rights." Another called it a "takeover" and a "step toward centralized control over medicine." A House of Delegates member from Louisiana declared: "The A.M.A. is wrong if it thinks we're going to turn in every doctor we haul up on the carpet in Louisiana." Much the same response met a proposal to strengthen medical discipline by granting original jurisdiction to the A.M.A. The Medical Disciplinary Committee reported that state medical associations generally act on disciplinary matters only on appeal from the county level, while county societies are generally slow to take action against offenders.

To fill the gap left by county and state societies, the committee proposed that the A.M.A. as a national association be empowered to initiate action against offending doctors. The committee urged that "the bylaws of the American Medical Association be changed to confer original jurisdiction on the Association to suspend or revoke the A.M.A. membership of a physician guilty of a violation of the Principles of Medical Ethics or the ethical policy of the American Medical Association regardless of whether action has been taken against him at local level."

The A.M.A. Judicial Council, which came out strongly for the change, made clear that it did not intend to make irresponsible use of this power. Nor did the council expect to use the power very often. But, it reasoned, the mere fact that the national association had it would make state and county societies more willing to act on their own.

At the annual A.M.A. meeting, the House of Delegates gave tentative approval to the measure. The necessary changes in the bylaws were to be drawn up for final passage at the A.M.A. clinical meeting in November. But between June and November opposition to the proposal grew. In November the original-jurisdiction bylaw was attacked on the grounds that it would destroy the confederacy principle of the A.M.A. and would "invade the domain of individual rights." A delegate from New York rose to say: "At a time when medicine is struggling against centralized authority in Washington, it would be ridiculous for us to centralize control of medical discipline in Chicago." The delegates thus voted the bylaw back for further study.

A supporter of original jurisdiction, a Judicial Council member, said: "Unless they give us the authority to initiate disciplinary action, they'll have taken the guts right out of our campaign" to strengthen medical discipline.

But the following June, the delegates passed an emasculated version of the bylaw, leaving discipline in the hands of county and state societies. The A.M.A. was limited to acting against an offender only at the invitation or with the approval of the state society, or after the county or state society has taken action.

The A.M.A. News misrepresented the new bylaw in its headline, "A.M.A. Authorized to Enforce Ethics." Closer to reality was the comment of a Judicial Council member: "Before this, the A.M.A. had its hands and feet bound. Now maybe a couple of fingers are loose, but we still can't do anything."

PART VIII

A Call to Action

THERE ARE FIFTEEN practical steps that would bring about much
needed reforms in medical discipline. All the proposals are derived from
existing programs that have proved successful. If adopted they would
retain the present system of a predominantly private practice of medicine
licensed by states, with federal activity in discipline kept to a necessary
minimum. With medicine's existing instrumentalities expanded and improved, the profession could at last be governed in the public interest
with no hardship to the typical physician.

25
What Needs to Be Done

SOME LAYMEN HATE doctors with bitterness. They distrust individual physicians and are scornful of the profession at large. They refuse to believe that the typical doctor is a good person who feels harassed but is trying to do the right thing. More likely, they are convinced, except for a rare saint all doctors are rich and inhuman and daily in conspiracy against patients.

Many of the people who are anti-doctor bear grudges against the profession as a result of a disappointment in treatment. A handful of patients who feel persecuted by their psychiatrists have formed an association to place therapists under surveillance. Another group is being organized by a woman who advertises in the *New York Times* for malpractice victims. She telephones people who reply and, often refusing to give her name, goes into detail about "what they did to me."

People who are anti-doctor commonly regard federal regulation of medicine as a cure-all for the profession's disciplinary problems. Other laymen, while more moderate in their views about physicians, similarly feel that the profession cannot or will not regulate itself, so the only hope lies in federal control. Organize a Federal Department of Medicine and Hospitals, goes one frequent proposal. This agency would license physicians nationwide and thereafter police their performance. If a doctor were unskillful or untrustworthy, his license would be withdrawn. With centralized administration there would be few of the close personal ties that now paralyze disciplinary activity.

This proposal is rooted in enough fact to be deceptively reasonable. There *is* a need for more federal activity in medical discipline. Local colleagues *are* loath to discipline one another. But as a practical program for improvement, federal regulation of the private practice of medicine can realistically be considered only as a remote last resort. For the foreseeable future, it has not the slightest chance of becoming law. Opposition is so overwhelming that people interested in resolving the profession's disciplinary problems would do better to work on solutions that are closer at hand.

Nor is it even desirable that a federal agency take over medical licensing and discipline. There is no assurance that a federal bureaucracy

333

would do a more effective job than is being done at present by medicine's many private and public instrumentalities. Lost in the process would be much of the initiative and direct action now possible through a pluralistic approach.

If medicine's existing mechanisms were expanded and improved upon, they could do most of what is needed—while retaining the present system of a predominantly private practice of medicine licensed by the states. Here, drawing on the experience of disciplinary programs already in existence, are broad proposals that promise major reforms. These measures would:

1. *Plug loopholes in medical practice acts.* In the words of the Federation of State Medical Boards: "The practice of medicine is a privilege granted by legislative authority and is not a natural right." Where the medical practice act is muddy, the state legislature should amend it to make clear that the licensing board has the effective authority to withdraw a license from an offender.

This may require shifting of powers. In some states, the medical examining board is merely an advisory body. Revocation and suspension of physician's licenses rests in the hands of a parent department, usually a large multipurpose agency handling all types of licensing or all matters pertaining to health. Medical discipline often gets bogged down. Better results are had where the board is empowered to initiate proceedings and revoke or suspend licenses, with the parent agency retaining merely a veto, if even that.

To stand up in court, a medical practice act must be clearly worded. In most states this requires defining "unprofessional conduct" before it can be cited as an actionable offense. Every state needs also to broaden its grounds for disciplinary action. One of the best medical practice acts is the State of Washington's. It lists no less than fourteen offenses constituting unprofessional conduct and requiring disciplinary action.

A medical practice act is a bad joke if it permits a physician to retain a license he got by fraud or if it allows a doctor to remain licensed even while he is in prison for a felony. Virtually every state needs to add as grounds for discipline fee gouging, overtreating, and other forms of exploitation of patients. So also should specific provision be made for disciplining physicians who are guilty of gross or repeated negligence or who commit willful acts of abandonment and assault.

Mental illness cries for new handling. Every medical practice act should provide for suspending the license of an alcoholic or narcotic addict. Insofar as a physician's sexual deviation is a hazard to patients, medical practice acts should treat it as a symptom of mental illness. Most boards are unable to proceed against a sex offender until he is convicted of a criminal offense. Regarding him as a psychiatric rather than a criminal problem would not only be more enlightened; it also would permit action to be taken where none can be now.

To withdraw a mentally disabled physician's license, a board should not have to wait until a court declares him insane, or until he is committed to a mental institution—extreme measures that often never come to pass. The board should be empowered to take independent action. Few agencies are more qualified than a body of physicians to determine if a doctor is mentally competent to practice medicine.

Senility presents a special problem. It would benefit everyone if annual relicensing were required after age sixty-five, a compromise age between doctors who are young at seventy and those who start fading at sixty. Before an elderly physician's license can be renewed he should need to present the results of a complete physical examination, including a psychiatric consultative examination to detect mental failing. Periodic physical examinations are already required in the relicensing of aircraft pilots. Psychiatric examinations are standard in many disability programs when mental incapacity is at issue.

2. *Make discipline the state boards' main function.* At present, the members of most state boards have little time for disciplinary activity, largely because they are too busy writing and grading licensing examinations. Their efforts produce an uneven product. Knowledgeable physicians often complain that state licensing exams are often unskillfully drafted, with questions that are ambiguous, irrelevant, unfair.

By contrast, the examinations given by the National Board of Medical Examiners are universally respected for their sophistication and comprehensiveness. The National Board is an independent nonprofit agency set up to test the competence of medical graduates. Its examination, drafted each year by some ninety medical educators, is to medical licensure much as the College Boards are to college admissions: a standard yardstick by which an applicant's qualifications may be judged. Already some forty-four states plus the District of Columbia honor National Board test scores and license successful candidates exactly as if they had passed the state board's own exam.

The A.M.A. Medical Disciplinary Committee has urged the profession to "reappraise the primary function" of state boards away from examining and toward discipline. The state boards now should delegate all testing to the National Board of Medical Examiners. Freeing state board members of the burden of writing and grading exams would give them more time for professional discipline while generally getting a better exam. Many state board members resist this proposal, fearing it would lead to the abolition of state boards. On the contrary, state boards are essential to maintaining discipline, whereas, since the National Board offers a better system, they are superfluous to administering exams.

The State of Washington's Medical Disciplinary Board suggests the shape state boards should take once they are divested of examinations. The Disciplinary Board was formed to concentrate disciplinary functions in a body separate from the board administering licensing examinations. All state boards should move quickly toward Washington's emphasis on discipline. (As a guide for reform, a copy of the Washington State Medical Disciplinary Board Act appears in Appendix C.)

Every board should have Washington's authority to initiate investigations. In many states, the board cannot take action until it receives a formal public charge, which an offender's colleagues are usually reluctant to file. In Washington, a quiet word to a Disciplinary Board member suffices to launch an investigation. The board can issue subpoenas, backed up by the courts, to compel attendance at an investigation or hearing.

In California, another state with a promising disciplinary program, the board has a system for uncovering offenders without waiting for complaints to come in. The board is in touch with local police, courts, medical societies. Mental hospitals in the state notify the board whenever they admit a physician as a patient. The California board makes about five hundred investigations a year. In Oregon, liaison with the police brought to light a doctor who was still practicing although he was about to be sentenced for stabbing a man in the stomach in a fit of jealousy.

Ample funds and staff are necessary if a board is to operate successfully. Almost invariably, a board is better off if it has its own investigators and legal counsel. These cost money. California employs over a dozen investigators and has an annual budget of half a million dollars.

Board members should be well paid for their services, for there are limits to how active a physician can afford to be if he must sacrifice income by being away from his practice. Payment of $150 a day plus expenses is not excessive considering what the doctor would otherwise gross. Taking the financial sting out of serving on the board would make service attractive to many more physicians, probably raising the overall caliber of board members.

The additional money should come from medical licensing fees. The medical profession, uniquely a nation within a nation, can be expected to pay for its own policing. No longer should state boards scrape along, financed by a merely nominal registration fee. Nor should states short-change medical boards by funneling substantial fees into the public coffers, to be divided up along with miscellaneous revenues. Licensing fees should go into a fund earmarked for board functions, and the board should be authorized to raise or lower fees as expenses warrant. Dr. William F. Quinn, of the California board, has said this self-financing system permits "guarding the integrity of the licenses we're empowered to grant."

3. *Require doctors to keep pace with medical progress.* Once a physician receives his license he should no longer be able to go to sleep on medicine. His incompetence should be uncovered before he has injured or killed a patient.

At the minimum, every physician should be required to take part in an organized program of continuing education like that of the American Academy of General Practice, the only society in medicine that has a continuation-study requirement. Each A.A.G.P. member must complete one hundred fifty hours of acceptable postgraduate study every three years or lose his academy certificate, a hallmark of great distinction among G.P.s. Following the A.A.G.P. pattern, the A.M.A. is seeking to develop a "lifetime learning" curriculum for practicing physicians. The A.M.A. envisions physicians keeping abreast of medicine by voluntarily taking A.M.A.-certified courses given by schools, hospitals, medical societies.

While voluntary postgraduate study would be ideal, an element of compulsion almost certainly will be needed. A.A.G.P. membership is lagging because some 500 members a year drop out after failing to meet the academy's modest study requirement. At the First National Conference on Continuation Medical Education, one panelist said of physicians who fail to take advantage of present educational opportunities: "They'll never keep up without some threat of regulation." Furthermore, the doctors who fail to take courses are generally those who are least fit to practice. Dr. Edward C. Rosenow, Jr., executive director of the American College of Physicians, has observed: "Men who resist postgraduate education are generally those who don't make the first team."

State boards therefore should make continuation study a requirement for retaining a license. The optimum system would have physicians take a licensing reexamination every three years—G.P.s, perhaps the clinical parts of the National Board exam; specialists, the current certification exam of their boards (or a special exam if the doctor is in a subspecialty). If a doctor failed part of an examination, he would have a year's grace to make it up. Thereafter his license would be suspended until he passed. One effect of this system would be the prompt development of a comprehensive program of postgraduate education. Lifetime learning would at last be a reality, for few doctors could afford not to keep up.

Periodic re-examination and relicensing of physicians is gaining increasing support. It was, for example, a primary recommendation of President Johnson's National Advisory Commission on Health Manpower. But the overwhelming majority of physicians are doggedly opposed to licensing re-examination. Studies show that under 10 percent of board-certified specialists favor periodic examinations for recertification, a much less revolutionary proposal than periodic relicensing. While Dr. Gunnar Gundersen was A.M.A. president he came forth with an idea for compulsory postgraduate work, saying that physicians need "some definite stimulus" to force them to keep abreast. The A.M.A. immediately disavowed the Gundersen plan—and today still stands foursquare against any compulsion in continuing education.

To increase the public's protection, the best compromise for the interim is for state licensing boards to require A.A.G.P.-type continuation study —i.e., in cycles of three years a doctor would take a minimum number of credit-hours of approved courses in his field. A year's probation would be granted if he failed to meet this requirement. Then his license would be suspended until he completed the required study. With this modest beginning, periodic re-examination or its equivalent would come closer to reality.

4. *Open licensing boards to public review.* A model medical practice act drafted by the National Conference of Commissioners on Uniform State Laws calls for laymen to be included on state medical licensing boards. One argument for this is that the public has a right to be included on a board whose primary purpose is to safeguard public welfare. It is also reasoned that nonmedical members could act as observers to see that the boards function properly.

This proposal could do more harm than good, for it ignores idiosyncrasies of medicine. Lay members of a board would need to excuse themselves on matters pertaining to medical competence, since only M.D.s are qualified to judge most clinical questions. An aggressive layman on a board in all likelihood would prompt the M.D.-members to close ranks against him. Laymen would thus be neither effective representatives of the public nor fully functioning members of the board.

A much better system would be to open the board itself to the public eye like any other judicial body. The Texas board has a policy of inviting the press to disciplinary proceedings, and has reported that "publicity helps deter violation-prone doctors." The news coverage also tells the public the names of wrongdoers, an effective form of caveat.

Press attendance is important but should not be relied on as the exclusive means of having the public review the workings of the board. All board hearings should be open to the public and should be attended by representatives of health insurance plans, hospital associations, government health-care programs, and other parties who have a stake in professional discipline. These large, knowledgeable purchasers of medical services are in effect patients' representatives. They can exert considerable political pressure if the board is remiss. Holding hearings in public may embarrass a defendant, but it assures that the proceeding is neither a whitewash nor a star chamber.

A related change needs to be made in states where board members are appointed by the state medical society or appointed by the governor solely on the basis of a medical society recommendation. This makes the board a function of the state medical society. The society is not the only organization in medicine worth hearing from. The public, in the person of the governor, should not be limited to only the society's choices.

Likewise, many states need to abolish laws that prohibit medical school professors from sitting on boards. Experience shows that educators help to maintain high board standards. Another restriction that many states should do away with is the requirement that board members be private practitioners. Other ways of practicing medicine are becoming more and more prevalent and should be represented. At the same time, it is reasonable to expect board members to themselves be licensed.

5. *Accent rehabilitation.* On one hand, state laws should provide for meaningful penalties. California has the right idea in making the unlicensed treatment of a serious illness a felony punishable by up to ten years' imprisonment. State boards should be empowered to suspend and revoke licenses—and medical societies and hospitals should be able to expel offenders. Only if a disciplinary body carries a big stick can it afford to speak softly. Dr. Leo T. Heywood, of the Nebraska board, has observed that warnings and dressing-downs are "not likely to be effective" if a disciplinary body is not also equipped to take severe action.

A punitive approach alone is not the answer, and disciplinary bodies should have the broadest latitude in dealing with offenders. New amendments to the California medical practice act give board members virtual free rein in handling a case—for example, if a physician is practicing beyond his skills, the board can limit his practice or require him to take additional training. Rehabilitation measures can be highly imaginative. In Washington State a physician was found guilty of income tax fraud. The board ruled that his license could be restored after he served a period as a medical missionary without compensation.

More disciplinary bodies should recognize that probation and rehabilitation could salvage many offenders who now are simply cast adrift—deprived of their licenses, tossed out of their medical societies, expelled from their hospitals. These castaways tend to get deeper into trouble, often injuring patients. One state medical association has queried 127 physicians who were disciplined by the state board. Nine out of ten feel that their local medical societies provided only "criticism and rejection" and failed to assist in restoring them to the profession or community. These doctors urge that societies have "rehabilitation committees" to give advice and help, especially in finding employment while a license is suspended.

The kind of counseling and supervising that should be used more widely is illustrated by how some enterprising state boards handle narcotic addiction. Most states take away the addict's narcotics permit and leave him to shift for himself, generally with poor results. But Colorado, California, and North Carolina put him on probation. He is required to get psychiatric treatment, privately or in a special hospital. If feasible, he continues practice or does supervised medical work. He is tided over with loans and other financial aid. When he can show he is cured, he can return to practicing without supervision—but with the understanding that his license will be revoked if he again takes drugs. In California, over 90 percent of former doctor-addicts stay cured, compared to a general rehabilitation rate for addicts estimated at as little as 10 percent.

In Minnesota the board places an addict on the staff of a state institution, usually a mental hospital. There he can do useful work while being under the care of a staff psychiatrist. One Minnesota addict has responded so well to his therapy that he has become an administrator of a state hospital.

6. *Coordinate discipline throughout medicine.* County medical societies should retain jurisdiction over violations of purely local rules, as on advertising and solicitation. More county societies also should take responsibility for putting new members on the right track. In Texas an extensive orientation program is part of a two-year probation for all new members, even those transferring from other counties in the state. Such guidance is in keeping with medicine's practice of supervising newcomers rigorously. As a deterrent, probation gives a society plenty of disciplinary muscle, for dropping a probationary member is far easier than expelling a regular one.

Because of the pressures that go with friendship and close professional contact, it is unrealistic to expect most county medical societies to discipline members of long standing. This failing—a hazard to patients, an agony to many doctors—should be resolved by taking discipline out of the exclusive control of an offender's local colleagues. Needed for all but the largest counties are *regional* grievance committees, whose members would represent several county societies. Physicians from other counties would thus always constitute a committee majority. They would be more likely to judge a case on its merits than would colleagues who must see an accused doctor every day.

This plan is similar to a proposal for a Judicial Commission with "district councils" put forward in the Michigan State Medical Society. Most regional proposals founder on the rock of county society autonomy. Though county disciplinary committees are largely nonfunctioning, the local societies refuse to give them up to regional authority. Such counties should note the remarks of Dr. H. Sheridan Baketel in the *Bulletin* of the Pottawatomie County (Oklahoma) Medical Society: "The aim of a grievance committee—whether some committee members know it or not—is simple and sufficient: To clean medicine's house and to better public relations."

To be effective, a disciplinary committee should be a consolidated entity able to initiate investigations on any matter pertaining to discipline. This will call for basic revisions in societies that now hamstring disciplinary committees by dispersing weak powers among several separate committees. Most societies also load discipline down with cumbersome procedures involving several committees. A disciplinary committee should be like a court, empowered to mete out penalties it finds warranted. The member, of course, would have the right of appeal to the state society.

To assure that a disciplinary system functions, original jurisdiction should be possible from above. State societies should be empowered to initiate action when local societies are lax. The Michigan society is well ahead of most other states in pushing for its Judicial Commission to exercise original jurisdiction at the request of any component society or any member. One of the Medical Disciplinary Committee's strongest proposals was that the A.M.A. be permitted to enter a case that state and local societies were failing to act on.

If the A.M.A. and state societies had the authority to intervene, most likely they would seldom need to. Heretofore, original-jurisdiction proposals have been resisted by local societies unwilling to surrender a fraction of their authority. Robert M. Cunningham, Jr., publisher of *The Modern Hospital*, has cautioned such societies: "It is better to lose autonomy than respect."

More states should institute methods of closing the gap between state-board and medical-society disciplinary areas. California is divided into five districts, each with a "district review committee." Three of the committee's five members are appointed from nominees of local medical societies, so that physicians of the area represent the major element of the committee. The other members are a nominee of the state board, and a faculty member of a medical school. Cases are referred to the committee by the board for hearing and recommendation. It is expected that the committees will strengthen the disciplinary authority of medical societies and hospitals. An offender's knowledge that complaints would be heard quickly by a body empowered to restrict his license would encourage his compliance with regulations.

Disciplinary bodies at all levels should report actions against offenders to a nationwide clearinghouse. This would help overcome the fragmentation that now permits a violator to move freely among state boards, medical societies, and hospitals. With a central repository for disciplinary reports, a problem doctor could be exposed in a routine check of the files.

Some precautions are needed lest this system develop into a *1984*-style monster. So that a physician's record would not be marred unfairly or by accident, he should get a copy of any report going into his file. So that improvement may be noted, provision should be made for updating a former offender's record.

The Federation of State Medical Boards and the A.M.A. each has the rudiments of such a clearinghouse. At present the Federation serves state boards almost exclusively, and not all these report to it or use it. So it is with the A.M.A. and medical societies. The A.M.A. and Federation files should be combined and expanded to include actions of all boards, societies, and hospitals. The important thing is that the file be reported to and used.

7. *Tighten hospital controls.* The hospital, with its day-to-day overseeing of physician performance, is the most effective body to control the incompetent or persistently negligent doctor. If a hospital fails to take action against an offender, or if he proves refractory, his case should be taken before the medical society grievance committee, possibly to the state licensing board.

Hospitals have an existing policing agency in the Joint Commission on Accreditation of Hospitals. Standards promulgated by the Joint Commission and enforced by periodic inspections have succeeded in greatly raising the level of hospital care. An institution seeking the laurel of accreditation must either meet the Joint Commission's standards, which usually require upgrading, or be denied. The Joint Commission can take the credit for requiring hospitals to establish such disciplinary bodies as tissue committees to detect needless or unskillful surgery and medical audit committees to evaluate the work of individual physicians.

Now the Joint Commission should insist that disciplinary committees function to the hilt. Where a hospital staff is too small to police itself effectively, the Joint Commission should require it to form combined committees with other hospitals. Already in operation are regional utilization committees, which review patients' charts for overlong stays and excessive services.

Hospitals need especially to face up to problems posed by elderly and by mentally ill physicians, whose errors often show up in the hospital but are likely to be ignored. The Joint Commission should spur institutions to curtail privileges. Marginal practitioners should be required to work under supervision, if necessary to seek psychiatric help.

Unaccredited hospitals are often havens for shoddy practitioners. The state agencies that license hospitals should require all institutions to come up to Joint Commission standards. In New York City, substandard hospitals were placed under the administrative control of first-rate institutions. Around the country unsatisfactory hospitals should similarly be absorbed by medical centers and by community hospitals meeting Joint Commission standards. Where conditions in a hospital are hopeless, the state should shut its doors.

Licensing and board authority should be extended to require hospital staffs to have meaningful discipline. Recent amendments to the California medical practice act make it an offense for a physician to be a member of a medical staff that does not have the fundamentals of a working disciplinary system. The California law requires hospital staffs to grant privileges only on an annual basis, review the competence of staff members, make fee splitting grounds for dismissal, enforce the proper maintenance of medical records.

8. *Expand third-party insistence on discipline.* Here, by exercising its power of the purse, is how the federal government can be most effective. Merely by requiring that hospitals have utilization committees for participation in Medicare, Congress made these disciplinary bodies a fixture throughout medicine. Advocates of "dollar diplomacy" in discipline are convinced that the surest way of getting high-caliber performance is to make it—and only it—pay.

Medicare provides one mechanism for upgrading the discipline in hospitals. As the law is written, an institution may participate even though it is not accredited by the Joint Commission. The program should be changed to require that every hospital meet Joint Commission standards, and should push for augmented disciplinary controls.

Physicians, too, should be qualified before they can get payments from Medicare, Medicaid, and the multitude of other federally financed health programs. In the main, the federal government avoids interfering in the private practice of medicine by working through existing channels—through private insurers acting as Medicare paying agents, through state and local welfare plans. The federal government should, however, set high standards for these intermediaries to enforce. Recent child-health programs have been highlighted by the federal government's setting, and the state's enforcing, rigorous standards for the training and performance of participating physicians.

So also should other third parties be strict in their insistence on medical discipline. Health insurers should refuse to honor claims from physicians of questionable competence. The insurers should disqualify hospitals that fail to exercise adequate disciplinary controls. Blue Cross in some states demands that participating hospitals have review committees and has kicked offending institutions out of the plan.

Insurers should prosecute physicians submitting fraudulent claims. In New York, Group Health Insurance found that local societies would not take action against offenders. Now G.H.I. files fraud charges directly with the state licensing board. In Oregon, Blue Shield received fourteen claims from a doctor for services he had not performed. Blue Shield helped postal authorities convict the doctor of mail fraud.

9. *Shield disciplinary officials from suit.* After receiving a six-month suspension from the Fulton County Medical Society, an Atlanta physician sued the members of the grievance committee for $2.5 million, charging

conspiracy. The committee members won the case, but the threat of such suits makes many physicians reluctant to prosecute a case vigorously, even to get involved in medical discipline.

Doctors who are on disciplinary bodies—whether on state boards or in medical societies or hospitals—should be granted civil immunity on decisions that are reached without malice. Precedents already exist in states that protect licensing-board members from suits based on official acts and in states that grant immunity to physicians who inform authorities of child abuse, gunshot wounds, and other reportable cases.

As interim protection, disciplinary bodies should buy for their members a special rider to malpractice policies. Pioneered by an insurer in northern California, the additional coverage protects disciplinary officials against reprisal suits.

10. *Make malpractice litigation fairer.* Patients should not have to fear they will be unable to collect damages if injured by a physician. Physicians can be spared the worry that although free of blame they will be bankrupted by a malpractice suit.

To make sure that all doctors have adequate coverage, New York State's assigned-risk plan of compulsory insurance for automobile registrants should be adapted to professional liability: As a condition for licensing, every doctor should be required to have malpractice insurance. Rising award trends make $500,000/$1,000,000 not too much protection. For most doctors, the increase in premium would amount to a few cents per patient. Poor risks, paying higher premiums, would be assigned among all the companies writing malpractice policies in the state.

Current malpractice law errs in requiring that the physician be at fault before the patient can collect. Doctors and patients thus are automatically made adversaries in personal injury proceedings, and injustices are often suffered by both. This needless legal combat is reminiscent of the conflict between employers and employees before Workmen's Compensation came into being. The courts were flooded with injured workers suing employers for negligence. At last every state decided that on-the-job accidents were inevitable, and that it mattered little if the employer were actually at fault—the worker was still injured. Worker's Compensation insurance became a requirement, and commissions now decide what payment, if any, should be given the worker.

A Workmen's Compensation-type system, funded by physicians' malpractice insurance, should cover injuries that would not ordinarily occur to patients during a treatment. Negligence would not be at issue, merely that the injury resulted from medical care. As with Workmen's Compensation, physicians and their insurers could contest claims before the commission. The judicial proceeding would be faster and cheaper than a comparable case before the courts. If either side disputed the commission's finding or the amount of the judgment, the ruling could be appealed to the courts. If Workmen's Compensation experience is a guide, professional liability judgments would be more uniform, with relatively few contests and appeals.

Meanwhile, as long as there must be malpractice litigation, patients should not lose cases merely because no local physician will testify for them. State legislatures should end this inequity by abolishing the community rule. Thereby legislators would recognize that the standards of good medicine are nationwide and local boundaries are largely irrelevant. Further, the legislatures should have the law reflect that the common knowledge of juries allows them to draw reasonable conclusions in many cases of patient negligence. Simply because no physician will testify against an obvious offender, a jury should not be forced to become part of the conspiracy and find in the wrongdoer's favor.

More medical societies and bar associations should help patients and physicians get a fairer shake. The Pima County Screening Plan, originated in Tucson, Arizona, keeps many baseless suits from going further. A doctor-lawyer committee reviews the evidence in malpractice claims. If the committee finds insufficient evidence to support a reasonable suit, it recommends against taking the claim to court. In most cases, the patient's attorney agrees with the panel's evaluation and advises his client to drop the suit. But if the committee finds that the patient may have a case, it recommends court action and the medical society helps the patient get a medical witness.

Another plan, initiated by medical societies and bar associations in several California cities, revolves around a panel of doctors whom malpractice plaintiffs may consult. After an examination, the panel physician reports his findings as to possible negligence. If the report shows malpractice, the patient can count on having the panel physician testify for him. Often this prods a prompt settlement from the malpractice insurer.

A word of caution: Such a plan must be above reproach. The slightest hint of tampering will cause litigants to abandon it. In Los Angeles, a single incident of lying by a supposedly impartial witness (the episode is recounted in Chapter 23, "Conspirators in Silence") soured plaintiffs' attorneys by the score on an otherwise promising program.

11. *Orient medical students.* "I think many young doctors drift into trouble simply because they weren't taught to avoid it," says Dr. Harold E. Jervey, Jr., of the Federation of State Medical Boards. Only fourteen schools have formal instruction in ethics or in their state's medical practice act. When young physicians enter the everyday life of practice, they often are not prepared to withstand, or even recognize, the temptations they find.

In a required course, every medical school should drive home the principles of proper conduct. The University of Maryland Medical School offers a program that should be widely copied. Besides discussing socioeconomic rights and wrongs, the course has the head of the Pharmacology Department spell out in horrifying detail the hazards of narcotic addiction. In twenty-six years only one graduate of the school has had a narcotics problem.

12. *Outlaw fee splitting.* In states that make fee splitting a criminal offense, penalties range up to a year's imprisonment and $1,000 fine. Such laws belong on the books if only to register the public's disapproval of the practice. But an assistant attorney of New York State has summed up the practical situation in states that have them: "It's a nice law, but it doesn't mean anything. It's totally inoperative. We haven't had a single case under the law since it was enacted."

One reason for the law's ineffectiveness is that fee splitting does not lend itself to the kind of evidence that clinches cases in criminal court. Neither of the doctors engaged in a fee split is likely to testify to the offense, and the multiple ruses—the feeder receives the assistant's fee, he gets to handle the aftercare—are too circumstantial for prosecutors to try to prove.

Even more important than making fee splitting a misdemeanor is specifying it as a ground for license revocation. State licensing boards can prove a case without being restricted by the rules of evidence that govern criminal courts. Moreover, their goal is to change the fee splitter's ways, not send him to jail. In this they can be far more constructive than the courts.

In every community where fee splitting exists, ethical surgeons should implement the widely hailed plan begun in Columbus, Ohio. To present a united front against G.P.s who had long demanded kickbacks in exchange for referrals, surgeons formed the Columbus Surgical Society. This association requires members to have a certified public accountant audit their financial records, patient lists, and income tax returns every year. If a surgeon refuses, or if an audit shows he is splitting fees, the society goes after his hospital privileges and invites the attention of the Internal Revenue Service to his income.

The society has claimed 100 percent effectiveness in wiping out fee splitting in Columbus. With the endorsement of the American College of Surgeons, the Columbus plan has spread to other cities. In Detroit the Surgical Society enforces audits of over five hundred members, including not only general surgeons but gynecologists, ophthalmologists, and ear, nose, and throat surgeons.

Hospitals hold one key to ending fee splitting, for they can refuse to grant privileges to any surgeon who is not a member of his local Columbus plan society. Where fee splitting is common and no local surgical society requires audits, the hospital itself should make an annual audit a condition of every surgeon's reappointment. By setting this requirement, hospitals in Bloomington, Illinois, stamped out fee splitting that had long been rife. As a precautionary measure, every institution should amend its bylaws so that on request any staff member must submit to an audit or lose his privileges.

Longer-range action in hospitals is needed to relieve the glut of surgeons, whose struggle to survive in an overcrowded specialty is a major reason for fee splitters' willingness to pay kickbacks. A.M.A.-approved residencies in surgery should be cut back. Concurrently, an effort should be made to develop residencies in specialties with critical shortages of manpower. The federal government already offers a number of grants each year to practicing physicians who take specialty training in psychiatry and in physical rehabilitation. Similar incentives should be offered to practicing general surgeons who wish to go into pediatrics or internal medicine, where practitioners are urgently needed.

Medical societies also should seek to end widespread fee splitting. In addition to punishing offenders, a local society can play a valuable role as an intermediary.

Often a surgeon is eager to stop splitting fees, not only because of high motives but because it takes money out of his pocket. ("The well of good deeds may be fed by a spring of selfishness," a College of Surgeons official has noted.) But he is likely to feel he cannot quit unless other local surgeons do also, for otherwise they would gain the referrals he would lose. Surgeons in arch-competition hardly trust one another, and so a go-between like the medical society can bring about an agreement that mutually suspicious surgeons will live up to. In Scranton, Pennsylvania, where virtually every surgeon and G.P. once split fees, the Lackawanna County Medical Society and the Pennsylvania Medical Society handled negotiations that have curtailed the practice.

The most effective policeman against fee splitting is often the patient himself. Before agreeing to surgery, he or a responsible relative should discuss who gets how much for what. The College of Surgeons calls this "a matter of self-protection." A fee is unlikely to be split if: The referring physician does *not* assist in the surgery or administer the anesthesia. The postoperative care is included in the surgical fee and handled by the surgeon. Each doctor on the case submits a separate itemized bill.

13. *Bar physicians from owning pharmacies and drug companies.* Congress should pass with modifications the Medical Restraint of Trade Bill introduced by Senator Philip A. Hart of Michigan. The Hart Bill prohibits physicians from owning drugstores or leasing space to a pharmacy for

a percentage of the store's income. It would be illegal also for physicians to own drug companies for the exploitation of patients, or for a drug company to pay off physicians so they will prescribe company products.

Enforcement would be flexible, as in other antitrust proceedings: U.S. attorneys could seek an injunction in federal district court. Injured individuals or businesses could sue for triple damages. Permitted under the bill would be physician-owned pharmacies in areas where no other one exists. The bill would not interfere with drugs administered by physicians or hospitals in the course of treatment. Nor would it affect the physician's right to own stock in big drug houses such as Pfizer and Squibb.

The Hart Bill needs amendment insofar as it bans only ophthalmologists from dispensing eyeglasses. Ideally no physician should be able to profiteer from his prescriptions, for eyeglasses no less than drugs. But *optometrists* prescribe—and dispense—more than half of all eyeglasses, and optometry is in no way regulated by the bill. As the Hart Bill now stands, optometrists would inherit most of the dispensing that would be surrendered by ophthalmologists. Yet optometrists can no less profiteer. It would be impracticable to bar both groups from prescribing and dispensing. Thus the best alternative would be for every state licensing law to include a no-exploitation provision with teeth. A profiteering ophthalmologist or optometrist should be faced with loss of license if he deliberately overprescribes.

Laws limiting physician ownership of profiteerable businesses are already on the books in California, Maryland, North Dakota, and Pennsylvania. Every state should have such statutes. A condition of licensing pharmacies should be that they be free of doctor proprietors. Regulating ownership of retail businesses is customary in the licensing of liquor stores, and the principle can be extended to cover pharmacies.

Licensing statutes should prohibit physician participation in drugstores and drug companies. The practice is as venal as fee splitting and should be no less outlawed. Some medical organizations, notably the A.M.A., protest that such regulations limit the doctor's rights as a citizen. Seen another way, these restrictions are a small price for the physician to pay for the extraordinary privileges he already receives.

Meanwhile, patients can discourage profiteering by keeping their prescriptions from becoming captive. For drugs or for eyeglasses, a patient can demand the written prescription and then shop around dispensaries known to be independently owned. The A.M.A. says the doctor is unethical if he refuses to hand over the prescription.

In drug purchases, patients will foil profiteers and at the same time will usually save money if they ask the doctor to prescribe generically, by chemical term rather than brand name. An obliging physician who does not know the generic name can usually look it up in *Physicians' Desk*

Reference, a directory of drugs most doctors receive. If the doctor insists on prescribing by trade name, the patient can ask that the manufacturer at least be one of the big reliable houses. If the doctor says no on all counts, the patient will be forgiven if he smells a rat.

14. *Overhaul emergency-care systems.* A licensing condition for every hospital should be that it maintain a twenty-four-hour emergency room. Hospitals that have attending physicians on call should make the assignment more than nominal. To have good emergency coverage, institutions need to obligate doctors on call to keep in touch and stay close by. Other arrangements for round-the-clock coverage are getting good results. Some hospitals are hiring physicians full time to run the emergency service. In Alexandria, Virginia, and in Norwalk, Connecticut, physicians have left regular private practice to take over hospital emergency services on a partnership contract.

Every county medical society should have a system enabling patients without regular doctors to locate a physician in an emergency. The best emergency-call systems formally schedule when doctors must stay available. Advertisements and publicity notices inform the public and police over and over again that medical help can be found any time of day by dialing the society's number. The Alameda-Contra Costa Medical Association, across the bay from San Francisco, achieved national fame for its pioneering work in setting up day-and-night emergency services, guaranteeing medical care regardless of a patient's ability to pay, and protecting patients from exorbitant bills for emergency care.

Many desperate calls for help can be averted by societies' taking a strong stand against abandonment in all its forms. Physicians should be reminded that while away from their practice they are ethically required to have a colleague covering for them. Doctors who leave patients in the lurch should be disciplined.

To allay doctors' fears that they will be sued if they treat an emergency case, every state should pass a Good Samaritan law giving physicians civil immunity for emergency care rendered in good faith. Granted that doctors' fears of suit are unfounded, and that Good Samaritan laws give physicians no more protection against unjust claims than the courts do already. Laws often codify the status quo.

The Good Samaritan law may be merely a psychological cure for an imaginary ill. But as every physician knows about the placebo, it well may work. *Northwest Medicine* has remarked in an editorial: "The fact that the fear is groundless seems to have little to do with the problem, which fundamentally, of course, is that of making good medical care available when and where it is needed. The fear remains, and the care people may need is being withheld from them."

15. *Form a National Commission on Medical Discipline*. The most significant reform to take place in American medicine—the top-to-bottom reorganization of medical education—got its impetus from outside the profession. Abraham Flexner was not a physician; indeed, before embarking on his survey he had never set foot inside a medical school. Laymen headed and staffed the Carnegie Foundation for the Advancement of Teaching, sponsor of the Flexner report. Their intention was to conduct a responsible study from the standpoint of the public.

Medical discipline now has few active proponents within the profession. The physicians who advocate disciplinary reform need the support of a well-financed organization, to be to them what the Carnegie Foundation was to reformers in medical education. A National Commission on Medical Discipline would be such a body: a gatherer of facts, a disseminator of information, a pressure group for the instituting of disciplinary reform.

The National Commission should be an independent voluntary agency supported by foundations and by individual donations. It should represent the public as well as the profession—for medicine is a public utility, medical knowledge a public resource, medical discipline a public concern. The commission's policy should be guided by the major professional associations and also by the organized consumers of medical care—health insurers, labor and business groups, state and local health officials.

The reforming of medical discipline calls for much activity at the local level. So, following the pattern of existing voluntary health associations, there should be local chapters of lay and physician members. These would bring to the cause of disciplinary reform the vigor and intelligence of an alerted citizenry.

APPENDIXES

APPENDIX A

MAJOR OFFENSES SUBJECT TO DISCIPLINARY ACTION

This table is based on an A.M.A. Medical Disciplinary Committee survey updated to 1968. √ indicates statutes exist. ✕ indicates no statute is reported.

STATE	1 Unprofessional conduct generally	2 Conviction of felony	3 Conviction of an offense involving moral turpitude	4 Drug addiction	5 Alcoholism	6 Committing or assisting in an abortion	7 Fraud in application, examination, or obtaining license	8 Specified types of advertising	9 Mental illness	10 Betrayal of a professional secret
Ala.	√	√	√	√	√	√	√	√	√	√
Alaska	✕	✕	√	√	√	√	√	√	✕	√
Ariz.	√	√	√	√	√	√	√	√	√	√
Ark.	✕	√	√	√	√	√	√	√	√	√
Calif.	√	√	√	√	√	√	√	√	√	✕
Colo.	√	√	√	√	√	√	√	√	√	✕
Conn.	√	√	√	√	√	✕	√	√	√	√
Del.	√	√	✕	√	√	✕	√	√	√	√
D.C.	√	√	✕	✕	✕	✕	✕	✕	✕	✕
Fla.	√	√	√	√	√	√	√	√	√	✕
Ga.	√	✕	√	√	√	√	√	√	√	✕
Hawaii	√	√	√	√	√	√	√	√	✕	√
Idaho	√	√	√	√	√	√	√	√	√	√
Ill.	√	√	✕	√	√	√	√	√	√	✕
Ind.	√	√	√	√	√	✕	√	✕	✕	√
Iowa	√	✕	√	√	√	√	√	√	✕	√
Kan.	√	√	√	√	√	√	√	√	√	√
Ky.	√	✕	√	√	√	√	√	✕	√	√
La.	✕	√	√	√	√	√	√	√	√	√
Maine	√	√	√	√	√	√	√	√	√	√
Md.	√	✕	√	√	√	√	√	√	√	√
Mass.	√	√	√	√	√	✕	√	√	√	✕
Mich.	✕	√	√	√	√	√	√	√	√	√
Minn.	√	√	√	√	√	√	√	√	√	√
Miss.	√	√	√	√	√	√	√	√	✕	✕
Mo.	√	✕	√	√	√	√	√	√	√	✕
Mont.	√	✕	✕	✕	✕	✕	✕	✕	✕	✕
Neb.	√	√	✕	√	√	√	√	√	√	√
Nev.	√	√	√	√	√	√	√	√	√	√
N.H.	√	√	✕	✕	✕	✕	✕	✕	√	✕
N.J.	✕	✕	√	√	√	√	✕	√	√	✕
N.M.	√	√	√	√	✕	√	√	√	√	√
N.Y.	√	A	A	√	√	√	√	√	√	√
N.C.	√	√	√	√	✕	√	√	√	√	√
N.D.	√	√	✕	√	√	√	√	√	√	√
Ohio	√	√	✕	√	√	✕	√	√	√	√
Okla.	√	√	√	√	√	√	√	√	√	√
Ore.	√	√	√	√	√	√	√	√	√	√
Pa.	√	✕	√	√	√	√	✕	✕	B	✕
R.I.	√	C	C	√	✕	√	√	√	√	✕
S.C.	√	D	D	√	√	✕	✕	✕	✕	√
S.D.	√	√	√	√	√	√	✕	√	√	√
Tenn.	√	√	√	√	√	√	√	√	✕	√
Tex.	√	√	√	√	√	√	√	√	✕	✕
Utah	√	✕	√	√	√	√	√	√	✕	√
Vt.	√	✕	√	√	√	√	√	√	✕	✕
Va.	√	√	√	√	√	√	√	√	√	✕
Wash.	√	✕	√	√	√	√	√	√	√	√
W.Va.	√	√	✕	√	√	✕	√	✕	✕	✕
Wis.	√	√	√	√	✕	√	√	√	✕	√
Wyo.	√	√	✕	√	√	√	√	√	√	√
TOTAL	46	39	36	48	44	41	46	43	35	25

A = Conviction of crime
B = Any condition which impairs intellect and judgment to such extent as to incapacitate for performance of professional duties
C = Violation of state law
D = Conviction of illegal practices

AMERICAN MEDICAL ASSOCIATION
PRINCIPLES OF MEDICAL ETHICS

PREAMBLE. These principles are intended to aid physicians individually and collectively in maintaining a high level of ethical conduct. They are not laws but standards by which a physician may determine the propriety of his conduct in his relationship with patients, with colleagues, with members of allied professions, and with the public.

SECTION 1. The principal objective of the medical profession is to render service to humanity with full respect for the dignity of man. Physicians should merit the confidence of patients entrusted to their care, rendering to each a full measure of service and devotion.

SECTION 2. Physicians should strive continually to improve medical knowledge and skill, and should make available to their patients and colleagues the benefits of their professional attainments.

SECTION 3. A physician should practice a method of healing founded on a scientific basis; and he should not voluntarily associate professionally with anyone who violates this principle.

SECTION 4. The medical profession should safeguard the public and itself against physicians deficient in moral character or professional competence. Physicians should observe all laws, uphold the dignity and honor of the profession and accept its self-imposed disciplines. They should expose, without hesitation, illegal or unethical conduct of fellow members of the profession.

SECTION 5. A physician may choose whom he will serve. In an emergency, however, he should render service to the best of his ability. Having undertaken the care of a patient, he may not neglect him; and unless he has been discharged he may discontinue his services only after giving adequate notice. He should not solicit patients.

SECTION 6. A physician should not dispose of his services under terms or conditions which tend to interfere with or impair the free and complete exercise of his medical judgment and skill or tend to cause a deterioration of the quality of medical care.

SECTION 7. In the practice of medicine a physician should limit the source of his professional income to medical services actually rendered by him, or under his supervision, to his patients. His fee should be commensurate with the services rendered and the patient's ability to pay. He should neither pay nor receive a commission for referral of patients. Drugs, remedies or appliances may be dispensed or supplied by the physician provided it is in the best interests of the patient.

SECTION 8. A physician should seek consultation upon request; in doubtful or difficult cases; or whenever it appears that the quality of medical service may be enhanced thereby.

SECTION 9. A physician may not reveal the confidences entrusted to him in the course of medical attendance, or the deficiencies he may observe in the character of patients, unless he is required to do so by law or unless it becomes necessary in order to protect the welfare of the individual or of the community.

SECTION 10. The honored ideals of the medical profession imply that the responsibilities of the physician extend not only to the individual, but also to society where these responsibilities deserve his interest and participation in activities which have the purpose of improving both the health and the well-being of the individual and the community.

A GUIDE FOR REFORM

THE WASHINGTON STATE Medical Disciplinary Board is the nation's only quasijudicial body concerned exclusively with medical discipline, with broad powers to conduct investigations and discipline offenders. The act creating the board suggests legislative changes that would gain comparable disciplinary authority for licensing boards across the country. For purposes of readability, references to other statutes and similar technical material have been deleted.

WASHINGTON STATE MEDICAL DISCIPLINARY BOARD ACT

BE IT ENACTED BY THE LEGISLATURE OF THE STATE OF WASHINGTON:

SECTION 1. This act is passed:

(1) In the exercise of the police power of the state to protect public health, to promote the welfare of the state, and to provide an adequate public agency to act as a disciplinary body for the members of the medical profession licensed to practice medicine and surgery in this state;

(2) Because the health and well-being of the people of this state are of paramount importance;

(3) Because the conduct of members of the medical profession licensed to practice medicine and surgery in this state plays a vital role in preserving the health and well-being of the people of the state; and

(4) Because the agency which now exists to handle disciplinary proceedings for members of the medical profession licensed to practice medicine and surgery in this state is ineffective and very infrequently employed, and consequently there is no effective means of handling such disciplinary proceedings when they are necessary for the protection of the public health.

SECTION 2. Terms used in this act shall have the meaning set forth in this section unless the context clearly indicates otherwise:

(1) "Board" means the medical disciplinary board.

(2) "License" means a certificate or license to practice medicine and surgery in this state . . . .

(3) "Members" means members of the medical disciplinary board.

(4) "Secretary" means the secretary of the medical disciplinary board.

SECTION 3. The term "unprofessional conduct" as used in this act shall mean the following items or any one or combination thereof:

(1) Conviction in any court of any offense involving moral turpitude, in which case the record of such conviction shall be conclusive evidence;

(2) The procuring, or aiding or abetting in procuring a criminal abortion;

(3) Fraud or deceit in the obtaining of a license to practice medicine;

(4) All advertising of medical business which is intended or has a tendency to deceive the public or impose upon credulous or ignorant persons and so be harmful or injurious to public morals or safety;

(5) All advertising of any medicine or of any means whereby the monthly period of women can be regulated or the menses reestablished if suppressed;

(6) The personation of another licensed practitioner;

(7) Habitual intemperance;

(8) The use or prescription for use of narcotic drugs in any way other than for therapeutic purposes;

(9) The offering, undertaking or agreeing to cure or treat disease by a secret method, procedure, treatment, or medicine, or the treating, operating, or prescribing for any human condition by a method, means, or procedure which the

licensee refuses to divulge upon demand of the board;

(10) The willful betrayal of a professional secret;

(11) Repeated acts of immorality, or repeated acts of gross misconduct in the practice of the profession;

(12) Unprofessional conduct as defined [elsewhere in the statutes];

(13) Aiding or abetting an unlicensed person to practice medicine; or

(14) Declaration of mental incompetency by a court of competent jurisdiction.

SECTION 4. There is hereby created the "Washington state medical disciplinary board," which shall be composed of one holder of a valid license to practice medicine and surgery from each congressional district now existing or hereafter created in the state. The board shall be an administrative agency of the state of Washington. The attorney general shall be the advisor of the board and shall represent it in all legal proceedings.

SECTION 5. Members of the board shall be elected by secret mail ballot by the holders of licenses to practice medicine and surgery residing in each congressional district and shall hold office until their successors are elected and qualified. Members from even-numbered congressional districts shall be elected in even-numbered years and members from odd-numbered congressional districts shall be elected in odd-numbered years.

SECTION 6. Nominations to the board may be made by petition signed by not less than twenty-five license holders residing in the nominee's district, and shall be submitted to the board at least four weeks prior to the date of the election. Votes cast for license holders not so nominated shall be valid.

SECTION 7. The election shall be held in September and shall be conducted in accordance with rules and regulations adopted by the board under the rule-making power hereinafter provided for. Terms of office of members shall commence on October 1st.

SECTION 8. Vacancies in the board shall be filled by the governor and a member appointed to fill a vacancy on

the board shall serve until the naming of his successor in the next district election and until his successor takes office on the October 1st following the election.

SECTION 9. Any member of the board may be removed by the governor for neglect of duty, misconduct or malfeasance or misfeasance in office, after being given a written statement of the charges against him and sufficient opportunity to be heard thereon.

SECTION 10. Members of the board shall be paid twenty-five dollars per diem for time spent in performing their duties as members of the board and shall be repaid their necessary traveling and other expenses while engaged in business of the board, with such per diem and reimbursement for expenses to be paid out of the general fund on vouchers approved by the director of licenses: PROVIDED, that the amount for expense will not be more than fifteen dollars per day, except for traveling expense which shall not be more than eight cents per mile.

SECTION 11. The board may meet, function, and exercise its powers at any place within the state.

SECTION 12. The first board shall be organized in this manner: Within ten days after the effective date of this act the director of licenses shall appoint five holders of licenses to practice medicine and surgery in this state to serve as members of a temporary commission which shall, within ninety days thereafter, organize and hold the election to name the first members of the medical disciplinary board. The temporary commission shall adopt such rules and regulations as it deems necessary to govern the holding of the first election. After the election is completed and the first members of the board have qualified and taken office, the temporary commission shall be abolished and all of its records shall be turned over to the board.

SECTION 13. The board shall elect from its members a chairman, vice-chairman, and secretary, who shall serve for one year and until their successors are elected and qualified. The board shall meet at least once a year or oftener upon the call of the chairman at such times and places as the chairman shall designate. Five members shall constitute a quorum to transact business.

SECTION 14. Members of the board shall be immune from suit in any action, civil or criminal, based upon any disciplinary proceedings or other official acts performed in good faith as members of such board.

SECTION 15. The board shall have the following powers and duties:

(1) To adopt, amend and rescind such rules and regulations as it deems necessary to carry out the provisions of this act;

(2) To investigate all complaints and charges of unprofessional conduct against any holder of a license and to hold hearings to determine whether such charges are substantiated or unsubstantiated;

(3) To employ necessary stenographic or clerical help;

(4) To issue subpoenas and administer oaths in connection with any investigation, hearing, or disciplinary proceeding held under this act.

(5) To take or cause depositions to be taken as needed in any investigation, hearing, or proceeding.

SECTION 16. Any person, firm, corporation, or public officer may submit a written complaint to the secretary charging the holder of a license to practice medicine and surgery with unprofessional conduct, specifying the grounds therefor. If the board determines that such complaint merits consideration, or if the board shall have reason to believe, without a formal complaint, that any holder of a license has been guilty of unprofessional conduct, the chairman shall designate three members to serve as a committee to hear and report upon such charges.

SECTION 17. When a hearing committee is named, the secretary shall prepare a specification of the charge or charges of unprofessional conduct made against a license holder, a copy of which shall be served upon the accused, together with a notice of the hearing, as provided in section 19 of this act.

SECTION 18. The time of hearing shall be fixed by the secretary as soon as convenient, but not earlier than thirty days after service of the charges upon the accused. The secretary shall issue a notice of hearing of the charges, which notice shall specify the time and place of hearing and shall notify the accused that he may file with the secretary a written response within twenty days of the date of service. Such notice shall also notify the accused that a stenographic record of the proceeding will be kept, that he will have the opportunity to appear personally and to have counsel present, with the right to produce witnesses and evidence in his own behalf, to cross-examine witnesses testifying against him, to examine witnesses testifying for him, to examine such documentary evidence as may be produced aaginst him, and to have subpoenas issued by the board.

SECTION 19. Subpoenas issued by the board to compel the attendance of witnesses at any investigation or hearing shall be served in accordance with the provisions . . . governing the service of subpoenas in court actions. The board shall issue subpoenas at the request and on the behalf of the accused. In case any person contumaciously refuses to obey a subpoena issued by the board or to answer any proper question put to him during the hearing or proceeding, the superior court of any county in which the proceeding is carried on or in which the person guilty resides or is found shall have jurisdiction, upon application by the board, to issue to such person an order requiring him to appear before the board or its hearing committee, there to produce evidence if so ordered or there to give testimony concerning the matter under investigation or question. Any failure to obey such order of the court may be punished by the court as a civil contempt may be punished.

SECTION 20. Within a reasonable time after holding a hearing under the provisions of sections 18 and 19 of this act, the committee shall make a written report of its findings of fact and its recommendations, and the same shall be forthwith transmitted to the secretary, with a transcript of the evidence.

SECTION 21. If the board deems it necessary, the board may, after further notice to the accused, take further testimony at a second hearing before the full board, conducted as provided for hearings before the three man hearing committee.

SECTION 22. In any event, whether the board makes its determination on the findings of the hearing committee or on the findings of the committee as supplemented by a second hearing before the board, the board shall determine the charge or charges upon the merits on the basis of the evidence in the record before it.

SECTION 23. If a majority of the members of the board then sitting vote in favor of finding the accused guilty of unprofessional conduct as specified in the charges, or any of them, the board shall prepare written findings of fact and may thereafter prepare and file in the office of the director of licenses a certificate or order of revocation or suspension, in which case a copy thereof shall be served upon the accused, or the board may reprimand the accused, as it deems most appropriate.

SECTION 24. If the license holder is found not guilty, or if less than a majority of the members then sitting vote for a finding of guilty, the board shall forthwith order a dimissal of the charges and the exoneration of the accused. When a proceeding has been dismissed, either on the merits or otherwise, the board shall relieve the accused from any possible odium that may attach by reason of the charges made against him by such public exoneration as is necessary, if requested by the accused to do so.

SECTION 25. The filing by the board in the office of the director of licenses of a certificate or order of revocation or suspension after due notice, hearing and findings in accordance with the procedure specified in this act, certifying that any holder of a license has been found guilty of unprofessional conduct by the board, shall constitute a revocation or suspension of the license to practice medicine and surgery in this state in accordance with the terms and conditions imposed by the board and embodied in the certificate or order of revocation or suspension: PRO-

VIDED, that if the licensee seeks judicial review of the board's decision pursuant to the provisions of this act, such revocation or the period of such suspension shall be stayed and shall not be effective or commence to run until final judgment has been entered in any proceeding instituted under the provisions of this act and the licensee's judicial remedies exhausted hereunder.

SECTION 26. The certificate or order of revocation or suspension shall contain a brief and concise statement of the ground or grounds upon which the certificate or order is based and the specific terms and conditions of such revocation or suspension, and shall be retained as a permanent record by the director of licenses.

SECTION 27. The director of licenses shall not issue any license or any renewal thereof to any person whose license has been revoked or suspended by the board except in conformity with the terms and conditions of the certificate or order of revocation or suspension, or in conformity with any order of reinstatement issued by the board, or in accordance with the final judgment in any proceeding for review instituted under the provisions of this act.

SECTION 28. Any person whose license has been revoked or suspended by the board shall have the right to a judicial review of the board's decision. Such review shall be initiated by serving on the secretary a notice of appeal either in the superior court of Thurston county, or in the superior court of the county in which the appellant resides, within thirty days after the filing of the certificate or order of revocation or suspension in the office of the director of licenses.

SECTION 29. The secretary shall, within twenty days after the service of the notice of appeal, transmit to the clerk of the superior court to which the appeal is taken a transcript of the record before the board, certified under the seal of the board, together with a certified copy of the board's written findings.

SECTION 30. The findings of the board, if supported by the preponderance of evidence, shall be final and conclusive. The review in the superior court shall be limited to determining whether the findings of the board are supported by the preponderance of evidence and whether the proceedings of the board were erroneous as a matter of law, or in violation of due process, or so arbitrary or capricious as to amount to an abuse of discretion, or contrary to any constitutional right, power, privilege or immunity.

SECTION 31. The procedure governing appeals to the superior court shall govern in matters of appeal from a decision of the board, insofar as applicable and to the extent such procedure is not inconsistent with the type of review provided in this act.

SECTION 32. Appeal shall be from the decision of the superior court.

SECTION 33. If the board finds the holder of any license guilty of unprofessional conduct and fails to file a certificate or order of revocation or suspension in the office of the director of licenses within thirty days, the license holder shall have the right to a judicial review of such finding of the board in the same manner and to the same extent as if the certificate or order had been filed.

. . .

SECTION 35. Every applicant for a certificate to practice medicine and surgery shall pay a fee of twenty-five dollars.

SECTION 36. Every person licensed to practice medicine and surgery in this state shall register with the director of licenses annually, and pay an annual renewal registration fee of seven dollars, on or before the first day of July of each year, and thereupon the license of such person shall be renewed for a period of one year. Any failure to register and pay the annual renewal registration fee shall render the license invalid, but such license shall be reinstated upon written application therefor to the director, and payment to the state of a penalty of ten dollars, together with all delinquent annual license renewal fees.

. . .

SECTION 38. The director must refuse a certificate to any applicant guilty of unprofessional conduct: PROVIDED, That any person whose license has been suspended or revoked under the provisions of this act may apply to the board for reinstatement at any time and the board may hold hearings on any such petition and may order reinstatement and impose terms and conditions thereof and issue a certificate of reinstatement to the director of licenses.

. . .

SECTION 40. Before refusal of a license upon the ground of unprofessional conduct a hearing must be had before the medical disciplinary board. Such hearing shall be governed by the procedure set forth in the medical disciplinary board act and the applicant shall have all the rights accorded to an accused license holder under such act, including the right to appeal from an adverse decision.

. . .

SECTION 44. In case of the refusal of a license, the medical disciplinary board shall file a brief and concise statement of the grounds and reasons therefor in the office of the director of licenses, which, together with the decision of the hearing committee of the medical disciplinary board, in writing, shall remain of record therein.

SECTION 45. There is appropriated from the general fund the sum of fifteen thousand dollars, or so much thereof as shall be necessary, for the purpose of carrying into effect and administering the provisions of this medical disciplinary board act during the biennium ending June 30, 1957.

SECTION 46. If any section, sentence, clause or phrase of this act should be held invalid or unconstitutional, the invalidity or unconstitutionality thereof shall not affect the validity or constitutionality of any other section, sentence, clause or phrase of this medical disciplinary board act.

. . .

Approved by the Governor March 16, 1955. (House Bill #365)

APPENDIX D

NOTES ON SOURCES

THE FOLLOWING CHAPTER NOTES document most of the material in this book taken from written sources. To avoid footnotes and the riffling back and forth they require, we employ a system of key-word notations. A word or phrase identifies what in each chapter a source refers to.

One type of source citation is familiar mainly to users of law libraries. In the hypothetical Dombey v. Smith, 216 P.2d 199 (Ore.): Dombey and Smith are litigants in a court in the state of Oregon. A report on the case begins on Page 199 of Volume 216 in the 2nd Series of the Pacific-region court reporter published by the West Publishing Company of St. Paul, Minnesota. Warning: To be sure of the precise roles of Dombey and Smith, you need to consult the source. Either may be the defendant doctor or the plaintiff patient; the plaintiff's name usually, but not always, comes first. To avoid embarrassment and possible false identifications of litigants, we cite the cases by page, volume and state only. Deleting names is fairest to the litigants but in no way impairs substantiation of the cases.

Other regional groupings of states are covered by the widely used West Company publications labeled A., So., N.E. (Atlantic, Southern, Northeastern), and so on. Separate reporters are also published for every state (Ore., Tenn., Wyo., etc.). Some additional designations are F., F. Supp., Cal. Rptr., and A.D.—for Federal, Federal Supplement, California Reporter, and the Appellate Division of New York.

If you wish to learn more about medical discipline, you may care to use these chapter notes as a working bibliography. Cited here are most of the major works published in this field since 1950, earlier where still valid. The most important basic work to consult is the two-volume study of the A.M.A. Medical Disciplinary Committee (its *Report* and its *Exhibits*), a panoramic view of the weaknesses in professional discipline. Reports of hearings by the Senate Subcommittee on Antitrust and Monopoly are similarly enlightening as to business abuses by physicians.

For keeping abreast of developments in medical discipline, the best publications are the *Federation Bulletin, Medical Economics,* and the *Journal of the American Medical Association.* Each of these has an excellent periodic index, which eases research.

To find out about medical discipline in your community, you'd do well to get a copy of your state's medical practice act from the medical licensing board (often called the Board of Medical Examiners). The state medical association is worth querying, although you may learn only that it has little disciplinary authority. You are likely to be referred to your county medical society and local hospitals. Here chances are you will get the frankest, most detailed responses if you *talk* to members of the disciplinary committees.

359

NOTES

Chapter 1. A Crisis for Patients
Summary of Medical Disciplinary Committee conclusions: "The Status of Discipline in the Medical Profession," *Federation Bulletin*, January 1960.

Tuberculosis mistreatment: "He's a Menace to the Public and the Profession," by Frank Suiter, M.D., *Medical Economics*, Aug. 14, 1961.

Committee summary on substandard physicians: Section IV: "Regional Conferences," *Report of the Medical Disciplinary Committee to the Board of Trustees, American Medical Association*, June 1961.

Borderline cases: Section X: "Background and Observations," *Report of the Medical Disciplinary Committee*.

Grounds for malpractice claims: In *Journal of the American Medical Association*: "Analysis of Professional Liability Claims and Suits," Oct. 5, 1957, and "How State Medical Society Executives Size Up Professional Liability," June 1, 1957.

Major disciplinary problems in states: Appendix D: "Analysis of Replies Received From State Medical Associations," *Report of the Medical Disciplinary Committee*.

Review of state board actions: Drawn from 1964 reports in *Federation Bulletin*.

Heywood study of complaints against physicians: "Discipline in the Medical Profession: Sources and Types of Complaints—Processing of Charges," by Leo T. Heywood, M.D., *Federation Bulletin*, June 1961.

Jervey estimate of problem physicians: "A Survey of Medical Discipline," by Harold E. Jervey Jr., M.D., *Federation Bulletin*, April 1961.

A.M.A. Law Department survey results: In *J.A.M.A.*: "First Results: 1963 Professional-Liability Survey," Sept. 14, 1964; "Review of Medical Professional Liability Claims and Suits," May 10, 1958; "Opinion Survey on Medical Professional Liability," Aug. 3, 1957.

Fisher: "Bad Care is Commoner Than You Think," *Medical Economics*, Aug. 14, 1961.

Corio: "We Need MORE Malpractice Suits," by Michael V. Corio, M.D., *RISS*, December 1963.

Trussell study of Teamsters program: *The Quantity, Quality and Costs of Medical and Hospital Care Secured by a Sample of Teamsters Families in the New York Area*, by Ray E. Trussell, M.D. (1962, Prepared for the Teamsters Joint Council No. 16 and the Management Hospitalization Trust Fund).

Medelman: "President's Letter," by J. P. Medelman, M.D., *Minnesota Medicine*, November 1964.

Lull and McCormick: "Why Some Doctors Should Be in Jail," by Howard L. Whitman, *Collier's*, Oct. 30, 1953.

Larson: "Medicine's Role in Self-Discipline and Continuing Education," by Leonard W. Larson, M.D., *Federation Bulletin*, June 1962.

Appel: "Medicine—Profession or a Business," by James Z. Appel, M.D., presented before First National Conference on Medical Ethics, March 5, 1966.

Research assistance: Deena Burton

Chapter 2. Legacy of Loopholes
Connecticut M.D.: 137 Conn. 535.

"Little legal status": "The Fate of Discipline," *Federation Bulletin*, January 1961.

Medical board officials: Appendix D: "Analysis of Replies Received From State Boards of Medical Examiners," *Report of the Medical Disciplinary Committee to the Board of Trustees, American Medical Association*, June 1961.

History of licensing: *History of Medicine in the United States*, by F. R. Packard (1963, Hafner); "The History and Philosophy of Occupational Licensing Legislation in the United States," by William L. Frederick, *Journal of the American Dental Association*, March 1959;

"History of Medical Training and Licensing," by H. M. Karn, M.D., *New Zealand Medical Journal,* August 1957.

Advice of Benjamin Rush: "The Doctor and the Public Circa the American Revolution," by Irving Frederick Burton, M.D., *Journal of the Michigan State Medical Society,* January 1961.

Medical theories, early medical schools: Articles in *Encyclopaedia Britannica* (1894, Werner): "Medicine," "American Medical Association," "Medical Colleges of the United States."

Difficulty in securing licensing: "Medical Licensure in Rhode Island," *Rhode Island Medical Journal,* December 1962.

Womack, historic review: "The Evolution of the National Board of Medical Examiners," by Nathan A. Womack, M.D., *Journal of the American Medical Association,* June 7, 1965.

States with no licensing exam: "States Not Requiring Examination," Queries and Minor Notes, *J.A.M.A.,* Sept. 28, 1901.

J.A.M.A. editorial: "National Board of Medical Examiners," Jan. 11, 1902.

Chapter 3. License to Do Wrong

Medical board officials: Appendix D: "Analysis of Replies Received From State Boards of Medical Examiners," *Report of the Medical Disciplinary Committee to the Board of Trustees, American Medical Association,* June 1961.

Offenses cited in medical practice acts: "The Law of Medical Practice," by Sidney Shindell, *J.A.M.A.,* Aug. 16, 1965. See Appendix A, "Major Offenses Subject to Disciplinary Action."

U.S. Supreme Court: 170 U.S. 189.

Discussion of felonies: "Study of Attitudes and Opinions of State Boards of Medical Examiners Regarding Income Tax Evasion and Other Felonies," by Albert M. Deal, M.D., *Federation Bulletin,* December 1960; Appendix Q: "Laws Relating to Medical Discipline," *Report of the Medical Disciplinary Committee.*

Derbyshire study on mental illness statutes: "Mental Illness as a Problem in Discipline" (editorial) and "Current Attitudes Towards Mental Illness in Physicians," by R. C. Derbyshire, M.D., *Federation Bulletin,* October 1960.

Merchant: "Mental Illness—A Follow-Up," by Frederick T. Merchant, M.D.,

Federation Bulletin, September 1966; "Physicians Called Upon to Police Themselves," *Medical World News,* March 4, 1966.

General weaknesses in law: "Problem Areas in Medical Discipline," by Carl E. Anderson, M.D., *California Medicine,* November 1964.

Derbyshire study on incompetence: "Medical Incompetence," by R. C. Derbyshire, M.D., *Journal of the American Medical Association,* Dec. 20, 1965.

Anderson on professional conduct statutes: "State Boards and State Medical Associations," by Carl E. Anderson, M.D., *Federation Bulletin,* March 1966.

Unprofessional conduct generally: "The Complex of Unprofessional Conduct," by Edwin S. Holman, *Federation Bulletin,* March 1961.

District of Columbia abortionist: 261 F.2d 68.

Narcotics user: 307 S.W.2d 317 (Tex.).

Numbers of disciplinary actions: "Disciplinary Action in the Medical Profession," report of the Judicial Council, *J.A.M.A.,* Dec. 21, 1964.

"Why Ask the Legislatures: Discipline and the Doctor—The View From Atlanta," *J.A.M.A.,* Jan. 23, 1960.

Jervey on penalties: "Medical Quackery as Viewed by State Boards of Medical Examiners," by Harold E. Jervey, Jr., M.D., *Federation Bulletin,* December 1961.

Sales tax on fee: "Note on Overspecialization," *Federation Bulletin,* January 1967.

Impostor: *Federation Bulletin:* "Medical Impostors," by H. Doyl Taylor, August 1966; General Note, October 1966.

Jervey on board laxity: "A Survey of Medical Discipline," by Harold E. Jervey, Jr., M.D., *Federation Bulletin,* April 1961.

"Suppression of criticism": 293 P.2d 424 (Nev.).

"No derogatory information": article in *Federation Bulletin,* November 1966.

Lage: "Suggestions for the Future," by George H. Lage, M.O., *Federation Bulletin,* April 1967.

General situation of boards: "Board of Medical Examiners," by Justin J. Stein, M.D., *California Medicine,* November 1964.

"A license to abuse": "Status of Discipline in the Medical Profession," *Federation Bulletin*, January 1960.

Chapter 4. Disorganized Medicine
McMahon: "Re: Medical Licensure," by Rhett McMahon, *J.A.M.A.*, June 19, 1967.
Medical Disciplinary Committee: Unless otherwise noted, all references to the Committee and to statements of medical society spokesmen and officials are from the *Report of the Medical Disciplinary Committee to the Board of Trustees, American Medical Association*, June 1961.
"To them we're all doctors"; "unless their licenses are revoked"; "more hard-boiled": "Discipline and the Doctor—The View from Atlanta," *J.A.M.A.*, Jan. 23, 1960.
Garceau: *The Political Life of the American Medical Association* (1941, Harvard University Press).
Medical students: *Boys in White: Student Culture in Medical School*, by Howard S. Becker, Blanche Geer, Everett C. Hughes, and Anselm L. Strauss (1961, University of Chicago); "Medical Education," by Howard S. Becker and Blanche Geer, in *Handbook of Medical Sociology*, edited by Howard E. Freeman, Sol Levine, and Leo G. Reeder (1963, Prentice-Hall); *Learning the Doctor's Role*, by Constance A. Nathanson, unpublished M.A. Thesis (1958, University of Chicago), reported in "Medical Education," above.
Society benefits: "The American Medical Association: Power, Purpose and Politics in Organized Medicine," by David R. Hyde and Payson Wolff, with Anne Gross and Elliott Lee Hoffman, *Yale Law Journal*, May 1954.
"Largest, most influential": *It's Your A.M.A.* (1953, A.M.A.)
A.M.A. organization and activities: Special section, *J.A.M.A.*, Oct. 24, 1966.
McKeown: "Present Status of Medical Discipline," Raymond M. McKeown, M.D., *Federation Bulletin*, May 1961.
Smith: "Opinion of the Judicial Council Concerning the Complaints Received Against Charles E. Smith, M.D. (1963, A.M.A.); "A.M.A. Rules on Walker Case M.D.," *Medical World News*, June 21, 1963.
Original jurisdiction: Opinions and Reports of the Judicial Council (1966, A.M.A.).
Derbyshire: "What Should the Profession Do About the Incompetent Physician?" by Robert C. Derbyshire, M.D., *J.A.M.A.*, Dec. 20, 1965.
Number of disciplinary actions: 1964 Medical Disciplinary Report, *J.A.M.A.*, Dec. 27, 1965.
McGuire: H. Thomas McGuire, M.D., in *Delaware Medical Journal*, August 1961.
"Present dilemma": "The County Medical Society in Discipline," *Federation Bulletin*, July 1961.
Doctor pockets cigarettes: "Medicine at Work," *J.A.M.A.*, April 5, 1958.
Prevalence of grievance committees, size of societies: *Nationwide Survey on County Medical Society Activities*, (1967 and 1963, A.M.A.).
Grievance committee publicity: "Toward 'Heightening the Proper Practice of Medicine,'" *J.A.M.A.*, May 23, 1959.
Evans: "Ethics and the Medical Profession," by Franklin J. Evans, M.D., *Journal of the Florida Medical Association*, Oct. 1963.
Buck-passing: "Enforcing Ethics Called Local Doctors' Duty," *Medical Economics*, Feb. 3, 1958.
Stetler: "Court Decisions Involving State Medical Board Actions," by C. Joseph Stetler, *Federation Bulletin*, April 1963.
Brooke; $5,000 gallbladder: "Self-Discipline Starts at the Top," by Robert L. Brenner, *Medical Economics*, Aug. 14, 1961.
Heywood: "Discipline in the Medical Profession: Sources and Types of Complaints—Processing of Charges," by Leo T. Heywood, M.D., *Federation Bulletin*, June 1961.
Cotton: "Doctors Act to Improve Care," by Earl Ubell, *New York Herald-Tribune*, May 5, 1965.
Regan: "Physical Disability and Professional Incompetence," by James F. Regan, M.D., *Federation Bulletin*, October 1966.
Buerki: "Discipline Found Lacking on Hospital Staffs," *Medical Economics*, May 1956.
Myers: "Euphemisms of Pathology—An Unnecessary Evil," by Robert S. Myers, M.D., *American College of Surgeons Bulletin*, May–June 1954.
A.C.S. audit: "See No Evil," by Paul

R. Hawley, M.D., *American College of Surgeons Bulletin,* July–August 1953.

Blum: *Hospitals and Patient Dissatisfaction,* by Richard H. Blum (1958, California Medical Association).

Aged surgeon: "Force M.D.s to Retire?" (letter), by W. S. Pennington, M.D., *Medical Economics,* Sept. 7, 1964.

Resident and ulcer case: "When You and the Attending Disagree," by Warren Elfast, M.D., *RISS,* March 1964.

But He Rejects A.C.R.'s Suggestion," *American College of Radiology Bulletin,* September 1959.

W. C. Fields: "What's a Reasonable Fee?" by Hugh C. Sherwood, *RISS,* November 1958.

Settlement of $1,939: 126 So.2d 423 (La.).

Charge of $5,500: "The Case of the $5,500-or-Nothing Fee," *Medical Economics,* Aug. 27, 1962.

Missing will: 65 N.W.2d 852 (Mich.).

"Daines": 104 A.2d 890 (Conn.).

Chapter 5. The Fee Gougers: "Vultures in Medicine"

"Medical vultures": "Let's Face It," *Massachusetts Physician,* November 1959.

Milligan: "President's Address," by Gatewood C. Milligan, M.D., *Rocky Mountain Medical Journal,* November 1957.

Dowell: "Doctors Who Overcharge . . ." (Professional Briefs), *Medical Economics,* May 7, 1962.

Burgin: *Report of the President-Elect,* by George A. Burgin, M.D., presented to the House of Delegates, Medical Society of the State of New York, 1964.

Johnson: "President Urges Medicare Support," by Harold M. Schmeck, Jr., *New York Times,* June 16, 1966.

Examples of extremely high charges (internist, surgeon, gynecologist); standardizing of fees: " 'Going Rates' Are the Coming Thing," *Medical Economics,* Feb. 12, 1962.

Congress on Medical Ethics: "Report of Workshop on Grievance Committees," by Henry A. Crawford, M.D., presented at the First National Congress on Medical Ethics, March 5, 1966.

College football team: " 'Your Fees Are Hurting Us All!' " by James Alexander, M.D., *Medical Economics,* Jan. 28, 1965.

Emergency-room absentee: "Charge Only for Actual Service Rendered, Say Trustees," *Bulletin—Multnomah County Medical Society,* May 1964.

A.M.A. ruling: *Opinions and Rulings of the A.M.A. Judicial Council,* 1966.

Washington hospitals: Series by Charles G. Brooks, *Washington Star,* Jan. 11–19, 1959.

Radiologist's negotiations with hospital: "College Member Requests Counsel,

Chapter 6. The Overtreaters: Pouring It On

Liver injections: "He's a Menace to the Public and the Profession," by Frank Suiter, M.D., *Medical Economics,* Aug. 14, 1961.

Washington State girl: "Larcenous Large Clinics" (Letter), *Medical Economics,* Jan. 4, 1960.

Emergency surgery: "Effectiveness of Hospital Tissue Committees in Raising Surgical Standards," by Henry V. Weinert, M.D., and Robert Brill, M.D., *J.A.M.A.,* Nov. 8, 1952. A similar case, involving an Ohio hospital, is cited in the *New Republic,* May 11, 1953.

Foreign gynecologist; Alvarez; workings of medical audits; incidence of unjustified appendectomies, hysterectomies: "Unjustified Surgery," by Greer Williams, *Harper's,* February 1954.

Difficulties in diagnosis: "The Justification for Surgery," by Robert S. Myers, M.D., *Bulletin of the American College of Surgeons,* July–August 1956.

Appendectomies in children: "Patients for Sale," by Steven M. Spencer, *Saturday Evening Post,* Jan. 16, 1954.

Incidence of unnecessary surgery: "Too Much Unnecessary Surgery" (interview with Dr. Paul Hawley), *U.S. News & World Report,* Feb. 20, 1953. Also "Is the Operation Necessary?" by George Crile Jr., M.D., *Science Digest,* July 1956.

Unnecessary hysterectomies: "Unnecessary Ovariectomies: Study Based on Removal of 704 Normal Ovaries From 546 Patients," by James C. Doyle, M.D., *J.A.M.A.,* March 29, 1952, and "Hysterectomy: Therapeutic Necessity or Surgical Racket" by Norman F. Miller, M.D.,

American Journal of Obstetrics and Gynecology, p. 804, 1946.

Chapter 7. The Fee Splitters: Patients For Sale

Graham; A.C.S. estimates; mother superior; $10,000 in 6 months; chief of surgery: "Patients for Sale," by Steven M. Spencer, *Saturday Evening Post,* Jan. 16, 1954.

Medical Disciplinary Committee: Section II, *Report to the Board of Trustees,* American Medical Association Medical Disciplinary Committee, 1961.

New York State Commission (called The Moreland Commission); Johnson, Blodgett; Bromme; Hoffman; eyeglasses and other nonsurgical splits: "Why Some Doctors Should Be in Jail," by Howard L. Whitman, *Collier's,* Oct. 30, 1953.

Eastern city surgeon who "didn't fit in"; "The Whole Town's Splitting Fees!" by John R. Lindsey, *Medical Economics,* Nov. 9, 1959. For a discussion of questions raised by community-wide fee splitting, see "Economics or Ethics?" by Russell B. Roth, M.D., delivered before First National Congress on Medical Ethics, March 5, 1966.

Ghost introduced as assistant: "Ghosts in the Surgery," *Time,* June 14, 1954.

Hawley; "shudder for the patient"; "surgeon's gravy": "Two Doctors Speak Their Minds on Fee Splitting," *American College of Surgeons Bulletin,* November–December 1952.

Dr. McKittrick: "Split Fees for Post-Operative Care?" by Leland S. McKittrick, *Medical Economics,* Sept. 1, 1958.

Hospital inspection; price war: "Better Surgery in Bloomington?" by Greer Williams, *The Modern Hospital,* September 1952.

Kickbacks as a deductible expense: 72 Sp. Ct. 497. For a case involving kickbacks to an insurance company employee who selected examining physicians, 241 N.Y.S. 2d. 540. For comments on abuse of laboratories, see "Ethics in Private Office Practice," by H. Russell Fisher, M.D., *Bulletin of the College of American Pathologists,* January 1964.

DeWall: "The Surgical Educator's Responsibility to His Student in the Postresidency Period," by Richard A. DeWall, M.D., *Surgery Gynecology and Obstetrics,* March 1966.

Visits by thirty-three G.P.s: "How Prevalent Is Fee Splitting Today?" by John R. Lindsey and Pearl Barland, *Medical Economics,* Oct. 13, 1958.

Surgeon's experience on tour; lost operations: " 'Out of the Mouths of Babes,' " by Paul R. Hawley, M.D., *American College of Surgeons Bulletin,* March–April, 1953.

Limbert: "A Letter From Iowa" [from Dr. Edwin M. Limbert], *American College of Surgeons Bulletin,* September–October 1953.

Wade: "Fee-Splitting Still an Evil—Medic," by Arthur J. Snider, *Chicago Daily News,* March 4, 1966.

Tax evader: "The Columbus Five-Year Cure for Fee-splitting," by Greer Williams, *The Modern Hospital,* June 1952.

Dr. Hawley on legalizing fee splitting: "The Truman Committee Report," by Paul R. Hawley, M.D., *American College of Surgeons Bulletin,* September–October, 1955.

Truman Committee Report (which cites Dr. J. Ray Thomas study): "The A.M.A. Report on Unethical Practices," *Medical Economics,* July 1955.

The following are additional discussions of fee splitting: "Fee-Splitting Doctors, Menace to Health," by Arch J. Beatty, M.D., *Coronet,* September 1952; "Professional Misconduct—Fee Splitting as Grounds for Revocation of License," by David J. Eardley, *Notre Dame Lawyer,* May 1956; "Two Physicians Speak Their Minds on Fee Splitting," *A.C.S. Bulletin,* November–December 1952; "What is Wrong with Fee-Splitting," by John H. Budd, M.D., *J.A.M.A.,* Jan. 10, 1966.

Chapter 8. The Profiteers: Captive Prescriptions

Principal sources: *Physician Ownership in Pharmacies and Drug Companies* in two parts—the 1964 *Hearings* and the 1965 *Report* of the Subcommittee on Antitrust and Monopoly of the Senate Committee on the Judiciary. Plus the 1967 *Hearings* on the Hart Bill.

Excellent summaries of Committee findings appear in "The Rx Racket: Medical Ethics v. Profits," by Keith Wheeler and William Lambert, *Life,* June 24, 1966, which adds reports on the southern Illinois clinic, and "Should Eye Doctors

Sell Glasses?" by Irwin Ross, *Reader's Digest*, December 1966.

Drugstore statistics: "Physicians' Ownership of Drugstores Stirs New Debate on Ethics," by Jerry Landauer, *Wall Street Journal*, Dec. 17, 1964.

Federation Bulletin quote: "The Beginning of the End?" *Federation Bulletin*, February 1965.

Other sources include: "Physician Ownership in Pharmacies," by Martin F. Idzik, *Notre Dame Lawyer*, November, 1965; "Physician Owned Pharmaceutical Companies—A Wrong Without a Remedy," by Robert W. Hammel, Maven J. Myers, *Food Drug Cosmetic Law Journal*, August, 1966.

Chapter 9. The Quacks: Practitioners of Witchcraft

California Committee: California Senate Interim Committee on Public Health, *Progress Report on Medical Quackery 9*, by State Senator Richard Richards, 1958; cited in "Quackery in California," *Stanford Law Review*, March 1959.

"Wagmann": 133 N.E.2d 551.

"Putty": 61 Dauphin County Reports 260; 94 A.2d 121; 63 Dauphin County Reports 243.

"Mondell": 24 Cal. Rptr. 568.

Chapter 10. The Swindlers: Blank Form, Blank Check

Willingness of carrier to pay: "The Insurance Fraud," *Federation Bulletin*, July 1961.

Recent cases of fraud: Section IV, *Report to the Board of Trustees*, American Medical Association Medical Disciplinary Committee, 1961.

Vitamin injections: "Doctors Who Do Practice Need Watching," by Henry A. Davidson, M.D., *Medical Economics*, Aug. 24, 1964.

Otolaryngologist; Dr. Fischl: "They're Turning In Unethical Doctors," by Robert L. Brenner, *Medical Economics*, July 17, 1961.

Carbuncles; breast tumor; dislocations; foreign bodies: "Sword and Buckler, Part I," *New York State Journal of Medicine*, Jan. 15, 1964.

Halverson; $200 bill for wart; bills cut by $3,000; $3,500 for hernia: "Abuses of Health Insurance," by A. B. Halverson, *Best's Life Insurance News*, July 1956.

Appendectomy reported for wart: " 'Little Dishonesties' in Health Insurance Add Up to Trouble," by John L. Fletcher, M.D., *Journal of the Arkansas Medical Society*, March 1960.

Berk: "It's Easy to Abuse," *Medical Economics*, June 4, 1962.

Mail fraud: "Professional Briefs," *Medical Economics*, April 20, 1964.

Adelizzi: *New York Times*, Feb. 27, 1957.

Health Insurance Council: Appendix F, *Report to the Board of Trustees*, American Medical Association Medical Disciplinary Committee, 1961.

Repeated disputes: 166 So.2d 532 (La.); 169 So.2d 544 (La.).

Baltimore hospital: "Blue Shield Probes Fraud in Maryland Hospitals," by Jerry Cartledge, *Baltimore News-American*, Feb. 13, 1965.

Newark doctor: *New York Times*, Dec. 18, 1957.

Dead veteran: *New York Times*, April 9, 1956.

$100,000 fraud: *New York Times*, April 2, 1964; *Newsday* (Garden City, L.I.), Dec. 30, 1965.

Physician tax evasions: Report of Terence F. Gastelle, Public Information Division, Internal Revenue Service. During the fiscal year ending June 30, 1965, 1,422 persons were convicted of tax fraud. Twenty of them were physicians, who were fined a total of $174,000 plus other penalties. In the previous year, 2,408 persons were sentenced for tax violations, 24 of whom were physicians.

Van Fossan: "Some Reflections by a Retired Judge," by Ernest H. Van Fossan, *Alumni Bulletin of the Columbia University Law School*, March 1958.

Deliberate concealment; secret books; recording wrong fees; coded payments; Report of Intelligence Division, Internal Revenue Service, on physicians sentenced to prison for tax evasion during fiscal year ending June 30, 1964. For a published report, see "Why 9 M.D.s Were Jailed as Tax-Dodgers," by James P. Gifford, *Medical Economics*, Dec. 28, 1964.

Converting to cashier's checks: 41 Cal. Rptr. 351, and "Doctor's License Suspended for Attempted Tax Evasion," *Federation Bulletin,* June 1965.

Trust accounts: 29 T.C. 940 (N.Y.).

Informer: "Tax Informers Can Put You on the Spot," by M. J. Goldberg, *Medical Economics,* Nov. 21, 1960.

Background on medical licensure and convicted tax evaders: "Study of Attitudes and Opinions of State Boards of Medical Examiners Regarding Income Tax Evasion and Other Felonies," by Albert M. Deal, M.D., *Federation Bulletin,* December 1960. For cases in which tax evasion was held grounds for suspension of license, see 101 N.E.2d 294; 308 P.2d 924 (Cal.); and 319 P.2d 824 (Wash.), plus a report on the Kindschi decision, "Willful Evasion of Federal Taxes as an Offense Allowing Summary Action by a Discipline Board," *Vanderbilt Law Review,* October 1958. For a case in which a physician was granted a stay of revocation pending his appeal of a tax-fraud conviction, see 280 P.2d 415 (Idaho).

Chapter 11. The Perjurers: Witness for the Highest Bidder

Hawley quotes, surgeon in $6,300,000 of claims: *New York Times,* May 26, 1955.

Brown: "You Do Have Medical-Legal Responsibility, Doctor," by Kent L. Brown, *J.A.M.A.,* March 1, 1965.

Arkwright Commission: *New York Times,* Jan. 9, 1959; Aug. 27, 1960; Dec. 31, 1960; July 25, 1961; Sept. 7, 1961; Jan. 13, 1962; Jan. 17, 1962; June 27, 1963.

Guilty doctor, good reputation: Application of, 212 N.Y.S.2d 701.

Bills of over $100: 246 N.Y.S.2d 867.

31 office visits: 218 N.Y.S.2d 226.

One accident, two reports: 230 N.Y.S. 2d 286.

Kickbacks from lawyer: 128 N.E.2d 789 (Mass.).

Sale of questions: *New York Times,* April 6, 1962; May 12, 1962; May 26, 1962.

Hospital head: *New York Times,* March 17, 1966.

Dismembered body: 266 A.D. 894, 42 N.Y.S. 2d 801.

Mayhem with saw: 120 S.E.2d 580.

Mayhem by castration: "This M.D.

Made a $500,000 Mistake," by Robert L. Brenner, *Medical Economics,* Aug. 29, 1960.

Dr. Spain: "Mississippi Autopsy," by D. M. Spain, M.D., In "Mississippi Eyewitness," *Ramparts,* Special Issue, 1964.

Another discussion of perjury among doctors can be found in: "Exposure of Doctors' Venal Testimony," by Logan Ford and James H. Holmes III, *Insurance Counsel Journal,* April 1965.

Chapter 12. The Drug Traffickers: "To Gratify The Appetite"

Giordano: *The Physician and the Federal Narcotic Law,* by Henry L. Giordano (Federal Bureau of Narcotics, April 1967).

Harrison Act: *Prescribing and Dispensing of Narcotics Under Harrison Narcotic Law* (Treasury Department Pamphlet 56).

"Gratify the holder's appetite": 262 Fed. 849.

"At his peril": 258 U.S. 250.

Nassau County: "Doctors to be Urged to Report Addicts," by Linda Charlton, *Newsday* (Garden City, N.Y.), Dec. 15, 1965.

Ruses: *Narcotic Don'ts For the Physician* (publication of Federal Bureau of Narcotics).

Bloomquist: "The Doctor, the Nurse and Narcotic Addiction," by Edward R. Bloomquist, *GP,* November 1958.

Doctor who got gifts: "Ethics and Patients' Gifts" (letter), *RISS,* June 1965.

"A perversion of meaning": 249 U.S. 96.

Narcotics Bureau on drug clinics: "The Official Position of the Federal Bureau of Narcotics on Handling Narcotics Addicts," by Henry L. Giordano, *American Professional Pharmacist,* January 1964.

White House Conference on Narcotic and Drug Abuse: *Proceedings,* Sept. 27–28, 1962 (Government Printing Office).

Joint-committee report: "Joint Statement on Narcotic Addiction by A.M.A. and N.R.C.," *New York Medicine,* Aug. 20, 1962.

A.M.A. on ambulatory treatment: In *J.A.M.A.:* "Report on Narcotic Addiction," May 4, 1957; "A.M.A. Restates Position on Ambulatory Clinics for Addicts," Oct. 13, 1962.

Attracts like "magnets": "Bronx Doctor Held on Prescriptions Issued to Addicts," *New York Times*, March 10, 1967.

Alexander King: *Mine Enemy Grows Older* (1958, Simon and Schuster).

3,000 percent profit: 206 P.2d 1085.

88 counts: *New York Times*, March 4, 1955, p. 16.

Reputable physician exploits addiction: 239 P.2d 78.

"Renal colic": 299 N.Y. 469.

Going through motions of physical: 277 P.2d 859.

Physician-druggist collusion: *New York Times*, Nov. 11, 1961, p. 49.

"Opportunity to invest": *Traffic in Opium and Other Dangerous Drugs—Report by the Government of the United States of America* (1962 and 1963).

New Jersey grand jury: *New York Times*, Feb. 22, 1964, p. 23.

Selling opiates to school children: *New York Times*, Feb. 15, 1964, p. 1

Truck crashes: 83 S.E.2d 460.

Study of addicts at P.H.S. hospital; addicted children's book illustrator: "Doctors and Dope," *Pageant*, May 1967.

Morphine for nausea: 81 N.E.2d 838.

Masking inadequate treatment with drugs: 275 P.2d 175.

Contributing to addiction for nine years: 18 Cal. Rptr. 196.

Addict turns to prostitution: *New York Times*, July 14, 1955, p. 46.

For additional information about the negligent prescription of narcotics, see: "Damages for Patients' Drug Addiction," by Sheldon Seligsohn, *Temple Law Quarterly*, Fall, 1955; "Negligent Prescription of Habit Forming Drugs," *Vanderbilt Law Review*, April, 1955.

Chapter 13. The Assaulters: Trespassing on the Patient

Judicial statement: 211 N.Y. 125.

Ratner: "Doctors' Views on What to Tell the Patient," *RISS*, September 1962.

Mix-up with boys; Illinois, California, Michigan cases: "Medicine's Legal Nightmare (Part 2)," by Milton Silverman, *Saturday Evening Post*, April 18, 1959.

Removal of kidney: "They Operated on the Wrong Patient," by Robert L. Brenner, *Medical Economics*, Feb. 29, 1960.

Removal of testicle: D.C., E.D., June

6, 1962. For a report of this case see "Operation in Confusion," *Time*, Dec. 1, 1958.

Fulguration of tumor: Section 101: "Malpractice Prophylaxis—Operation, Autopsy, Hazardous Therapy," in *Doctor and Patient and the Law*, by Louis J. Regan, M.D.

Spinal anesthetic: 261 P.2d 199 (Okla.). For a similar case see 96 So.2d 716 (Fla.).

Ovaries removed: "Your Legal Risks in Sterilization," by John H. Tovey, *Medical Economics*, Jan. 24, 1966.

Woman trying to conceive: 119 So.2d 649 (La.).

Botched hysterectomy: 288 P.2d 1003 (Calif.).

For discussions of informed consent, see: "Consent to Medical and Surgical Treatment," by Anna I. Shinkle, *Drake Law Review*, May, 1965; "Consent to Medical Treatment," by Diana M. Kloss, *Medicine, Science and the Law*, April, 1965; "Informed Consent: A Plaintiff's Medical Malpractice 'Wonder Drug,'" by William H. Karchmer, *Missouri Law Review*, Winter, 1966.

Chapter 14. The Abandoners: Bad Samaritans

Law of abandonment: "The Abandoned Patient," by Maurice Levin, *Insurance Law Journal*, May 1965. "Action of Abandonment in Medical Malpractice Litigation," by Leon L. McIntire, *Tulane Law Review*, June 1962; "Recent Cases of Interest—Tort—Malpractice—Abandonment of Patient," by John S. Langford Jr., August 1958; "What Is Abandonment?" *Texas Journal of Medicine*, April 1963.

"Jerry Robins": 47 S.E.2d 314 (Va.).

Psychiatrist who refuses patients: From *Medical Economics*: "Why Take on 'Impossible' Patients," by Roswell Porter, M.D., Jan. 28, 1963; "Like a hobby": Letter from William F. Quinn, M.D., June 3, 1963; "Anti-human-being": Letter from Henry A. Davidson, M.D., March 25, 1963.

Thrope: "Trouble in Paradise," *Federation Bulletin*, June 1962.

Boston University poll; Donnelly; A.M.A. comments: "Those Good Samaritan Laws: Are They Really Necessary?"

by William N. Jeffers, *Medical Economics,* July 27, 1964.

A.M.A. survey: "1963 Professional Liability Survey," *J.A.M.A.,* Sept. 14, 1964.

Good Samaritan laws: "Good Samaritans and Liability for Medical Malpractice," *Columbia Law Review,* November 1964; "Pennsylvania's Good Samaritan Statute: An Answer to the Medical Profession's Dilemma," by Joseph F. Busacca, *Villanova Law Review,* Fall 1964; "Wisconsin's 'Good Samaritan' Statute," by David A. Suemnick, *Marquette Law Review,* Summer, 1964.

Liability in emergencies: "Exemption From Civil Liability," by William E. West Jr., *Boston University Law Review,* Winter 1963; "Civil Liability for Treatment Rendered at the Scene of an Emergency," *Wisconsin Law Review,* May 1964; "Liability in Rendering Emergency Aid," *Memphis Medical Journal,* September 1962.

Hassard: Reported in "Emergency Care," *Medical Economics,* Sept. 23, 1963.

Plant: "Good Samaritans Needn't Fear Suits," News Briefs, *Hospital Physician,* July 1966.

A.M.A. Law Department on specialism: *The Citation,* Jan. 16, 1961.

Postman: *New York Times,* Sept. 28, Dec. 12, Dec. 17, 1964.

"Grady": 202 N.Y.S.2d 436. Judgment dismissing complaint reversed and new trial ordered on grounds questions should have gone to jury.

Letourneau: Professional Briefs, *Medical Economics,* Aug. 27, 1962.

Sending patient to neurosurgeon: 9 Cal. Rptr. 634.

Veteran bleeding to death: 146 So.2d 882 (Miss.).

Abandonment in hospitals: Law Forum, *Hospital Progress,* November 1963.

Berry: "The Responsibility Is Yours, Doctor," *American College of Surgeons Bulletin,* May–June 1959.

Boy left in hospital: 54 N.W.2d 639 (Minn.).

Doctor out to lunch: 374 S.W.2d 645 (Tenn.).

Itinerant surgery: "Policy on Itinerant Surgery," *A.C.S. Bulletin,* May–June 1962.

Tonsillectomy: "The Anatomy of Malpractice: The Throat," by John H. Tovey, *Medical Economics,* Feb. 24, 1964.

For additional discussions of Good Samaritan laws, see: "Should a physician be required to render aid in emergencies?" by Albert M. Horn, *Alabama Law Review,* Spring 1956; "Suit or Samaritan?" by R. L. Gouge, *Journal of the American Medical Women's Association,* November 1964; "Negligence–Medical Malpractice–Criticism of Existing Good Samaritan Statutes," by Jacob E. Vilhauer, *Oregon Law Review,* June 1963; "Good Samaritan Laws–Good or Bad," by William Wheeler Bryan, *Mercer Law Review,* Spring 1964.

Legal implications of cardiac arrest can be found in: "Cardiac Arrest and Cardiac Massage," by Maurice Levin, *Insurance Law Journal,* October 1965.

Additional discussions of abandonment: "Abandonment of Patient," by Howard Newcomb Morse, *J.A.M.A.,* Nov. 28, 1966; "Abandonment of the Patient," by N. L. Chayet, *New England Journal of Medicine,* January 7, 1965; "Standard of Care of Medical General Practitioners," by Milton Oppenheim, M.D., *Marshall Law Review,* May 1960.

Chapter 15. The Toll of Ignorance

Medical impostor: "Layman, 29, Posed 4 Years as Doctor; Practiced in Detroit," *New York Times,* Sept. 5, 1964.

Taft: 78 Fed. 442.

Law of negligence: "Medical Malpractice," *Tennessee Law Review,* Summer 1959; *Doctor and Patient and the Law,* by Louis J. Regan, M.D. (Mosby, 1956).

Curran: "Professional Negligence–Some General Comments," by William J. Curran, *Vanderbilt Law Review,* June 1957.

Sadusk: "Hazardous Fields of Medicine in Relation to Professional Liability," by Dr. Joseph F. Sadusk Jr., *J.A.M.A.,* March 16, 1957.

A.C.S. official: "Medicine's Legal Nightmare," by Milton Silverman, *Saturday Evening Post,* April 11, 1959.

Hawley: "The General Practice of Medicine," by Paul R. Hawley, M.D., *A.C.S. Bulletin.*

"Day of rapid transportation": 196 P.2d 52, 205 P.2d 3 (Cal.).

Lee: *A Doctor Speaks His Mind,* by Roger I. Lee (Little, Brown, 1958).

A.A.G.P. study; Delp: "Continuing

Education—Too Little and Too Late?" *J.A.M.A.*, Vol. 189, No. 9.

Leg fracture: "Must a Physician Refer a Patient to a Specialist" by Alexander Schambam, *Medical Times*, October 1964.

Myers: "Who Should Do Surgery?" by Robert S. Myers, M.D., *A.C.S. Bulletin*, March–April 1954.

"Any fool can take out an appendix": "Medicine's Worst Sin," by Charles Thurd, M.D., *Medical Economics*, Jan. 6, 1958.

Letourneau: "Board Certification Isn't Good Enough, He Says," *Medical Economics*, March 17, 1958.

Burned boy: 33 Cal. Rptr. 673.

For a case of a drainage tube left in a lung for 19 years see 249 S.W.2d 791 (Ky.).

Broken filiform: 92 N.W.2d 57 (Mich.).

"Mrs. Densen": 184 F.Supp 944 (Va.).

For discussions of statutes of limitations, see: "Statute of Limitations—Fraudulent Concealment," by Edward H. Feege, *Villanova Law Review*, November 1957; "Statute of Limitations for Undiscovered Malpractice," by J. E. Stenfield, *Wyoming Law Journal*, Fall 1957: "Statute of Limitations," by John H. Anderson Jr., *Insurance Counsel Journal*, April 1958.

Discussions of the standard of care required of doctors can be found in: "Malpractice and the Physician—Lack of Diligence," by O. C. Schroeder Jr., *Postgraduate Medicine*, September 1965; "Medical Malpractice—Standard of Care," by John H. Harris, *Tennessee Law Review*, Spring 1962; "Contributory Negligence of Incompetents," by Joseph P. Flynn, *Washburn Law Journal*, Spring 1964; "Care Required of Medical Practitioners," by Allan H. McCoid, *Vanderbilt Law Review*, June 1959; "Standard of Care of Medical General Practitioners," by Milton Oppenheim, *Cleveland-Marshall Law Review*, May 1960.

Chapter 16. Where Physicians Blunder
Failures in diagnosis: "The Standard of Care," by Oliver C. Schweder Jr., *Postgraduate Medicine*, February 1964.

Observer error: "Detecting 'Observer Error' by Doctors in Personal Injury Cases," *Current Medicine for Attorneys*, May 1961.

Dr. Guttmacher: *Pregnancy and Birth* by Alan F. Guttmacher, M.D. (Viking, 1958).

Robson: "The Inquiring Mind," by H. N. Robson, *Australasian Annals of Medicine*, May 1960.

Hospital study: "Diagnostic Errors: A Study of Clinical and Autopsy Findings," *Law and Medicine*, by William J. Curran (1960, Little, Brown).

Hemoglobin test: "The Case of the Outmoded Blood Test," by Xavier F. Warren, *Medical Economics*, January 1957.

Rh incompatibility: 320 F.2d 674 (Va.).

Staphylococcal pneumonia: 241 N.Y.S. 2d 373.

Court on x-ray: 186 P.2d 450 (Cal.).

Dye injection: 180 F. Supp. 172 (Va.).

Unger; Geiger; transfusion care: "The $150,000 Blood Transfusion," by John R. Lindsey, *Medical Economics*, Sept. 28, 1954.

Transfusion case; evaluation of mother's life: 173 N.E.2d 791, 205 N.Y.S.2d 274; "Why You Can Expect More $150,-000 Malpractice Suits," by John R. Lindsey, *Medical Economics*, Aug. 3, 1954.

Treatment of wart: 112 N.E.2d 175 (Ill.). For other cases of x-ray burns see 76 So.2d 599 (La.).

Archambault: "Professional Briefs," *Medical Economics*, May 3, 1965.

Doctors' responsibility: "Physician Responsibility for Drug Prescription," by Don Harper Mills, M.D., *J.A.M.A.*, May 10, 1965; Dr. Joseph F. Sadusk Jr., talk before American College of Physicians, New York City, April 19, 1966.

Salt solution too strong: *Doctor and Patient and the Law.*

Child with bronchitis: *The Citation*, Nov. 24, 1961 (D.C.).

Office worker gets TAT: 363 P.2d 438 (Kan.) For a fatal reaction to a nasal spray see 102 A.2d 352 (Conn.).

Patient's protest ignored: 153 A.2d 255 (Pa.). This case is well reported in "How to Get Hit with a $75,000 Malpractice Verdict," by William N. Jeffers, *Medical Economics*, Feb. 2, 1959.

Tinnitus: 145 A.2d 809 (N.J.); *The Citation*, Feb. 25, 1959; "Current Observations on Medical Malpractice," by William F. Martin, *Insurance Counsel Journal*, July 1959.

For a general discussion of malpractice in the administration of drugs and blood transfusions, see the following: "Blood Transfusion Accidents," by William S. Henley and John Land McDavid, *Insurance Counsel Journal*, April, 1965; "Incompatible Blood Transfusions," by Maurice Levin, *Insurance Law Journal*, April, 1965; "Malpractice and the Administration of Drugs," by Don Harper Mills, M.D., *Medical Times*, June, 1965.

Chapter 17. . . . And Surgeons Go Astray

"Mrs. Joy": 2 Cal. Rptr. 167. Reported in "Do Bad Results Prove You're Negligent?" by John R. Lindsey, *Medical Economics*, Sept. 24, 1962.

"No inference of negligence": 31 Cal. Rptr. 633.

Surgical clamp: "Damages Recovered for Death Caused by Leaving Clamp in Patient," *The Citation*, August 1961.

Humphrey case: 160 S.W.2d 6 (Ky.).

"Why was a foreign substance left?": 64 P.2d 409(Cal.).

Forceps piercing colon: 166 F. Supp 296 (N.D.).

Sponge count: 362 S.W.2d 926 (Tenn.).

Gauze in tonsil depression: 227 P.2d 772 (Utah).

Previous difficulty with anesthesia: "New Malpractice Danger: Cardiac Arrest," by John Herbert Tovey, *RISS*, August 1963.

The rights of unborn infants are discussed in many judicial rulings. For a good review, contained in a case brought in behalf of an unborn infant, see 38 N.W.2d 838 (Minn.).

For general discussions of the physician's liability in surgery, see: "Surgeons Liability for Negligence—Removal of Swabs or Packs," by J. P. Eddy, *The Law Times*, Dec. 16, 1955; "The Liability of Physicians for Negligent Acts of Others," by Charles U. Letourneau, M.D., *Hospital Management*, December, 1964; "Surgeon Responsible for Pre-Operative Negligence of Anesthesiologist," by Edwin M. Larkin, *Georgetown Law Journal*,

Winter 1961; "Malpractice Problems in Anesthesia," *Medical Annals of the District of Columbia*, 33:108, March, 1964.

Chapter 18. The Mentally Ill: "Our Biggest Problem"

Committee summary on substandard doctors: Section IV: "Regional Conferences," *Report of the Medical Disciplinary Committee to the Board of Trustees of the American Medical Association*, June 1961.

Suicide: "High Rates of Suicide Among Physicians," *Medical World News*, July 3, 1964.

Oregon study: "Suicide in Professional Groups," by P. H. Blachly, M.D., H. T. Osterud, M.D., and R. Josslin, *New England Journal of Medicine*, June 6, 1963.

"Pelvic massage": 308 S.W.2d 261.

"Sleeping woman" doctrine: 292 S.W. 422 (Mo.).

Psychiatrist: 22 Cal. Rptr. 419.

Woman drugged: 337 P.2d 192 (Calif.) .

In own home: 336 P.2d 913 (Okla.).

Tax evader: 124 N.W.2d 37 (Wis.).

Derbyshire: "What Should the Profession Do About the Incompetent Physician?" by Robert C. Derbyshire, M.D., *J.A.M.A.*, Dec. 20, 1965.

"Dr. Kowalski": "Warning to All State Boards of Medical Examiners," by C. J. Glaspel, M.D., *Federation Bulletin*, October 1957.

Sally Benson: "Sally Benson's Doctor Indicted; She Says He Made Her an Addict," *New York Times*, Dec. 12, 1965.

Tenery: "Society Must be Protected From Unethical Physicians," by Robert Mayo Tenery, M.D., *Texas State Journal of Medicine*, July 1954. See also "Psychological Problems in Medical Students," by C. H. Hardin Branch, M.D., *Federation Bulletin*, October 1964.

Suit-prone doctors: *The Psychology of Malpractice Suits*, by Richard H. Blum, (1957, California Medical Association); *Hospitals and Patient Dissatisfaction*, by Richard H. Blum (1958, California Medical Association).

Filthy office: Quoted in "Doctor's 'Filthy Office' Draws Public Rebuke," *Medical Economics*, April 28, 1958.

Regan: "Physical Disability and Professional Incompetence," by James F. Regan, M.D., *Federation Bulletin*, October 1966.

"Your License and the Law," by James F. Regan, M.D., *California Medicine*, June 1962.

Chapter 19. The Narcotic Addicts: Doctors' Disease

Occupational disease: In *Federation Bulletin:* "Panel on Problems of Discipline—I. Narcotic Addiction in Physicians," by John M. Fiorino, M.D., August 1960; and "Problems in Narcotic Addiction," by C. J. Glaspel, M.D., July 1958.

Rate; Modlin: "Psychiatrists Probe Personality of MD-Addict," *Medical World News*, June 5, 1964.

Garb; Demerol: "Narcotic Addiction in Nurses and Doctors," by Solomon Garb, M.D., *Nursing Outlook*, November 1965.

Winick: "Physician Narcotic Addicts," by Charles Winick, in *The Other Side*, edited by Howard S. Becker (1964, Free Press of Glencoe).

Eastern hospital; postgraduate study; roller-skating; medical-school dean: "Narcotic Addiction Among Physicians," by J. DeWitt Fox, M.D., *Journal of the Michigan State Medical Society*, February 1957.

Chronic painful disease: 178 N.E.2d 741 (Ind.).

Terminal cancer; doctor addicted to amphetamines: "How One M.D. Helps Doctors in Trouble," by Claron Oakley, *RISS*, November 1962.

Wall study: "The Results of Hospital Treatment of Addiction in Physicians," by James H. Wall, M.D., and "Narcotic Addiction as a Problem," both in *Federation Bulletin*, May 1958.

Typical relapse: 15 Cal. Rptr. 879 (Cal.).

Prescriptions for addicts: Annual Report, Federal Narcotics Bureau (1965).

"Charles Kay": "Hindsight in Disciplinary Problems," by Joseph J. Combs, M.D., *Federation Bulletin*, December 1964.

"Bailin": 115 A.2d 448. For a case discussing the definition of "addicted"—in which a doctor's use of drugs was described as "heroic"—see 87 N.E.2d 301 (N.Y.).

Surgery by addict: 327 P.2d 131 (Cal.).

Types of narcotic offenses under law:

Chapter 20. False Alarm

McKeown: "A.M.A. Disciplinary Committee: Toward Heightening the Proper Practice of Medicine," *J.A.M.A.*, May 23, 1959.

Hollings: "Legislative Concern Over Discipline," by Hon. Ernest F. Hollings, *Federation Bulletin*, August 1961.

Roemer: "The Future of Social Medicine in the United States," *The Pharos of Alpha Omega Alpha*, April 1967.

Annis: "Who's the Winner in Surgical Squabbles," by Edward R. Annis, M.D., *Medical Economics*, Jan. 29, 1962.

Current Medicine for Attorneys: "The Lawyers' Bill of Complaint," September 1962.

Swanson: "Blurring of the Image," by E. C. Swanson, M.D., *Federation Bulletin*, May 1964.

Rocky Mountain Medical Journal: "Mass Media and the Physician . . . Or How Sick Is Our Image?" by Clyde E. Stanfield, M.D., July 1961.

"The Doctor's Image Is Sickly"; Petrarch quote: article by Walter Goodman, *New York Times Magazine*, Oct. 16, 1966.

Harper's: "The Crisis in American Medicine," October, 1960.

Doctors and Supreme Court Justices: "Jobs and Occupations: A Popular Evaluation," National Opinion Research Center, *Opinion News*, Oct. 1, 1947.

Massachusetts Physician: "Delusions of Grandeur," May 1957.

Gamson and Schuman: "Some Undercurrents in the Prestige of Physicians," by William A. Gamson and Howard Schuman, *American Journal of Sociology*, January 1963.

Lee: "The Social Dynamics of the Physician's Status," by Alfred McClung Lee, *Psychiatry*, November 1944.

Murray: Medicine, *Newsweek*, June 17, 1957.

Cahal; Opinion Research Corp.: "The Image," by Mac F. Cahal, *J.A.M.A.*, July 20, 1963.

Gaffin: *What Americans Think of the Medical Profession: Report on a Public*

Opinion Survey (1956, American Medical Association).

Dichter: *The Doctor-Patient Relationship—A Psychological Study,* published in *GP,* October 1951.

Medical Economics survey: "Patients Speak Out About Doctors' Methods," *Medical Economics,* April 20, 1964.

Konold, Cox: *A History of American Medical Ethics: 1847–1912,* by Donald E. Konold (1962, Department of History, University of Wisconsin).

Feldman: "What Americans Think About Their Medical Care," by Jacob J. Feldman, American Statistical Association Proceedings of the Social Statistics Meeting, Dec. 27–30, 1958.

Unseconded motion: "The Doctor and the Public," by Irving Frederick Burton, M.D., *Journal of the Michigan State Medical Society,* January 1961.

Chapter 21. The Medicolegal Nightmare

History: "Why the Increase in Malpractice Litigation," by Dr. Joseph S. Stewart, A. Lee Bradford and Edward J. Kelly, *Insurance Counsel Journal,* October 1960; "The Care Required of Medical Practitioners," by Allan H. McCoid, *Vanderbilt Law Review,* June 1959.

Mort: Y. B. Hill, 48 Edw. III, f. 6, pl. 11 (1374).

Cross v. Guthrey: 2 Root 90 (Conn.).

Lincoln: Ritchey v. West, 23 Ill. 329.

A.M.A. surveys; high-litigation states: In *J.A.M.A.*: "First Results: 1963 Professional Liability Survey," Sept. 14, 1964; "Review of Medical Professional Liability Claims and Suits," May 10, 1958; "Opinion Survey on Medical Professional Liability," Aug. 3, 1957; "Court Decisions—Medical Professional Liability," July 20, 1957; "Analysis of Professional Liability Claims and Suits," Oct. 5, 1957.

Iowa and California rates: Aetna Insurance Co.

$650,000: "Paralyzed Veteran Awarded $650,000," *New York Times,* Feb. 4, 1965.

"Michaelson": 230 F. Supp. 536.

Williams and Louisell: *Trial of Medical Malpractice Cases,* by David W. Louisell and Harold Williams, M.D. (1966, Bender).

Broken arm; statute of limitations; pin swallower: *Doctor and Patient and the Law,* by Louis J. Regan, M.D. (1956, Mosby).

New York State Malpractice Insurance and Defense Board: Report by T. M. D'Angelo, *New York Journal of Medicine,* April 15, 1953.

A.M.A. Committee on Medicolegal Problems: "Problems on Professional Liability and the Law," *J.A.M.A.,* Feb. 23, 1963.

"Poppycock": "Malpractice Suits Are an Increasing Hazard," *American College of Surgeons Bulletin,* May–June 1956.

Blum: *Malpractice Suits: Why and How They Happen,* by Richard H. Blum (1958, California Medical Association).

Ashe; Morris; Hirsh on "stigma"; expanding grounds: "Suing the Doctor: Recent Court Decisions Help Patients Seeking Malpractice Damages," by Donald Moffitt, *Wall Street Journal,* July 12, 1965.

Results of suits: "Review of Medical Professional Liability Claims and Suits," *J.A.M.A.,* May 10, 1958.

Largest settlement: Carvainis v. Montefiore Hospital for Chronic Diseases, Supreme Court, New York County, Index No. 11907; "Medical Teamwork—or Malpractice," by Robert L. Brenner, *Medical Economics,* Sept. 11, 1961.

Age of Absolute Liability; Bloustein; Hurd: "The Liability Revolution," by Peter Vanderwicken, *Esquire,* August 1966.

Pyoderma gangrenosum: "Pyoderma Gangrenosum, Peptic Ulcer, and a $625,-000 Award," by Isadore Kaplan, M.D., *J.A.M.A.,* Dec. 7, 1964.

Holman: "Doctors Urged to Fight Unjust Court Awards," *Medical Economics,* June 1957.

Tow truck: "$400,000 Awarded for Leg Lost Due to Hole in Street," *New York Times,* Jan. 15, 1966.

Law reviews: 71 *Scottish Law Review* 177 (1955).

Hirsh on "patients think that doctors can guarantee results": "Shift in Malpractice Decisions," *Medical World News,* April 24, 1964.

Belli: "Inflation, Courtroom Histrionics Hike Injury Case Awards to New Highs," by Kenneth G. Slocum, *Wall Street Journal*, July 7, 1958.

"Wald": "Summation in Ergas vs. Barricini," by Jacob D. Fuchsberg, *Plaintiff's Advocate*, April 1964; *NACCA Newsletter*, Oct. 1963.

Expanding grounds: "Trends in Professional Liability—What You Need to Know," by Thomas Allen, *New Physician*, November 1963; "Changing Legal Concepts," by Carl E. Wasmuth, M.D., *Anesthesia and Analgesia*, September–October 1962; "Changing Concepts of Malpractice Laws," by Thomas A. Martin, M.D., *Journal of the Maine Medical Association*, August 1962; "Recent Trends in Malpractice," by Arthur H. Clephane, *Pennsylvania Medical Journal*, June 1960.

Evans: "Judicial Trends—Effect Upon Malpractice Litigation," by Franklin J. Evans, M.D., *GP*, December 1963.

"Malpractice is hard to prove": Judge Rutledge in 124 F.2d 825.

Cancerophobia: 176 N.Y.S.2d 996 (N.Y.).

Heart attack: "Cause of Death: Fright," *Newsweek*, Dec. 27, 1965.

Prenatal injury: 367 P.2d 835 (Wash.).

Pentothal: 173 A.2d 48 (Pa.).

Res ipsa: "Res Ipsa Loquitur," by Howard Newcomb Morse, *J.A.M.A.*, May 23, 1966; "Res Ipsa Loquitur in California," by David S. Rubsamen, M.D. *Stanford Medical Bulletin*, November 1962; "The Use of the Legal Doctrine 'Res Ipsa Loquitur' in Medical Malpractice Suits," *Journal of the Louisiana State Medical Society*, April 1962; "The Problem of Res Ipsa Loquitur," by Carl E. Wasmuth, M.D. *Annals of Internal Medicine*, March 1960. "Malpractice and the Clinical Laboratory," by Don Harper Mills, M.D., *Science*, May 8, 1964.

"No longer innocent": "Current Trends and Problems in Medical Malpractice Litigation," by Horace F. Turner, M.D., *Journal of the Medical Society of the State of Alabama*, December 1959.

Tovey: "The Most Inflated Malpractice Threat," by John H. Tovey, *Medical Economics*, June 14, 1965.

Byrne: 159 Eng. Rep. 299.

Human toe: Quoted in *The Doctors' Dilemmas*, by Louis Lasagna, M.D. (1962, Harper).

Bed warmer: 159 P. 436 (Cal.).

Ybarra: 154 P.2d 687 (Cal.) 208 P.2d 445.

"Attempt to equalize": 317 P.2d 170 (Cal.).

Self-protection: *Your Guide for Malpractice Protection*, by the Malpractice Insurance and Defense Program of the Medical Society of the State of New York (1963); "Prevention of Malpractice," by Henry A. Kiker, *Federation Bulletin*, January 1965; "Modern Medico-Legal Trends," by Anne M. Knisely, M.D., *Ohio State Law Journal*, Summer 1964; "These Are Rules for Avoiding Liability in Office Practice, Where Many Claims Originate," *American College of Surgeons Bulletin*, July–August 1956; "Contributory Negligence on the Part of the Patient May Safeguard the Surgeon in Malpractice Actions," American College of Surgeons Bulletin, May–June 1957.

Society executives: "How State Medical Society Executives Size Up Professional Liability," *J.A.M.A.*, June 1, 1957.

Wyckoff: "What to Expect If You're Sued," by Robert L. Wyckoff, M.D., *Medical Economics*, Nov. 7, 1960.

Physician sued for first time; "two diagnoses"; Dr. Clark: "When Your Doctor Fears His Patients," by William Peters, *Good Housekeeping*, September 1959.

Medical Economics survey; Barth: By Robert L. Brenner in *Medical Economics*: "Does the Malpractice Threat Inhibit Good Medicine," Aug. 15, 1960, and "How the Malpractice Threat is Changing Medicine," Aug. 1, 1960.

Wesson: "Medical Malpractice Suits: A Physician's Primer for Defendants," by Miley B. Wesson, M.D., *Cleveland-Marshall Law Review*, May 1959.

Mitty: "How Surgical Practice is Influenced by the Legal Profession," by William F. Mitty, Jr., M.D., *Medical Trial Technique Quarterly*, 1964 Annual.

Regan on "one chance in a thousand": "Medicine vs. Law," *Medical Economics*, January 1956.

Markowitz: "Judge Here Calls Doctors Fearful," by Robert E. Tomasson, *New York Times*, Sept. 21, 1966.

"Gradually the courts awoke"; Salgo; California District Court of Appeal: 317 P.2d 270; note in *Dickinson Law Review*, June 1958.

Allman: *New York Times*, April 29, 1961.

J.A.M.A. quote: "Medicine and the

Law: Medico-Legal Problems and Their Solution," *J.A.M.A.*, Oct. 12, 1957.

Comments on the award for cancerophobia: "Recovery for Mental Anguish in Malpractice Suits," *Fordham Law Review*, Winter 1959; "Damages for Mental Suffering," by Claude C. Kelly Jr., *Cornell Law Quarterly*, Summer 1959; "Damages for Mental Suffering," *N.Y.U. Law Review*, April 1959; "Recovery for Mental Anguish in Malpractice Suits," *Virginia Law Review*, June 1959.

Discussions of the doctrine of res ipsa loquitur: "Res Ipsa Loquitur—Its Future in Medical Malpractice Cases," by David W. Louisell and Harold Williams, *California Law Review*, May 1960; "Res Ipsa Loquitur—When Does It Apply?" by Joseph D. Bulman, *Insurance Law Journal*, January 1961; "Highlights on Res Ipsa Loquitur in Medical Malpractice Cases," by Donald R. Brophy, *Insurance Law Journal*, November 1964; "Res Ipsa—Superior Knowledge Factor," by W. R. Mackey, *Hastings Law Journal*, May 1958; "Res Ipsa Loquitur—As it Applies in Medical Malpractice," by Joseph D. Bulman, *Journal of the Bar Association of the District of Columbia*, March 1962; "Res Ipsa Loquitur in Medical Malpractice," by A. H. Coleman, *Journal of the National Medical Association*, January 1965.

Additional information on malpractice causes, problems and decisions can be found in "The Causes of Malpractice Action," by Carl E. Wasmuth M.D., *Anesthesiology*, September–October 1965; "Malpractice and the Physician—Damage Awards," by O. C. Schroeder Jr., *Postgraduate Medicine*, June 1965; "Proof and Procedures in Malpractice Cases," by Meyer H. Goldman, *Massachusetts Law Quarterly*, October 1955; "Malpractice Litigation: Recent Breaches in the Traditional Barriers," by Carl Wilson, *Texas Law Review*, December 1957; "Some Pertinent Court Decisions in the Field of Legal Medicine," by Maurice Levin, *Military Medicine*, November 1964; "Professional Liability Problems of the Medical General Practitioner," by Joseph F. Sadusk Jr., M.D., Insurance Law Journal, May 1958; 'Trial Judge: His Responsibility in Medical Malpractice Cases," by Eugene A. Wright, *Insurance Law Journal*, December 1964; "Medical Malpractice Litigation: A Plague on Both Houses," by Albert L. Cohn, *American Bar Association Journal*, January 1966; "Good Doctors Don't Shun Poor Risks— Or Fear Medical Audits," by Robert S. Myers, *Modern Hospital*, October 1964.

Chapter 22. Rules of the Guild

Guilds: "The History of Medical Training and Licensure," by H. M. Karn, *New Zealand Medical Journal*, August 1957.

"Do not look lecherously": "The Medical Code of Ethics," *Worcester (Mass.) Medical News*, January 1960.

Current ethical code: *Opinions and Reports of the Judicial Council* (1964, A.M.A.)

History of American medical ethics: *A History of American Medical Ethics: 1847–1912*, by Donald E. Konold (1962, Department of History, University of Wisconsin); *AMA: Voice of American Medicine*, by James G. Burrow (1963, Johns Hopkins); *Medicine and Society in America: 1660–1860*, by Richard Harrison Shryock (1960, Great Seal).

Early American ethics: *Physician and Patient*, by Worthington Hooker, M.D., (1849, Baker & Scribner); *Medical Ethics and Etiquette*, by Austin Flint, M.D., (1883, Appleton); *Professional Codes*, by Benson Y. Landis (1927, Teachers College, Columbia University).

Percival: *Percival's Code*, by Chauncey D. Leake (1923, A.M.A.).

"Respectable social position": 38 Ga. 608.

Stanfield; Fox: "Mass Media and the Physician . . . Or How Sick Is Our Image?" by Clyde E. Stanfield, M.D., *Rocky Mountain Medical Journal*, July 1961.

Pediatrician: "When It's Right to 'Steal' a Patient," by Charles E. Miller, M.D., *Medical Economics*, Feb. 2, 1959.

Dr. Gray: 24 Bar. (N.Y.) 570.

$2,500,000 damage suit: *New York Times*, Oct. 15, 1955.

Separate billing resolution: "Board Halts Action on Resolution," *A.M.A. News*, August 15, 1966.

Dr. "Barker": *Hospitals, Doctors and Dollars,* by Robert M. Cunningham, Jr. (1961, F. W. Dodge).

Dr. Shadid; Williston; Ross-Loos; Logan County; Tampa; Puget Sound: "The American Medical Association: Power, Purpose and Politics in Organized Medicine," by David R. Hyde and Payson Wolff, with Anne Gross and Elliott Lee Hoffman, *Yale Law Journal,* May 1954.

Group Health Association: "How D.C. Health Plan Fought the A.M.A.—and Stayed Healthy," by William V. Shannon, *New York Post,* May 28, 1954.

H.I.P.: "Medicine and the Law," *J.A.M.A.,* Feb. 26, 1955; "Monopoly in medicine: it cuts both ways," by Robert L. Brenner, *Medical Economics,* Sept. 12, 1960.

Baehr: "Ethical Standards of the Medical Profession," by William T. Fitts, Jr., M.D., *A.C.S. Bulletin,* May–June 1956.

Stacey: "What I Learned From the Doctors of Bloody Harlan," by John R. Lindsey, *Medical Economics,* Feb. 16, 1959.

Draper: "Report to the Conference on Medical Care in the Bituminous Coal Mine Area," by Warren F. Draper, M.D., *J.A.M.A.,* March 7, 1953.

Novy; A.M.A. convention: "Medicine v. the Mine Workers," by John R. Lindsey, *Medical Economics,* July 21, 1958.

Kentucky: "Doctors Honor Sponsor of Anti-U.M.W. Bill," *Medical Economics,* Nov. 10, 1958.

For additional background material, see: "Sources of Medical Morals," by Richard Thomas Barton, M.D., *J.A.M.A.,* July 12, 1965.

Chapter 23. Conspirators in Silence
"Price"; Lercara; survey: "Doctors in Court," by Milton Silverman, *Saturday Evening Post,* April 18, 1959.

Hall: "Malpractice and the A.M.A.: Let's Understand Each Other," by George E. Hall, *Illinois Bar Journal,* 1954.

A.M.A. ethics code: *Principles of Medical Ethics* (A.M.A., 1956).

A.M.A. survey: *What Americans Think of the Medical Profession* (A.M.A., 1955).

Roundtable discussion: "Medical Mistakes," *Medical Economics,* Sept. 23, 1963.

Rubsamen: "The California Medical Malpractice Picture," by David S. Rubsamen, M.D., *California Medicine,* November 1963.

Trial of Medical Malpractice Cases, by David W. Louisell and Harold Williams, M.D. (1966, Bender).

Original records; blood transfusion; boy dying of appendicitis; Belli's neurosurgeon: *Blood Money: Ready for the Plaintiff,* by Melvin M. Belli (1956, Grosset & Dunlap).

1903: 94 N.W.607 (Neb.).

Carter: 234 P.2d 34 (Cal.).

Orthopedist has no malpractice insurance: 393 P.2d 497 (Okla.).

N.A.C.C.A.: *New York Times,* Feb. 13, 1955.

A.B.A. Report of the Committee on Improvements in the Law of Evidence, 62 A.B.A. Rep. 590 (1938).

Polsky: "The Malpractice Dilemma: A Cure for Frustration," by Samuel Polsky, *Temple Law Quarterly,* Summer 1957.

"In Stockton"; typical instructions to jury: 209 P.2d 98 (Cal.).

Man with a briefcase: "An Ancient Therapy Still Applied: The Silent Medical Treatment," by Melvin M. Belli, *Villanova Law Review,* May 1956.

A.M.A. Law Department: "First Results: 1963 Professional-Liability Survey," *J.A.M.A.,* Sept. 14, 1964.

Chairman of Malpractice Committee: "Malpractice: Medical—The Important Events of the Last Two Years," by R. Crawford Morris, *Insurance Counsel Journal,* Jan. 1963.

Impartial witness: 313 P.2d 118 (Cal.).

Special evidence rules for medical malpractice: "Public Responsibility of the Learned Professions," by John W. Wade, *Louisiana Law Review,* December 1960.

Community rule: "Diminishing Importance of Community Rule as to Expert Witnesses," by Howard Newcomb Morse, *J.A.M.A.,* Dec. 5, 1966.

Chicago physicians in Florida: 84 So.2d 34.

San Francisco doctor in Utah: 329 F.2d 53.

Philadelphia expert in Baltimore: 237 F. Supp. 787.

"I generally won't take a case"; Albert Averbach in "Trends in Trials," *Medical Economics,* Sept. 20, 1965.

Medical texts as evidence: "A Medico-legal Experiment and Its Failure," by David Rines, *Trial and Tort Trends,* 1961 Belli Seminar (Bobbs-Merrill Co.).

Murphy: "Medical Malpractice," by Walter G. Murphy, *Defense Law Journal,* 1960.

Alternatives to medical witness: "Is It Error to Discuss Conspiracy of Silence in a Malpractice Trial," by Robert L. Starks, *Cleveland-Marshall Law Review,* September 1965; "Malpractice and Medical Testimony," *Harvard Law Review,* 1963.

Meritorious cases: "Comments on Recent Important Personal Injury (Tort) Cases," by Thomas F. Lambert Jr., *NACCA Law Journal,* May 1958.

Second fetus: Reported in "Can We Trust All Our Doctors?" by Sidney Shalett, *Ladies' Home Journal,* March 1953.

Broder: "Lawyer Attacks Hospital Secrecy," by David Bird, *New York Times,* Feb. 24, 1966.

For additional discussions about medical society pressure on doctors not to testify, see: "Coercion by a Medical Association to Preclude Availability of Expert Testimony in a Medical Malpractice Action," by William Y. Webb, *Michigan Law Review,* March, 1960; "Expulsion from Medical Association for Testimony in a Judicial Proceeding Held Unreasonable," by James W. Rawlings, *Utah Law Review,* Fall, 1956; "Disparaging Remarks of One Doctor About Another as a Basis for Revocation of License," by Edward W. Mullins, South Carolina Law Quarterly, Spring, 1957.

Other valuable discussions include: "Expert Testimony in Medical Malpractice Cases," by Elliott L. Miller, *University of Miami Law Review,* Winter, 1962; "Conspiracy of Silence: Physician's View," by Carl E. Wasmuth, *Cleveland-Marshall Law Review,* January 1966; "Neutralizing the Systematic Suppression of Expert Medical Testimony in Malpractice Suits," by Robert Gittleman, *Wayne Law Review,* Spring, 1966.

Chapter 24. Resistance to Reform
Omaha-Douglas County Medical Society Bulletin: "How Do You Stand?" by John D. Coe, M.D., March 1964.

Colcock: "Medical Linen," by Bentley P. Colcock, M.D., *Surgery, Gynecology and Obstetrics,* February 1964.

Allman; Gregg: "Quotes on Conduct . . . ," *J.A.M.A.,* May 23, 1959.

Federation Bulletin on "facing the problem squarely," "swept under the rug": "Under the Rug or Out in the Open?" March 1966.

Lull; Hawley: "The Ideals and Ethics of Medicine," by Paul R. Hawley, M.D., *American College of Surgeons Bulletin,* July–August 1953.

San Francisco: *San Francisco Call Bulletin,* Jan. 13, 1954: "S.F. Doctors Deny Unethical Practice Charge" and "Exposure Has Its Purpose" (Editorial).

RISS article: "What You Have to Go Through to Get a License!" by Lois Hoffman, *RISS,* July 1963; reprinted with "As Others See Us" (Editorial) in *Federation Bulletin,* October 1963.

Percival: *Percival's Code,* by Chauncey D. Leake (1923, A.M.A.).

"Our disciplinary system is O.K.": Robert M. Metcalfe, M.D., quoted in " 'He's a Menace to the Public and the Profession;' " by Frank Suiter, M.D., *Medical Economics,* Aug. 14, 1961.

Lasagna: *The Doctors' Dilemmas,* by Louis Lasagna, M.D. (1962, Harper). Review by R. C. Derbyshire, M.D., *Federation Bulletin,* January 1963.

Davis: *American College of Surgeons Bulletin:* "The Strange Case of Loyal Davis," by Greer Williams, July–August 1953; "Regents and Reporters Discuss Ethics," January–February 1954.

Hawley: "Gen. Paul Hawley, Physician, 74, Dies," *New York Times,* Nov. 26, 1966; "Paul Hawley: the Man Who Raised His Voice," by Lois R. Chevalier, *Medical Economics,* Jan. 30, 1961.

U.S. News & World Report: "Too Much Unnecessary Surgery," Feb. 20,

1953; "Too Many Wrong Ideas About Doctors," April 3, 1953.

Northwest Medicine: "Hawley and His Press," January, 1957.

A.M.A. resolutions: *Report of the Reference Committee on Legislation and Public Relations to the A.M.A. House of Delegates,* June 3, 1953.

Baughn: "Should Doctors Police Each Other?" by William L. Baughn, M.D., *Medical Economics,* Dec. 28, 1964.

Tissue committees: " . . . For the Triumph of Evil," by Edward H. Daseler, M.D., *American College of Surgeons Bulletin,* January–February 1955.

Fear of legislature; recommendations: *Report of the Medical Disciplinary Committee to the Board of Trustees,* American Medical Association, June 1961.

Physician Ownership in Pharmacies and Drug Companies: Title of 1964 *Hearings* and 1965 *Report* of Subcommittee on Antitrust and Monopoly of the Committee on the Judiciary, U.S. Senate.

A.M.A. News: "The Hart Bill's Effect," March 13, 1967.

Louisiana delegate: Rhett McMahon, M.D., quoted in "Self-Discipline Starts at the Top," by Robert L. Brenner, *Medical Economics,* Aug. 14, 1961.

"A.M.A. Authorized to Enforce Ethics": *A.M.A. News,* July 9, 1962.